Action Stations Revisited

Action Stations Revisited

The complete history of Britain's
military airfields:
No. 7 Scotland and Northern Ireland

Martyn Chorlton

Crécy Publishing Limited

First published in 2012 by Crécy Publishing Limited
All rights reserved

© Martyn Chorlton 2012
Martyn Chorlton is hereby identified as the author of this work in accordance with
Section 77 of the Copyright, Designs and Patents Act 1988

A CIP record for this book is available from the British Library

ISBN 9 780859 791557

Printed and bound in
England by MPG Books

Crécy Publishing Limited
1a Ringway Trading Estate, Shadowmoss Road, Manchester M22 5LH
www.crecy.co.uk

CONTENTS

Acknowledgements...6

Introduction 7

Glossary 14

The military airfields of Scotland 22

The military airfields of the Orkney Islands.........25

The military airfields of Northern Ireland............26

The military airfields of the Republic of Ireland ...28

The military airfields of the Shetland Islands......30

The airfields 31

Bibliography 316

Index 317

ACKNOWLEDGEMENTS

Special thanks to my wife Claire, who proofed the full text. Also, mainly for photographs and moral support, I would like to thank the following: Niall Hartley, Bill McConnell, Keith Grinstead, Stuart Leslie, A. P. Ferguson and the Museum of Flight, East Fortune.

INTRODUCTION

I feel very privileged to have been asked to write the latest in the series of *Action Stations Revisited*. Although slightly realigned from the original, which was first published in 1983 and revised in 1989, this volume has given me the opportunity to present several new 'Action Stations'. With a remit of 100,000 words, I applied my blinkers, got my head down and began writing away without a care, thinking that I would struggle to reach that number. By the time I had finished I had actually written 275,000 words and, if I had not been given a deadline, could have probably continued indefinitely! I then had to endure the heart-sinking experience of chopping the work down to size, which has obviously meant that many of the stones that I turned over had to be put back into place. So please, before you write that letter telling me that I have missed out this fact and that fact, please bear in mind that the information is probably laying on the cutting-room floor.

The RAF in Scotland

Much has changed over the past twenty-odd years, the most significant change being the end of the Cold War. While UK air defence patrols did not come to an end, the 'enemy' was no longer greeted on a regular basis high over the North Sea. Battles were now being fought over Middle Eastern skies and, together with North Africa, continue to do so today. Between the publications of the original editions and this one, the existence of Kinloss, Lossiemouth and Leuchars has been pretty solid. But despite our commitments overseas seeming to be no less busy, we now see the fall of Kinloss and the Nimrod force with it, leaving an alarmingly large hole our maritime capability, and our ability to continue being a major player in actions abroad. Aircraft such as the Jaguar and Tornado F.3 have now been consigned to history, both replaced by the Typhoon FGR.4, which now serves with 6 Squadron at Leuchars. In the background the Tornado continues to serve in the bomber role, but recent sweeping cuts have seen squadron strength significantly reduced. Lossiemouth remains a busy place, but it is only a fraction of its former self. Today, four Tornado GR.4 units serve at Lossiemouth, namely 12, 14, 15 (Reserve) and 617 Squadrons, as well as the all-important presence of D Flight, 202 Squadron, and its Sea Kings. Only Lossiemouth now as a reasonably secure futures, while Kinloss begins a lengthy and costly run-down. The present timetable runs at the airfield closing by 31 July 2011; no longer an RAF station by 31 March 2013; and one year later Kinloss will be in the hands of Defence Estates. If that was not enough for Scotland, the Defence Secretary Liam Fox announced on 18 July 2011 that Leuchars would also close. The Typhoon force based here, was only stood up in March 2011 but now this will have been moved to Lossiemouth by 2013. Leuchars future, like so many ex-RAF stations looks to now be in the hands of the Army from 2015.

In the meantime RAF Alness was closed in 1986, RAF Turnhouse followed in 1996 and, despite millions being spent over the years, in 1998 the RAF no longer had a requirement for Stornoway. Both Turnhouse and Stornoway were already being used considerably more for civilian flying than military, and their transition to all-civilian operations was fairly seamless.

There is still an RAF Benbecula, which has also had a great deal of money spent on it over the years. More recently the airfield was upgraded to provide a low-profile home for weapons testing for the Eurofighter Typhoon and BAe Systems projects and trials in general. Benbecula's use as a military airfield relies on the existence of the United Kingdom's largest air and sea range at South Uist. Unfortunately, it was announced in 2009 that the range was to close, but an unusual U-turn seems to have taken place and it appears that South Uist may remain open as options for marketing the range to worldwide customers are studied. Its closure, if it was to occur, would devastate the island community, which relies so heavily on the QinetiQ-run facility for employment.

Prestwick retains an RAF presence with the Scottish Air Traffic Control Centre (Military), and while military aviation is not a patch on what it was during the Second World War, several aircraft still stage through.

One station often overlooked is RAF Kirknewton, which is the home to 661 VGS and looks as though it will be for many years to come. Intriguingly, Kirknewton may have been an option for the USAF as a Contingency Hospital up to 1991 (post-Gulf War 1). It is most likely that a hangar would have been converted into the hospital to deal with large numbers of casualties; several airfields were allocated this role throughout the UK, but this is believed to have been the only one Scotland.

Finally, the name RAF Tain also lives on in the coastal bombing range that continues to serve the Lossiemouth Tornados and visiting RAF, USAF and European air forces. Its existence hinges on Lossiemouth, which seems fairly secure at the moment.

The MoD

It is certainly not unusual for the Army to take over airfields that the RAF no longer requires, especially since the military has steadily withdrawn from bases in Germany. This scenario sometimes occurs with ex-FAA airfields as well, Arbroath being a good example. Since 1971 the airfield has remained in the hands of the MoD and has enjoyed a new lease of life as Condor Barracks. The local economy has benefited no end from it now being the home of 45 Commando, which employs more than 600 civilian staff to help run the barracks.

A military presence remains at Balado Bridge, thanks to the 'golf ball' and its clandestine listening. Dounreay, despite its lack of aviation history, remains in military hands but today is going through the lengthy process of decommissioning, which will continue until at least 2036.

Machrihanish's days as a large NATO facility came to an end in 1995, but today an MoD presence remains. The airfield now provides a large playground for Army exercises, although these are becoming increasing rare. BAe Systems has made use of the airfield for UAV testing, but how much longer the MoD will cling on here is open to scrutiny.

Edzell is also a delicate place that still serves as home to several different communication and listening facilities, as does Milltown, but the HF operations there were due to end by 2006. The MoD is more active at West Freugh, which sees more activity from BAe Systems than the RAF. Various weapons systems are tested here, but since QinetiQ took over in 2001 the airfield is becoming less busy. The nearby bombing range at Luce Bay is not regularly manned but is opened as and when it is needed, and up to recent years has been used for NATO exercises. On the airfield several large 'golf balls' have appeared in recent years. These are for a satellite ground station that has already been used to control several micro-satellites, and it is planned that they will support QinetiQ's new TopSat satellite.

Rattray looks as though it will remain in military hands for the foreseeable future, following a £200 million upgrade of its HF communication systems.

The RAF in Northern Ireland

Across the water, Aldergrove has seen some changes over the past few years as the situation in Northern Ireland continues to improve. Operation 'Banner' finally came to an end in 2007, which in turn would see the military aircraft movements in and out of Aldergrove reduce dramatically. A presence still remains, but rather than being an RAF station it is now referred to as the Joint Helicopter Flying Station Aldergrove. The vast majority of helicopter bases throughout the province have also been closed, each of them a mini 'Action Station' in its own right. While aviation enthusiasts may mourn their loss, this must be viewed in a very positive light as talks and politics have replaced terrorism.

Ballykelly has only been recently vacated by the Army, although the local council has wasted no time in pronouncing that the former Shackleton Barracks is up for sale, while the airfield remains open to local helicopter movements. The entire 682-acre site has been offered under the title

Bessbrook in its heyday was the busiest helicopter station in the whole of Europe. Hardly a minute would pass without either a AAC or RAF helicopter coming and going. Here a Westland Lynx comes into land with a 230 Squadron Puma, home base Aldergrove in the foreground. Via author

'Expressions of Interest Sought', and part of what is on offer is a freehold with 126 years remaining. The chances of it being used in any great capacity for civilian aviation is remote, thanks to Eglinton being a few miles down the road.

The RAF has left Bishop's Court since the original book was published, and worthy of mention among the many mini 'Actions Stations' is the closure of Bessbrook Mill and St Angelo. The former, although never an airfield, was in its heyday the busiest helicopter base in Europe. The substantial ex-linen mill and its grounds were requisitioned by the Army in 1971, which required a large base within the heart of South Armagh. The Mill had nine helicopter pads capable of handling any helicopter from Scouts in the 1970s through to the RAF's Chinooks and every other AAC and RAF rotary type in between. This significant base was closed on 25 June 2007, bringing the first peace to this part of the country since 1845, when the mill was first built! St Angelo made use of one of the original airfield's runways as its operating area, albeit behind high wire. Long Kesh also had its own helicopter pad, remaining in use until the prison closed in 2000.

Finally, probably one of the most significant RAF units remaining in the province is 664 VGS at Newtownards. The school has been in residence since 1995 and looks as though it will remain for many years to come.

Early Days and the First World War

The vast majority of the new 'Action Stations' featured in this book are from the First World War era. This has given me an excuse to introduce some names that would otherwise have been overlooked, including many from the Republic of Ireland.

Remnants of Second World War airfields are prevalent throughout Scotland and Northern Ireland, while in general their First World War counterparts have returned to the soil. This does not mean that they did not make an impact, especially with regard to employing civilian contractors and bringing prosperity into the locality, albeit briefly.

In the Republic of Ireland, up to thirty-six airfields were active until 1922, ranging from ELGs through to complex airfields such as Baldonnel and Collinstown, the latter having been developed into Dublin International Airport. Prior to this, and by some margin, the only military flying recorded in the country was carried out by the British Army. The Royal Barracks in Dublin witnessed balloon launches from 1785, and Portobello Barracks, also in Dublin, was used for the same task from 1817.

No expense was spared with the large training stations during the First World War, which were made up of at least seven Belfast Truss-type aircraft sheds and anything up to a dozen Bessoneau hangars. Technical buildings were very often brick-built and centrally heated, and the accommodation was no less comfortable. Having only been surveyed by Sholto Douglas in 1917, several were barely open by the end of the First World War, by which time the fledging RAF was already in decline. The majority of Ireland's sites remained in use until 1922, by which time they were either closed or handed over to the Irish Air Corps.

Across the border Aldergrove was chosen as another training station for the RFC, which luckily though tentatively remained in military hands, eventually thriving in the late 1920s. Northern Ireland was not seen as an important location during the First World War for the siting of airfields, and only token LGs at Ballycastle, Bangor, Bryansford and Slidderyford Bridge were brought into limited use. The most notable site during this period was Bentra airship station, which carried out the only operational patrols from the province during the First World War.

Thanks to being within range of the Zeppelin, Edinburgh and the surrounding area was littered with LGs for the use of 77(HD) Squadron from 1916 through to early 1919. The first experience for the Scottish people of a Zeppelin attack took place on 2 April 1916. Two airships travelled up the Forth probably looking for targets but, after crossing the coast at Leith, the first dropped twenty-seven HE bombs and at least fourteen IBs. The first IBs set a bonded warehouse on fire in Leith and further bombs fell on the shoreline there. One struck St Thomas's Parish Manse, Sheriff Brae, and another at Bonnington, killing a small child. The Zeppelins then turned for Edinburgh city centre, towards the castle. One bomb hit The Mound and another a house in Lauriston Place.

Several onlookers rushed out of the White Hart Hotel in the Grassmarket to see what was going on, only for a bomb to fall in front of them. Four were injured, and one later died from injuries sustained. The County Hotel on Lothian Road was also hit, and a wing of George Watson's College was levelled by a direct hit. Marshall Street saw the worst of it, when six people were killed and seven others seriously injured. The final casualty of the night was a young child who was killed after a bomb struck a tenement in St Leonard's Hill.

The raid could have been much worse because the original plan was to meet up with two other airships before reaching the Firth of Forth. Luckily for the people of Edinburgh, one turned back and another got lost and dumped its bombs in Northumberland before heading home.

The extra squadrons that were formed following the spate of early Zeppelin attacks used up more than 10,000 personnel alone, all of whom would have been more useful closer to the front line. 77 (HD) Squadron first formed at Edinburgh on 1 October 1916 with a collection of aircraft, including the BE.2C, BE.2E, BE.12 and BE.12b. None of these aircraft were capable of tackling an airship, mainly due to their poor climb rate and altitude.

Drem Lighting System

During June 1940 Wg Cdr Richard 'Batch' Atcherley became Drem's station commander. Atcherley was an ingenious character, with a head full of ideas, and was always prepared to experiment with something new. Pilots of Hurricanes and Spitfires found it very difficult to land at night or in poor weather because of the glare given off from the exhausts and the nose-high attitude of the fighter on approach. Also, the low-wing design of both fighters did not lend itself to good downward visibility.

Atcherley designed a set of shrouded approach lights that would help the pilots see the runway much more clearly. The lights, set far outside the circuit, guided the pilot to a set of curved lights, which in turn led him, via a set of 'funnel' lights, to the end of the runway. A combination of better baffles on the fighter's exhaust and the curved approach helped pilots throughout the war. Officially known as the Drem Airfield Lighting System, it went on to be installed at eighty fighter and bomber airfields.

The *Tirpitz*

The sister ship of the *Bismarck*, the 42,900-ton *Tirpitz*, was destined never to be involved in a single naval action during her 3½-year existence. Her presence alone caused naval and RAF resources to be tied up until her final destruction in November 1944. Her importance was emphasised by Winston Churchill, who stated that, 'The destruction, or even crippling, of this ship is the greatest event at sea at the present time. No target is comparable to it.'

In January 1942 the *Tirpitz* was moved to Trondheim to help protect Norway from an invasion that Hitler was convinced would inevitably occur. The Germans also planned to use her to attack the Arctic convoys that were vital to the Russian war effort; in the event, neither invasion or convoy attacks took place.

In response to the ship's movement into Norway, several Bomber Command operations were organised in an attempt to sink her. From January through to March 1942 several operations were flown from Lossiemouth, and Kinloss was also used during April. None of the attempts to bomb the giant battleship were successful, but a failed attempt to torpedo the vessel using Fairey Albacores convinced the Germans that the ship was vulnerable to air attack.

The threat of what the ship would do next remained throughout 1943 and, despite several brave attacks by the FAA's Barracudas, in the summer of 1944 she remained afloat, now residing at Tromsö. Attacks by Bomber Command began again in September 1944 and on 29 October, when 9 and 617 Squadrons, taking off from Lossiemouth, Kinloss and Milltown, dropped thirty-seven 12,000lb 'Tallboys' on her. Cloud cover moved over the ship just moments before the Lancasters were due to bomb, and all of the bombs missed her. On 12 November another force of thirty Lancasters from 9 and 617 Squadrons took off from Lossiemouth, each carrying a 'Tallboy'. The *Tirpitz* was hit by at least two 'Tallboys' in this final attack, one managing to explode her magazine. A large hole was ripped into her hull and she capsized, trapping more than 1,000 of the 1,900 crew aboard. The *Tirpitz*, which had been nicknamed the 'Lone Queen of the North', was no longer a threat.

The German battleship Tirpitz seen attempting hiding in a Norwegian fjord, as captured by the cameras of a 540 Squadron Spitfire.

The capsized Tirpitz lies off Hakoy Island near Tromso in June 1945. She was eventually broken up in a joint Norwegian and German salvage operation which lasted from 1948 to 1957.

Lest we forget

Despite the passing years it is very nice to see an increasing number of memorials appearing on or near airfield sites today. However, the impressive double Celtic Cross that was erected by the people of Kirkoswald Parish in 1923 showed great foresight. Many young airmen lost their lives training at Turnberry during the First World War and this fact was immediately recognised. Those who lost their lives during the Second World War are also commemorated, but their names were not placed on the memorial until forty-five years after the conflict ended.

Other significant aircraft memorials, many of which had been erected since the publication of the original *Action Stations* volume, include Banff (Strike Wing and 14 PAFU), Charterhall, Dallachy, Donibristle, Dumfries, Dundonald (cairn in Frasers Garden Centre), East Fortune, Elgin, Ganavan Sands/Oban, Grangemouth (two memorials, one at the entrance to the BP site and the second remembering seventy-four pilots killed with 58 OTU on the old perimeter), Longman, Peterhead, Renfrew, Skitten (Operation 'Freshman') and Stornoway. Untold individual crash sites and notable aviation people and events have also been marked over recent years. Captain Ted Fresson OBE (1891-1965) has been recognised outside Inverness Airport Terminal with a striking statue.

Even individual buildings are now being recognised, such as the old aircraft sheds at Leuchars, which have received a plaque declaring them to be the oldest of their kind still in use in Scotland. Churches obviously harbour a host of memorials, and notable are the stained-glass windows in St Columbus Church, Kinloss, recognising 120, 201 and 206 Squadrons. The church at Longside is home to an airship propeller in memory of the nearby airship station.

Museums also help to keep the memories alive, and three at Dumfries, Montrose and East Fortune make use of original airfield buildings. All three also display memorials, and East Fortune is home to a very nice plaque to the R 34. Across the water, Long Kesh is now the home of the Ulster Aviation Society, after having spent many years at Langford Lodge.

Tragic events, such as aircraft crashes, were all too common during the Second World War, and many are remembered throughout Great Britain. Being so close to Forres, it was almost expected that at least one Whitley would crash on or very near the town. Not only was it in line with the main north-eastern runway, it was also regularly over-flown by Whitleys climbing out of Kinloss. Even before the SLG opened, the town suffered its first serious accident when Whitley N1440 dived into Tolbooth Street on 7 November 1940. Incredibly, there were no civilian casualties, but the crew of six on board stood no chance of escape when the bomber stalled at only 1,200 feet. Today a plaque is in place at Tolbooth Street in memory of the aircrew.

An attempt a few years back tok acknowledge Ayr resulted in a replica Spitfire taking flight during a gale one night. However, the replica Spitfire at Edinburgh Airport seems to be fairly well established and remembers 603 (City Edinburgh) Squadron, which served from 1925 to 1957.

GLOSSARY

AA	Automobile Association	AOP	Air Observation Platform
AAC	Army Air Corps	AOS	Air Observers School
AACF	Anti-Aircraft Co-operation Flight	APC	Armament Practice Camp
		A/Plt Off	Acting Pilot Officer
AACU	Anti-Aircraft Co-operation Unit	APS	Armament Practice Station
		ARD	Aircraft Repair Depot
A&AEE	Aeroplane & Armament Experimental Establishment	ARS	Aircraft Repair Shed
		A/S	Anti-Submarine
AAF	Auxiliary Air Force	ASAC	Air Surveillance and Control Systems Force Command
AAP	Aircraft Acceptance Park/Air Ammunition Park		
		ASDU	Armament Synthetic Development Unit
AAPC	Anti-Aircraft Practice Camp		
AATE	Air Armament Trails Establishment	ASH	Air-to-surface-vessel radar (American Type)
AAU	Air Assembly Unit	AST	Air Service Training
ABS	Air Base Squadron	ASWDU	Anti-Submarine Warfare Development Unit
A/C	Aircraftsman		
ACC	Aircraft Control Centre	ASL	Above Sea Level
ACAC	Air Crew Allocation Centre	ASR	Air-Sea Rescue
ACHU	Air Crew Holding Unit	ASRE	Air Signals and Radar Establishment
ACLANT	Allied Command Atlantic		
ADDL	Aerodrome Dummy Deck Landing	ASRTU	Air-Sea Rescue Training Unit
		ASU	Aircraft Storage Unit
ADG	Air Depot Group	ASV	Air-to-surface-vessel radar (British Type)
ADGB	Air Defence of Great Britain		
ADLS	Air Delivery Letter Service	ASWDU	Air-Sea Warfare Development Unit
AFC	Air Force Cross		
AFSC	Air Force Servicing Command	ATA	Air Transport Auxiliary
		ATC	Armament Training Camp/Air Traffic Control/Air Training Corps
AFU	Advanced Flying Unit		
AG	Air Gunner		
AGS	Air Gunnery School	ATCC	Air Traffic Control Centre
AHU	Aircraft Holding Unit	ATFERO	Atlantic Ferry Organisation
AI	Aeronautical Inspection & Airborne Interception	ATG	Air Transport Group
		ATS	Armament Training Station/Armament Training Squadron
ALG	Advanced Landing Ground		
ALT	Attack Light Torpedo		
AMMT	Air Ministry Meteorological Flight	AVM	Air Vice Marshal
		BAD	Base Air Depot
ANS	Air Navigation School	BATF	Blind/Beam Approach Training Flight
AOC	Air Officer Commanding	BB	Balloon Base
AONS	Air Observers Navigation School	BDTF	(Bomber) Defence Training Flight

BEM	British Empire Medal	DPHU	Day Pilot Holding Unit
BFI	Bulk Fuel Installation	DRS	Depot Repair Squadron
B&GS	Bombing & Gunnery School	DSC	Distinguished Service Cross
BOAC	British Overseas Airways Corporation	DSO	Distinguished Service Order
		DSS	Depot Support Squadron
BTU	Bombing Trials Unit	EAF	Enemy Aircraft Flight
B&V	Blohm & Voss	EDD	Equipment Disposal Depot
CAG	Carrier Air Group	EFTS	Elementary Flying Training School
CANS	Civil Air Navigation School		
CAS	Chief of Air Staff	ELG	Emergency Landing Ground
CASTS	Combined Anti-Submarine Tactical School	EO	Extra Over
		E&RFTS	Elementary and Reserve Flying Training School
CCA	Carrier Controlled Approach		
CCDU	Coastal Command Development Unit	ESD	Equipment Supply Depot
		FAA	Fleet Air Arm
CCFIS	Coastal Command Flying Instructors School	FB	Flying Boat
		FBDF	Flying Boat Development Flight
CCIS	Coastal Command Instructors School		
		FBFU	Flying Boat Fitting Unit
CCRC	Combat Crew Replacement Centre	FBSU	Flying Boat Servicing/Storage Unit
CF	Communications Flight/Conversion Flight	FBTS	Flying Boat Training Squadron
C&M	Care & Maintenance	FCSU	Fighter Command Servicing Unit
CODF	Combined Operations Development Flight		
		FF	Fighter Flight
(C)OUT/COTU	(Coastal) Operational Training Unit	FG	Fighter Group/Fighter Gunnery
CPF	Coastal Patrol Flight	Fg Off	Flying Officer
Cpl	Corporal	FIS	Flying Instructors School
CRO	Civilian Repair Organisation	FLP	Forced Landing Practice
CTP	Chief Test Pilot	Flt Lt	Flight Lieutenant
CTW	Combat Training Wing	Flt Sgt	Flight Sergeant
CU	Conversion Unit	FOB	Forward Operation Base
CWGC	Commonwealth War Graves Commission	FOCTF	Flag Officer Carrier Training Flight
DARA	Defence Aviation Repair Agency	FPP	Ferry Pilots Pool
		FP	Ferry Pool
DCC	Deputy Chief Constable	FRU	Fleet Requirement Unit
DFC	Distinguished Flying Cross	FS	Fighting School/Fighter Squadron/Ferry Squadron
DFM	Distinguished Flying Medal		
DFR	Dounreay Fast Reactor	FSoAFG	Fleet School of Aerial Fighting and Gunnery
DLCO	Deck Landing Control Officer		
DLP	Deck Landing Practice	FTC	Flying Training Command
DLT	Deck Landing Training	FTS	Flying Training School
DMTR	Dounreay Materials Test Reactor	FTU	Ferry Training Unit
		FW	Fighter Wing
DOE	Department of the Environment	GA	General Aviation
		Gen.	General

GIR	Glider Infantry Regiment	LG	Landing Ground
GOC	General Officer Commanding	LOC	Lockheed Overseas Corporation
Gp	Group		
GP	General Purpose	LORAN	LOng RAnge Navigation
Gp Capt	Group Captain	LRM	Leading Radio Mechanic
GR	General Reconnaissance	Lt(A)	Lieutenant (Acting)
GS	Gliding School	Lt Cdr	Lieutenant Commander
HAAPC	Heavy Anti-Aircraft Practice Camp	LTU	LORAN Training Unit
		MAC	Merchant Aircraft Carrier
HCU	Heavy Conversion Unit	MAEE	Maritime Aircraft Experimental Establishment
HD	Home Defence		
HE	High Explosive	MAP	Ministry of Aircraft Production
HF	High Frequency		
HFDF	High Frequency Direction Finding	MATS	Military Air Transport Service
		MCBU	Marine Craft Base Unit
HIAL	Highland and Islands Airports Limited	MCU	Marine Craft Unit/Meteorological Unit
HQ	Headquarters	MCRU	Marine Craft Repair Unit
HM	His Majesty	MoA	Ministry of Aviation
HMA	His Majesties Airship	MoCA	Ministry of Civilian Aviation
HMAS	His Majesties Australian Ship	MoD	Ministry of Defence
HMCS	His Majesties Canadian Ship	MOTU	Maritime Operational Training Unit
HMP	Her Majesties Prison		
HMS	His/Her Majesties Ship	MRS	Maritime Reconnaissance School
HSL	High Speed Launch	MTSU	Mechanical Transport Storage Unit
IAC	Irish Air Corps		
IB	Incendiary Bomb	MU	Maintenance Unit
ICCS	Integrated Command and Control System	MV	Merchant Vessel
		NAFS	Naval Air Fighter School
JASS	Joint Anti-Submarine School	NAS	Naval Air Station
Jg	Jagdgeschwader	NASS	Naval Anti-Submarine School
KLM	Koninklijke Luchtvaart Maatschappij	NATS	Northern Air Transport Service
Kptlt.	Kapitänleutnant	NCB	National Coal Board
Kts	Knots	NEAM	North East Aircraft Museum
OAFU	Observers Advanced Flying Unit	NFW	Naval Fighter Wing
		NITS	Northern Ireland Training School
Oblt	Oberleutnant		
(O)FIS	(Operational) Flying Instructors School	NOTU	Naval Operational Training Unit
ORB	Operations Record Book	NRTE	Naval Reactor Test Establishment
ORP	Operational Readiness Platform		
		(O)FIS	Operational Flying Instructors School
OS	Observer School		
OTU	Operational Training Unit	OHMS	On His Majesties Service
LAAPC	Light Anti-Aircraft Practice Camp	ORB	Operational Record Book
		ORP	Operational Readiness Platform
LASSS	Low-Altitude Space Surveillance System		

OS	Observers School	(S)FPP	Service Ferry Pilots Pool
(P)AFU	(Pilots) Advanced Flying Unit	SFS	Service Ferry Squadron
PFR	Prototype Fast Reactor	SFTS	Service Flying Training School
PLC	Public Limited Company		
Plt Off	Pilot Officer	Sgt	Sergeant
PM	Prime Minister	SGR	School of General Reconnaissance
PMC	Parachute Maintenance Company		
		SHQ	Station Headquarters
POW	Prisoner of War	SIS	Secret Intelligence Service
PR	Photographic Reconnaissance	SLG	Satellite Landing Ground
QDM	Magnetic heading (of runway for this book)	SMO	Station Medical Officer
		SMT	Scottish Motor Traction
QRA	Quick Reaction Alert	SoAF	School of Aerial Fighting
RAAF	Royal Australian Air Force/Royal Auxiliary Air Force	SoAF&G	School of Aerial & Gunnery
		SoAG	School of Aerial Gunnery
		SOE	Special Operations Executive
RAE	Royal Aircraft Establishment	Sqn Ldr	Squadron Leader
RAFNI	Royal Air Force Northern Ireland	SSP	Sea/Submarine Scout Pusher
		SSS	Storage Sub-Site/Space Surveillance Squadron
RCAF	Royal Canadian Air Force		
RCN	Royal Canadian Navy	SSWT	Supplementary School of Wireless Telegraphy
RDF	Radio Direction Finding		
RDFS	Radio Direction School	STF	Seaplane Training Flight
RFA	Royal Fleet Auxiliary	STS	Seaplane Training Squadron
RFS	Reserve Flying School	SU	Servicing Unit/Signals Unit
RFTS	Refresher Flying Training School	SW	Servicing Wing
		TAC	Transatlantic Aircraft Control
RFTU	Refresher Flying Training Unit	TAF	Tactical Air Force
		TAG	Telegraphist Air Gunner
RFU	Refresher Flying Unit	TAT	Torpedo Attack Trainer
RIC	Royal Irish Constabulary	TB	Torpedo Bomber
RLG	Relief Landing Ground	TBR	Torpedo Bomber Reconnaissance
RMU	Radio Maintenance Unit		
RN	Royal Navy	TCA	Trans-Canada Airlines
RNAS	Royal Naval Air Service/Station	TCC	Troop Carrier Command
		TDS	Training Depot Station
RNHF	Royal Navy Historic Flight	TE	Twin Engined
RNorAF	Royal Norwegian Air Force	TEU	Tactical Exercise Unit
RNVR	Royal Navy Volunteer Reserve	THUM	Temperature and Humidity
		TRF	Torpedo Refresher School
RNZAF	Royal New Zealand Air Force	TS	Training Squadron
RS	Radio School	TSR	Torpedo Spotter Reconnaissance
RSM	Radio Squadron Mobile		
RSS	Radio Servicing Section	TTF	Target Towing Flight
SAL	Scottish Aviation Ltd	TTS	Torpedo Training Squadron
SAS	Scandinavian Air Service	TTU	Torpedo Training Unit/ Tactical Trials Unit
SD	Special Duties		
SE	Servicing Echelon/Single Engined	TU	Training Unit

UAS	University Air Squadron
UCCS	United Kingdom ASCACS Command and Control System
UCMP	United Kingdom Air Defence Ground Environment Capability Maintenance Programme
UKADGE	United Kingdom Air Defence Ground Environment
UKAEA	United Kingdom Atomic Energy Authority
UKMATS	United Kingdom Military Air Traffic Service
USAAF	United States Army Air Force
USAFSS	USAF Security Service
USCG	United States Coast Guard
USN	United States Navy
USNAS	United States Naval Air Service
VGS	Volunteer Gliding School
VR	Volunteer Reserve
WAAF	Womens Auxiliary Air Force
WDU	Wireless Development Unit
WEU	Wireless Experimental Unit
Wg Cdr	Wing Commander
W/O	Warrant Officer
WO/AG	Wireless Operator Air Gunner
W/T	Wireless/Transmitter

Military Airfields of Scotland and Ireland

1 Abbotsinch, Strathclyde

2 Aldergrove, Down

3 Alloa (Forthbank/Caudron), Clackmannanshire

4 Alness (Invergordon/Dalmore), Ross-shire (Ross and Cromarty)

5 Annan, Dumfries and Galloway

6 Arbroath (Aberbrothock), Tayside

7 Armagh (Farmacaffly), Armagh

8 Askernish (South Uist), Western Isles

9 Athlone (Ballydonagh), Roscommon

10 Aught Point (Rinenore Point), Donegal

11 Auldbar (Albar), Angus/Forfarshire

12 Ayr (Heathfield), South Ayrshire

13 Ayr (Racecourse), Strathclyde/South Ayrshire

14 Balado Bridge, Tayside

15 Baldonnel (Casement)

16 Balhall, Angus

17 Ballincollig, Cork

18 Ballycastle, Antrim

19 Ballyhalbert, Down

20 Ballykelly, Londonderry

21 Ballyliffin, Donegal

22 Ballymena, Antrim

23 Ballyquirk (Killeagh), Cork

24 Ballywalter Park (Millisle), Down

25 Balmain, Kincardineshire/Angus

26 Balta Sound (Unst), Shetland

27 Banff (Boyndie), Grampian

28 Bangor (Groomsport), Down

29 Bantry, Cork

30 Barassie, Ayrshire

31 Barrhead, East Renfrewshire

32 Barry, Angus

33 Belhaven Sands, East Lothian

34 Benbecula (Balivanich), Western Isles

35 Bentra (Whitehead, aka Larne), Antrim

36 Berehaven aka Bearhaven (Castletownbere), Cork

37 Berneray, Western Isles

38 Birr (Crinkill), Offaly

39 Bishops Court, Down

40 Black Isle (Blackstand Farm/Fortrose), Highland

41 Blaris (Lisburn), Antrim

42 Boa Island (Rock Bay), Fermanagh

43 Bogton (Dalmellington), Ayrshire

44 Bowmore, Strathclyde

45 Brackla, Highland

46 Brims Mains, Highland

47 Broughty Ferry, Dundee

48 Bryansford (Newcastle), Down

49 Buddon (Barry Buddon), Tayside

50 Buttergask, Tayside

51 Buttevant, Cork

52 Cairncross, Borders

53 Caldale, Orkney

54 Campbeltown, Strathclyde (Argyll and Bute)

55 Cardross, Argyll and Bute

56 Carmunnock (Cathcart/Glasgow), Strathclyde

57 Castlebar, Mayo

58 Castletownroach, Cork

59 Castle Archdale (Lough Erne), Fermanagh

60 Castle Kennedy, Dumfries and Galloway

61 Castletown, Highland

62 Catfirth, Shetlands

63 Charterhall, Borders

64 Clongowes Wood College, Kildare

65 Clonmel (Abbeyfarm), Tipperary

66 Cluntoe (Kinrush), Tyrone

67 Colinton (Edinburgh), Mid-Lothian

68 Collinstown (Dublin), Dublin

69 Connel (Oban Airport/North Connel), Strathclyde

70 Crail, Fife

71 Creetown, Kirkcudbrightshire

72 Cromarty, Ross-shire

73 Dalcross, Highland

74 Dallachy, Grampian (Morayshire)

75 Dalmuir (Robertson Field), Strathclyde

76 Delny House, Highland

77 Donibristle, Fife

78 Dornoch, Highland

79 Downhill (Benone Strand/Coleraine), Londonderry

80 Dounreay (Thurso), Caithness

81 Drem (West Fenton/Gullane), East Lothian

82 Dumfries (Heathhall/Tinwald Downs), Dumfries and Galloway

83 Dundee (Stannergate), Tayside

84 Dundonald (Gailes), Strathclyde

85 Dundrum (Murlough), Down

86 Dungavel, East Ayrshire

87 Dunino, Fife

88 Dyce, Aberdeenshire/Grampian

89 East Fingask, Aberdeenshire

90 East Fortune, East Lothian

91 East Haven, Tayside

92   Eccles Tofts, Borders
93   Edzell, Tayside/Angus
94   Eglinton (Londonderry Eglinton/City of Derry Airport), Londonderry
95   Elgin (Bogs O'Mayne/ Miltonduff), Grampian
96   Errol, Perthshire/Tayside
97   Evanton (Novar), Highland
98   Fair Isle, Shetland
99   Fearn (Balintore/Clays of Allan), Highland
100 Fermoy (Carrignagrogher), Cork
101 Fifteen Acres (Phoenix Park), Dublin
102 Findo Gask, Tayside
103 Fordoun, Aberdeenshire/ Grampian
104 Forres, Grampian (Moray)
105 Fort George, Highland
106 Fraserburgh (Inverallochy/ Cairnblug), Grampian
107 Ganavan Sands (Oban), Argyllshire
108 Gifford (Townhead), Lothian
109 Gilmerton, Edinburgh City
110 Gormanston, Meath
111 Grangemouth, Falkirk (Central Region)
112 Granton Harbour, Edinburgh
113 Greencastle (Cranfield), Down
114 Greenock (Caird's Yard and Gourock Bay), Renfrewshire
115 Hatston, Orkney
116 Hawkcraig, Fife
117 Helensburgh (Rhu), Strathclyde
118 Hoprig Mains (Penston/ Tranent), East Lothian
119 Houton Bay (Including Orphir), Orkney

120 Inchinnan, Strathclyde/ Renfrewshire
121 Inverkeithing Bay, Fife
122 Johnstone Castle (Wexford), Wexford
123 Kayshill, Ayrshire
124 Kidsdale (Burrow Head), Dumfries and Galloway/ Wigtownshire
125 Kilconquhar, Fife
126 Kilkenny, Kilkenny
127 Killadeas, Fermanagh
128 Kinloss, Moray/Grampian
129 Kinnell, Tayside
130 Kirkandrews, Dumfries and Galloway
131 Kirkcolm (Corsewall), Dumfries and Galloway
132 Kirkistown, Down
133 Kirknewton
134 Kirkpatrick, Dumfries and Galloway
135 Kirkton (Golspie), Highland
136 Kirkwall (Grimsetter), Orkney
137 Kirkwall Bay, Orkney
138 Langford Lodge, Antrim
139 Largs Channel, Strathclyde
140 Leanach (Culloden Moor), Inverness-shire
141 Lennoxlove (Haddington), East Lothian
142 Lerwick, Shetland
143 Leuchars, Fife
144 Leven, Fife
145 Limavady (Aghanloo), Londonderry
146 Limerick, County Limerick
147 Loch Baghasdail (Lochboisdale), South Uist
148 Loch Doon, Strathclyde
149 Long Kesh, Down
150 Longman (Inverness), Highland

151 Longside (Lenabo/ Peterhead), Aberdeenshire
152 Lossiemouth, Grampian
153 Low Eldrig, Dumfries and Galloway
154 Luce Bay, Dumfries and Galloway
155 Machrihanish (Strabane/ Campbeltown Airport), Strathclyde
156 Macmerry, Lothian
157 Maghaberry, Antrim
158 Malahide, Dublin
159 Maydown, Londonderry
160 Methven, Tayside
161 Millisle, Down
162 Milltown, Grampian
163 Montrose (Broomfield), Tayside
164 Montrose (Upper Dysart), Angus
165 Mullaghmore, Londonderry
166 Musgrave Channel (Belfast Harbour), Belfast City
167 Myreside, Edinburgh
168 Newtownards (Ards), Down
169 Nigg, Highland
170 North Queensferry, Fife
171 Nutt's Corner, Antrim
172 Oban, Strathclyde
173 Omagh (Straughroy), County Tyrone
174 Orangefield, Belfast City
175 Oranmore, County Galway
176 Paisley, Renfrewshire
177 Perth (Scone), Tayside
178 Peterhead (Longside), Grampian
179 Peterhead Bay, Grampian/Aberdeenshire
180 Pierowall (Westray), Orkney
181 Port Ellen (Islay/ Glenegedale), Strathclyde

182 Port Laing (Carlingnose), Fife

183 Portobello Barracks (Cathal Brugha Barracks), Dublin

184 Prestwick (Prestwick Ayr/Glasgow Prestwick), Strathclyde

185 Queenstown (Cobh/Aghada), Cork

186 Raeburnfoot, Dumfries and Galloway

187 Rathbane House (Banemore or Bawnmore), Limerick

188 Rathmullan (Lough Swilly), Donegal

189 Rattray (Crimond), Grampian

190 Renfrew (Moorpark), Strathclyde

191 Rerrin (Bear or Bere Island), Cork

192 River Bann (South Landagivey), Derry

193 River Foyle, Derry

194 Rosyth, Fife

195 Royal Barracks (Collins Barracks), Dublin

196 St Angelo (Enniskillen Airport), Fermanagh

197 Sandy Bay (Lough Neagh), Antrim

198 Scapa, Orkney

199 Scatsta, Shetland

200 Scone Park, Perthshire

201 Skateraw (Innerwick), East Lothian

202 Skeabrae, Orkney

203 Skitten, Caithness

204 Slidderyford Bridge, Down

205 Smoogroo, Orkney

206 Snelsetter/Hoy & Longhope, Orkney

207 Sollas (North Uist), Western Isles

208 South Belton (Dunbar), Lothian

209 South Kilduff (Kinross), Fife

210 Stenness Loch, Orkney

211 Stirling (Kincairn/Gargunnock), Central

212 Stirling (Raploch/Falleninch Farm), Central

213 Stornoway (including HMS Mentor [Lews Castle]), Western Isles

214 Stracathro, Tayside

215 Strathaven (Couplaw Farm), South Lanarkshire

216 Strathbeg, Aberdeenshire

217 Stravithie, Fife

218 Sullom Voe (Garth's Vow), Shetland

219 Sumburgh, Shetland

220 Sydenham (Belfast), Down

221 Tain, Highland

222 Tallaght (Cookstown), Dublin

223 Tealing, Tayside

224 The Curragh, Dublin

225 Thurso, Highland

226 Tiree, Strathclyde (Argyllshire)

227 Toome, Londonderry

228 Turnberry, Strathclyde/Ayrshire

229 Turnhouse (Edinburgh), Mid-Lothian

230 Twatt, Orkney

231 Tynehead, Midlothian

232 Urquhart, Invernesshire

233 Valencia Harbour, Kerry

234 Wakefield, Kincardineshire

235 West Cairnbeg, Aberdeenshire

236 West Freugh, Dumfries and Galloway

237 Wexford (Ferrybank), County Wexford

238 Whelans Field (Ballymullen Barracks), Kerry

239 Whiddy Island, Cork

240 Whiteburn (Grantshouse), Borders

241 Whitefield, Perth & Kinross

242 Wick, Highland

243 Wig Bay and Stranraer (including Cairn Ryan), Dumfries and Galloway

244 Wigtown (Baldoon), Dumfries and Galloway

245 Winfield (Horndean), Borders/Berwickshire

246 Winterseugh, Dumfries & Galloway

247 Woodhaven, Fife

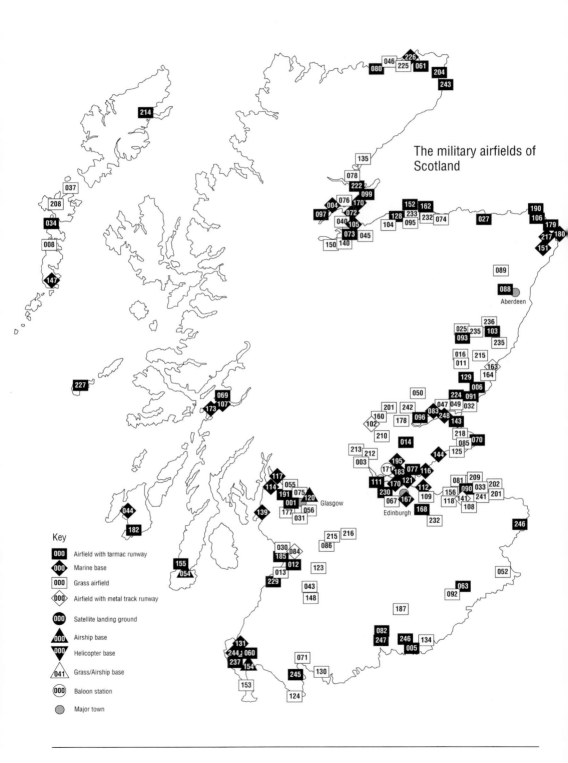

The military airfields of
Scotland

Key

000   Airfield with tarmac runway

000   Marine base

000   Grass airfield

000   Airfield with metal track runway

000   Satellite landing ground

000   Airship base

000   Helicopter base

041   Grass/Airship base

000   Baloon station

●   Major town

1	Abbotsinch, Strathclyde	54	Campbeltown, Strathclyde (Argyll and Bute)	91	East Haven, Tayside
3	Alloa (Forthbank/Caudron), Clackmannanshire			92	Eccles Tofts, Borders
				93	Edzell, Tayside/Angus
		55	Cardross, Argyll and Bute	95	Elgin (Bogs O'Mayne/Miltonduff), Grampian
4	Alness (Invergordon/Dalmore), Ross-shire (Ross and Cromarty)	56	Carmunnock (Cathcart/Glasgow), Strathclyde		
				96	Errol, Perthshire/Tayside
		60	Castle Kennedy, Dumfries and Galloway	97	Evanton (Novar), Highland
5	Annan, Dumfries and Galloway	61	Castletown, Highland	99	Fearn (Balintore/Clays of Allan), Highland
6	Arbroath (Aberbrothock), Tayside	63	Charterhall, Borders		
		67	Colinton (Edinburgh), Mid-Lothian	102	Findo Gask, Tayside
8	Askernish (South Uist), Western Isles			103	Fordoun, Aberdeenshire/Grampian
		69	Connel (Oban Airport/North Connel), Strathclyde	104	Forres, Grampian (Moray)
11	Auldbar (Albar), Angus/Forfarshire				
12	Ayr (Heathfield), South Ayrshire	70	Crail, Fife	105	Fort George, Highland
		71	Creetown, Kirkcudbrightshire	106	Fraserburgh (Inverallochy/Cairnblug), Grampian
13	Ayr (Racecourse), Strathclyde/South Ayrshire	72	Cromarty, Ross-shire		
		73	Dalcross, Highland	107	Ganavan Sands (Oban), Argyllshire
14	Balado Bridge, Tayside	74	Dallachy, Grampian (Morayshire)		
16	Balhall, Angus			108	Gifford (Townhead), Lothian
25	Balmain, Kincardineshire/Angus	75	Dalmuir (Robertson Field), Strathclyde	109	Gilmerton, Edinburgh City
27	Banff (Boyndie), Grampian	76	Delny House, Highland		
		77	Donibristle, Fife	111	Grangemouth, Falkirk (Central Region)
30	Barassie, Ayrshire	78	Dornoch, Highland		
31	Barrhead, East Renfrewshire	80	Dounreay (Thurso), Caithness	112	Granton Harbour, Edinburgh
32	Barry, Angus	81	Drem (West Fenton/Gullane), East Lothian	114	Greenock (Caird's Yard and Gourock Bay), Renfrewshire
33	Belhaven Sands, East Lothian				
34	Benbecula (Balivanich), Western Isles	82	Dumfries (Heathhall/Tinwald Downs), Dumfries and Galloway	116	Hawkcraig, Fife
37	Berneray, Western Isles			117	Helensburgh (Rhu), Strathclyde
40	Black Isle (Blackstand Farm/Fortrose), Highland	83	Dundee (Stannergate), Tayside	118	Hoprig Mains (Penston/Tranent), East Lothian
43	Bogton (Dalmellington), Ayrshire	84	Dundonald (Gailes), Strathclyde		
44	Bowmore, Strathclyde	86	Dungavel, East Ayrshire	120	Inchinnan, Strathclyde/Renfrewshire
45	Brackla, Highland	87	Dunino, Fife	121	Inverkeithing Bay, Fife
46	Brims Mains, Highland	88	Dyce, Aberdeenshire/Grampian	123	Kayshill, Ayrshire
47	Broughty Ferry, Dundee			124	Kidsdale (Burrow Head), Dumfries and Galloway/Wigtownshire
49	Buddon (Barry Buddon), Tayside	89	East Fingask, Aberdeenshire		
50	Buttergask, Tayside	90	East Fortune, East Lothian	125	Kilconquhar, Fife
52	Cairncross, Borders			128	Kinloss, Moray/Grampian

129 Kinnell, Tayside
130 Kirkandrews, Dumfries and Galloway
131 Kirkcolm (Corsewall), Dumfries and Galloway
133 Kirknewton
134 Kirkpatrick, Dumfries and Galloway
135 Kirkton (Golspie), Highland
139 Largs Channel, Strathclyde
140 Leanach (Culloden Moor), Inverness-shire
141 Lennoxlove (Haddington), East Lothian
143 Leuchars, Fife
144 Leven, Fife
147 Loch Baghasdail (Lochboisdale), South Uist
148 Loch Doon, Strathclyde
150 Longman (Inverness), Highland
151 Longside (Lenabo/Peterhead), Aberdeenshire
152 Lossiemouth, Grampian
153 Low Eldrig, Dumfries and Galloway
154 Luce Bay, Dumfries and Galloway
155 Machrihanish (Strabane/Campbeltown Airport), Strathclyde
156 Macmerry, Lothian
160 Methven, Tayside
162 Milltown, Grampian
163 Montrose (Broomfield), Tayside
164 Montrose (Upper Dysart), Angus
168 Myreside, Edinburgh
170 Nigg, Highland
171 North Queensferry, Fife
173 Oban, Strathclyde
177 Paisley, Renfrewshire

178 Perth (Scone), Tayside
179 Peterhead (Longside), Grampian
180 Peterhead Bay, Grampian/Aberdeenshire
182 Port Ellen (Islay/Glenegedale), Strathclyde
183 Port Laing (Carlingnose), Fife
185 Prestwick (Prestwick Ayr/Glasgow Prestwick), Strathclyde
187 Raeburnfoot, Dumfries and Galloway
190 Rattray (Crimond), Grampian
191 Renfrew (Moorpark), Strathclyde
195 Rosyth, Fife
201 Scone Park, Perthshire
202 Skateraw (Innerwick), East Lothian
204 Skitten, Caithness
208 Sollas (North Uist), Western Isles
209 South Belton (Dunbar), Lothian
210 South Kilduff (Kinross), Fife
212 Stirling (Kincairn/Gargunnock), Central
213 Stirling (Raploch/Falleninch Farm), Central
214 Stornoway (including HMS Mentor [Lews Castle]), Western Isles
215 Stracathro, Tayside
216 Strathaven (Couplaw Farm), South Lanarkshire
217 Strathbeg, Aberdeenshire
218 Stravithie, Fife
222 Tain, Highland
224 Tealing, Tayside
226 Thurso, Highland
227 Tiree, Strathclyde (Argyllshire)

229 Turnberry, Strathclyde/Ayrshire
230 Turnhouse (Edinburgh), Mid-Lothian
232 Tynehead, Midlothian
233 Urquhart, Invernesshire
235 Wakefield, Kincardineshire
236 West Cairnbeg, Aberdeenshire
237 West Freugh, Dumfries and Galloway
241 Whiteburn (Grantshouse), Borders
242 Whitefield, Perth & Kinross
243 Wick, Highland
244 Wig Bay and Stranraer (including Cairn Ryan), Dumfries and Galloway
245 Wigtown (Baldoon), Dumfries and Galloway
246 Winfield (Horndean), Borders/Berwickshire
247 Winterseugh, Dumfries & Galloway
248 Woodhaven, Fife

The military airfields of the Orkney Islands

Key

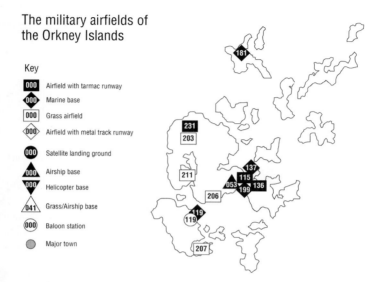

000   Airfield with tarmac runway

000   Marine base

000   Grass airfield

000   Airfield with metal track runway

000   Satellite landing ground

000   Airship base

000   Helicopter base

041   Grass/Airship base

(000)   Baloon station

⬤   Major town

53   Caldale, Orkney

115   Hatston, Orkney

119   Houton Bay (Including Orphir), Orkney

136   Kirkwall (Grimsetter), Orkney

137   Kirkwall Bay, Orkney

181   Pierowall (Westray), Orkney

199   Scapa, Orkney

203   Skeabrae, Orkney

206   Smoogroo, Orkney

207   Snelsetter/Hoy & Longhope, Orkney

211   Stenness Loch, Orkney

231   Twatt, Orkney

The military airfields of
Northern Ireland

Key

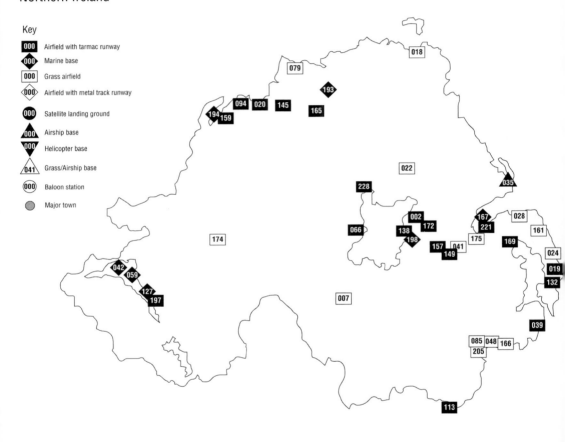

000	Airfield with tarmac runway
◆000◆	Marine base
000	Grass airfield
◇000◇	Airfield with metal track runway
●000●	Satellite landing ground
▲000	Airship base
▼000	Helicopter base
/041	Grass/Airship base
(000)	Baloon station
●	Major town

2	Aldergrove, Down	79	Downhill (Benone Strand/Coleraine), Londonderry	167	Musgrave Channel (Belfast Harbour), Belfast City
7	Armagh (Farmacaffly), Armagh	85	Dundrum, Down	169	Newtownards (Ards), Down
18	Ballycastle, Antrim	94	Eglinton (Londonderry Eglinton/City of Derry Airport), Londonderry	172	Nutt's Corner, Antrim
19	Ballyhalbert, Down			174	Omagh (Straughroy), County Tyrone
20	Ballykelly, Londonderry	113	Greencastle (Cranfield), Down	175	Orangefield, Belfast City
22	Ballymena, Antrim	127	Killadeas, Fermanagh	193	River Bann (South Landagivey), Derry
24	Ballywalter Park (Millisle), Down	132	Kirkistown, Down	194	River Foyle, Derry
28	Bangor (Groomsport), Down	138	Langford Lodge, Antrim	198	Sandy Bay (Lough Neagh), Antrim
35	Bentra (Whitehead, aka Larne), Antrim	145	Limavady (Aghanloo), Londonderry	205	Slidderyford Bridge, Down
39	Bishops Court, Down	149	Long Kesh, Down	197	St Angelo (Enniskillen Airport), Fermanagh
41	Blaris (Lisburn), Antrim	157	Maghaberry, Antrim	221	Sydenham (Belfast), Down
42	Boa Island (Rock Bay), Fermanagh	159	Maydown, Londonderry	228	Toome, Londonderry
48	Bryansford (Newcastle), Down	161	Millisle, Down		
59	Castle Archdale (Lough Erne), Fermanagh	165	Mullaghmore, Londonderry		
66	Cluntoe (Kinrush), Tyrone	166	Murlough (Dundrum), Down		

The military airfields of the Republic of Ireland

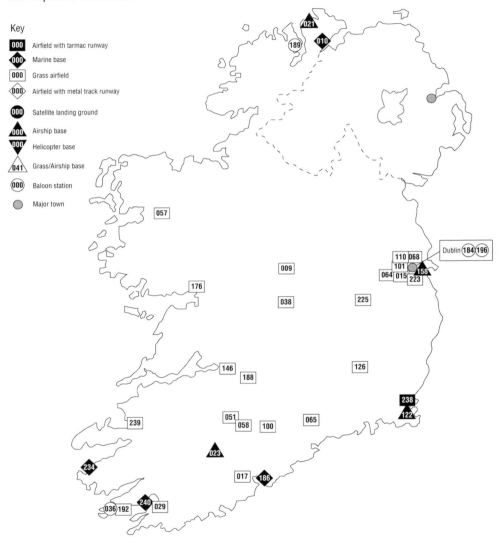

Key

000	Airfield with tarmac runway
000	Marine base
000	Grass airfield
000	Airfield with metal track runway
000	Satellite landing ground
000	Airship base
000	Helicopter base
041	Grass/Airship base
(000)	Baloon station
⬤	Major town

9   Athlone (Ballydonagh),   68   Collinstown (Dublin),   188 Rathbane House
     Roscommon   Dublin   (Banemore or
10   Aught Point (Rinenore   100 Fermoy   Bawnmore), Limerick
     Point), Donegal   (Carrignagrogher), Cork   189 Rathmullan (Lough
15   Baldonnel (Casement)   101 Fifteen Acres (Phoenix   Swilly), Donegal
17   Ballincollig, Cork   Park), Dublin   192 Rerrin (Bear or Bere
21   Ballyliffin, Donegal   110 Gormanston, Meath   Island), Cork
23   Ballyquirk (Killeagh),   122 Johnstone Castle   196 Royal Barracks (Collins
     Cork   (Wexford), Wexford   Barracks), Dublin
29   Bantry, Cork   126 Kilkenny, Kilkenny   223 Tallaght (Cookstown),
36   Berehaven aka Bearhaven   146 Limerick, County   Dublin
     (Castletownbere), Cork   Limerick   225 The Curragh, Dublin
38   Birr (Crinkill), Offaly   158 Malahide, Dublin   234 Valencia Harbour, Kerry
51   Buttevant, Cork   176 Oranmore, County   238 Wexford (Ferrybank),
57   Castlebar, Mayo   Galway   County Wexford
58   Castletownroach, Cork   184 Portobello Barracks   239 Whelans Field
64   Clongowes Wood   (Cathal Brugha Barracks),   (Ballymullen Barracks),
     College, Kildare   Dublin   Kerry
65   Clonmel (Abbeyfarm),   186 Queenstown   240 Whiddy Island, Cork
     Tipperary   (Cobh/Aghada), Cork

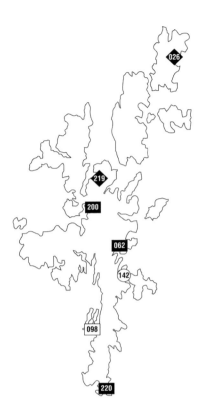

The military airfields of the Shetland Islands

Key

000	Airfield with tarmac runway
◀000▶	Marine base
000	Grass airfield
◀000▶	Airfield with metal track runway
000	Satellite landing ground
▲000	Airship base
▼000	Helicopter base
041	Grass/Airship base
(000)	Baloon station
⬤	Major town

26   Balta Sound (Unst), Shetland
62   Catfirth, Shetland
98   Fair Isle, Shetland
142   Lerwick, Shetland
200   Scatsta, Shetland
219   Sullom Voe (Garth's Vow), Shetland
220   Sumburgh, Shetland

THE AIRFIELDS

ABBOTSINCH, Strathclyde

55°52'49"N/04°25'49"W; NS479670. 5 miles W of Glasgow city centre off J28 of M8

For the first thirty years of its existence, Abbotsinch lived under the shadow of its neighbour at Renfrew. Thanks to a decision made in the 1960s, the airfield has blossomed into one of Scotland's most successful international airports and continues to thrive today.

The story began in 1932 when an airfield was established between Black Cart Water and White Cart Water. Completed ahead of schedule, the first unit was 602 (City of Glasgow) AAF Squadron, which moved in from Renfrew on 20 January 1933 with Wapitis. Since its formation the squadron had been operating in the bomber role, but with the arrival of the Hector in November 1938 it changed to Army Co-operation. However, it was announced on 14 January that the squadron was to transfer to fighters and re-equip with the Gauntlet. By May 1939 the unit received the Spitfire and was embodied into the RAF, its part-time days now behind it. On the outbreak of war, 602 Squadron moved to Grangemouth, destined to achieve great things but not to serve here again until peacetime.

Despite being formed at Renfrew in 1925, 602 (City of Glasgow) made Abbotsinch its home from 1933 flying a range of types from the DH.9 to the Spitfire. The Hawker Hart I was introduced from February 1934 and served until June 1936.

The first of nearly forty FAA squadron movements took place on 17 December 1939 when 816 and 818 Squadrons' Swordfish arrived from HMS *Furious*. Their stay was brief, both having departed for Campbeltown by 19 February 1940. Another unit with a naval theme arrived here from Gosport on 19 March. The TTU's job was to train torpedo-bomber crews flying the Shark and Swordfish; the unit trained both naval and RAF crews for this dangerous occupation. Torpedo drops were carried out over the Firth of Clyde, but not without loss to man and machine. As the Royal Navy increased its own units in the role, the TTU re-equipped with Beauforts and Wellingtons before it was merged into 1 TTU at Turnberry on 1 January 1943.

Avro Anson I K6318 of 269 Squadron, which served at Abbotsinch for three tours of duty from 1936 to 1938.

The first front-line RAF unit to be formed here was 309 Squadron on 7 October 1940 with Lysanders. It was the first of several Army Co-operation squadrons to be formed as the 'winged arm' of the Polish Army. The vast majority of its personnel were Polish, all having served in their own air force before the outbreak of the war. During its stay here the new squadron was inspected by Gen W. Sikorski, the GOC of the Polish Army, before it moved to Renfrew on 6 November 1940.

232 Squadron's Hurricanes made an appearance in July, having made a rather indirect transit from Montrose to Ouston. As the year progressed the airfield became busier, with the Blackburn aircraft company making full use of Abbotsinch to test-fly its aircraft built at its Dumbarton factory. These were mainly Bothas, which were a common sight through to early 1942. The airfield became a storage area, with nearly 130 aircraft being recorded here during October 1941, although it would be developed as part of the CRO system. It was this influx of aircraft that instigated the departure of the TTU to the comparative calm of Turnberry.

The CODF, or 1441 Flight, was formed here on 20 January 1942. It flew the Anson and Lysander and was tasked with providing co-operation for 'Combined Operations' training units stationed in western Scotland. For those pilots serving on the flight, its activities would have been as close as you could get to action without being shot at! Sorties included practice attacks on shipping and landing craft, low-level reconnaissance, smoke screen laying, gas spraying and providing aircraft for demonstrations to Army units on the ground. The Mustang and Hurricane were also introduced before the busy flight departed for Dundonald in October.

RAF units were by now becoming few and far between, so the formation of another flight here on 24 May 1943 could only have been pertinent to western Scotland. 1680 Flight CF was just that, specifically to ferry VIPs to the Hebrides, Orkney and Shetland islands. Equipped with three Dominie and a Walrus, this flight moved to Prestwick on 6 March 1944.

An FAA presence continued through May and June 1943 when 819 Squadron's Swordfish came and went via Ballykelly before embarking on HMS *Archer*. 892 Squadron's Martlets also made a brief appearance in June as Abbotsinch was being prepared for new ownership. The transition to Royal Navy control would have almost gone unnoticed, as a Maintenance Yard on the airfield known as HMS *Sanderling* had been established since June 1940. This same name was given to the entire airfield when it came under complete Royal Navy control from 11 August 1943. The day-to-day life of the station changed very little as RAF Maintenance Command continued its activities until it made a move to Renfrew.

832 Squadron visited with Avengers in February 1944, and 730 Squadron was formed on 17 April 1944. Initially equipped with the Reliant, a Q.6 followed in July, and in September the Firefly, Sea Otter and Walrus were also added. On 20 November 1944 the squadron moved to Ayr.

Throughout the summer and autumn of 1944, several FAA squadrons came and went. These included the Wildcats of 813 and 852 Squadrons, the Sea Hurricanes of 835 Squadron and the Swordfish of 824 Squadron, although none of them stayed for very long.

Only a detachment of Barracudas from 821 Squadron passed through HMS *Sanderling* in January 1945 before peace descended upon the airfield again. Post-war residents included the return of 821 Squadron and two visits in July and August of 802 Squadron's Seafires; they would return again on detachment in October 1947. 1702 Squadron also arrived in September when it moved up from Lee-on-Solent, only to leave for HMS *Trumpeter* eight days later.

Despite being an established RNAS airfield by now, the re-formation of 602 Squadron on 10 May 1946 was welcomed by both services. The unit was embodied on 11 June, but did not receive its first aircraft, the Spitfire F.14, until October. The F.21 and F.22 followed until, in January 1951, the squadron entered the jet era with the Vampire, which it retained for the remainder of its existence. Detached to Leuchars from April to July 1951, the squadron moved to Renfrew in April 1952, only to return here on 18 June 1954. It continued to operate from Abbotsinch until 10 March 1957, when the RAAF was abruptly brought to an end by sweeping defence cuts.

Other post-war units included the arrival of Glasgow UAS from Renfrew in October 1946, which had moved to Perth by 1 December 1950. A different pace of life descended upon Abbotsinch on 5 December 1952 when 666 Squadron with Austers arrived from Renfrew under the guise of 1968 Flight. They were joined on the same day by 1967 (Reserve) AOP Flight, also from Renfrew flying Austers. Both had gone by 1954, 1967 Flight moving to Perth on 2 September 1954. 663 VGS was also formed here on 16 November 1959 but had gone by the early 1960s, becoming the last significant RAF flying presence on the airfield.

Meanwhile the FAA presence continued to grow and the airfield was expanded into one of the Royal Navy's largest AHUs. This began in 1950 when a Reserve Aircraft Storage unit was established and a Royal Navy Maintenance Yard. The latter helped to prepare new types for service with the FAA, including the Sea Vixen. The storage element was responsible for anything up to 400 aircraft at a time, and also had the task of scrapping aircraft. From any direction aircraft such as Avengers, Sea Hawks, Sea Venoms and Skyraiders could be seen parked side by side with the wings folded, awaiting their fate.

While several FAA squadrons continued to come and go, a few were a little more permanent. One of these was 1830 Squadron, which was re-formed here on 15 August 1947. Equipped with Seafires and Fireflies, its role was a fighter A/S squadron in the RNVR. It moved to Donibristle on 2 December 1950, but was back here by 1 November 1952. After a brief spell at Culham, the squadron returned in mid-1953 and remained here until it disbanded on 10 March 1957.

When 1830 Squadron returned from Renfrew on 1 November 1952 'A' Flight was formed, which by 28 March 1953 had been redesignated into another squadron. 1843 Squadron was an A/S unit that used the Avengers from 1830 Squadron. The unit's life was cut short on 10 March 1957 when it fell victim to defence cuts. By now the AHU's workload was in decline as the FAA was rapidly shrinking and its needs compared to wartime were considerably less. On 31 October 1963 the Royal Navy paid off HMS *Sanderling* as the airfield was now being planned with a civilian aviation future in mind.

In a typical scene at Abbotsinch during the Royal Navy's AHU period, aircraft such as the Sea Venom and Sea Hawk, as seen here, were stored in the open, most likely never to fly again.

In 1960 the future of Abbotsinch as Glasgow's new airport had already been decided. Renfrew continued as Glasgow Airport until 2 May 1966, when the first civilian aircraft, a BEA Viscount piloted by Captain Eric Starling, landed. Incredibly, in its first year of operation the new Glasgow Airport handled 1.5 million passengers and 34,000 aircraft movements.

By the 1970s the package holiday boom helped the airport grow, and by 1976 a £2 million extension was begun to the international area of the terminal building. By the 1980s annual passenger numbers were about to breach four million and it was clear that the airport was going to have to expand again to keep pace. This began in 1989 with a large terminal development programme, which would increase its size by 70%. Not long after this work had begun, Prestwick lost its monopoly on international flights and the big carriers from the USA and Canada began moving into Glasgow. The 21st century brought continued growth, with eight million passengers being handled by 2003. The following year a second terminal was opened and, in August 2004, Glasgow became the first Scottish airport to handle one million passengers per month.

Glasgow Airport describes itself today as 'Scotland's principal long-haul gateway', which is a difficult statement to dispute.

Main features:
WW2 FAA period: *Concrete runways:* QDM 173-353 1,730 yards, 058-238 1,400 yards, 103-283 1,030 yards. *Hangars:* three Callender Hamilton 180 x 90 feet, five Bellman and one 60 x 70 feet. *Accommodation:* RN: 1,486; WRNS: 311.

ALDERGROVE, Down

54°39'12"N/06°13'77"W; J145795. 2 miles N of Crumlin

By the time Aldergrove opened, the RFC had passed into history and it was only thanks to aircraft production at Harland & Wolff that a role was found. On 15 October 1918, 16 AAP was formed to accept Harland & Wolff-built V/1500s, but only a handful arrived. Hangars and several technical and domestic buildings were built for the AAP but their full potential use was yet to be established. 16 AAP was closed on 4 December 1919, but the RAF retained the airfield for annual exercises.

The F.2bs of 4 Squadron were first to arrive from Farnborough in August 1920, remaining until 4 May 1921. 2 Squadron then brought F.2bs from Digby on 31 May 1922, in an Army support role in the event of any trouble in the province. The squadron left for Farnborough in

September but returned the following year. Aldergrove then languished for a few years before an Air Ministry decision in 1924 approved the formation of several Special Reserve Squadrons.

On 15 May 1925 502 (Bomber) Squadron began to form here. Volunteers were plenty and all airmen were billeted in Crumlin, which is where the squadron also had its own office in Old Town Hall Street. The first of several Vimys arrived on 9 June and remained in use until July 1928. Before the year was out, the unit had changed its name to 502 (Ulster) Squadron and displayed the distinctive red hand on its badge and aircraft. The Vimy was replaced by the Hyderabad, followed by the Virginia in December 1931. From October 1935 the squadron remained a night bomber unit but now flew the Wallace and, from April 1937, the Hind. 502 Squadron also became part of Coastal Command on 28 November 1938, where it would continue to serve until the end of the war.

Looking south-west towards Lough Neagh, this 1930s view of Aldergrove shows a large grass landing area and the fledgling RAF camp. The rifle range in the foreground is still in situ.

On 6 October 1936 2 ATC was re-formed and the first operational unit, 85 Squadron, brought its Hurricanes from Debden on 18 October 1938. 2 ATC became 2 ATS from 1 April 1938, with a range located at Loch Neagh. The unit would change its name again on 17 April 1939, when 1 ATS at Catfoss combined with 2 ATS to become 3 AOS, and once more on 1 November, becoming 3 B&GS.

502 Squadron received a more appropriate aircraft when the Anson arrived in January 1939. By the end of August the auxiliaries were already mobilised and flying convoy escort and A/S patrols.

Aldergrove become the home of 23 MU from 1 December. Its main task was as an ASU and a Repair & Salvage Unit. The first types handled were Blenheims, Hampdens and Wellingtons, which were all prepared for front-line service. The workload would grow as the war progressed to such a point that, at its peak, Aldergrove had a further six SLGs under its control in Northern Ireland.

Up until now there was a distinct lack of fighter protection against enemy raids on Belfast, but this was rectified when 245 Squadron moved in from Turnhouse on 20 July 1940. The squadron flew convoy patrols and, all too often, abortive scrambles.

Several detachments from Coastal Command served here in 1940. The Blenheims of 235 Squadron from Bircham Newton were the first to arrive, followed by the Hudsons of 233 Squadron from Leuchars on 3 August. Both squadrons flew convoy escort and A/S patrols until they were relieved by 224 Squadron's Hudsons and 253 Squadron's Blenheims following 233 Squadron's return to Leuchars on 14 September.

Hurricanes of 245 Squadron taxi in the sunshine at Aldergrove in May 1941. By now the unit was off the mark with several enemy kills under its belt.

Armourers replenish the .303 Browning machine guns of a 245 Squadron Hurricane at Aldergrove.

In the meantime 502 Squadron was still flying patrols in its Ansons, but despite its best efforts was never up to the task of sinking a U-boat. In August the squadron began to receive ASV Mk II-equipped Whitleys. These aircraft formed their own flight and, despite being fitted with radar, the target was often spotted visually before the radar operator picked it up. By the time the squadron got to grips with the Whitleys it had moved to Limavady on 27 January 1941.

245 Squadron saw some action during the Belfast Blitz, which began on 7/8 April 1941. The squadron had switched to the night role and it was on that night that it began to score by shooting down an He 111 off Larne. The enemy raids continued and the following night another He 111 was destroyed, but it was not until 6 May that a third was shot down near Ardglass. The squadron had already taken part in detachments to Limavady and Ballyhalbert, and it was to the latter that the squadron moved on 14 July 1941. The Fighter Sector HQ had already moved to Ballyhalbert in June, and now Aldergrove was all set for a long period with Coastal Command.

252 Squadron arrived from Chivenor on 6 April with Blenheims, but began to receive the Beaufighter not long after. Few Beaufighter sorties were flown before the squadron was earmarked for service overseas. The aircraft were flown out to the Mediterranean from late May, and on 15 June the squadron was disbanded and redesignated the same day as 143 Squadron, still at Aldergrove.

252 Squadron's duties were taken over by 254 Squadron from Sumburgh on 29 May, which was still equipped with the Blenheim. The squadron flew shipping escorts until it was moved to Dyce on 10 December 1941. 143 Squadron had inherited some of 252 Squadron's Beaufighters, but before the unit was fully worked up it was moved to Thornaby on 5 July 1941.

On 12 August 1941 it was the turn of 206 Squadron from St Eval with Hudsons. The Wellingtons of 311 Squadron arrived from East Wretham on 28 April and flew their first patrol about a month later, only to leave for Talbenny on 12 June. This move was to make way for 9 OTU, which was formed on 7 June; the unit's role was to train crews on the Beaufighter and Beaufort. Plans were already afoot for Aldergrove to become a Coastal Command airfield, and on 6 September 9 OTU was moved to Crosby-on-Eden. In the meantime 206 Squadron was carrying out several attacks on U-boats, but could not confirm any before it moved to Benbecula on 1 July 1942.

120 Squadron's Liberators from Ballykelly served here in mid-1942, and on 14 February moved in permanently. The same day 220 Squadron, flying the Fortress, arrived from Ballykelly and both squadrons began A/S patrols. The following day 120 Squadron was in action when Fg Off R. Turner and crew attacked and sunk U-529. More success followed on 21 February when Sqn Ldr Isted and crew were escorting convoy ON166. A pair of U-boats were spotted near the convoy, and Isted attacked the nearest with depth charges, sinking U-623.

120 Squadron scored another success on 5 April when Fg Off G. Hatherley and crew sank U-635 south-west of Iceland after attacking with depth charges. The following day Fg Off G. Moffat and crew attacked two U-boats while they were escorting convoy HX231 off Iceland. One of them, U-594, was seriously damaged and was forced to return to port earlier than planned. 120 Squadron was making such an impression while operating from Iceland that it moved there on 15 April, although elements remained at Aldergrove during the summer of 1943. 220 Squadron did not achieve the same level of success during its tour before it moved to Benbecula on 20 March 1943.

Two days earlier 86 Squadron brought its Liberators from Thorney Island, and it was not long before its tally was on the increase. On 6 April Plt Off C. Burcher and crew managed to take U-632 by surprise and sunk it with several depth charges. A second U-boat was also attacked before the end of the patrol, but its demise could not be confirmed. U-109 fell victim to an 86 Squadron Liberator on 4 May when it was attacked by four depth charges south of Ireland.

Aldergrove took on a training role from 10 October 1943 when 1674 HCU was formed to provide conversion training for crews for long-range patrol squadrons. The majority of equipment needed was provided by 1 (Coastal) OTU at Silloth. The OTU's Liberator CF, which had been here since 9 September, formed the core of the new HCU. Only nine days later the unit was moved to Longtown while the Liberator Flight remained here. The HCU trained hundreds of Coastal Command aircrew during its long tour, which came to an end on 10 August 1945 with a move to Milltown.

On 9 August 1945 Aldergrove's original meteorological unit, 1402 Flight, returned from Ballyhalbert and was joined by 518 Squadron from Tiree on 18 September. Twelve days later the flight was absorbed into 518 Squadron, whose Halifaxes had been flying its own Bismuth sorties since mid-1943.

502 Squadron returned when it was re-formed here on 10 May 1946 with the Mosquito B.25, which had been replaced by the NF.30 by December 1947. The squadron would remain in the fighter role, later receiving the Spitfire, followed by three marks of the Vampire, before being disbanded for good on 1 March 1957.

One of many aircraft test-flown from Aldergrove was the Short Sperrin. The 'fourth' V-bomber is seen on its maiden flight on 10 August 1951.

518 Squadron was renumbered as 202 Squadron in October 1946, retaining the Halifax until 1950, when it was superseded by the Hastings. 224 Squadron was also re-formed here with the Halifax on 1 March 1948, but moved to Gibraltar on 18 October. 120 Squadron returned on 1 April 1952, now flying the Shackleton MR.1. A month after 120 Squadron's arrival several of its MR.1s were transferred to 240 Squadron, which re-formed here, then moved on to St Eval on 27 May. 120 Squadron operated the MR.2 alongside the earlier mark until both were superseded by the MR.3 from September 1958. On 1 April 1959 the squadron returned to Kinloss.

The 1950s saw several detachments from 275 Squadron, flying the Sycamore HR.14 on ASR duties. Aldergrove briefly gained its own Sycamore unit when 118 Squadron was re-formed here on 1 February 1959. However, the unit was to be short-lived and was disbanded on 14 April 1961, leaving just 202 Squadron as the only RAF flying unit here. The latter squadron, which could trace its lineage to the pre-war AMMT, was finally disbanded on 28 August 1964.

The airfield was now the domain of 23 MU, which had continued to be busy through the post-war years. On 1 December 1963, while retaining its original name, the MU was referred to as the Aircraft Supply & Servicing Depot. At a similar time, Aldergrove was about to enter a new phase of its history thanks to a decision to turn it into Belfast Airport. Unlike Nutt's Corner, from which it was taking over, the new airport would have a brand new terminal building.

Aldergrove duly became Belfast Airport and its new terminal was opened by HM Queen Elizabeth the Queen Mother on 28 October 1963. Within three years the airport began its first regular jet service to Gatwick, and later both Aer Lingus and BOAC introduced scheduled services

The prototype Short Belfast lands at Aldergrove on 5 January 1964 after its maiden flight from Sydenham.

across the Atlantic. The airport's facilities continued to expand during the 1970s including larger aprons, enabling the airport to handle all aircraft up to Boeing 747 size.

In the meantime half the airfield was still under military, control and 23 MU continued to serve here until it was disbanded on 30 June 1978. 845 Squadron was detached here from Yeovilton with its Wessex helicopters from October 1977 to May 1982. The long association between Aldergrove and 72 Squadron began when it arrived from Benson on 12 November 1981. The squadron flew its Wessex HC.2s to every corner of Northern Ireland until it was disbanded here in April 2002. Various RAF and FAA helicopter units were detached here through the 1980s and 1990s, but Aldergrove ceased to exist as an RAF station on 20 September 2009. However, the military are far from finished with this airfield as it is now under tri-service control, and is currently under the control of the Joint Helicopter Command. The AAC has also been quietly operating from here since the early 1970s, flying a host of different rotary types as well as the Beaver and Islander in the photographic and surveillance roles, which it continues to do.

The airport, which has been known as Belfast International since 1983, continues to go from strength to strength, and during 2010 more than four million passengers passed through its gates from more than 40,000 aircraft movements. Aldergrove's future as a civilian airport, we can safely say, looks pretty secure.

Main features:
Concrete runways: QDM 256 2,000 yards, 356 2,000 yards. *Hangars:* eighteen various. *Hardstandings:* thirty loop. *Accommodation:* RAF: 2,752; WAAF: 537.

Modern-day Belfast Airport, with the civilian terminal on the north side, while the military retains the south.

ALLOA (FORTHBANK/CAUDRON), Clackmannanshire

56°6'50"N/03°46'02"W. 1 mile E of A907/A910 Clackmannan Road, S of A907/B909 junction on northern bank of Firth of Forth

More associated with flying at Hendon during the pre-First World War period, W. H. Ewen Aviation Co Ltd had opened a flying school in 1911 at Lanark. Later, from 1913, the company was registered at 28 Bath Street, Glasgow, then the outbreak of the Great War saw the company expand.

W. E. McEwen in a Caudron G.2, after landing near Peterborough en route to Scotland.

Contracts for the supply of aircraft were being undertaken at the Hendon Factory, so Ewen looked for another plant further north. The company's second site, described as the 'Scottish factory and aerodrome', was established at Alloa in 1914. The same year the company was renamed the British Caudron Co Ltd, showing its alliance to the French manufacturer.

The production focused on Caudron types, a single G.2 and the more prolific G.3, of which sixty-one were built here. As pressure for more aircraft increased, the factory became a sub-contractor for other companies for the rest of the war. Fifty BE.2C/Es, twenty-two 504Bs and 100 Camels were built here.

The Armistice brought an end to the factory, but the airfield was licensed for a short period during the 1920s for recreational flying. Sir Alan Cobham brought his 'flying circus' to the 'Old Aerodrome' for a display on 14 September 1932.

Unusually the site has not been developed thanks in part to the area just coming under the wing of the Trossachs National Park. The site remains much the same as it was, although there is no physical evidence of a factory or airfield remains.

ALNESS (INVERGORDON/DALMORE), Ross-shire (Ross and Cromarty)

57°40'47"N/04°15'56"W; NH655675. 1 mile S of Alness off A9

The RAF had a presence at Alness for more than fifty years, but now the sound of flying boats roaring down the Cromarty Firth has long gone. This flying boat station was one of the busiest during the Second World War, but could trace its roots back a lot further.

On 8 July 1924 two aircraft from the FBDF at Felixstowe alighted on the Cromarty Firth, a Felixstowe F.5 and Saro A.7. At this time the station was known as Invergordon, despite being positioned just a mile south of Alness along Teaninich Beach at Alness Point. Gone in just a few weeks, the site used by the FBDF must have been noted for future use.

The years passed until early 1938, when the military presence began to increase. The first customers were 209 Squadron's Singapores, once again from Felixstowe, on 27 October 1938. Two days later they were joined by Londons of 201 Squadron from Calshot, and the same day 228 Squadron's Stranraers arrived from Pembroke Dock. The activity was short-lived, however, with all three leaving by 9 October, but an RAF presence remained, and work began on expanding Invergordon.

209 Squadron returned on 12 August 1939, now with the Stranraer. It was joined the same day by 240 Squadron from Calshot with Londons and Lerwicks. After some detachments, both squadrons saw Invergordon enter the war. 209 Squadron left first for Oban, on 7 October 1939. 240 Squadron, whose Lerwicks had gone by September, moved to Sullom Voe on 4 November 1939. In the meantime 210 Squadron's Sunderlands had arrived from Pembroke Dock on 23 October. They returned on 6 November, but were replaced the same day by 201 Squadron from Sullom Voe flying the London. Rejoined by 210 Squadron on 24 November, both squadrons settled into a period of operations, which continued until May 1940. 240 Squadron also returned, staying from 12 February to 27 March 1940 before returning to Sullom Voe.

4 (Coastal) OTU moved here on 21 June 1941, bringing Invergordon back to life again. The familiar sight of the Stranraer and the London graced the Cromarty Firth again, as well as the odd Lerwick. The Catalina also made an appearance, and by August 1941 more than forty flying boats spread across the four types served the OTU, as well as several Lysanders operating from Evanton.

This Saro Lerwick I of 4 COTU is on a training sortie from Invergordon.

On 20 February 1942 five Sunderlands and seven Catalinas were dispersed to Wig Bay, to reduce temptation from the Luftwaffe. This still left a large number of flying boats here, so the OTU was divided into two. Basic flying training was carried out on the Stranraer, seven Londons, three Sunderlands and three Catalinas, which were detached to Stranraer. Operational training would be carried out here on Catalinas and Sunderlands, while observer training would continue on the Singapores and Stranraers that remained. However, by September 1942 Invergordon had its own servicing unit, 5 FBSU, located at Dalmore, until it was disbanded in December 1944.

When 4 OTU first arrived it was training up to ten crews per course, but the new split system had increased this to an average of twenty-two crews per month. Further progress was hindered by the lack of Sunderlands and Catalinas, which were not arriving very quickly. By late 1942 the problem was aggravated by the withdrawal from RAF service, after many faultless years, of the Singapore, Stranraer and London.

The arrival of 228 Squadron's Sunderland III W4026 from Oban on 23 August 1942 would not have turned many heads as it was refuelled ready for a flight to Iceland two days later. However, on board the aircraft that day was HRH the Duke of Kent. After a long take-off, the Sunderland clambered into the air and set course for Dunnet Head, following the Caithness coast en route. Unfortunately, a combination of factors developed, the Sunderland drifted off course and, now too far inland, crashed into a ridge known locally as the Eagles Rock near Dunbeath, killing all on board except the rear gunner, whose turret broke away after the initial impact.

On 10 November 1942 the Stranraer detachment returned as part of a plan to take over the new site near Dalmore, which was still not complete. Regardless, several of the Nissen huts on the site began to be occupied by the influx of airmen.

A reshuffle of several of the RAF's OTUs followed, and from October 1943 Alness (its name changed on 10 February 1943) became an all-Sunderland unit. The Catalinas left for 131 (C)OTU at Killadeas, and by March 1944 the OTU's establishment had been adjusted to forty-one Sunderlands, five Martinets and an Oxford. The number of Sunderlands was further increased the same month when 302 FTU arrived from Stranraer and stayed until June.

All land-based support aircraft were moved to Tain on 10 December, and by the New Year there was a slightly reduced establishment. 302 FTU returned on 1 July 1945, but with the war at an end all operations ceased; it clung on until it was disbanded on 1 April 1946.

One of the final units to move here was the CCFIS from Turnberry on 16 July 1945, returning on 29 October of that year. 4 OTU continued training crews as there was still a demand in the Far East, and the Sunderland was many years away from retirement. However, 4 OTU was not destined to remain and the unit was moved to Pembroke Dock on 15 August 1946.

This was certainly not the end for Alness as an RAF station, and its reprieve came not from a flying unit but from a marine one. On 1 July 1946 1100 MC was formed here to provide ASR for the many aircraft that were still operating over the Moray Firth. This small but important unit continued this task until it was disbanded on 1 April 1986.

Very few buildings were erected at Invergordon with long-term use in mind, including the unique watch office, pictured here in 1945.

Sunderland Vs of 3 OTU moored in the Cromarty Firth in 1945.

Today the main site is a business park, while Dalmore is occupied by a distillery. However, the remnants of one slipway remain and the usual tell-tale remnants of concrete roads still meander among the more modern buildings.

ANNAN, Dumfries and Galloway

55°01'04"N/03°13'46"W; NY218700. 3 miles NE of Annan off B722

There is no doubt that the position of this airfield, whatever its purpose was to become, was not given the greatest of thought. The area suffered from poor weather, more often than not with fog and mist, a regular hazard, aggravated by its proximity to the Solway Firth and the River Annan. But this was early 1941 and the Air Ministry was hungry for more airfields if it was going to meet its own targets for more qualified RAF pilots.

Annan received its first unit when 55 OTU arrived from Usworth on 28 April 1942 to find the airfield resembling a building site rather than a new training station. Once the move was complete, more than seventy-five Hurricanes, twenty Masters, several Lysanders and a Dominie were parked around the perimeter, a lucky few finding shelter in the hangars and blisters.

No self-respecting OTU could operate without a batch of Masters, 55 OTU being no exception.

It was impractical for all of these aircraft to operate safely from one airfield, so from early May Annan gained a satellite at Longtown. 'A' and 'B' Flight of the OTU would operate from Annan while 'C' and 'D' Flights, for the more advanced stages of training, would fly from Longtown.

From 15 April 1943 the OTU was under the control of 9 Group based at Barton Hall. Its task was the defence of North West England and, despite being based in Scotland, Annan's fighters could be called upon to fly a defensive role.

Longtown had to be relinquished on 20 October 1943 to make way for the Wellingtons of 6 OTU from Silloth and the Halifaxes of 1674 HCU from Aldergrove. Both 'C' and 'D' Flights, made up of just eight Hurricanes and a Master, made a seamless transition to Great Orton.

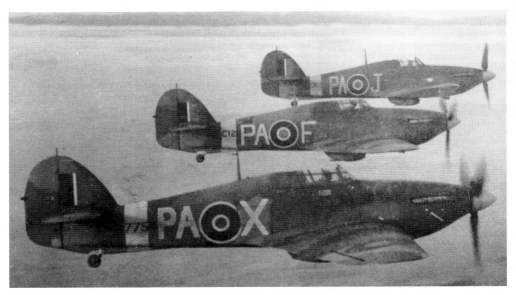

'EH' and the 'PA' coding on these Hurricanes was introduced to 55 OTU from its formation in November 1940 and was retained when the unit became 3 TEU in March 1944.

The arrival of the Typhoon brought about several changes to 55 OTU including its disbandment and reincarnation as 4 TEU on 26 January 1944. Before this change had occurred, the unit was briefly designated as a DPHU, but when it became a TEU the intention was to operate the unit as a fighter-bomber OTU. It was also briefly made a temporary Typhoon CU, but a lack of the type rendered this title instantly obsolete, with only two of them still on station by February 1944.

A reshuffle saw the new TEU reduced to three flights, with 'B' operating from Great Orton. Nearly ninety Typhoons were operated by 4 TEU, the majority of which were still early Mk Is, the rest being made up of Mk IIas and IIbs. The latter were useful for specialised training such as rocket-firing, dive-bombing and tactical formation bombing, all of which were planned for a Typhoon unit. Aerial gunnery had been the 'bread and butter' of the unit since the start, while the local coastline lent itself as a makeshift French coast where pilots could carry out dummy low-level attacks using gun cameras.

4 TEU was designated as 3 TEU on 21 March 1944 and was now tasked with the training of fighter-bomber pilots. By this time there were sufficient Typhoons to fully equip 'B' and 'C' Flights. The former was tasked with type conversion while the latter trained its pilots in the art of attacking shipping, tactical bombing and low-level cross-country exercises. Hurricanes were still the dominant type; fifty-eight were used, together with twenty-five Typhoons and the usual collection of support aircraft.

The TEU's aircraft were now more useful along the English South Coast than in south-west Scotland, and on 10 May 1944 'C' Flight's Typhoons headed for Honiley. Under the guise of 555 Squadron, the Flight provided fighter defence cover over Tyneside from Acklington, while the operational squadrons began to congregate for the invasion of Europe. 'C' Flight was never to return to Annan and, with forty-five aircraft remaining, 3 TEU left on 17 July 1944 for Aston Down.

This was the end for flying, but Annan's use as a military establishment was not quite over. From 17 August 1944 the airfield was taken over by 14 MU as an ESD sub-site. On 27 May 1945 it was joined by 249 MU, which used all available concrete surfaces for the storage of ordnance. Both MUs ceased to use Annan on 15 August 1952 and the site and all its remaining buildings were sold off.

However, Annan continued to be used for a different military role when it became the home of a Magnox nuclear power plant, aka Chapelcross. Completed in 1959, the foremost purpose for the plant was to produce plutonium for WE.177, the United Kingdom's main nuclear weapons programme. The electricity produced by the plant was seen as a by-product to help disguise the plant's true purpose. Four giant 300-foot cooling towers dominated the skyline for many years until the plant ceased to operate in 2004. Against a great deal of local opposition, the cooling towers were demolished in 2007 and the long process of decommissioning continues.

Main features:
Runways: QDM 240 1,600 yards, 150 1,600 yards. *Hangars:* three T1, eight blister. *Hardstandings:* seventy-four. *Accommodation:* RAF: 1,900; WAAF: 322.

ARBROATH (ABERBROTHOCK), Tayside

56°34'57.37"N/2°37'19.04"W; NO620435. 2 miles NNW of Arbroath off A933

Arbroath is a unique airfield that has stood the test of time, thanks to its continuous occupation since it opened in 1940. It remains a time capsule of what an FAA airfield looked like during the war, with a huge range of original preserved and sympathetically modernised buildings.

Arbroath was commissioned on 19 June 1940 as HMS *Condor*, becoming the home of 2 OS and a DLT School. The first unit to arrive was 778 Squadron from Lee-on-Solent, bringing a huge range of aircraft to Arbroath until its departure to Crail on 5 March 1943.

It was the remnants of 767 Squadron that arrived here on 8 July 1940 from HMS *Ark Royal* with the Swordfish and Albacore. Regrouping, the unit became a DLT squadron from parts of 763 Squadron, later known as the DLT School. As well as making full use of an inhouse DLT runway, further training was also carried out from HMS *Furious* and *Argus*. The DLT work was also shared with 768 Squadron, which formed on 13 January 1941. As well as operating Swordfish, the squadron also provided fighter training on the Fulmar, Sea Hurricane and Martlet using HMS *Activity*, *Furious* and *Argus*. 768 Squadron moved to Machrihanish on 1 March 1943, followed by 767 Squadron, which moved to East Haven on 5 May 1943. This did not bring an end to DLT work because a third unit, 769 Squadron, re-formed here on 29 November 1941. Once again, a large array of current FAA types was operated until the unit joined 767 Squadron at East Haven on 7 November 1943.

2 OS grew with the arrival of three more squadrons during August and September 1940 thanks to the efforts of the Luftwaffe along the English South Coast. First to arrive was 751 Squadron, flying the Walrus from Ford on 19 August after a serious German raid. The Luftwaffe also forced 753 Squadron out of Lee-on-Solent ten days later. The squadron brought Seals and Sharks, followed later by the Swordfish. It was a similar story for 754 Squadron, which arrived on 7 September, also from Lee-on-Solent. Its main task was to train observers and air gunners in ASV equipment using the Proctor until the end of 1941.

Two further training squadrons arrived in October with 758 Squadron on the 14th and 791 Squadron, formed here on the 15th. 758 Squadron was a TAG Training squadron with the Skua, Roc and Proctor, only to disband on 1 February 1941. 791 Squadron served here a lot longer as an Air Target Towing unit with two Rocs. It would grow in size with the addition of various types before disbanding on 10 December 1944.

The final training unit that would make up 2 OS was formed on 9 January 1941. 783 Squadron was created as an ASV Radar Training squadron, which would become Arbroath's longest-serving unit. Its main type was the Swordfish, which would continue to serve until July 1945. The squadron also operated a DH.86, AX840, until it was damaged by 'friendly fire' from a minesweeper off Bell Rock in July 1942.

Early 1944 was interrupted by the brief sound of Merlins as both 820 and 841 Squadrons passed through Arbroath with Barracudas. Another Barracuda unit, 814 Squadron, arrived during the year as the torpedo-bomber rapidly rose to becoming the most common FAA type in the region.

1944 also saw the demise of 754 Squadron, which was disbanded on 27 March, but before the year was over more training squadrons were established here. 'Y' Flight of 787 Squadron formed on 13 June as a Fighter Affiliation Flight with Seafires, but had left for Burscough by 6 August. Next to arrive was 778 Squadron, a Service Trials Units, which as its name suggests performed tests on all new aircraft that were about to enter service with the FAA. Every single service type of the day passed through the unit, which arrived from Crail on 15 August 1944. It was an incredibly busy unit and its workload was far from over when it left for Gosport on 9 August 1945.

By now the Naval Air Signals School had also been established during early 1944, and by 1945 the two training squadrons were still 753 and 783, both now flying the Barracuda, Avenger and Firefly.

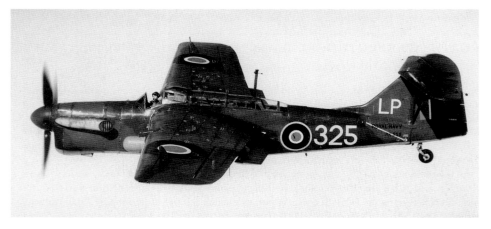

A lovely shot of 783 Squadron Barracuda V RK558 out of Arbroath in early 1945.

With the end of the war in Europe only days away, the first operational squadron created here was 802 Squadron on 1 May 1945, re-formed with Seafires. The unit moved to Twatt on 21 June not long after another operational squadron was re-formed. It was now the turn of 803 Squadron, which re-formed on 15 June 1945 with Seafires. The plan was for 803 Squadron to join the 19th CAG for service on an 'Implacable' Class carrier, but the end of the war in the Far East brought that idea to a close and the unit moved instead to Nutt's Corner on 23 September.

2 OS began to wind down from this point. 753 Squadron moved to Rattray in November 1945, but it was not until 15 May 1947 that 783 Squadron moved to Lee-on-Solent. In the meantime, 772 Squadron, an FRU, arrived from Burscough in January 1946 with various aircraft, only staying until July. It returned again on 26 June 1947, this time from Anthorn with the Mosquito, and remained here until 13 October 1948, when 772 Squadron was disbanded. 801 Squadron also made Arbroath its home during the post-war period when it brought its Sea Hornets from Culdrose on 30 April 1948, only to leave for Anthorn on 21 May. The pace of units coming and going finally began to slow and the sound of aircraft engines began to fade for the first time in more than eight years.

It was not quite over yet, though, and with HMS *Condor* still in Admiralty hands 802 Squadron was re-formed again on 2 February 1953 with Sea Furies, leaving on 20 April for HMS *Theseus*. The last FAA flying unit to pass through Arbroath was 'A' Flight, 703 Squadron, which arrived from Ford on 17 February 1954. The flight was operating as an independent unit, with six ex-825 Squadron Fireflies as 'clockwork mice' for Ferranti's new CCA system. The trial came to an end on 30 June 1954 when the flight returned to Ford. This brought an end to flying operations, but this did not stop an RAF unit, 662 VGS, from making Arbroath its home on 10 May 1958 after moving in from Edzell; it still flies from here today.

Arbroath remained under the control of the Admiralty until it was paid off on 31 March 1971, but it would remain in military hands even before the FAA had decided it had no further use for the airfield. It was immediately taken over by 45 Commando, Royal Marines, and today is known as Condor Barracks.

Main features:

Various hard surface runways: QDM 079-259 1,320 yards, 169-349 1,150 yards, 124-304 1,130 yards, 034-214 1,100 yards, 079-259 530 yards. *Hangars:* five squadron, one storage. *Accommodation:* RN: 1,962; WRNS: 561

Arbroath remains in military hands today and is now the home of 45 Commando as Condor Barracks.

ARMAGH (FARMACAFFLY), Armagh

54°19'91"N/06°39'90"W. 2 miles S of Armagh, approached via Keady Rd

This field was brought into use as an ELG from early 1940, but the site was abandoned in 1941.

ASKERNISH (SOUTH UIST), Western Isles

57°11'01"N/07°24'59"W. 10 miles NNW of Erriskay off A865

During the war Askernish was requisitioned by the RAF as a small ELG until at least 1945. Owing to the surrounding terrain, it would have been very difficult to find, and any emergency landing could have been similarly achieved in the surrounding countryside.

ATHLONE (BALLYDONAGH), Roscommon

3 miles ESE of Athlone railway station at Fardrum, N of Ballydonagh near N6

This was an LG during the First World War, later developed for the IAC.

AUGHT POINT (RINENORE POINT), Donegal

Seaplane station: 55°06'25"N/07°12'71"W; C50177 28838. 3 miles NE of Muff

LG: 55°06'35"N/07°12'81"W; C50142 29020; part of Aught Point

This dual-purpose site was constructed for the USNAS. Combining a seaplane station and LG, it appears that the RNAS used both sites at the same time. RFC operations are recorded as taking place only months before it became the RAF, but by January 1919 it was closed.

AULDBAR (ALBAR), Angus/Forfarshire

56°41'38"N/02°42'10"W. 3½ miles SW of Brechin

Auldbar was a mooring-out station for Lenabo. Four airship bases were carved out of Montreathmont Forest and the area was cleared to allow for the operation of SS airships. The remaining trees formed a natural barrier for those that sought shelter from poor weather or could not make it safely back to Lenabo. The site was only operated from July 1918 to mid-1919 and was then abandoned. Vegetation rapidly reclaimed the site, but four mooring pits still remain and local efforts are being made to restore them.

AYR (HEATHFIELD), South Ayrshire

55°29'08"N/04°35'50"W. NE of Heathfield region of Ayr

There is very little to show for this once important fighter station. This is partly due to the development of Prestwick and the need for more housing and industry as Ayr continues to sprawl.

While construction began in late 1940, Prestwick was hosting fighter squadrons that were mainly operating over central Scotland. Considering the proximity of the two airfields, it is surprising that Prestwick did not retain this role, although it was being considered for bigger and better things.

Ayr was opened on 7 April 1941 but, as was typical with most wartime-built airfields, it was far from ready. Grass areas were unprepared and electrical cables littered the site only days before the first fighters arrived. When 602 Squadron did move in from Prestwick on 15 April, there was still no power on site and fuel had to be brought in until Ayr's facilities were finally finished.

602 Squadron's Spitfires were joined by 141 Squadron from Gravesend on 29 April. 602's uneventful tour came to an end on 10 July when it moved Kenley. However, 141 Squadron, which was now operating the Defiant in its intended role as a night-fighter, would achieve success above Glasgow and Tyneside. It had also been providing night-fighter cover on detachments to Acklington and Drem, which, combined with operations from here, would gain the squadron a further eight enemy kills. Having arrived in June, 141 was operational on the Beaufighter by August, by which time the enemy bombing raids had subsided and no further success was achieved before the unit moved to Acklington on 29 January 1942.

A new Defiant unit was formed here on 20 June 1941. 410 Squadron, the third Canadian night-fighter unit, would go on to be one of the top-scoring squadrons. However, it had barely worked up when it was moved to Drem on 6 August.

More Canadians arrived on 10 July when 402 Squadron brought its Hurricanes from Martlesham Heath. The squadron carried out local defensive patrols during its stay, which ended on 19 August when it moved to Southend. The same day the patrols were taken over by another Hurricane unit, 312 Squadron from Martlesham Heath. However, not many were flown before the squadron was pronounced non-operational while it traded in its Hurricanes for Spitfires from October onwards. On 1 January 1942 the squadron moved to Fairwood Common.

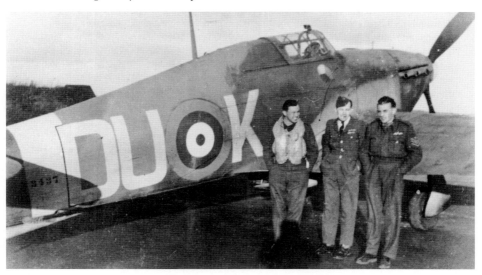

Pilots of 312 Squadron at Ayr in September 1941, only weeks before being declared non-operational to convert to the Spitfire.

A small unit that would shape the future of air operations at Ayr arrived from Ouston on 25 January 1943. 1490 Flight had a variety of aircraft including the Lysander, Master, Henley and Martinet, and not long after arriving Spitfires were also received for air-firing practice. The flight was committed to a large detachment at Catterick from May to July, but once it settled back at Ayr it prepared itself to become the nucleus of the airfield's new and important role.

652 Squadron's Austers moved in from Methven on 2 July 1943 and remained until 7 December, moving then to Ipswich. Not long after, the first of many FAA squadrons arrived. 835 Squadron, with the Swordfish and Sea Hurricane, arrived from HMS *Battler*, and before it left it was joined by 819 Squadron from Maydown, also with Swordfish. 186 Squadron and its Hurricanes spent time working up here after arriving from Drem on 3 August. After getting used to the type, the unit began to re-equip with the Typhoon before leaving for Tain in January 1944. Several more operational RAF and FAA Squadrons arrived during September, and on 1 October 169 Squadron was re-formed here.

Equipped with a handful of Mosquitoes and a Beaufighter, the unit began its training working with 'Gee'. The squadron's ground personnel, who were left at Middle Wallop following its disbandment there on 30 September, were posted in over the following days. 169 Squadron moved to Little Snoring on 8 December, from where it flew its first operational sortie on 20 January 1944.

1490 Flight's destiny was fulfilled when 14 APC was formed from it on 18 October 1943. The new APC was equipped with only a handful of Martinets, but over the following ten months nearly fifty RAF and FAA squadrons would make use of it, making Ayr one of the busiest airfields in Scotland during this period. There simply is not enough space within this book to mention every squadron that passed through, but two Free French squadrons that were formed here in 1944 are worthy of note: 329 Squadron, GC I/2 'Cicognes', and 345 Squadron, GC II/2 'Berry', both formed in January. 329 Squadron left for Perranporth without any aircraft on 22 January, while 345 Squadron received its first Spitfire, AB986, on 30 March.

The number of FAA squadrons that passed through Ayr during 1944 increased as the year progressed. Lodger facilities had been given to the FAA by 13 Group since 1943, but as the RAF workload began to decline it was clear that the airfield was about to change hands. 14 APC was closed down on 27 August, but prior to this one of the FAA's largest squadrons moved in from Machrihanish on 2 July. Its work at Ayr was stepped up when the airfield was transferred to the Admiralty on 6 September and commissioned as HMS *Wagtail* on 20 October.

Sixteen more FAA Squadrons served at Ayr during 1945; the last, 824 Squadron, arrived from HMS *Activity* on 20 October with its Fireflies, but had left for Burscough by 18 December. This was the last operational squadron to serve at Ayr. Meanwhile, 772 Squadron's days were also numbered, but its work would continue and it also moved to Burscough on 10 January 1946. The same day the airfield was paid off, reduced to C&M and closed to flying later in the year.

Ayr was taken over by the USAF in 1951 to become the home of the MATS 1631st ABS. This unit began to expand its operations at Ayr while maintaining a separate detachment at Prestwick. However, the location of 1631st was directly in line with the proposed extension of Prestwick's main runway, and in 1957 the ABS abandoned its location here in favour of its larger neighbour.

With the USAF's departure Ayr was closed, and it was not long before the heavy plant started to rip up the northern half of the airfield for the new extension. Housing and industry quickly claimed the remainder of the airfield, and by the mid-1990s the Heathfield Retail Park had been established on the rest. The entrance to the park briefly displayed a replica Spitfire, which decided to fly away in 1996 following a severe storm, leaving only its propeller behind.

The modern runway encroaching from the north in this aerial view is one of Prestwick's, giving and idea how close these two wartime stations were to each other.

Areas of runway 13/31 remain, providing a border between the houses and the Prestwick St Cuthbert Golf Course. A clutch of decaying technical buildings can also be seen from Wheatpark Road.

Main features:
Tarmac and asphalt runways: QDM 065-245 1,600 yards, 004-184 1,380 yards, 131-311 1,200 yards. *Hangars:* three 180 x 90 feet, one Bellman, seventeen over-blister. *Hardstandings:* sixteen double pen, six hardstandings. *Accommodation:* RAF: 2,075; WAAF: 451.

AYR (RACECOURSE), Strathclyde/South Ayrshire

55°27'54"N/4°36'91"W; NS350220. NE side of town

Established in 1907, it is possible that several aircraft visited the flat expanse of grass before the arrival of the RFC on 17 September 1917.

The first occupant, which would continue to re-manifest itself at Ayr in several different forms, was 1 SoAF. Virtually every type of aircraft in service with the RFC carried out this dangerous phase of a pilot's training, which was shared with a similar unit at Turnberry. On 10 May 1918, 1 SoAF became 1 SoAFG, only to be redesignated again on 29 May to become 1 FS.

Visits by operational squadrons were rare, with only two short occurrences recorded in May 1918. 105 Squadron was the first to arrive from Andover on 16 May, only staying three days before continuing on to Omagh with its RE.8s. 106 Squadron followed on 21 May, also from Andover, staying slightly longer en route to Fermoy with its RE.9s on 31 May 1918.

The North-Western Area FIS was the next and final unit to be formed, on 1 July 1918, with 504J/Ks. Both of Ayr's resident units survived long enough to become part of the new RAF. The instructors' school disbanded in January 1919 and 1 FS closed in April.

Little, if any, evidence of continued aviation activity has been recorded, although it can be safely said that the original flying field is fairly well preserved today, in the shape of Ayr Racecourse.

BALADO BRIDGE, Tayside

56°12'33"N/03°27'21"W. 1 mile W of Kinross, between A91 and A977

Since its formation in October 1940, 58 OTU had struggled to train fighter pilots. The situation deteriorated further when the unit expanded in February 1941 to almost 100 aircraft. It was obvious that it needed a satellite and preferably one with better weather conditions than Grangemouth.

Work began at Balado Bridge, which was referred to as Kinross, in mid-1941. Probably many weeks before the airfield was ready, personnel from 58 OTU arrived on 20 March 1942; Balado had opened three days earlier. The OTU wasted no time and the first group of pupil pilots began their advanced flying training on 23 March with a few Spitfires and Masters for familiarisation training. By April the OTUs air-to-air firing squadron, which was originally split between Macmerry and Grangemouth, made Balado its home. Those senior pupil pilots who were close to completing their course were also dispatched to Dyce to gain early experience of flying in an operational environment.

Balado established itself as an Advanced Training Centre for trainee pilots, and almost every conceivable ground training aid was made available to 58 OTU. Because of this, the airfield was known as 'Synthetic City', which made it the envy of the many OTUs that had been established by late 1942. Night-flying began in August, although this was also simulated with the pilots wearing dark goggles during daylight hours, with the runway in use being marked by sodium flares.

On 5 October 1943 58 OTU became 2 CTW before being redesignated 2 TEU ten days later. The TEU provided operational training for both fighter and fighter-bomber pilots. It still operated the early Spitfires with the addition of the Hurricane, while air-to-air firing was supported by the Martinet and the Master. Much of the work the TEU was putting in was geared towards the forthcoming invasion of Europe, and when the big day finally arrived the unit's tasking was effectively complete. On 12 June 1944 2 TEU was disbanded and for just a few weeks the airfield was silent.

The interesting mix of hangars was a result of the CRO setting up here from late June 1944. T. McDonald & Sons established two factories (the other at Kirkcaldy) for the repair of the Hudson, Boston, Mustang, Fulmar, Tomahawk and Blenheim. A host of component repairs and refurbishment was also carried out by the company, but exactly what role Balado had to play in this is not known. McDonald's completed its final contracts in January 1946, but it can be presumed that the company's association with Balado would probably have come to an end by May 1945.

Balado became an RLG for 9 PAFU from 12 September to 3 November 1944. The rasping engines of the Harvard filled the air at this time, and it became the last RAF unit to operate from here.

Following the war the airfield was a dumping ground for old airframes, specifically FAA examples, which were being broken up by McDonnells, located at Milnathort. By 1947 the task was at its peak but continued into the early 1950s. Light aircraft and the Scottish Gliding Club operated from here until 1957, when they were relocated to Portmoak.

This is Balado Bridge after the war, with at least 200 aircraft in open storage probably awaiting the scrapman's axe. Note how work appears to have begun on a third runway running in a north-westerly direction.

Sections of the airfield remained in the hands of the MoD and in 1985 a NATO communication facility was established on the southern side of the airfield close to the B918. Known locally as the 'Golf Ball', the facility was closed in 2006.

From a runway and perimeter track point of view the airfield is well preserved. The runways now form the bases of the Balado Bridge Poultry Farm and the control tower is preserved as a private dwelling. The airfield is now more famously known as the venue for 'T in the Park', which has been held annually here since 1997 and draws up to 140,000 music fans.

Main features:
Hardcore and concrete runways: QDM 275 1,650 yards, 217 1,400 yards. *Hangars:* one B1, four EO blister, one Super Robin. *Hardstandings:* twenty-five. *Accommodation:* RAF: 723; WAAF: 109.

BALDONNEL (CASEMENT), Dublin

53°18'06"N/06°27'04"W. 7 miles WSW of Dublin city centre

Baldonnel was one of several airfields in Ireland surveyed by Capt W. Sholto Douglas in mid-1917. Within days of his visit, building work began on the airfield, which was ready by 1 September 1918. 23 TDS was the first resident, formed from 31 and 51 TSs. The TDS, as with all units of this type, was very busy training new pilots using various aircraft including the 504, DH.9 and SE.5A; it was disbanded in February 1919.

Further expansion began in December 1918, with the establishment of 8 (Irish) ARD. However, by 1 May 1919 it was still not complete. One unit that was established was Delivery Station (Storage), which formed on 25 February 1919. As its name suggests, its main task was to store the many surplus aircraft with which the country was now awash following the end of the war. The unit continued to serve here until its disbandment in May.

The first operational RAF unit to arrive was 100 Squadron, although it was little more than a cadre. Arriving from St Inglevert on 12 September 1919, it soon re-established itself by absorbing 141 Squadron on 1 February 1920. The unit's aircraft were the DH.9a and F.2b, which took part in several detachments from Baldonnel to Castlebar and Oranmore.

At Baldonnel on 11 January 1919 seven hangars are in various states of construction, with at least nine Bessoneaus in the foreground. A lone Avro 504K is the only aircraft visible.

Looking from the top of one of the main hangars, the quality of these brick-built technical buildings is clearly evident.

The Met Flight was formed here with F.2bs in January 1920, and was disbanded exactly two years later. 4 Squadron was here in late 1920 from Farnborough with its F.2bs, becoming the last RAF unit to do so. Finally, the Irish Flight was formed on 18 January 1922 flying the DH.9a and F.2b before moving to Collinstown on 1 May.

Already established at Merrion Square was 11 (Irish) Group, which, before moving to 65 Fitzwilliam Square, Dublin, arrived on 22 November 1919. It was redesignated 11th (Irish) Wing in April 1920 to control 2 and 100 Squadrons as well as 'A' Flight, 4 Squadron, from August 1920. In February 1922 11 Wing moved to Spittlegate and was replaced by RAF Ireland. This unit remained here until May, when it was relocated to Island Bridge Barracks in Dublin.

BALHALL, Angus

56°45'06"N/02°47'11"W

Originally a First World War LG and an ELG for Montrose, Balhall was also used during the Second World War as an FLP. As such, it was first used by 2 FIS. It could be one of any number of fields located around the Bogs, Milton or Mains of Balhall area.

BALLINCOLLIG, Cork

51°53'45"N/08°36'09"W; W58584 71122. Half a mile NW of Ballincollig

An LG was located near the town from 1916. No RFC or RNAS squadrons were permanently based here, but it was used for communication flights to the barracks in the town. Remaining in RAF hands until the early 1920s, it later became a civilian strip, which operated until 1952.

Alan Cobham's Air Flying Circus operated from here on 5/6 July 1933. Ballincollig was also the birthplace of Edward Mannock VC; his father was serving at the barracks at the time.

Edward 'Mick' Mannock VC is believed to have been born in Ballincollig Barracks on 24 May 1887.

BALLYCASTLE, Antrim

55°12'21"N/6°15'28"W; D11100 41000. On SW edge of town

Another mysterious LG, this was believed to have been established in 1918. Closed by 1920, no RAF units were recorded being here, but it may have been used for the odd communication flight for the local barracks.

BALLYHALBERT, Down

54°29'54"N/05°28'21"W; J640638. SE of Ballyhalbert off A2

Ballyhalbert, positioned in the centre of the Ards Peninsula, originally played an important part in the aerial defence of Belfast.

Construction began in mid-1940, and twelve months later it was ready, complete with its own satellite at Kirkistown. The airfield was also allocated its own decoy at Kearney (aka Faughanvale at C577219), 8 miles south.

Opened on 28 June 1941, 245 Squadron's Hurricanes from Aldergrove were first to arrive on 14 July. They were joined by 256 Squadron from Squires Gate, also with Hurricanes. The fighter squadrons based here at this time were not only tasked with air defence duties but also convoy patrols, the latter being the most common. During its tour 245 Squadron was joined by 504 Squadron's Hurricanes on 26 August. Their arrival from Chilbolton was a dramatic one, with seven aircraft damaged as they battled a strong crosswind. 504 Squadron took over the local duties as 245 Squadron left for Chilbolton on 1 September, and 504's Hurricanes began to be superseded by Spitfires from October 1941. At least one enemy reconnaissance aircraft was forced down and another damaged. But local weather and accidents certainly claimed more aircraft than the enemy. The New Year saw the squadron move to Kirkistown.

While 153 Squadron continued working up to becoming an operational unit, it was joined by 25 Squadron on 16 January 1942 from Wittering with Beaufighters. 153 Squadron's Defiants remained here until April 1942, by which time the squadron had converted to the Beaufighter. 25 Squadron's tour of duty came to an end on 17 May 1942 when it moved to Church Fenton.

153 Squadron was now performing regular night patrols, but also saw very little contact with the enemy. Overseas duty beckoned, and on 18 December 1942 the squadron departed for Portreath, then on to North Africa.

Spitfires returned on 19 October 1942 when 501 Squadron arrived from Middle Wallop for a rest from operations. Shipping patrols were all that was demanded of the unit before it rejoined the fray on 30 April 1943 by moving to Westhampnett. 887 Squadron arrived from Sydenham with Fulmars the same day that 501 Squadron left, and moved to Kirkistown on 4 November to re-equip with the Spitfire pending the arrival of Seafires a few weeks later.

1943 saw more units, beginning with the Lysanders of 1493 Flight from Newtownards and a detachment of Mustangs from 231 Squadron at Nutt's Corner. 26 Squadron brought its Mustangs here on two occasions during 1943 and again in early 1944. 1493 Flight's responsibilities were taken over by 1494 Flight from Sydenham on 16 April, a unit that would remain here until 5 March 1945. Local fighter defence patrols were taken over by the Spitfires of 130 Squadron from Drem on the same day that 501 Squadron left. No enemy aircraft were encountered during 130's tour before it left for Honiley on 5 July 1943. 315 Squadron's Spitfires, from Hutton Cranswick, took up the task the following day. This squadron moved to Heston on 13 November, transferring its tasking to 303 Squadron, which had arrived from Northolt on the previous day. 303 Squadron's departure, on 30 April 1944 to Horne, marked the end of defensive patrols flown from here. Defence during the night-time hours from November 1943 to March 1944 was carried out by 125 Squadron's Beaufighters, which maintained a detachment here from Valley.

The Spitfires of 130 Squadron carried out local defence patrols from Ballyhalbert between April and July 1943.

From October 1943 an increased number of FAA squadrons began to arrive, which was a sign of things to come. 880 Squadron started by bringing in its Seafires from HMS *Stalker* on 7 October. Five days later, 898 Squadron disembarked its hook-fitted Spitfires from HMS *Hunter*. Both squadrons stayed until January and February of the New Year.

With the exception of a couple of detachments by 63 Squadron from Woodvale in May and July, and 1402 Flight from Aldergrove in December, all other squadron movements during the remainder of the war were by FAA units. The FAA's 24th FW, made up of 887 and 894 Squadrons, moved in from Burscough on 6 and 8 February respectively, both with Seafires. The Fulmar continued to appear with 784 Squadron during April, and the Hellcats of 894 and 1840 Squadrons arrived in May.

Barracudas arrived in January 1945 when 812 Squadron arrived from Fearn, and 1846 Squadron from Eglinton with Corsairs. The fighters were detached to HMS *Colossus* at the end of the month, before joining the ship in February. More Barracudas of 827 Squadron, also from HMS *Colossus*, arrived in late January, only staying until 20 February. Of the Royal Navy's flying units, this left just Y Flight of 787 Squadron, which served during February 1945, after which it returned to Machrihanish.

A small RAF contingent remained, and this decreased when 1494 Flight left. 1402 Flight was the only unit flying from here until 9 August 1945. In the meantime the airfield had been passed to the Admiralty on 14 July, and three days later became HMS *Corncrake*, home of 4 NAFS. The backbone of the new school was provided by 718 Squadron, which moved in from Henstridge on 17 August flying the Corsair and Seafire. 768 Squadron, a DT unit, brought in more Seafires and Corsairs from Ayr on 28 August. The DLT work was carried out with HMS *Premier* and *Nairana* during September, before the unit moved to East Haven in October 1945. The fighting school was to be a short-lived period of the airfield's history and was disbanded on 1 November, following which the Admiralty wasted no time in paying off the airfield on the 13th. By January 1946 Ballyhalbert belonged to Coastal Command, which appears to have made very little use of it and it was abandoned not long thereafter.

Large sections of runways and perimeter tracks remain, mainly on the western side of the airfield, while the eastern and northern side is now occupied by a caravan park and new housing. A few buildings can be still found, including the aircraft gun butts, and, more importantly, the Type 518/40 control tower still defiantly stands.

This aerial view of Ballyhalbert was taken in May 1992, since when the village has expanded steadily westwards.

Main features:

Tarmac and wood chipping runways: QDM 085 2,000 yards, 025 1,147 yards, 145 1,093 yards. *Hangars:* two Bellman, six over and six EO blister. *Hardstandings:* five fighter, six SE and six TE twin pens. *Accommodation:* RAF: 2,409; WAAF 327.

BALLYKELLY, Londonderry

55°03'37"N/07°01'13"W; C632245. 2 miles W of Limavady off A2

The choice of another airfield in Northern Ireland that was a mere 2 miles from Limavady may seem strange to us today. However, this was wartime and the RAF could not get its hands on enough of them during the early stages. First surveyed in 1940, Ballykelly was an excellent location for operational aircraft to fly out over the North Atlantic to protect the important convoys that were Great Britain's lifeline.

The RAF took over on 1 June 1941, even though the airfield was neither finished nor close to becoming operational. The first unit arrived on 6 December from Carew Cheriton, and the CCDU was formed to carry out service trials on aircraft and equipment. It brought the Whitley, Hudson and Beaufort here, before it moved to Tain on 18 June 1942.

The first of many operational Coastal Command squadrons arrived on 20 June 1942 with 220 Squadron from Shallufa via Nutt's Corner. The squadron operated the Fortress I, which was replaced by the more capable Fortress II from July. It was joined by 120 Squadron's Liberators, also from Nutt's Corner, on 21 July. Both squadrons flew A/S and ASR patrols from Ballykelly over the summer of 1942, and success for 120 Squadron came on 17 August. Liberator AM929 attacked a U-boat on the surface, inflicting damage, then the following day Sqn Ldr T. M. Bulloch and crew attacked U-653. As the submarine crash-dived one of its crew was lost and the U-boat was so seriously damaged that it was forced to return to Brest. On 19 August 120 Squadron was at it again when it forced U-214 to submerge, possibly hindering another attack on a convoy.

The Fortresses of 220 Squadron had been flying just as many operations as 120 Squadron, but it was not until 3 February 1943 that success came. FL456, flown by Plt Off Ramsden and crew, straddled U-265 with depth charges, sinking the submarine with the loss of all forty-six on board. Four days later Plt Off Robertson and crew dispatched U-624, which had sunk nine ships up to its demise.

On 14 February 1943 both 120 and 220 Squadrons were moved to Aldergrove to make way for airfield repairs and runway extension work. One runway was lengthened across the railway line, which meant that communication between the control tower and the nearest signal box was essential. Ballykelly had also been designated as a central airfield for major servicing of RAF Liberators, and two additional hangars were erected for this purpose.

It was several months before Liberators returned. First came 86 Squadron from Aldergrove on 6 September, joined nine days later by 59 Squadron, also from Aldergrove. At the same time the GR Pool was formed here to maintain a pool of Liberators to support all 15 Group squadrons; it would continue to do so until August 1945.

A stationary 120 Squadron Liberator makes an interesting mix with a Londonderry to Belfast train crossing the runway at Ballykelly in 1944.

86 Squadron moved to Reykjavik on 24 March 1944 to take over from 120 Squadron, which arrived here the same day, equipped with the Liberator V. Since its last tour 120 had sunk ten U-boats and shared three others. Both squadrons were now occupied with flying sorties along the Norwegian coast, which was not the most convenient of locations for units based in Northern Ireland. Up to eighty sorties per month were flown by both squadrons during this time. One of these, on 25 May, was an eventful one for a 59 Squadron crew in Liberator FL984. While off the Norwegian coast, fire was exchanged with an armed auxiliary vessel, without result for either party. It was a different story later in the patrol when U-990 was spotted west of Bodø. Just as the U-boat began to submerge, six depth charges were dropped, critically damaging the vessel, which floundered long enough for the fifty-one crew to escape. Three days later FL984 was in action again when it discovered U-292 on the surface west of Trondheim. The Liberator attacked and, after dropping its depth charges, a bright yellow explosion was seen and the bow of the U-boat rose out of the water before sinking with the loss of all fifty-one on board. 120 Squadron ended the war as Coastal Command's top U-boat killers, with sixteen to its name, but this did not save the unit from disbandment on 4 June 1945. The Liberator period came to an end when 59 Squadron left for Waterbeach on 14 September.

The unit that served here the longest was formed on 19 November 1945. The JASS operated a flight of aircraft specifically for practising A/S tactics with the Lancaster ASR.3 and Warwick GR.V. By the early 1950s several USAF Neptunes were working with the school, and during the mid-1950s the Shackleton, which was to become synonymous with Ballykelly during these post-war years, began to arrive. The JASS continued to operate from Ballykelly until 30 June 1971.

744 Squadron arrived from Eglinton with its Barracudas during late 1945 until May 1946. During this time 248 Squadron arrived from Chivenor with its Mosquitoes to take part in Operation 'Deadlight'. This was the code name for the scuttling of surrendered U-boats, the majority of which met their end in deep water off Lisahally. Various trials took place against the submarines, including 248 Squadron's contribution, which involved firing rockets or heavy cannon at the hulks. The Mosquitoes returned to Chivenor on 17 December 1945.

A similar scene a few years later, with a 269 Squadron Shackleton MR.2. The locomotive appears to be the same, but this time is heading for Londonderry.

The ASWDU served here from 26 May 1948, having arrived from Thorney Island. This unit operated a wide range of Coastal Command aircraft, but its stay was short, as Ballykelly was now being prepared once again for large numbers of four-engine heavies. First to arrive was 269 Squadron from Gibraltar with the Shackleton MR.1 on 24 March 1952. 240 Squadron, also flying the Shackleton MR.1, followed from St Eval on 5 June, and the airfield was filled when 210 Squadron brought its Lancaster ASR.3s from St Eval on 10 September. The latter only stayed until the end of September before leaving for Topcliffe, but both Shackleton squadrons would remain for many years.

Armourers load anti-submarine bombs into the bomb bay of a 224 Squadron Shackleton during Exercise 'Teamwork' at Ballykelly in September 1964.

Ballykelly became the only RAF station to support three operational Shackleton units at once when 204 Squadron was formed here with MR.2s on 1 January 1954. Both 269 and 240 Squadrons were also flying the MR.2 on long-range operations for hours on end over the open seas. On 1 November 1958 240 Squadron was renumbered as 203 Squadron, and one month later 269 Squadron was renumbered as 210 Squadron. Both served at Ballykelly for many years to come, the most significant change during this period being the arrival of Shackleton MR.3s for 203 Squadron from June 1966. There was no squadron movement until 1 February 1969, when 203 Squadron left Ballykelly for Luqa. Next came the disbandment of 210 Squadron on 31 October 1970, followed by 204 Squadron on 1 April 1971; the latter became the last RAF squadron to serve here.

Ever since mid-1945 lodger facilities had been made available to the Royal Navy. Minor units had been attached to Ballykelly, and three Avenger squadrons briefly served here in the 1950s. 831 Squadron's Gannets also served here in the early 1960s, followed by a host of brief visits through to early 1971. 819 Squadron, with Wessex HAS.1s, arrived from HMS *Centaur* on 7 February 1963, and there followed scores of detachments serving at Ballykelly until January 1971, when it was disbanded. The same day the Royal Navy relinquished its lodger facilities.

From the early 1970s and beyond Ballykelly was used by a variety of AAC units, including 655 Squadron's Lynxes, which were here from 1982 to 1991. On 2 June 1972 Ballykelly came under Army control as Shackleton Barracks. Several regiments served here until 2008, when the last, The Princess of Wales's Regiment, departed for Woolwich. Ballykelly is virtually complete from its wartime days and development during the Shackleton era. One legacy of this period was the construction of a 700-foot-long maintenance hangar, which, together with at least two wartime hangars, still survives today. A mix of wartime, post-war and modern buildings are spread all around the vast site, which is only now regularly use by a police helicopter. For those lucky enough

This view is possibly from 1966, when the MR.2 began to make way for the MR.3. The giant 700-foot-long servicing hangar is in place and four MR.3s and a single MR.2 can be seen on the ground.

A modern-day view of the aircraft servicing shed at Ballykelly, which, together with the whole site, is currently up for sale, its future in doubt. Niall Hartley

Today the control tower at Ballykelly remains inactive, and the chances of survival following redevelopment are slim. Niall Hartley

to get onto the site, a unique memorial, consisting of a fin and rudder from an MR.3, is on display as a tribute to the Shackleton years, although it may have since been moved. The entire airfield site, including domestic areas, is now in the hands of the Limavady Council, which has wasted no time in selling off the married quarters as private housing.

Main features:
Concrete runways: QDM 210 2,000 yards, 267 2,000 yards, 330 1,100 yards. *Hangars:* two T2, three half-size T2, eight 69-foot blister. *Hardstandings:* thirteen loop. *Accommodation:* RAF: 1,925; WAAF: 402.

BALLYLIFFIN, Donegal

Airship station: 55°18'03"N/07°22'11"W; C40100 50600. 1½ miles NNE of Clonmany

RAF FLP: 55°17'30"N/07°22'22"W; C40000 49242; 1 mile NE of Ballyliffin

Work began on an RNAS airship sub-station for Luce Bay in July 1916. The station would be for non-rigid airships, but by the time the RAF was formed it was still not complete. There had been no further progress by the time of the Armistice, and it was abandoned by 1919.

BALLYMENA, Antrim

54°52'25"N/06°14'44"W; D12924 03997. Three-quarters of a mile NE of Ballymena

This LG was being used by Lysanders from Newtownards for short-field and ELP training during 1940. 55 MU also had a sub-site here, which became 217 MU during March 1942.

BALLYQUIRK (KILLEAGH), Cork

51°55'84"N/08°01'36"W; W98432 75390. 7 miles W of Youghal

Work on this airship patrol station began in 1918. It took up 365 acres of flat land that was also accessible by rail, thanks to a spur off from the main Cork to Youghal line. No local labour was employed and all materials were shipped in from England, then on to Killeagh by train.

Progress was slow, and despite the war coming to an end construction carried on. It was not until 20 August 1919 that the project was brought to a close, almost complete. As the workforce were laid off, they left behind, among other things, one 840-foot-long rigid shed and one 456-foot-long coastal airship shed, a large generator house, offices, stores and accommodation for more than 300 personnel.

BALLYWALTER PARK (MILLISLE), Down

WW1: 53°33'18"N/05°29'40"W. Location based on old grid J/619 703

WW2: 54°32'36"N/05°29'04"W. Straddles A2, S of Ballywalter

The first of two flying sites near Ballywalter on the Ards Peninsula was active between 1918 and 1922. Its exact use is unclear other than that it was used by the RAF, probably as an ELG. The second location, which was established more than 20 years later, is much clearer.

23 MU at Aldergrove was growing during late 1940 and needed new SLGs to cope with the amount of aircraft arriving. A field not far from the original site was surveyed and prepared in early 1941. A test landing by an Anson took place on 25 April, which exposed an alarming trait involving crosswinds. The only way to rectify this was to extend the runway by 250 yards.

Once the work was completed, Ballywalter was opened on 1 June 1941 and named 16 SLG. Despite further land being requisitioned before it opened, only a handful of aircraft arrived during 1941. The following year did see an increase, and 23 MU made use of it until 14 March 1945.

Flying briefly returned to Ballywalter in 1990, when at least one light aircraft made use of the grass runway that remains in place today.

BALMAIN, Kincardineshire/Angus

56°50'17"N/02°35'29"W

This was another field that acted as an FLP from July 1940. 8 FTS would have made use of it, followed by 2 FIS until 1945.

BALTA SOUND (UNST), Shetland

60°45'32"N/00°50'18"W. Balta Sound, Shetland Islands

An advanced mooring station was here during the First World War for the use of Catfirth-based aircraft. There was very little activity beyond 1919, but a seaplane slipway was built by an Auxiliary Battalion of the Royal Marines along the edge of Balta Sound in April 1940.

BANFF (BOYNDIE), Grampian

57°40'06"N/02°38'15"W; NJ619643. 6 miles W of Banff off B9139

During the last few months of the war a separate little conflict was taking place from airfields along the North Grampian coast. Mosquito and Beaufighter squadrons were wreaking havoc against enemy shipping and military targets along the Norwegian coast. One of the airfields involved in this campaign was Banff.

Banff's first resident, 14 (P)AFU, arrived in May 1943 from Ossington with 168 Oxfords and a few Ansons. Dallachy and Fraserburgh were used as satellites, and Brackla was brought into use by 1944. 1512 BATF, with Oxfords, was also operated from here until August 1944.

In mid-1944 plans were afoot to move the Mosquito and Beaufighter Strike Wings to the North East of Scotland. All of the (P)AFUs by this stage of the war had produced a surplus of trained pilots, and some had to be disbanded. 1512 BATF, having now reduced in size, was disbanded on 31 August, followed the next day by 14 (P)AFU.

On 1 September 1944 Banff was taken over by Coastal Command, which controlled a mixed Strike Wing made up of 144 and 404 Squadron Beaufighters, and 235 Squadron operating Mosquitoes. The group also controlled a second Mosquito Strike Wing consisting of 248 Squadron and 333 Squadron, all under the command of Gp Capt J. W. M. 'Max' Aitken DSO DFC.

It was the Norwegian-crewed Mosquitoes of 'B' Flight, 333 Squadron, that were the first 'armed' aircraft to arrive. The squadron's main task was reconnaissance operations over Norway, and its first sortie from here was on 2 September. Being Norwegians themselves, their local knowledge was invaluable, and the squadron would also act as Pathfinders on many operations.

144 and 404 (RCAF) 'Buffalo' Squadron Beaufighters arrived from Strubby on 3 September. Both squadrons were in the air on the 6th, contributing twenty-six aircraft for a shipping strike. The same day 235 Squadron Mosquitoes arrived from Portreath to provide fighter protection for the two Beaufighter squadrons. By the time 235 Squadron returned from its first operation, 248 Squadron arrived from Portreath, also with Mosquitoes. Among the squadron's assets were the Mosquito FB.XVIIIs fitted with the 57mm Molins gun in the nose, which were nicknamed 'Tsetse'.

248 Squadron was equipped with the Mosquito FB.XVIII, which carried a weapon unique to Coastal Command. Just under the nose of the Mosquito can be seen a 57mm 6lb Class M cannon, more familiarly known as the Molins 'Tsetse' gun.

HR414 of 143 Squadron is seen at a chilly Banff in early 1945. Note the rails under each wing, which carried the deadly 25lb rocket projectiles.

Detachments from 281 Squadron's ASR Warwicks had been operating from here since March 1944 and would continue to do so until the war's end. On 22 October 1944 404 Squadron made the short flight to Dallachy, followed the next day by 144 Squadron. The same day 143 Squadron arrived from North Coates with its Mosquitoes.

235 Squadron had not even seen an enemy aircraft since August 1944. This was about to change when the Me 110s of 12/ZG moved from Ørlandet to Fliergerhorst Hedia and began to intercept shipping patrols. To meet this problem Coastal Command instructed two 235 Squadron Mosquitoes to fly a 'Rover' patrol from Marstein to Stadlandet in the hope of turning the tables on the German fighters. On 24 October 1944 four Me 110s were intercepted west of Bergen, and within minutes three of them were diving in flames towards the sea.

143 Squadron flew its first operational sortie on 7 November, but poor weather disrupted further flying until the 13th. On that day 235 and 248 Squadrons, together with 144 and 489 Squadrons' Beaufighters, attacked shipping off Egersund, west of Rekefjord, leaving one MV damaged and two small vessels sunk.

Another operation, on 16 December 1944, had mixed results. Twenty-two Mosquitoes took off, led by one from 333 Squadron, to attack shipping in the narrow sound at Kraakbellesund. An MV was left in flames and a small flak vessel was sunk for the loss of two Mosquitoes.

On 11 January 1945 fifteen Banff Mosquitoes joined twenty-one Beaufighters on an armed strike to Flekkerfjord. As the force prepared to attack, they were not only greeted with intense and accurate flak but also the Lista-based Bf 109s and Fw 190s. RPs were jettisoned and the more manoeuvrable Mosquitoes took on the fighters while trying to protect the escaping Beaufighters. At least four enemy fighters were shot down, although two aircraft failed to return.

Ålesund was notorious for being a heavily defended port, but this did not deter a force of thirty-one Mosquitoes setting out to attack it on 17 March 1945. Surrounded by four coastal batteries, a host of flak and machine-gun emplacements, a warm welcome was guaranteed. A 333 Squadron outrider reported to the main force that seven MVs were at anchor, and the weather was good enough to carry out an attack. The defenders would certainly have spotted the 333 Squadron Mosquito and would be ready for the inevitable attack that was to follow. Knowing this, the main force headed inland and approached Ålesund from the east to catch the defences off guard. The different approach worked and, within minutes of the attack beginning, three MVs were sunk and two others were damaged.

Banff gained a fifth squadron when 404 Squadron returned from Dallachy to re-equip with the Mosquito. Its conversion to the new aircraft was swift, and within three weeks the Canadians were ready for operations.

This final strike of the war, led by Wg Cdr Foxley-Norris, took place on 4 May 1945. It involved all five operational squadrons totalling forty-eight Mosquitoes plus eighteen Mustangs from 19 and 234 Squadrons with a pair Warwicks in ASR support. An E-boat was sunk en route, and before the day was over two more MVs had been sunk and another left on fire.

Sorties from Banff were now restricted to ASR searches and looking for surrendered U-boats. On 25 May 143 and 404 Squadrons were disbanded, only for 14 Squadron to rise from the ashes of the former the same day, still equipped with the Mosquito. The next day, the Mosquitoes of 333 Squadron were disbanded into 334 Squadron, which moved to Gardermoen on 8 June 1945 to become part of the RNorAF. 489 Squadron moved in from Dallachy to convert to the Mosquito, but this was to be short-lived as the squadron was disbanded on 1 August 1945, becoming the last Mosquito unit to operate from Banff. 235 Squadron was also disbanded on 10 July, and 248 Squadron temporarily escaped the axe when it was moved to Chivenor on 19 July. A detachment of Sea Otters of 279 Squadron from Thornaby made a brief appearance in late July to early 1946, becoming the last unit to operate from Banff.

The airfield was then placed under C&M, and by mid-1946 was closed to flying. When the Royal Navy took over Lossiemouth, it proposed that Banff could be used as a satellite, but in November 1953 the idea was scrapped and within a year the airfield was being disposed of.

An MV is under attack at Sandefjord on 2 April 1945. This Mosquito has already launched its RPs and can be seen firing its cannon at the vessel below the water line. Two MVs were sunk during this successful attack.

This photograph shows a typical Banff Strike Wing attack on Porsgrunn on 11 April 1945. Four MVs were sunk and two damaged before the formation was pounced upon by German fighters only minutes after this photo was taken. One 333 Squadron Mosquito failed to return.

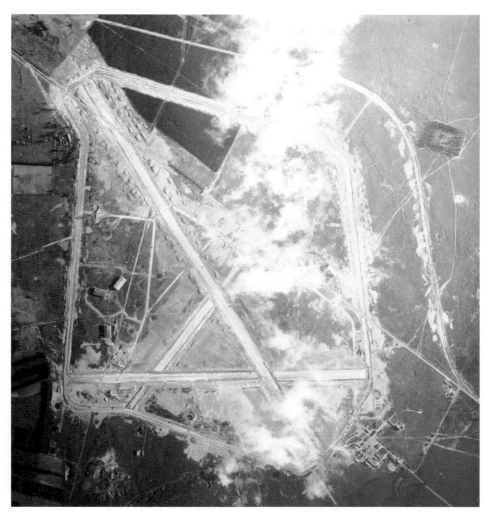

Taken towards the end of the Second World War, this view of Banff shows at least eighty Mosquitoes on the ground.

Aviation made a comeback when the Banff Flying Club was formed in 1976, and part of its opening ceremony saw a flypast by a Mosquito. By the early 1980s the club was no more, and Banff was left desolate and abandoned but not forgotten. On 23 September 1989 a memorial was dedicated to the Banff Strike Wing, and again a Mosquito made a flypast accompanied by a Kinloss-based Nimrod.

Thanks to the brief occupancy of the Banff Flying Club, the control tower still stands and the now faint letters of its last owner can still be seen across the top of it. Large sections of the runways, perimeter tracks and dispersals are still in place and the odd wartime building can still be found.

Today, Boyndie is dominated by a wind farm owned by a local co-operative made up of 716 members who purchased an area of the old airfield in 2006. The seven turbines can generate enough electricity to supply 8,500 homes, for an area made up of Banff, Portsoy, Whitehills and further homes in rural areas. While wind farms do have their critics, this one does serve the unintentional purpose of preserving the airfield on which it stands.

Main features:
Concrete runways: QDM 295 2,000 yards, 236 1,400 yards, 180 1,400 yards.
Hangars: three half T2, thirteen 69-foot double blister. *Hardstandings:* thirty-six
frying pan. *Accommodation:* RAF: 2,301; WAAF: 341.

BANGOR (GROOMSPORT), Down

WW1: 54°39'07"N/05°39'95"W; J50631 80630

WW2: 54°40'33"N/05°36'93"W; J538831. 1½ miles of NE Bangor

Two sites on the outskirts of Bangor were used for military aviation during the 20th century. The
first was an LG used by land-based aircraft from the USN serving in Ireland during 1918.

The second aerodrome started out as a civilian one. It was established around August 1930 and
was significant enough to be on the AA's airfield listing. Requisitioned at the outbreak of the war, it
has been suggested that it was used by several Lysanders during the early part of the conflict, which
undoubtedly would have hailed from Newtownards. Today it lies under a housing estate.

BANTRY, Cork

51°40'72"N/09°27'30"W. V99361 48352. 1 mile W of Bantry

Opened in 1920, Bantry was described as a field strip. It was used briefly by the RAF and the
RIC before being closed in March 1921. Very close to the original site is its modern
counterpart.

BARASSIE, Ayrshire

55°33'23"N/04°38'51"W. On Darley Golf Course, east of railway line

Under the CRO scheme, the LMS Railway Carriage & Wagon Works at Barassie found itself
repairing and overhauling Spitfires, and the first of 1,200 aircraft was ready for its test flight on
10 October 1941. Aircraft were towed from the factory across the railway onto a golf course where a
temporary runway had been laid out across the fairways. With a small amount of fuel on board, the
fighter took to the air and landed at Ayr, from where the full flight test was carried out.

A pair of Super Robin hangars was erected in early 1942; they were used for final assembly
work and were ready by the end of the year. The main factory had modified its operation to cater
for the Spitfire, and its paint shop could hold twenty-five fuselages at a time, another twenty-five sets
of wings, and ten aircraft in the hangars for final assembly.

Today the grass strip has returned to golf, while the factory, like the Super Robins, is long gone.

*Both the layout of the grass runway and the two
Super Robin hangars east of the railway line can
be seen in this wartime aerial view.*

BARRHEAD, East Renfrewshire

55°47'06"N/04°21'56"W

Worthy of mention, although not really an 'action station', is the founding home of the Scottish Aeronautical Society. In May 1911 land adjoining Cowan Public Park was leased to a Mr W. S. Duncan and two other members of the society for the purpose of creating an aerodrome.

There were plans to establish a training school and organise flying meetings here. King George V's Coronation was celebrated here in June 1911, but by 1912 the aerodrome had been closed down.

BARRY, Angus

NO532334. 8 miles E of Dundee

Barry was created during the early stages of the First World War for RNAS landplanes, and was used until 1916.

BELHAVEN SANDS, East Lothian

NT652792. W of Dunbar

When work began on this temporary LG, as well as preparing the beach several huts were erected as workshops in April 1918. Two Bessoneaus were also provided, with accommodation at East Fortune.

A Sopwith Cuckoo drops its torpedo in a scene representative of what took place off Belhaven Sands nearly 100 years ago.

In Belhaven Bay, Royal Navy torpedo boat destroyers acted as targets for Sopwith Cuckoos. RAF Marine Section boats also supported the Cuckoos' activities. As well as recovering the dummy torpedoes, the RAF 'sailors' were also on hand to help in the case of an accident. The dropping height of a torpedo from the Cuckoo was critical and had to be between 10 and 20 feet above the water: too high and the torpedo would not enter the water correctly, too low and the resulting splash could knock the Cuckoo out of the air, which happened to one pilot.

BENBECULA (BALIVANICH), Western Isles

57°28'39"N/07°21'59"W; NF787562. Due N of Balivanich off B892

One of the most windswept and bleakest locations in the entire British Isles, Benbecula had its roots in the 1930s. It was first used by Scottish Airways for services throughout the Western Isles. This came to an end after the beginning of the war and the land was requisitioned by the Air Ministry.

Work began in mid-1941 and was complete by May 1942, but there was no burst of activity associated with the arrival of a new unit. Finally, on 1 July, Benbecula came alive when 206 Squadron's Hudsons arrived from Aldergrove. The Hudson was an excellent aircraft but, not long after arriving, it began to be replaced by the even better Fortress II. A/S patrols were flown on a daily basis regardless of the weather, and several U-boats were attacked over the coming months. At least two of the attacks damaged the enemy, including one by Fg Off Owen and his crew on 11 December 1942, who depth-charged two U-boats and carried out a mock attack on a third in the same sortie.

Boeing Fortress II FL452 of 206 Squadron is seen at Benbecula in 1943.

220 Squadron's Fortresses arrived from Aldergrove on 20 March 1943, and the unit wasted no time in joining the hunt for the elusive U-boats; however, these would remain elusive as 220 Squadron's only contribution was assisting a Catalina attacking a submarine on 3 August.

Success came again for 206 Squadron on 11 June when the CO, Wg Cdr R. B. Thomson, and his crew caught U-417 on the surface, south-east of Iceland. On the run-in, the Fortress was hit by anti-aircraft fire, which caused damage to the nose, cockpit, wings, bomb bay and rear turret. Despite the damage, Thomson stuck to the task and accurately dropped his depth charges, causing U-417 to sink almost immediately. Such was the damage to the Fortress that Thomson was forced to ditch into the sea, and all eight crew managed to scramble into a dinghy. It was not until the 14th that the aircrew were spotted by a Catalina of VP-84. As it attempted to alight on the rough seas, it crashed, forcing its nine aircrew to take to their lifeboats. Later that day another Catalina of 190 Squadron managed to rescue the 206 Squadron crew, but it would be another five days before the USN crew were discovered. Sadly, all but one had died of exposure. On 18 October both 206 and 220 Squadrons moved to Lagens in the Azores to continue their fight against the U-boats.

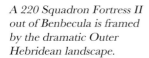

A 220 Squadron Fortress II out of Benbecula is framed by the dramatic Outer Hebridean landscape.

Despite being a useful location to carry out operations, Benbecula became a non-operational airfield. The odd aircraft continued to make use of it, including a few from across the Atlantic; in fact, during this period Benbecula was considered as an Atlantic Ferry staging post, but nothing ever came of it.

The arrival of two Wellington squadrons brought the airfield to life again to continue its part in the Battle of the Atlantic. Both 179 and 304 Squadrons moved in from Chivenor and both used the Leigh Lights to catch their prey. Their tours here were pretty fruitless, as the U-boats became harder to find, mainly thanks to the frequent use of Schnorchel underwater breathing apparatus. October 1944 was a classic example of 304 Squadron's efforts, with more than eighty sorties flown without sighting a single U-boat. The same month 179 Squadron returned to Chivenor, leaving 304 Squadron to continue flying for hours on end over seemingly empty seas. The poor success rate resulted in a detachment of Wellingtons moving to Limavady in late January 1945, but this move did not produce the hoped-for results either. On 6 March 304 Squadron left for good, and without a tear shed, for St Eval.

36 Squadron, also from Chivenor, with Wellingtons, replaced 304 Squadron on 9 March 1945. It was not an auspicious start, as it lost one aircraft and crew without trace en route when poor weather came down around the airfield. Once again no successes were achieved, and on 1 June 36 Squadron flew its last operational sortie. Eight days later it was disbanded, bringing an end to operational flying here.

By early 1946 the airfield had been reduced to C&M, but later in the year it began to be used by BEA. Its military surroundings steadily decayed and eventually only the two longer runways were maintained in a serviceable condition. None of the original hangars survived for any length of time after the war, and two of them were bought by KLM in 1949 and re-erected at Schiphol Airport.

The Cold War saw Benbecula being returned to the RAF in 1958. Since then, it has been used for several intriguing purposes, including the control centre for the South Uist Missile Range. The airfield also provided long-range surveillance of the North Atlantic for the use of the United Kingdom's ICCS, which was replaced by the UKADGE project in the 1970s. The system was still being modified and upgraded into the 21st century under another title, UCMP, which continues today.

As seen on 27 July 1995, Benbecula remains in regular use today under HIAL control.

A CRC was also located here under the control of Buchan throughout the Cold War. Buchan was closed down in 2005 to be replaced by RRH, as was the CRC at Benbecula. Both RRHs are under the control of the United Kingdom ASACS. Today the ASACS's UCCS is the main structure of all the country's ground, permanent, static, air command and control installations.

Recently upgraded, RAF Benbecula and the South Uist Missile Range are still very active today. Civilian flights operate regularly to and from Glasgow, Barra and Stornoway, and the airport is now operated by HIAL.

Main features:
Bitumen and compacted sand 'sand carpet' runways: QDM 111 1,990 yards, 003 1,410 yards, 071 1,050 yards. *Hangars:* ten half T2. *Accommodation:* RAF: 2,300; WAAF: 260.

BENTRA (WHITEHEAD, AKA LARNE), Antrim

Airship station: 54°45'89"N/05°43'64"W; J46249 93143. 1 mile NW of Whitehead railway station

LG: 54°45'84"N/05°43'35"W; J46569 93072

In 1917 an airship station and LG were opened here, positioned so that 'SS' Class airships and fixed-wing aircraft could patrol the Irish Sea looking for U-boats. It was an Airship Station Class A, and operated as a sub-station for Luce Bay for non-rigid RNAS and later RAF airships. Patrols were also flown from Luce Bay to help protect the Larne-Stranraer ferry, *Princess Maud*. Bentra was created so that the escorting airships could moor during the day while the wind dropped, making passage back to Luce Bay much easier. On 5 June 1917 the first airship, SS-20, arrived at Bentra, having flown across the Irish Sea; it returned safely to Luce Bay that evening.

Bentra had at least one 'portable' hangar and runways up to 400 yards long. Flying ceased in 1919, and on 20 February 1920 the site was closed.

Princess Maud, seen here under way between Larne and Stranraer, was one of the reasons for establishing an airship station at Bentra in 1917.

BEREHAVEN aka BEARHAVEN (CASTLETOWNBERE), Cork

51°39'25"N/09°51'63"W; V71251 46263. 2 miles E of Castletown Bearhaven pier

This station was located under the Slieve Miskish Mountains in South West Ireland. The naval base became the home to the Royal Navy Kite Balloon Station from early 1917, and was expanded when the unit was upgraded to 17 BB on 15 April 1918.

Later that year the station was handed over to the USN, which had a large presence here, including a submarine base. By 4 December 1918 it had been returned to the RAF and renamed Berehaven, but with the war now over the unit disbanded on 30 June 1919.

BERNERAY, Western Isles

57°43'21"N/07°11'09"W

Berneray was an ELG during the Second World War.

BIRR (CRINKILL), Offaly

53°04'51"N/07°54'10"W; N06580 02739. 1½ miles S of Birr

A landing area was believed to have been active here since 1913, but it did not see any military activity until the RAF arrived in 1919. The first unit was 106 Squadron from Fermoy in March, flying the F.2b. 141 Squadron arrived the following month from Tallaght, also flying the F.2b, remaining until May. 141 Squadron returned in December, only to depart for the last time in January 1920, bringing this LG's short history to an end.

BISHOPS COURT, Down

54°18'21"N/05°34'08"W; J580425. 4 miles NE of Ardglass off A2, E of Ballyhornan

Bishops Court was a late starter, and was allocated to the USAAF to be used as a CCRC on 28 February 1942. Not long after construction began, it was realised that all the planned CCRCs were well catered for and the airfield's future looked in doubt even before it was completed.

Built on land west of Bishops Court village, the airfield was constructed to a design similar to an 'A' Class bomber station. On 17 May 1943 the airfield's first unit, 7 AOS, was re-formed with Ansons, although it was not until 31 July that courses began. The following day, 12 AGS was also established, flying the Anson, Martinet and Master. On 15 February 1944 7 AOS was redesignated as 7 OAFU, still retaining the Anson as its main type.

Since 1943 the airfield had been handling an increasing number of diverted Coastal Command aircraft, thanks to its long runway that could easily cater for a Liberator. Initially, the task of handling these large aircraft was a little ad hoc, but by late 1944 the airfield was geared up for the task. Refuelling was the biggest challenge, followed by a lack of accommodation for the crews, but for almost two years the airmen here managed to turn around every Coastal Command aircraft that was diverted here with little trouble.

Wellingtons began to arrive for 12 AGS from November 1944, and the unit remained until it was disbanded on 31 May 1945. Forty-seven air gunner courses had passed through the AGS, and the final one continued its training at Barrow. The same day 7 AOS was redesignated as 7 ANS, by now also flying Wellingtons and several Ansons. It was redesignated again on 4 June 1947 to become 2 ANS, which was nothing more than an administrative change. On 1 October 2 ANS, which had been associated with the airfield since 1943, left for Middleton St George.

By January the following year the airfield was reduced to C&M, although there was no indication that it was about to be abandoned. In fact, it was reactivated on 3 March 1952 when 2 ANS, flying the Varsity, Valetta and Anson, was re-formed here. The resurgence of activity was short-lived, however, and the ANS was disbanded on 14 April 1954.

Various contractors arrived in 1955 when the airfield was one of many selected as an all-weather fighter station. It was upgraded with large ORPs, but no squadrons made use of it. A glider unit did take advantage of the empty airfield when 671 VGS moved in from Aldergrove on 22 January 1959, but only stayed until September 1962. It was another seven years before aviation briefly returned again; 819 Squadron Wessex from Ballykelly arrived on detachment on 30 September 1969, but only stayed a few days. The final flying here was by 664 VGS, which was formed on 1 August 1986 with the Venture, but by 31 October 1990 it had been disbanded.

For many years the airfield was used as part of UKMATS and was known as Ulster Radar, providing both military and civilian coverage across the Atlantic. This task was taken over by the

This is possibly the disbandment parade of 12 AGS at Bishops Court in June 1945.

2 ANS Valetta T.3 WG259 is on a training sortie over the Irish Sea out of Bishops Court in 1953.

ATCC at Prestwick from 1978, but the RAF would remain here until the late 1980s, and between 1991 and 1995 the airfield was systematically sold off. It was hoped that Ryanair would take over this substantial airfield after bidding for the site in 2003, but sadly nothing ever came of it.

Today the western half the airfield is used as a racetrack, and the rest, while still very much intact, is steadily decaying through lack of use. The control tower still stands, but housing is beginning to encroach on the southern side, slowly covering the area were a giant marshalling area was constructed.

Main features:
Concrete runways: QDM 060 2,000 yards, 180 1,400 yards, 120 1,400 yards.
Hangars: four T2, thirty-five EO blister. *Hardstandings:* ten 150-foot circular, eight
125-foot diameter, twelve spectacle, 800 x 1,000 feet marshalling area.
Accommodation: RAF: 2,177; WAAF: 584.

BLACK ISLE (BLACKSTAND FARM/FORTROSE), Highland

57°37'04"N/04°08'58"W; NH715605. 2 miles N of Rosemarkie off B9160

This SLG gained its name from being in the heart of the Black Isle, a large peninsula located 30 miles north-west of Lossiemouth.

Work began on making the site into an airfield in early 1941. On 1 July it was inspected by officers from 46 MU, and on 12 August an Anson made a trial landing. Ten days later 42 SLG was opened, and from 1 September the first of many Beaufighters from Lossiemouth began to arrive for dispersal. Despite the efforts of the main contractors, Rendall, Palmer & Tritton, the runway was far from level. In fact, it was often better for the MU's ferry pilots to land across the airfield and hope that the aircraft would stop before the boundary fence!

Facilities at the SLG were sparse, and all personnel working on site were accommodated in Fortrose. Those buildings that were built stood around Blackstand Farm, while aircraft were covered with camouflage netting and, where possible, made use of surrounding trees and foliage. Storage capacity for 42 SLG was restricted to fifty-five aircraft, but in August 1942 this was set to increase. The runway was extended and a successful test-landing by a Halifax took place, but despite the outcome no four-engined types were ever stored here.

With the war over, very few of the Beaufighters that had arrived were destined to be flown out again. Now surplus to requirements, the long process of scrapping them began. The work was aided by a working party from Bristol Aircraft, which was detached from Lossiemouth during the summer of 1945.

Although dates are unclear, Black Isle was also used briefly by 45 MU, but by September 1945 only a pair of shabby Warwicks remained. These were repaired to an airworthy condition and flown out to Lossiemouth, becoming the last aircraft to do so. Not long after, 42 SLG was closed and the land was placed under the control of the Forestry Commission.

Today, despite being such a small airfield, several buildings still survive, including the Robin hangar and others in various states of repair. Although difficult to imagine, the landing strip also remains virtually intact, only disrupted by the odd hedgerow and tree.

BLARIS (LISBURN), Antrim

54°31'N/06°06'W; J22884 64858. 2¼ miles W of Lisburn

Originally used as a dispersal field for Battles in late 1939, Blaris consisted of a few large fields opposite the old churchyard. It had a runway 770 yards long, which was created by removing a few hedgerows. Accommodation was a few tents around the perimeter.

Designated as an emergency dispersal site, it was upgraded to an RLG. By May 1943 the airfield had gained its own unit with 201 GS, which remained until April 1944, following a move to Newtownards. Blaris remained in military hands until January 1946.

BOA ISLAND (ROCK BAY), Fermanagh

54°30'58"N/07°49'16"W; H115635. 5 miles W of Kesh on A47

A sheltered bay south of Boa Island protected by Crunnish served as an area to moor 131 OTU's Sunderland Flight. Boa was brought into use as a satellite from 31 May 1944. Catalinas also took advantage of this peaceful mooring, which remained in use until 1 March 1945.

A few buildings were constructed and, together with a slipway, remain in place today.

BOGTON (DALMELLINGTON), Ayrshire

55°19'24"N/04°24'35"W; NS472057. SW of Dalmellington, on edge of Loch Bogton

After the failure of trying to build an aerodrome near Loch Doon, an alternative was found slightly further north. The site was still a marshy one and was prone to flooding, but it was hoped that, with time and drainage, the situation would improve.

Surveyed in March 1917, work was carried out swiftly, and by early April a pair of hangars had been erected and two aircraft had arrived. By the summer the aerodrome continued to develop, with workshops, stores, vehicle sheds and eighteen brick-built thirty-man accommodation buildings. Even the aeroplane sheds were centrally heated, which, combined with the comfortable accommodation, made this a very pleasant posting.

'Y' Squadron formed here as part of the SoAG, but the failure and eventual cancellation of the Loch Doon aerial gunnery range in December 1917 resulted in Bogton seeing very little use.

BOWMORE, Strathclyde

55°45'29"N/6°17'20"W. Off Bowmore, on Loch Indaal

It was a cold, miserable night on 24 January 1943 when a Sunderland of 246 Squadron fought its way back to Bowmore only to be told that it should divert to Oban. The wireless operator, Sgt E. G. Palmer, failed to receive the message and approaching from the north; the pilot, Capt. E. J. Lever SAAF, prepared to land regardless, although he had to circle Bowmore several times before committing. Miscalculating his approach, Lever descended too early, skimmed the top of a hill, destroyed a workshop and careered through some telephone wires before coming to a rest on the edge of the loch at Blackrock. Of the twelve crew on board, only two were injured and eleven managed to escape from the wreck, which still had its depth charges on board. Eight of the crew made their way towards the road up the beach, but they soon realised that one man, the rear gunner, 32-year-old Sgt G. C. Phillips, was still trapped in his turret. All eight returned to the aircraft to rescue their colleague, but as they entered the aircraft the depth charges exploded, killing all nine airmen. Debris was scattered far and wide, mainly across Blackrock Farm, and the blast was felt up to 20 miles away. This tragic accident has been marked by a small plaque laid by Margaret Reid, who was a friend of Sgt W. E. C. Heath, one of the two Navigator/Bomb Aimers killed in the blast. The plaque is being restored and a larger memorial consisting of a cairn overlooking the site is in the process of being constructed.

The first unit to arrive here was 'G' Flight from Stranraer with three ex-BOAC S.26/M 'G' Class flying boats and an S.23/M 'C' Class. These were ideal for patrols over the Atlantic, and would fill a useful gap in Coastal Command's capability at the time. 'G' Flight arrived at Bowmore on 24 December 1940 with a single 'G' Class, X8235, which had only entered RAF service nine days earlier. The other aircraft had all arrived by the beginning of 1941, achieving almost daily patrols from Bowmore.

The day after 'G' Flight's arrival, a second unit, SD Flight, arrived from Helensburgh. This flight was formed to carry out trials for the MAEE, and by January 1941 was also equipped with three S.23s. Both 'G' Flight and the SD Flight were redesignated on 13 March to re-form 119 Squadron.

Retaining their pre-war civilian names, 119 Squadron's S.26s were *Golden Fleece*, *Golden Hind* and *Golden Horn*, and a pair of S.23s were also retained, named *Clio* and *Cordelia*. The S.23s were relegated to transport duties while the S.26s were joined by Catalinas in April. These only remained until July 1941, and by 4 August the squadron had moved to Pembroke Dock and continued to operate its S.26s until October, being the only RAF squadron to do so.

It was not until 5 August 1942 that flying returned, when 246 Squadron was re-formed with Sunderlands. The squadron was not operational until 12 December, and on that day it began the first of many long-range A/S patrols over the Atlantic. Having achieved no success, the unit was disbanded on 20 April 1943, its aircraft being passed to 228, 330 and 422 Squadrons.

119 Squadron Short S.23/M flying boat AX660 Cordelia at her moorings at Bowmore.

Short S.23/M AX659 Clio, also of 119 Squadron, at Bowmore in early 1941.

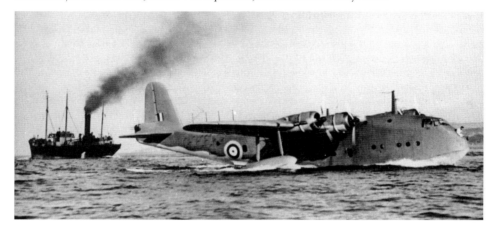

A Sunderland of 246 Squadron at Bowmore in late August 1942, not long after the unit was re-formed.

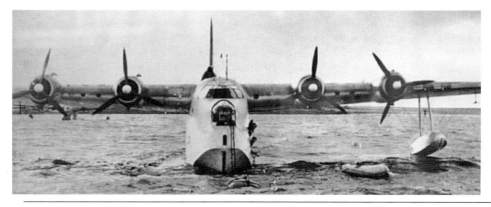

The latter all-Canadian-manned unit moved in on 8 May 1943, with Sunderlands. Flying daily patrols, it was not until 17 October that it achieved a partial success against the enemy. Flt Lt P. T. Sargent and crew attacked U-448 after achieving a radar contact close to a convoy. As Sargent lined up his Sunderland for the attack, a second enemy vessel, U-281, began to open fire. Four depth charges were dropped on the first pass but fell short, while the U-boat's fire also failed to find its mark. Sargent made a second pass, dropping two further depth charges on U-448, but this time the enemy's fire struck the Sunderland, killing the front gunner and mortally wounding the navigator. Sargent had no choice but to ditch near the convoy, but he was killed during the attempted forced landing. The seven surviving members of the crew were rescued by HMS *Drury*. At the expense of three crew and an aircraft, Sargent's last attack on U-448 had managed to heavily damage the U-boat, killing two of the crew and forcing the vessel to return to port early for repairs.

On 3 September 422 Squadron left for St Angelo, becoming the last operational unit to be based at Bowmore. Probably only now serving as a refuelling stop for lost flying boats, Bowmore did well to last as long as July 1945 before being closed down.

BRACKLA, Highland

57°32'30"N/03°54'38"W; NH858519. Immediately NE of Cawdor, off B9090

Developed over the war years, this RLG had a varied career, ending in 1946 when it was covered in hundreds of Halifaxes and Warwicks, none of which were destined to leave in one piece.

The War Office requisitioned land north-east of the Cawdor in May 1939 with the intention of using it for a factory for filling bombs and shells. The site was more suited as an airfield, however, and during late 1940 through to early 1941 an RLG was constructed by McAlpine at a cost of £890,000.

Flying is believed to have begun during the summer of 1941 with visits by the odd Defiant and Lysander from 2 AGS. Adopted by 2 AGS as its own RLG, the airfield became busier during the winter months as Dalcross was steadily becoming a quagmire, while Brackla remained dry and well-drained. Brackla also proved useful for 2 CFS from Church Lawford, which arrived on 1 November 1941 with its Oxfords.

The uncluttered circuit and ample runways had also not escaped the notice of 19 OTU, and it began to operate its Whitleys here from December 1941. On 7 January 1942 until 27 April 1944 19 OTU adopted Brackla as one of its satellites.

2 AGS continued to use Brackla during 1943, and it became another RLG for 19 PAFU from 20 October 1942. The unit's Oxfords continued to operate from here until 14 June 1943, and after a brief quiet period 14 PAFU arrived from Banff, also with Oxfords, on 7 September, and again on 17 June 1944. Dalcross still had its muddy problems and 19 PAFU returned on 3 December 1943, staying until 25 February 1944, when Brackla took on another role.

Brackla was surveyed by 45 MU as an ideal airfield for the open storage of four-engined types, such as the Halifax. During February 1944 a few arrived from Kinloss, while others arrived direct. By this time 19 OTU no longer had a use for the airfield, and 2 AGS continued to operate on only a very small scale. The activities of the MU grew and, to cope with the amount of aircraft now about to arrive at Brackla, 102 Super SLG was formed on 7 February 1945 with the task of being a dispersal centre for the Halifax. The same day the first of 130 Halifaxes arrived, and to cope still further with the influx of aircraft 102 SSS was also formed here in April 1945.

A few Halifaxes were prepped for the French Air Force, but with the war now at an end it was clear that the majority that arrived would be scrapped. A large number of Warwicks also ended their days here. On 15 September 1947 45 MU left, and the same month 102 SSS was closed down. 102 SLG closed on 31 December 1947, followed by the airfield not long after.

Today the majority of the perimeter track, all four T2 bases and several diamond-shaped dispersals remain, while the flying field is only disputed by a few free-range pigs.

Most likely seen in 1947 after its closure, Brackla is devoid of aircraft but its complete infrastructure remains, including all four T2 hangars and a host of buildings.

Main features:
Grass runways: QDM SW-NE 2,000 yards, N-S 1,450 yards, E-W 1,450 yards. *Hangars:* four T2. *Hardstandings:* thirty diamond. *Accommodation:* RAF: 2,117; WAAF: 447.

BRIMS MAINS, Highland

58°36'26"N/03°38'49"W. N of Bridge of Forss, S of Brims Castle, near West Brims Farm

Brims Mains was an ELG for Castletown-based fighters. It was possibly a decoy for Castletown during the early war years, although Barrock is the confirmed Q-site for this station.

BROUGHTY FERRY, Dundee

NO463303

This was a First World War LG.

BRYANSFORD (NEWCASTLE), Down

54°13'73"N/05°55'86"W; J34902 33108. 1½ miles NW of Newcastle

This small strip, which dates back to 1913, was in civilian hands before the outbreak of the war. It is not clear when, but Bryansford was later used by the RFC, but for how long is not known.

BUDDON (BARRY BUDDON), Tayside

56°28'46"N/02°45'34"W. 8 miles ENE of Dundee, between Monifieth and Carnoustie

In 1966 a large exercise took place when 600 soldiers were landed at Buddon by HMS *Fearless*. During 1-2 May this combined operation, supported by *Fearless*'s Wessex helicopters, began with the construction of a temporary airfield under simulated battle conditions. In just under two weeks a 5,000-foot-long runway was built complete with BFIs. The reward for the soldiers' efforts came on 13 May when a 47 Squadron Beverley carried out several take-offs and landings without incident.

A 47 Squadron Beverley C.1 on approach to Buddon in May 1966.

The Army continued to use of the airstrip until at least 1976, often with AAC Beavers. Today a 700-yard grass strip is visible running in a north-south direction, once again only a few hundred yards from the current Army camp, but whether this follows a similar line to the 1966 strip is debatable.

845 Squadron, from HMS *Albion*, operating the Wasp, is recorded as being detached to Barry Buddon from 29 May to 7 June 1973. The likelihood of these manoeuvrable helicopters needing to make use of a 5,000-foot runway is doubtful.

BUTTERGASK, Tayside

56°29'55"N/03°17'11"W. 1 mile E of Springfield off A94

By mid-1941 the number of aircraft then operated by 11 EFTS justified the need for a second RLG. Needing little more than a flat area of land without serious obstructions, this is exactly what Buttergask provided. With instructors, groundcrew and emergency services on hand, the trainee pilots could fly the endless 'circuits and bumps' in a relatively safe environment, away from Perth.

Buttergask was brought into operation from November 1941 and is believed to have remained active until at least the end of 1945. Today the area is exactly the same as it was before the RAF arrived – just another field that does not yield anything of its military past.

BUTTEVANT, Cork

52°14'02"N/08°40'79"W; R53555 09310

An RAF LG was present here from 1918 to 1922. There are very few details regarding its military use, although a civilian airstrip was established not far from the original site in 1998.

CAIRNCROSS, Borders

55°51'55"N/02°10'04"W. 1½ miles SSW of Coldringham, 3 miles W of Eyemouth

Cairncross was the most southerly of 77(HD) Squadron's LGs. The aerodrome was 1,000 yards long and 750 yards wide, and took up 115 acres.

77 Squadron first made use of Cairncross from October 1916. It is most likely that the BE.2C and RE.8 would have been the most common types seen there until the squadron departed in late 1918. The same year a detachment of 256 Squadron's DH.6s from Seahouse operated from Cairncross, which would have closed not long after the Armistice.

CALDALE, Orkney

58°58'41"N/03°00'54"W; HY417105; 2 miles W of Kirkwall, S of Caldale off minor road

Caldale was credited as being the most northerly airship station in the British Isles. Its main role was to provide A/S patrols and convoy escort around the Orkneys using the SS Scout Pushers. To accommodate these airships, a pair of large sheds was built; they were staggered and six giant windbreaks were erected to help when manoeuvring the airships in and out. A technical area was also built, as well as accommodation for at least 200 personnel.

The 146-acre site was opened in July 1916, although the large Coastal shed was not completed until September 1917. This was aggravated by the remote location and the difficulty in obtaining stores. Designated as a Class B Airship Station, the first airships to arrive were a pair of Submarine Scouts, SS-41 and SS-43. These began operating from late summer 1916, but sorties were often aborted owing to the regular high winds and unpredictable weather. The Scouts were joined in 1917 by the slightly more advanced Submarine Scout Pusher, SSP Nos 2, 4 and, later, 41. Two of these would be lost before the end of 1917. On 26 November No 2 came down in the sea off Westray

An early Submarine Scout airship about to embark on a patrol from Caldale.

following an engine failure, with the loss of all three crew. A similar fate befell No 4, which came down in heavy snow at night into the sea on 21 December. The wreckage was washed ashore at Westray, but sadly there was no sign of the three-man crew. In the space of a few weeks the station had lost two of its three non-rigid airships, and SS-41 could not be used because of a lack of gas to inflate it.

One of Caldale's two large airship sheds, which survived until the 1930s.

On 22 January 1918 an order was received from the Admiralty to close the airship station; it would now change roles and become a Kite Balloon Base. With the formation of the RAF, Caldale had another name change, this time becoming 20 BB, forming on 15 April 1918. At the end of the war the name was modified again, to Balloon Training Base. The unit was disbanded on 15 September 1919 and Caldale was closed, although several of the buildings, including the giant sheds, survived into the 1930s.

The site is still marked on modern maps as 'Camp Site (dis)' and all of the building bases and foundations are still in situ.

CAMPBELTOWN, Strathclyde (Argyll and Bute)

55°26'29"N/05°41'51"W. 3½ miles WNW of Campbeltown

Campbeltown can trace its roots back to the First World War, when it was the original site of an aerodrome and airship sub-station then known as Machrihanish. In its later form the airfield was known as The Strath, and was referred to as Strath Aerodrome by Midland & Scottish Air Ferries Ltd, which began services from here on 27 April 1933. Named after Strath Farm, south of the B843, the LG was in an area known as Mitchell's field, and the first aircraft to arrive was an AS.4 Ferry.

Midland & Scottish was wound up in 1934, but its service was taken over by Scottish Airways Ltd, which flew the Fox Moth and Dragon. Facilities were sparse during this period, but a single hangar was built and survives on Dalivaddy Farm next to the B843.

Still in civilian hands when war broke out, it was not until 12 February 1940 that Campbeltown was requisitioned for Admiralty use. Scottish Airways continued to operate from here and several civilian staff remained in their original jobs.

The first military aircraft here were those of 816 and 818 Squadrons, both arriving on 19 February 1940. 816 Squadron brought its Swordfish from Abbotsinch, but moved to Ternhill on 30 May. 818 Squadron, also equipped with the Swordfish, arrived from HMS *Furious*, only to return to her on 4 April. The squadron returned via Hatston on 26 May, only to move on to Sealand two days later.

Some continuity was achieved with the arrival of 772 Squadron from Portland on 14 July to provide target-towing facilities. The unit's first customer arrived the same day, with 829 Squadron from Ford with Albacores and Swordfishes. 815 Squadron from HMS *Illustrious* also squeezed in its Swordfishes on 23 July, but by August both units had left.

The Albacore and Swordfish units continued to arrive, mainly because they were the only types at the time that could safely operate from a small airfield. Before the year was over, 829, 818, 820, 826, 816 and 828 Squadrons had all sampled Campbeltown, which was described by many as 'quite primitive'. Wartime facilities had barely made a difference, the only major addition being a Bessonneau hangar. The situation had not improved a great deal when Campbeltown was taken over by the Royal Navy on 1 June 1940, now under the control HMS *Merlin* at Donibristle.

A Fairey Albacore of 826 Squadron at Campbeltown in 1940.

812 Squadron, from Topcliffe, once again with Swordfishes, saw the airfield's status rise slightly, although it was in administrative rather than physical form. On 1 April 1941 the airfield was commissioned as HMS *Landrail*, but by 15 June it had been downgraded to HMS *Landrail II* following Machrihanish becoming the parent.

The RAF made one appearance when Lysanders of 614 Squadron from Macmerry stayed during exercises in May. On their departure, activity here reduced and it was not until 29 February 1942 that another FAA unit arrived. This was 810 Squadron from High Ercall, which only stayed until 9 March. Limited activity returned with the allocation of Campbeltown to 766 Squadron, which had made Machrihanish its home from mid-April. Once again flying the Swordfish, the unit made regular appearances until its departure in July 1943 to Inskip.

One of the main benefits for the permanent staff was the comfortable accommodation at Machrihanish. By 1943 the airfield was little more than an overflow for Machrihanish, which quickly filled with front-line squadrons enjoying a spell of shore leave. Biplanes were landed straight into Campbeltown, while all other types were towed the short distance, their wings folded, along a minor road that traversed Machrihanish Water.

By mid-1945 HMS *Landrail II* had been paid off and flying, whether military or civilian, never returned, owing to the airfield's proximity to Machrihanish. As well as the previously mentioned pre-war hangar, a few brick wartime buildings remain, the only consolation being that the name Campbeltown, ironically, lives on today in the civilian side of Machrihanish.

Main features:
Grass runways: QDM ENE-WSW 850 yards, NNW-SSE 770 yards. *Hangar:* one civil.

CARDROSS, Argyll and Bute

NS33?77?

Percy Pilcher flew his 'Bat' glider from Wallacetown Farm near Cardross in the 1890s. An LG was recorded as being established here for more than twenty years – possibly at a similar location.

CARMUNNOCK (CATHCART/GLASGOW), Strathclyde

55°46'09"N/04°15'59"W

Hundreds of new aircraft took to the air from this aerodrome during the First World War. All were built by G. & J. Weir, an established engineering company founded in 1871 and operating from a factory in Cathcart. During the war this company, together with several others, combined to become the Scottish Group of Manufacturers, all engaged in the massed production of military aircraft. Contracts came in thick and fast for Weir, beginning with an order for 450 FE.2bs and 600 DH.9s, although 200 of these were later cancelled. As part of the Scottish Group, Weir also worked with Alexander Stephen, the North British Locomotive Company and Barclay, Curle & Company. Within this partnership, Weir helped to build at least 300 BE.2s and up to 300 FE.2bs.

By 1918 all Weir-built aircraft were test-flown from Renfrew, and Carmunnock's role was over.

CASTLEBAR, Mayo

53°51'10"N/09°16'86"W; M15700 89900. 1 mile E of Kilbar

Castlebar was the RFC's most westerly airfield and one of its remotest. Opened in May 1918, its first unit was 105 Squadron with RE.8s from Omagh, which returned in March 1919 with F.2bs. 2 Squadron's F.2bs stayed in March 1920, before returning to Oranmore. The following month saw the last unit to arrive, 100 Squadron, with F.2bs and DH.9s from Baldonnel. By mid-1920 the site had been abandoned by the RAF.

However, it does appear to have enjoyed civilian use, which ended on 7 June 1936.

CASTLETOWNROACH, Cork

52°10'46"N/08°28'01"W; R68065 02592

Castletownroach was selected as a forced-landing field on 11 April 1918. It was most likely used by the RAF until 1922.

CASTLE ARCHDALE (LOUGH ERNE), Fermanagh

54°28'52"N/07°43'51"W; H1755585. 4 miles W of Irvinestown off B82

This flying boat base was a real 'action station', playing a major role in the Battle of the Atlantic throughout the war. It not only contributed a great deal in protecting convoys from U-boat attacks, but could also lay claim to sinking several of them as well.

Opened in February 1941 on the western shore of Lough Erne, the first occupant was 240 Squadron from Stranraer, operating the Stranraer flying boat. Castle Archdale was supposed to be receiving the squadron permanently after it opened, but it would be a few more months before it would make the station its home. In the meantime Castle Archdale was renamed Lough Erne on 18 February 1941, but its original name would be reinstated in early 1943.

209 Squadron, flying the Lerwick, arrived from Stranraer on 23 March 1941. The Lerwicks did not remain here for long, and from April the more capable Catalinas replaced them. With greater confidence, 209 Squadron set out across the Atlantic, and before the month was over the unit would play a role in bringing about the demise of the *Bismarck*. On 26 May 1941 Fg Off D. A. Briggs and his crew in Catalina AH545 were on patrol over the Atlantic when Briggs's co-pilot, Ensign L. B. Smith USN, spotted the battleship. Thanks to this chance but crucial discovery, the *Bismarck* was hunted down and sunk the following day.

On 26 July 1941 209 Squadron left for Reykjavik, to be replaced by 240 Squadron's Catalinas on 23 August. The squadron joined in with seemingly endless patrols over the Atlantic, flying sorties that could last up to 17 hours.

Lough Erne gained a long-term resident when the Sunderlands of 201 Squadron arrived from Sullom Voe on 9 October 1941, although it would be a while before the first encounter with a U-boat. An unknown enemy submarine was attacked in April 1942, but whether it was damaged or not could not be confirmed. The following month 240 Squadron left for the Far East without having achieved a success, but the number of U-boats it had kept under the surface was immeasurable.

Lough Erne's long association with the RCAF began with the formation of 422 Squadron with Lerwicks on 2 April 1942. Re-equipped with the Catalina by August, the squadron left on 20 October for Long Kesh.

119 Squadron was re-formed on 16 April 1942 with Catalinas, which arrived in May. The squadron spent the summer working up before moving to Pembroke Dock on 6 September. 302 FTU was also formed here in August 1942, tasked with training crews to ferry flying boats to overseas units. Equipped with a few Sunderlands and Catalinas, the FTU moved to Stranraer on 1 December 1942.

Before the year was over two more squadrons, both flying the Sunderland, swelled the strength of the station. First was 423 Squadron on 2 November, followed by 228 Squadron on 11 December, both from Oban.

Catalina IB FP107 of 302 FTU, seen not long after the unit's formation at Castle Archdale in May 1942.

Now established as Castle Archdale again, 1943 would see a change of fortunes for several squadrons based here as U-boat detection improved. 228 Squadron left for Pembroke Dock empty-handed on 4 May 1943, but nine days later 423 Squadron was off the mark. Flt Lt J. Musgrave and his crew spotted U-753 on the surface 10 miles from convoy HX-237. The U-boat opened fire on the Sunderland, which shadowed it for 20 minutes and returned fire while HMCS *Drumheller* forced the boat to dive using gunfire. Musgrave took his opportunity and, after the spot was marked by a Swordfish from HMS *Biter*, he dropped his depth charges, followed by more from HMS *Lagan*. Although it was a shared victory for 423 Squadron, it was still celebrated.

201 Squadron also achieved its first success on 31 May when Flt Lt Hall and crew caught U-440 on the surface north of Cape Ortegal. A single pass and a stick of depth charges sunk the U-boat, with all forty-six hands lost. The following month, on 27 June, Fg Off E. H. Lane RNZAF and crew strafed and dropped four depth charges on U-518 west of Cape Finisterre. While the U-boat survived, it was so badly damaged that it had to return to its home base straight away.

Two more victories were claimed by 423 Squadron, the first on 4 August when Fg Off A. A. Bishop and crew fought an epic battle with U-489. The U-boat had already been damaged earlier in the day and had no choice but to fight it out on the surface against whomever wanted to finish her off. The aircraft was shot to pieces as it made its run, but it still managed to sink the U-boat, although it had to ditch immediately after. On 8 October Fg Off A. H. Russell and crew attacked U-610 with depth charges while it was on convoy escort duties. The U-boat was sunk with all fifty-one hands killed.

It was time for a reshuffle of units as many operations were geared to supporting the forthcoming invasion of Europe. 201 Squadron would play an important part in this, and on 8 April 1944 it moved to Pembroke Dock from where it achieved further success in the English Channel. It was replaced by another Canadian unit. 422 Squadron returned on 13 April 1944, by now with the Sunderland. Despite its best efforts, the squadron had a quiet tour and left for Pembroke Dock on 4 November without attacking, let alone sinking, a U-boat.

Sunderland III EK491 is seen serving with 422 Squadron at Castle Archdale, not long before the aircraft was transferred to 4 OTU.

202 Squadron brought its Catalinas from Gibraltar on 3 September 1944, and 201 Squadron returned from Pembroke Dock on 3 November. It was not long before the latter unit claimed another enemy scalp when U-297 was sunk on 6 December.

Of the wartime units, it was 202 Squadron that was the first to disband, but not until 4 June 1945. 423 Squadron flew its last operational sortie on 13 May, and on 8 August moved to Bassingbourn to re-equip with Liberators. Last to leave was 201 Squadron, which left for Pembroke Dock on 2 August, bringing the curtain down on Castle Archdale's wartime history. It was not, however, the end of the flying boat days, which were seen out here by 230 Squadron's Sunderlands on 10 August 1946. It was to be a short tour for the squadron, which moved to Calshot on 16 September after serving at one of the RAF's most pleasant stations.

A three-ship farewell, as 201 Squadron's Sunderland Vs leave Castle Archdale for the last time in August 1945.

The main site is now home to the Castle Archdale Caravan Park and Camping Site, although remnants of the RAF occupation still exist. At the entrance to the park, military buildings have been maintained in good order and the site office was the station's main operations and HQ building. All slipways are still in place, as well as a substantial purpose-built dock for Shetlands, which neither arrived here nor entered RAF service.

CASTLE KENNEDY, Dumfries and Galloway

54°54'00"N/04°56'03"W; NX119598. 3 miles ESE of Stranraer off A75

The flat ground at Castle Kennedy was ideal for an airfield, and was used for the first recorded landing by a fixed-wing aircraft in Galloway, in August 1913. The aircraft involved were one MF7 and five BE.2's of 2 Squadron from Upper Dysart, which were on their way to Ireland to take part in military manoeuvres. While here they were fitted with flotation bags in the event of ditching in the Irish Sea. The arrival of the aircraft created much local interest, and schools were closed and special trains organised to view the new machines.

Shortly after the outbreak of hostilities there was a need to move training establishments away from the South Coast of England. Castle Kennedy was chosen to house a gunnery school, and work began in mid-1940. On 23 June 1941 the CGS from Warmwell arrived, although it was clear from a very early stage that the grass runways were in no fit state due to being waterlogged. Much of the CGS's flying was done from West Freugh, but in the meantime more units were planned.

On 24 July 1941 10 AGS, with Defiants and Lysanders, was formed. It made the best of a bad job, but flying was dangerous enough without the complication of dealing with churned-up runways. On 5 December the CGS moved to Chelveston; 10 AGS left ten days later for Barrow, and the airfield was closed to flying while two runways were laid.

3 AGS was formed on 20 April 1942 with Bothas and twenty-seven Battles, the latter serving as target tugs. The new AGS suffered a high accident rate with the Botha as well as a poor serviceability record before it was moved to Mona on 19 December 1942 to make way for another new unit.

The same day 2 TTU was formed here to train torpedo-bomber crews on Beaufighters and Beauforts. Senior staff were never fully convinced that the RAF should be training its crews to drop torpedoes, feeling that this was really the domain of the FAA. With this in mind, by mid-1943 a decision was made to reduce all RAF torpedo training, and the first victim of this wind-down was 2 TTU. On 29 September 1943 the unit was absorbed into 1 TTU at Turnberry.

After a few weeks of inactivity, 3 AGS returned on 3 November 1943. The school was now operating Ansons with Martinets, and teaching up to ninety pupils per course, each of which would last for approximately seven weeks. By March 1945 the Ansons gave way to Wellingtons, which were still available in abundance despite it being so late in the war. On 21 June 1945 3 AGS was disbanded, having trained thousands of air gunners for both Bomber and Coastal Command service.

Castle Kennedy then followed the traditional route of being taken over by an MU, in this case 57 MU, on 16 July 1945. On the same day 104 SSS was also formed to provide additional storage for 57 MU, primarily for the storage and eventual scrapping of Mosquitoes and Wellingtons.

By early 1946 the airfield was closed, but could easily be called upon in the event of an emergency. 57 MU's tasking came to an end in August 1947, and not long after that Castle Kennedy was closed.

The airfield lay dormant until 1955, when Silver City Airways began flights from here with Type 170 Freighters and Dakotas. Services were mainly flown to Ireland, but were later expanded to include the Isle of Man. Unfortunately the flights came to a premature end in 1957, but light aircraft occasionally used the airfield and still do.

Three of the four hangars are still here, two of them now used by Scottish Milk Products. Both runways remain in reasonable condition at almost their original length.

Main features:
Tarmac-covered concrete runways: QDM 170 1,400 yards, 090 1,400 yards. *Hangars:* four Callender Hamilton, nine EO blister. *Hardstandings:* ten rectangular. *Accommodation:* RAF: 1,369; WAAF: 329.

Castle Kennedy is seen here more than twenty years ago, but the airfield remains in a similar condition today. The main technical site and surviving hangars are at the top of the photo.

CASTLETOWN, Highland

58°35'07"N/03°21'01"W; ND215669. 1½ miles SE of Castletown off B876

Castletown's role in the war was initially as an important one, helping to protect Scapa Flow and Northern Scotland. Built as a satellite for Wick, its first unit was 504 Squadron with its Hurricanes, which moved in from Wick on 21 June 1940. The squadron, which was recovering from action in France, flew many patrols, achieving success on 24 and 28 July when two He 111s were shot down. The unit left for Catterick on 2 September, its task being taken over by 3 Squadron's Hurricanes the following day; the squadron was joined by 808 Squadron's Fulmars from Worthy Down on 5 September. On the 14th 3 Squadron left for Turnhouse, to be replaced by 232 Squadron's Hurricanes from Sumburgh four days later.

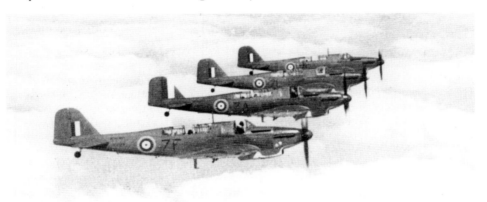

A rare shot of three Fulmars of 808 Squadron on patrol out of Castletown in 1940.

It was thought that a German invasion was imminent, and both 232 and 808 Squadrons stepped up their patrols over the next few weeks. This area of Scotland was thought to be one of many points where enemy forces might invade, although thanks to a local 4.7-inch naval gun called 'Big Bertha' at Dunnet Head, the Germans may have thought better of it. The gun, which was acquired by Castletown's station commander, Wg Cdr D. F. W. Atcherley, was part of the airfield's defence and was manned by a 'hijacked' group from the Pioneer Corps.

808 Squadron left for Donibristle on 2 October 1941, followed by 232 Squadron, which moved to Skitten on the 13th. The same day, the patrol duties were taken over by 3 Squadron, again returning from Turnhouse. Before the end of 1941 3 Squadron returned to carry out further air defence patrols over Scapa until it moved to Skeabrae on 7 January 1942. In the meantime, 260 Squadron was re-formed here with Hurricanes and, after moving to Skitten on 5 December 1940, returned to take over the patrols from 3 Squadron.

The Blenheims of 404 Squadron served here from 20 June 1941, having moved from Thorney Island. Other units that carried out patrol duties from here during late 1941 included 54, 123, 331 and 607 Squadrons. All had one thing in common: none had encountered or attacked a single enemy aircraft. Both 54 and 123 Squadrons settled here the longest, the latter leaving for Egypt from 11 April 1942 and 54 Squadron moving to Wellingore on 2 June.

167 Squadron's Spitfires arrived from Acklington on 1 June. During August, one of them spotted a Ju 88 and managed to get a burst of fire at it before it disappeared into the mist. 167 Squadron moved to Ludham on 14 October 1942, and was replaced by the Spitfires of 610 Squadron the following day from the same airfield.

123 Squadron, with its Spitfire IIAs, was one of many fighter units that took their turn at flying patrols over Scapa Flow from Castletown in 1941.

131 Squadron took over from 610 Squadron on 22 January 1943, and, after moving to Exeter on 26 June, was itself replaced by 310 Squadron. This squadron's main equipment was the Spitfire VC, but from July to September it also had several Spitfire VIs. The latter were introduced to combat high-flying enemy reconnaissance, but none was encountered from Castletown before the squadron moved to Ibsley on 19 September.

1490 Flight moved in from Skeabrae on 16 August, although its Lysanders and Masters had moved to Peterhead by October. 310 Squadron's duties were taken over by two Spitfire squadrons, 118 Squadron from Peterhead and 504 Squadron from Redhill. With the latter moving to Peterhead on 18 October 1943, 118 Squadron remained until 18 January 1944, having been relieved by 132 Squadron two days earlier. It was at Castletown that 132 Squadron also received additional Spitfire VIs during its tour, which came to an end when 504 Squadron returned from Hornchurch on 10 March. Success came for 504 Squadron on 22 April when Fg Off Waslyk and Sgt Thorne shot down a Ju 188 off the Pentland Skerries before their unit left for Digby eight days later.

The last fighter squadron to pass through Castletown during the war was 66 Squadron from Bognor on 8 May. It returned on 14 May, bringing an end to more than four years of patrols. It was almost as if the Luftwaffe was aware of this, because just four days later a pair of Ju 188s flew low over the airfield completely unmolested!

All attention seemed to be focused on events happening in mainland Europe from June 1944, and very little activity occurred here. The odd waif and stray was diverted here before the end of the war, and the Royal Navy showed some interest before the airfield was closed in June 1945.

Today the airfield is a bleak sight with the hangars removed and the control tower long demolished. Large sections of runway still exist, although the perimeter track is now little more than a gravel path. Six of the banked SE fighter pens still exist, together with a few technical buildings, including the generating house and decontamination centre.

Main features:
Asphalt runways: QDM 250 1,200 yards, 292 1,125 yards, 161 1,085 yards. *Hangars:* one Bellman, one T3. *Hardstandings:* six SE. *Accommodation:* RAF: 1,227.

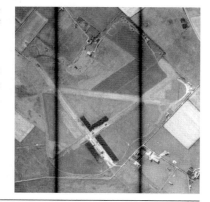

Thanks to its remoteness, Castletown remains in a reasonable state of preservation in this view taken in 2005.

CATFIRTH, Shetlands

60°15'51"N/01°11'28"W. Half a mile S of Freester

The Shetland Islands' first seaplane station arrived too late to play any significant role. Work began in early 1918 on a large slipway and hangar capable of housing the RNAS's largest flying boats. However, with the formation of the RAF plans to accommodate a flying boat unit were reduced to just a single flight. This was 300 Flight, which was formed within 28 Group on 15 June 1918 flying the Felixstowe F.3 and the Porte FB.2.

Five further units, 301 to 305 Flights, also operating the F.3, were due to arrive here as well. However, the end of the war was in sight and none of them were formed. 300 Flight continued to operate alone until the end of March 1919, and Catfirth was closed on 15 April.

Surprisingly, considering how long it was in service, a great deal remains today. The slipway and hangar base are easy to find and several accommodation huts still stand as the shoreline is approached. Its good condition during the Second World War attracted the attentions of Luftwaffe aerial reconnaissance – Catfirth was obviously giving the impression that it was still in use.

CHARTERHALL, Borders

55°42'25"N/02°22'37"W; NT765463. 3 miles NE of Greenlaw off B6460

The combination of an OTU, inexperienced aircrew, complex twin-engined aircraft and extensive night-flying earned Charterhall an unenviable reputation and the nickname 'Slaughter Hall'.

Requisition orders were served on local landowners in March 1941, and by June a contract to build a fighter training station had been drawn up with J. Miller & Partners of Edinburgh. Work began immediately and it was hoped that the airfield would be completed in seven months. However, poor weather and a changing remit resulted in the airfield not being ready until April 1942, but it would be several months before Charterhall was fully complete.

When Charterhall's first and longest-serving unit, 54 OTU, arrived from Church Fenton and the first courses began on 12 May, the airfield still looked like a building site. A satellite at Winfield, which was far more prepared than its parent, began flying operations the same day.

54 OTU's task was to train night-fighter crews on twin-engined aircraft, which were, at the time, the Blenheim and the Beaufighter. The same month the unit was reorganised, with conversion training being carried out by 'A' Squadron flying Oxfords and Blenheims, while 'B' Squadron was for intermediate training using the Blenheim and Beaufighter IIf. Once the successful crew members had passed both stages they would move to Winfield and fly with 'C' Advanced Squadron, where AI flying and armament training would be given.

The Blenheim, despite its withdrawal from night-fighter duties, was still a very useful aircraft, and several were on strength in 1943; at least two were still flying in early 1944. By this time, however, it was the Beaufighter, with more than seventy on strength, that was the most common type. Wellingtons arrived from 21 March 1944 when the unit took over a flight from 6 OTU, Thornaby; ten operated from Charterhall, all fitted with AI Mk X classrooms enabling several radar operators to be trained at once. Only weeks later the first of many Mosquitoes began to arrive, but it was not until February 1945 that they began to arrive en masse.

From July 1945 the Beaufighter was phased out, and Beauforts replaced the Wellington radar trainers. 54 OTU had achieved great things while serving here, including the output of 882 night-fighter crews, and 91,860 flying hours (65,774 of which had been at night) had been logged, which equated to an average of three aircraft being in the air both day and night for more than three years. As always, the successes had been achieved at a price – fifty-six were killed and 336 accidents recorded. 54 OTU left for East Moor on 1 November 1945.

Before the OTU's departure, the FAA had taken advantage of the unit's experience by moving 770 Squadron in from Drem on 1 July 1945. The Mosquito-equipped unit carried out radar trials

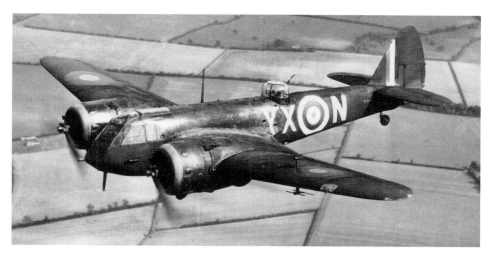

A Blenheim IF of 54 OTU out of Charterhall, similar to the aircraft that claimed the life of Richard Hillary in January 1943.

before returning on 1 October. The same day, another FAA unit, 772 Squadron from Ayr, carried out the same trials before returning on 16 October.

On the same day as the OTU's departure, 3 APS arrived from Hawkinge with Martinets, Masters and Spitfires. This unit's experienced instructors gave a host of lectures on all forms of armament fitted to fighter-bomber aircraft of the day. Air-to-ground firing was carried out at St Abbs, Goswick Sands and Fenham Flats, all along the Northumbrian coast. 130 Squadron from Manston, with its Spitfires, was the first unit to take part in a course from 1 December 1945, with 165 Squadron's Spitfires from Vaernes following on the 30th. When these squadrons' courses were completed on 24 January, their place was taken by 263 Squadron's Meteors from Acklington. The jets returned on 1 March and the final unit to take advantage of the course was 303 Squadron from Wick, with its Mustangs. 303 Squadron left for Hethel on 23 March 1946, and not long afterwards 3 APS was disbanded. For some unknown reason, it was then re-formed on 7 November with Martinets, its duties being target-towing over one of the Northumbrian ranges; on 26 March 1947 it was disbanded again.

The airfield survives in reasonable condition and two Bellman hangars remain on the north side, now owned by Tarmac. Within this area several original wartime buildings are extant. Just off the B6460 at the junction of two minor roads, the original entrance to the site, a lovely memorial to Charterhall and Richard Hillary sits on the edge of the road. The Battle of Britain ace was killed here on 8 January 1943, just one of many who lost their lives at Charterhall.

Main features:
Hardcore and tarmac runways: QDM 077 1,600 yards, 024 1,600 yards. *Hangars:* four Bellman, seven blister. *Hardstandings:* thirty-eight. *Accommodation:* RAF: 1,392; WAAF: 464.

CLONGOWES WOOD COLLEGE, Kildare

53°18'75"N/06°40'86"W; N87901 29950. N of Clane

This field strip was located in the grounds of the college. Founded in 1814, the college boasted at least 150 acres of land, and the 'strip' was first documented on 15 December 1917. Used briefly by the RAF, it would be almost sixty years before aviation returned. Since 1978 the grounds have been used as a balloon launch site, virtually from the same spot where the biplanes once operated.

CLONMEL (ABBEYFARM), Tipperary

52°15'16"N/07°47'16"W; S17612 22512. 1½ miles W of Clonmel railway station

An LG was here from April 1921. It was briefly used by the RAF before passing into civilian hands, operating until 4 June 1937.

CLUNTOE (KINRUSH), Tyrone

54°37'26"N/06°32'00"W; H945755. 4 miles ESE of Coagh off B161

A large number of the airfields planned for Northern Ireland were to be Bomber Command OTUs, and Cluntoe was no exception. Construction began in December 1940, but before completion the RAF no longer had any use for it. With no incentive to hurry, the civilian contractors took their time and Cluntoe was not completed until June 1942. It was with reluctance that the RAF took over the airfield with a C&M party, which arrived on 20 July. It was a well-equipped airfield with good long runways as expected for an OTU, and a large array of technical training buildings, and these facilities would not be overlooked by a different air force the following year.

As the US 8th AF began to arrive at its bases in England, it was soon realised that the crews had never experienced Britain's foul weather, let alone the RAF Flying Control procedures and rules for flying in a war zone. All the American crews had been trained in clear skies, and it was decided to set up several introductory centres that would give them the information for operating safely over Britain.

The answer came with the formation of the CCRC. Cluntoe was one of many locations that were earmarked to become CCRCs, and it was inspected by American personnel on 4 February 1943 when it received its first aircraft, a pair of L-4s. The process of opening Cluntoe continued to be slow, and it did not come under full USAAF control until 30 August, when the 8th Composite Command took over the now redesignated Station 238.

4 CCRC was established here on 21 November 1943 and the airfield came alive with a large influx of personnel and aircraft. From its formation to February 1944 alone, fifty-seven B-17 crews passed through the centre, as well as forty-five pilots from the 311th Ferrying Squadron and 103 radio operators received special training.

From late February 1944 the first of many B-24 crews also passed through the centre, before it was redesignated as 2 CCRC on 7 March. Very little changed within the centre, which not only taught whole crews but also individuals within their specialist fields. By the end of March air gunners were being taught separately at Greencastle, and high-altitude bombing and tactics was also added.

By the summer of 1944 the number of crews began to decline, although 210 still passed through in August. On 8 November 2 CCRC was closed and control of the airfield was returned to the RAF. No units were placed here, so the airfield saw out its wartime days under C&M and was closed to flying by June 1945.

Cluntoe remained in military hands following the war, and from 1 April 1947 was a reserve airfield for the FAA, being renamed HMS *Gannet*. It was then reactivated thanks to an RAF recruitment drive for the Korean War. The station was refurbished, and on 1 February 1953 2 FTS was re-formed, complete with an RLG at Toome. The school flew the Harvard and Prentice and taught pilots the basics through to gaining their wings. Cluntoe's new-found role was to be short-lived, however, and 2 FTS moved to Hullavington on 1 June 1954. By 1957 the airfield had been closed.

Cluntoe today has been taken over by a host of different businesses mixed in with the odd private dwelling. All three runways are still virtually intact and can be accessed with little trouble, although the last of the complex dispersals were lifted a few years ago. The most significant building remaining is a Type 12779/41 control tower, which from the state of it has an uncertain future.

Main features:
Concrete runways: QDM 240 2,000 yards, 360 1,400 yards, 100 1,400 yards.
Hangars: four T2. *Hardstandings:* thirty 125-foot frying pan, fifty fighter.
Accommodation: RAF: 2,512.

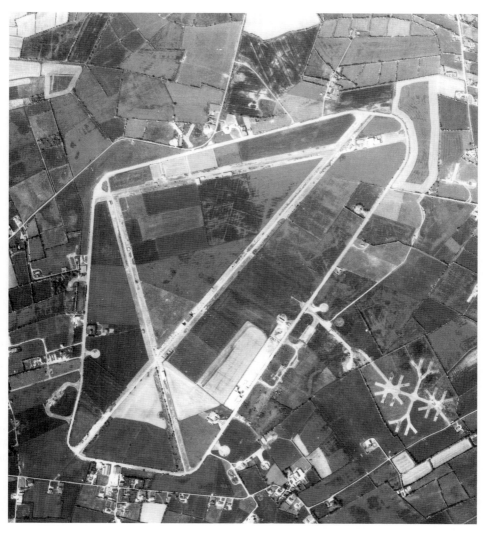

Cluntoe, seen in May 1992, is still in a reasonable state, most likely thanks to the expensive refurbishment that took place in the 1950s.

COLINTON (EDINBURGH), Mid-Lothian

55°53'55"N/03°15'53"W; NT 219689

Colinton was established in 1916 for 77(HD) Squadron in response to the Zeppelin threat.

COLLINSTOWN (DUBLIN), Dublin

53°25'68"N/06°15'33"W; O15936 43410. 5½ miles N of O'Connell Street Bridge

One of several sites surveyed by Sholto Douglas in 1917, Collinstown would grow into Dublin International Airport.

Collinstown is seen here only six days before the end of the First World War. Seven large hangars are under construction, while Bessoneaus serve as an interim with 504s all around.

With no expense spared, work began in late 1917, and by August 1918 Collinstown was ready. 24 TDS was formed on 15 August from 24 and 59 TS, and came under the charge of the 3rd Wing, which was located at 9 Merrion Square, Dublin. However, by May 1919 the wing had moved to Collinstown House, before disbanding.

24 TDS was a large unit with almost 900 personnel and more than seventy aircraft on strength. American personnel were also prevalent, with several under flying instruction and many more employed by a large repair section.

On 13 April 1919 24 TDS was redesignated 24 TS, by now only flying the 504K. The unit moved to Tallaght on 1 May and Collinstown was wound down. The Irish Flight arrived from Baldonnell on 1 May 1922 with F.2bs and DH.9as, but by 31 October had been disbanded.

A 24 TDS 504K and a DH.9a at Collinstown in early 1919.

CONNEL (OBAN AIRPORT/NORTH CONNEL), Strathclyde

56°27'44"N/05°24'04"W. 5 miles NE of Oban, 1 mile NW of Connel

Positioned under Beinn Lora and shoehorned into a strip of land on the shoreline of Ardmucknish Bay, Connel is not located in one of the most ideal spots.

Connel was a pre-war civilian airfield but, following a survey of potential fighter stations for protecting naval installations at Loch Ewe and the Kyle of Lochalsh, it was looked at in more detail. Tiree came up as the final choice, with Connel put forward as the nearest mainland option for a forward airfield. However, owing to poor approaches the airfield was barely used.

It was expanded in 1941 for land-based aircraft supporting the flying boat base at Oban. It would also serve as an important ELG for several aircraft that were lost or low on fuel over western Scotland, where airfields were few and far between.

Completed by 1942, the airfield hosted the odd visitor but it never really found a useful purpose until early 1944, and even this was not for a flying unit. On 1 February 244 MU was formed as an AAP, and by 21 February the airfield was closed to flying.

244 MU's tenure here was short, as it had moved to Cottom by September 1944. Connel had already reopened as an ELG in August, and during the remainder of the war several aircraft made use of it.

Some time during 1945 2 GS served here, becoming the last military unit to do so. Its departure is sketchy, but it appears that the site had been certainly abandoned by the Air Ministry some time in the late 1940s, but was still owned by the MoD.

By 1967 the site was in civilian hands, having been purchased by Oban Council for development. A brief service by Loganair was established from 1 September, flying a route that linked Glasgow, Oban and Mull, but this was to be short-lived, although the airfield still remained active. By the early 1980s regular light aircraft flying was begun and continues today. The airfield, which is now referred to as Oban Airport, boasts a modern tower and terminal building and is run by Argyll & Bute Council. At present the main operator from here is Hebridean Air Services, which flies routes to Colensay, Islay, Coll and Tiree.

Main features:
Tarmac runways: QDM 202 1,400 yards, 214 1,050 yards. *Hangars:* two T3. *Accommodation:* RAF: 109; WAAF: 31.

CRAIL, Fife

56°16'08"N/02°36'22"W; NO625085. 1 mile NNE of Crail

The village of Crail, located at Fife's most easterly point, lent its name to two airfields during the 20th century. The first opened during the latter stages of the First World War, only to be reopened during the early months of the Second. Supporting at least thirty-six FAA squadrons alone during the Second World War, Crail became the most important airfield for training aircrews in the art of attacking the enemy using a torpedo.

The first build began in 1918 and was commissioned for use by the RFC and RNAS, but by the time it opened the RAF had been formed. The first units to arrive were 58 TS from Spittlegate on 15 July 1918, followed by 64 TS from Harlaxton. Both squadrons were destined to be disbanded into 27 TDS, which was formed here on 15 August.

27 TDS had a short life, and with the end of the war the RAF was wound down. 27 TDS was disbanded on 31 March 1919, leaving Crail with only a Delivery Station (Storage), which had been formed on 1 March. 104 Squadron arrived on 3 March as a cadre, and the personnel remained until the squadron was disbanded on 30 June 1919. This was the end, and, despite a lot of money, time and effort having been put into building this aerodrome, it closed in late 1919. By the early 1920s Crail had returned to the plough, and all hangars and buildings were demolished not long after.

F.2b Fighters and a 504K belonging to 27 TDS are seen at Crail in early 1919. Note the substantial hangar behind, which was razed to the ground only months later.

Crail's rebirth came about as a result of Donibristle's need for an RLG. Unlike Crail, Donibristle had managed to survive the post-First World War closures, retaining a foothold for the Royal Navy in Scotland. After surveying the original site, work began on a larger one from 1 September 1939, and it would take more than a year before it was completed.

Crail was re-opened on 1 October 1940 to train TBR aircrews for FAA squadrons. However, the first flying squadron to pass through here was a fighter unit, when 800 Squadron's Rocs arrived on 8 October 1940 from HMS *Ark Royal*; three weeks later the squadron left for Prestwick. Albacores were next, with 827 Squadron from Yeovilton on 2 November, followed the next day by 829 Squadron from St Eval. This squadron only stayed a couple of weeks, while 827 Squadron departed to HMS *Argus* for DLT on 14 March 1941.

On 4 November 1940 the first of two squadrons was formed for TBR training. 785 Squadron was the first, with Sharks and Swordfishes, while 786 Squadron was the second, formed here on 21 November with Albacores.

Crail was commissioned as HMS Jackdaw *on 1 October 1940.*

Albacores of 785 and 786 Squadrons await another batch of practice torpedoes at Crail. Via the late R. C. Sturtivant

831 Squadron was formed here on 1 April 1941 as a TBR squadron with Albacores; after working up, the squadron moved to Machrihanish for weapons training on 26 August. Another long-term resident, 770 Squadron, with Rocs, arrived from Donibristle on 1 June. Two Rocs were used as target tugs, the others for target marking.

Throughout the remainder of 1941 two Albacore units, 820 and 828 Squadrons, together with two Swordfish units, 819 and 823 Squadrons, were here for a few weeks. The latter was re-formed on 1 November as a TBR unit with Swordfishes, only to leave for Fraserburgh on 6 December. 819 Squadron arrived from Lee-on-Solent on 10 December, remaining slightly longer. Training began with the focus on torpedo-dropping and night-flying. Poor weather in January 1942 almost wiped out the squadron when six Swordfishes were damaged in a gale. The squadron left on 27 January for Twatt.

820 Squadron Albacores out of Crail during late 1941. Via the late R. C. Sturtivant

From December 1942 both 785 and 786 Squadrons began to receive the Barracuda. 785 continued to use the Swordfish and Albacore, but 786 Squadron retired its Swordfishes and Albacores within weeks of the Barracuda arriving. By the war's end, 785 Squadron had more than fifty Barracudas, and 786 Squadron more than eighty.

The Barracuda was a common sight here by late 1943, but it was not until 18 October that the first operational unit, 810 Squadron, arrived from HMS *Illustrious*. The unit did not stay long, moving to Machrihanish for weapons training before returning to HMS *Illustrious* in late November.

The airfield's long association with 770 Squadron came to an end on 29 January 1944, although it only moved as far as Dunino, and its aircraft were still quite often seen here until it was disbanded in October 1945.

Early 1944 saw several operational units arrive, the majority with Barracudas. 820 and 826 Squadrons, the most notable of these, stayed from February to June 1944. After leaving for HMS *Indefatigable*, both were involved in an unsuccessful torpedo attack on the *Tirpitz*.

The last unit to arrive here during the war was 711 Squadron, which re-formed as a TBR unit with Barracudas on 9 September 1944. By this stage 786 Squadron was training crews on A/S courses and Barracuda familiarisation. At the end of 1944 the squadron became part of 1 NOTU and, with the end of hostilities in Europe, started to receive the Avenger. 711 Squadron had become an Avenger OTU by August 1945, but this task reduced and it was disbanded into 785 Squadron on 21 December. 786 Squadron was also disbanded into 785 Squadron on the same day. Despite the swelling of 785 Squadron, the need for torpedo crews had long expired. Having served at Crail for 5½ years, 786 Squadron disbanded on 1 March 1946.

711 Squadron was the last unit to be re-formed at Crail during the Second World War, initially with the Barracuda II.

The airfield was now running down and the last FAA flying unit to arrive was 780 Squadron, with Oxfords, in December 1946 from Hinstock for instrument training before moving to Donibristle on 27 March 1947.

On 28 April 1947 the airfield ceased to be HMS *Jackdaw*, becoming HMS *Bruce* for ground training purposes and as a boys' training establishment. More than 1,300 passed through HMS *Bruce* during the late 1940s and early 1950s in preparation for joining the senior service. The airfield gained a giant replica tall ship's mast during the period, located next to the parade ground. The base and approximately 10 feet of the mast are all that remains today.

Aircraft returned in the 1950s when 1830 Squadron moved from Donibristle with Fireflies. This squadron, which used the airfield for circuit training, was active here from December 1950 through to November 1952. The Army took over in 1952, with the 1st Battalion of the Black Watch taking up residence. It was from here that the battalion was mobilised before being deployed to fight in Korea; it returned in 1955 but left for good for service in British Guiana not long after.

The last military aviation use of Crail occurred between March 1953 and August 1957. Initially moved because of extension work at Leuchars, St Andrews UAS made use of Crail's quiet runways for many years after the work was completed.

The first of several sales to return Crail to civilian use began in 1961, and by 1963 all had been returned to its original owners or purchased by others. The airfield has been used for a variety of different tasks since becoming civilianised. Farming dominates, and several film companies have used the surviving hangar over the years. The runways have been used for motor sport and a permanent karting circuit is in situ today. The runways also provide a good location for Sunday markets.

The three-storey Standard control tower dominates Crail, with an increasingly rare Aircraft Repair Shed in the background. Author

With few exceptions, the runways, perimeter track and dispersal areas remain and are overlooked by the three-storey control. Behind, row upon row of buildings can be seen, very few of which are approaching dereliction. The Bellmans have found homes elsewhere or have been scrapped, but the single ARS remains in use. Altogether more than 150 buildings remain in generally good condition. This makes Crail the best-preserved disused airfield in Scotland, possibly also ranking as one of the most impressive in Great Britain.

Main features:

Tarmac runways: QDM 247 1,200 yards, 209 1,000 yards, 297 1,000 yards, 337 1,000 yards. *Hangars:* eight 60 x 70 feet, one 185 x 110 feet ARS, eight super blisters. *Accommodation:* RN: 1,447; WRNS: 700.

This view gives an idea of how many buildings are still standing at Crail, together with the well-preserved runways, perimeter track and dispersal roads.

CREETOWN, Kirkcudbrightshire

54°55'00"N/04°22'45"W. Off A75 E of Spittal

Creetown was active during the early 1930s in civilian hands, and was on the AA aerodrome list in 1932. It was requisitioned by the military some time during the war, but did not host any unit until the end. In June 1945 8 GS moved in from Ayr, flying the Cadet. By March 1947 the school had been disbanded and no further use by the RAF is recorded.

CROMARTY, Ross-shire

57°41'01"N/04°02'09"W. Near old lighthouse and coastguard station in Cromarty

The Cromarty Firth is a natural deep harbour that provided the Royal Navy with safe anchorage for many years. On 7 May 1913 one of the officers on board HMS *Hermes*, Lt Cdr A. Longmore, was appointed as commander of Cromarty Air Station. At this time no such place existed, but it was up to Longmore to establish one to support ships operating from the Firth.

It was not the easiest of tasks, and Longmore eventually chose a site near the lighthouse and coastguard station. Used by local fishermen to dry their nets, it was large enough to accommodate a hangar and close enough to the foreshore to launch seaplanes. It was not clear who actually owned the land, but the Admiralty had already allocated up to £10,000 to be spent on the new station, which would have easily covered the purchase of land and any construction needs.

A Bessoneau hanger arrived on a lighter from Sheerness on 4 July 1913. Recruitment at the time was fascinating, with only half of the twenty ratings taken on for the station having actually seen an aircraft before. Fitter and rigger training was carried out inhouse, with most rectification faults cured by trial and error!

Aircraft began arriving by rail and boat in dribs and drabs, the first being Maurice Farman Seaplane No 117 followed by Sopwith Seaplane No 59 and Borel Seaplane No 85. Longmore wasted no time in using these aircraft in Fleet exercises, proving that air-sea co-operation was feasible when he spotted a periscope off Nairn on 26 July 1913. Using an Aldis lamp, Longmore signalled his find to a nearby ship, much to the enthusiasm of senior officers taking part in the exercise.

Despite quickly establishing Cromarty as a seaplane station, it was never meant to be. The barracks at Fort George were found to be more than adequate, and from October 1913 Cromarty was moved, piece by piece, by boat across to its new location.

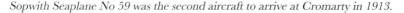

Sopwith Seaplane No 59 was the second aircraft to arrive at Cromarty in 1913.

DALCROSS, Highland

57°32'25"N/04°03'00"W; NH775521. 8 miles NE of Inverness off A96

Thanks to Capt Fresson of Scottish Airways, the Air Ministry found itself an excellent airfield, which could have been in service quicker if it had listened to his advice.

Unable to expand Longman, Fresson looked elsewhere. He did not have to look far, and with the war fast approaching he offered his findings to the military, which was searching for sites in the area. Fresson's advice was that tarmac runways were essential as the area would become very boggy in winter. His advice was ignored, an airfield was established and, funnily enough, during the winter of 1940 the grass runways turned into the predicted quagmire. Dalcross was closed and by early 1941 three solid runways had been laid.

Reopened on 15 June 1941, the first unit to use Dalcross was 2 AGS with Defiants, which was formed on 10 July and would remain until the end of 1945. Several Lysanders were used for target-towing, and at first there were insufficient drogue operators, but this was overcome when thirty airmen from the station went on a short course of instruction at Evanton.

It was not until 16 August that training began, by which time an RLG had been made available at Brackla until 14 June 1943. August also saw a detachment of 13 Group AACF from Turnhouse, and 19 OTU's Whitleys also carried out night-flying. Oxfords from 11 SFTS made use of Dalcross while Shawbury's runways were built, and in December two flights from 2 CFS were also here pending a move to Church Lawford.

New Year 1942 saw a detachment of 1 FIS from Church Lawford, which was transferred to 2 FIS control on 1 February. Flying the Oxford, the FIS would form the nucleus for the second training unit to be formed here, 19 PAFU, which was formed on 20 October 1942 from the 2 FIS Flight, which was expanded from a handful of aircraft to 145 Oxfords and four Ansons before the end of the year.

RAF Dalcross was a neat-looking airfield from the air, but this design with all three runways crossing at the same point was very vulnerable to air attack. Rows of 19 PAFU Oxfords are visible in front of the hangar line.

A lack of RLGs was one of the early problems encountered by the PAFU, but by May 1943 both Forres and Elgin were available. This relieved the pressure on Dalcross, which was further alleviated when Leanach was also allocated from 6 June. Elgin was lost on 31 July 1943, but an alternative was found at Tain, which offered a few Oxfords at a time. The use of Brackla had also been lost the previous month, but would be returned briefly from 3 December. At Tain a Night Flying Flight was formed on 18 November, but as 1944 approached senior staff were made aware that their unit would be disbanded in the New Year. On 25 February the PAFU was duly disbanded, with all aircraft, pupils and nearly all of its instructors posted to 21 PAFU.

In the background, 2 AGS had been getting on with its own workload despite its strength being reduced in 1943. It had also begun a new course designed for WAAF balloon operators who were re-training as flight mechanics, creating its own School of Technical Training. By November 1944 the AGS had replaced its Ansons with Wellingtons and Spitfires, and went on to serve until disbandment on 24 November 1945.

On 5 December 1945 Dalcross became the home of 13 Group HQ, which moved in from Inverness with its CF. During this time the Spitfires of 122 Squadron moved in from Wick on 3 January 1946, only to be renumbered as 41 Squadron on 1 April before moving to Wittering two weeks later.

13 Group and its CF was disbanded on 20 May 1946, and the airfield was briefly placed under C&M. From 1 September 1947 Dalcross was controlled by the MoA as Inverness Airport, and BEA, which had taken over Scottish Airways, began to transfer from Longman to Inverness. Early flights by BEA used Ju 52s, C-47s and Rapides but, despite civilian operations rapidly building, the RAF was not quite finished with Dalcross.

Thanks to the Korean War and increasing tension across Europe, the RAF went through another expansion period. Part of this was the re-formation of several flying schools to cater for increased pilot training, and 8 FTS was one of them formed here on 1 May 1951. The new arrival saw the return of the ubiquitous Oxford, up to sixty of which were on strength during the school's tenure. From 1 July 1952 the unit was renamed as 8 AFTS, and by 12 May had acquired Edzell, Fearn and Evanton as RLGs. By 1 December 1953 the school had been disbanded.

Civilian operations continued unabated during this period, but it was not until the 1970s that Dalcross began to develop into the Inverness Airport we know today. In 1974 the main runway was upgraded to accommodate the Tridents of BEA, which also continued to operate the Viscount from here. Dan-Air maintained a service with One-Elevens and Boeing 737s, and was in turn taken over by British Airways in the 1990s. The BAe 146 was the most common and cost-effective airliner used, and is still a common sight today. Now owned by HIAL, more than half a million passengers pass through Inverness every year via a diverse range of airlines.

Inverness Airport's general layout has not altered a great deal over the years, but the wartime buildings have slowly made way for more modern counterparts.

The airfield layout is much the same as it was during the war, but very few buildings from that period now remain apart from a pair of Bellman hangars, which are still in use.

Main features:
Concrete runways: QDM 240 1,833 yards, 120 1,366 yards, 200 1,300 yards. *Hangars:* two AR or VR(?), two Bellman, nine EO blister. *Hardstandings:* 300 x 100 feet hardcore area. *Accommodation:* RAF: 1,631; WAAF: 306.

DALLACHY, Grampian (Morayshire)

57°39'22"N/03°04'01"W; NJ365635. 2 miles N of Fochabers on B9104

The operations that took place from Dallachy during the last few months of the war are often overshadowed by those at Banff. It was not until 25 May 1943 that a use for Dallachy was finally found. 14 (P)AFU was already preparing to move from Ossington into Banff with its large fleet of Oxfords. Before it arrived Dallachy was allocated as an RLG and this was to be the airfield's role for the next 15 months. By 8 July 1943 1542 BATF was formed here with Oxfords to provide advanced training and refreshers for pilots until the end of August 1944. On 1 September the (P)AFU was disbanded and Dallachy would enter a new and more intensive period of operations.

The first unit to fly from here belonged to the FAA – 838 Squadron arrived from Benbecula on 28 September 1944 with Swordfishes. The following day a detachment of Warwicks from 281 Squadron arrived from Thornaby. The first operational sortie, an A/S patrol, was flown on the 30th by two Warwicks, while the Swordfishes began the first of 106 unsuccessful sorties. 838 Squadron moved to Fraserburgh on 22 October, followed by 281 Squadron returning to Thornaby on the 25th.

In the meantime Dallachy was prepared for the arrival of several units as Coastal Command began to move its strike squadrons to North East Scotland. It was 455 Squadron that became the first of four Beaufighter units to arrive, on 20 October. Two days later the second unit, 404 Squadron, arrived from Banff. 404 Squadron had already gained valuable experience operating as part of the Strubby and Banff Strike Wings, since arriving at the latter in early September. On 23 October they were joined by 144 Squadron's torpedo-fitted Beaufighters, which had already seen considerable action from Strubby and briefly at Banff. The final unit, 489 Squadron, also from Langham, arrived on 24 October, giving the new Dallachy Strike Wing a Commonwealth feel.

404 (Buffalo) Squadron RCAF and four of its Beaufighter Xs are on a sortie out of Dallachy in December 1944.

The wing's first operation took place on 25 October 1944, an attack on shipping at Kristiansand involving twenty-two Beaufighters of 144 and 404 Squadrons, accompanied by two Mosquitoes of 235 Squadron from Banff. On this occasion, poor weather forced the group to abandon the operation.

A well-aimed batch of RPs could easily dispatch the average MV, and the Dallachy Strike Wing often did.

Success came on 8 November when twenty-five Beaufighters of 144, 404 and 455 Squadrons set course for Utvaer. The force made landfall near Bremanger then headed north and attacked the main target, a civilian Norwegian ferry. Caught in the open, it was so badly damaged that it had to be beached. The force continued on to the Midtgulenfjord, where five MVs were attacked. Luckily, the enemy flak positions were asleep as the two largest MVs were hit by the first wave, one being sunk outright and the second left burning. A pair of escort ships were also damaged and, despite many Beaufighters being damaged by flak, all returned to complete this successful raid.

It was as a result of a reconnaissance operation on Friday 9 February 1945 that one of the largest strikes flown from Dallachy took place. Several MVs and a 'Narvik' Class destroyer had been spotted by two 489 Squadron Beaufighters in the Fordefjord and five more MVs to the north in Nordgulen. On receiving the reports, it was decided that a strike should be prepared on the two targets. The wing was already on standby, and in a very short time thirty-two Beaufighters were prepared. They were joined by twelve 65 Squadron Mustangs together with two Warwicks following behind. Meanwhile, over in Norway, the sighting of the two 489 Squadron Beaufighters during the morning had alerted the five MVs, which moved into a safer position, close to the steep sides of the mountains at Vindspollen, in the south part of Midtgulen. The crew of destroyer and escort were also wise to the fact that an attack was on the cards and were on high alert. All non-essential crew onboard the MVs were put ashore.

MVs Aquila *and* Helga Ferdinand *are under attack in Midtgulenfjord on 8 November 1944. This was the Dallachy Strike's first successful attack.*

The strike wing was not in a good position to attack and all had to orbit above the fjord before diving down on their newly positioned targets. This gave the defenders an opportunity to open fire early, and the Beaufighters began to drop down into the fjord into a hail of flak. While this was taking place, 404 Squadron was bounced by Fw 190s, and in no time at all six had been shot down. Down in the fjord the flak was relentless and the Beaufighters, attacking in threes because of the lack of room, were being hit from all directions. Three more aircraft were lost to flak, having only managed to damage the destroyer; all were observed crashing into the sides of the fjord after being hit. A single 65 Squadron Mustang was also shot down trying to defend one of the 404 Squadron Beaufighters. The operation was nothing less than a disaster for the Dallachy Strike Wing and the single worst day of the war for 404 Squadron – it became infamously known as 'Black Friday'. Many questions were asked as to how an operation could take place against such a heavily defended target, and within days of it happening. the shipping target priority list was changed.

Despite being depleted by a squadron, the wing continued its operations at pace during April 1945 and achieved some success. One MV was damaged on the 4th and a trip to Ytteroerne on the 7th was also successful. Twenty-four Beaufighters with a Mosquito outrider and 19 Squadron's Mustangs found two MVs moored in the harbour. By the time the Beaufighters had finished, the larger vessel was burning and the smaller had been hit several times with RPs and cannon fire. All aircraft returned safely, probably frustrated that their targets had not been sunk, but only a few days later the wing did send a minesweeper to the bottom of a fjord. Further success came on 22 April when an MV was sunk at Maaloy and another was sent to the bottom at Sognefjord the following day.

With the end of the war now only days away, the Dallachy Beaufighters continued their attacks and succeeded in sinking another minesweeper on 2 May. The same day a U-boat was sunk and another damaged in the Kattegat. On 4 May a pair of Danish freighters were sunk in Kiel Bay, bringing an end to the operations of the Dallachy Strike Wing.

The wing had flown 2,230 sorties, sunk fifteen ships and damaged fifty-five others during its existence. A few more operations were flown by the wing during May, one of the most significant being an escort for HMS *Devonshire* as she returned the Norwegian Crown Prince Olav back to his homeland. Further sorties were flown during the month, trying to round up any surrendering U-boats, the last of which was flown on 21 May.

Three days later, both 144 and 455 Squadrons were disbanded, and on 15 June 1945 489 Squadron left Dallachy for Banff, bringing to an end all military flying from the airfield. An RAF presence remained briefly during the summer when 21 ACHU was established from 1 June, only to leave for Haverfordwest on 15 August.

Only one aircraft is visible in this view of Dallachy in the summer of 1945 as the airfield approaches closure.

Now under C&M, the airfield was taken over by the Army as a Territorial training centre on 24 November 1945. During the Army's tenure the FAA squadrons based at Lossiemouth also used the airfield for simulated bombing practice. In 1958 the Army had gone and no further use for this once important wartime airfield could be found.

Today the airfield is well-preserved with both runways intact and the entire perimeter track in place. The section from Nether Dallachy round the north-eastern edge is now the route of a minor road, appropriately named Beaufighter Road. Virtually all of the dispersals still exist, although surviving buildings are restricted to the control tower and the operations block.

The original entrance to the airfield, off the B9104 in Bogmoor, was selected as the location for a memorial to the Dallachy Strike Wing. Unveiled on 30 July 1992, the ceremony was attended by many surviving personnel with a flypast by a Nimrod and two Buccaneers. The memorial is a fitting tribute to the many airmen who gave their lives during those hectic final few months of the war.

Main features:
Concrete runways: QDM 228 1,600 yards, 290 1,400 yards. *Hangars:* two T2, five 69-foot double blister. *Hardstandings:* one frying pan, thirty-six concrete loop. *Accommodation:* RAF: 1,530; WAAF: 408.

DALMUIR (ROBERTSON FIELD), Strathclyde

55°54'25"N/04°26'04"W

Beardmore-built BE.2C 8336 at Dalmuir.

To meet the massive orders for aircraft that had fallen upon Beardmore's shoulders, the company constructed a large building on the north bank of the Clyde. It was called the 'Seaplane Sheds' and, once complete in 1915, contained more than 63,000 square feet of floor space. At a similar time a small airfield was established at Dalmuir near the shipyard known as Robertson's Field after the local farmer, Peter Robertson. By 1916 two hangars had been built and the first aircraft arrived. The initial batch of sixty BE.2Cs to be reassembled were test-flown then transferred to Inchinnan. Beardmore went on to produce the Camel in great numbers and its own WB.2, and a few V/1500s were also flown from here.

Beardmore also produced hundreds of seaplanes, and these were also built in the 'Seaplane Sheds' and launched onto the Clyde for their first flights via a slipway at Dumbarton.

Beardmore designed and built the WB.1 and WB.2. Both were constructed and test-flown from Dalmuir.

DELNY HOUSE, Highland

57°43'11"N/04°07'49"W; NH730720. Between Delny and Balintraid

Established during early part of the First World War, this LG was used by aircraft flying off warships that were anchored in the Cromarty Firth, and was still in use by June 1920. At that time a DH.9A took part in wireless and range-finding experiments with HMS *Barham* and HMS *Warspite* on moving targets.

Delny was inspected in 1921 with expansion plans in mind, but nothing ever came of it and Novar (Evanton) was chosen instead.

DONIBRISTLE, Fife

56°02'29"N/03°20'59"W; NT155834. 2 miles E of Rosyth off A92

Affectionately known as 'Donibee', this airfield had a diverse history that dated back to 1917 and continued, almost uninterrupted, for a further forty-two years.

In late 1916 sites surrounding Rosyth were surveyed for the location of an LG and a storage area for large numbers of RNAS aircraft. In early 1917, as part of the aerial defence of the Firth of Forth and Edinburgh, 77(HD) Squadron established a small ELG on land belonging to the Earl of

Moray at Donibristle House. Several trees had to be removed to clear a runway, then a single guard hut and a few ancillary buildings were constructed.

No aircraft used the LG before the arrival of the RNAS in August 1917. Allocated to the Admiralty on 17 September, work began on building a large ARD. This task brought about the formation of the Fleet Aircraft Acceptance Depot in October 1918, which later became the Fleet ARD. Highlighting the importance of its first major role, Donibristle was kept open after the Armistice and continued to overhaul carrier-based aircraft until it was reduced to C&M in 1921.

It was reopened in 1924 as a shore base for aircraft leaving aircraft carriers anchored in the Firth of Forth. Built on land that was loaned to, then purchased by, the Air Ministry, the airfield was transferred to the Admiralty on 24 May 1939 and commissioned as HMS *Merlin*.

These are Horsleys of 36 Squadron at Donibristle, a unit that was formed from the Coastal Defence Torpedo Flight until it was redesignated in 1928.

The first task for HMS *Merlin* was the formation of two new DLT squadrons. 767 Squadron with Swordfishes, Albacores and Sharks was formed by renumbering 811 Squadron, and took part in several DLT detachments on HMS *Furious* before leaving for the Mediterranean in 1940.

769 Squadron was the second DLT, formed as a Fighter DLT squadron by renumbering 801 Squadron with Skuas, Rocs and Sea Gladiators. Like 767 Squadron, the unit carried out the majority of its training on HMS *Furious* before four of its Gladiators formed 804 Squadron at Hatston in November 1939. 769 Squadron was disbanded not long after, on 1 December.

Having been associated since the end of the First World War with overhaul and storage, it was a logical step for Donibristle to become a Royal Navy Aircraft Repair Yard during the Second World War. Located on the north-western side of the airfield, the yard was autonomous. Its main task was to carry out major maintenance on all types of aircraft, with minor, or basic, maintenance still being carried out by the surrounding RNAS stations. As the war progressed aircraft carriers arriving at Rosyth delivered battle-damaged aircraft for repair here.

Donibristle would also continue throughout the war to be the starting point for many squadrons that were either forming or re-forming. 801 Squadron was a good example when it re-formed at Donibristle on 15 January 1940 with six Skuas; by 2 February it had moved to Evanton.

782 Squadron Dominies, Merlin I *and* Merlin IX, *stand outside one of Donibristle's hangars.*
Via the late R. C. Sturtivant

This was typical of the 'here today, gone tomorrow' squadrons that passed through the airfield during the war years. No fewer than thirteen units passed through in 1940 before the only long-term resident squadron to be based here was formed.

Before the end of the war more than fifty-five FAA Squadrons had passed through. Many of them returned several times and a large proportion were operational. Swordfish units included a detachment of 825 Squadron from Arbroath in March 1941, and 819 Squadron from Hatston for three weeks in March 1942. The last operational Swordfish squadron to be formed did so here on 15 June 1943, when 860 Squadron was formed as a Royal Netherlands Navy-manned TBR squadron. The unit received its first six Swordfishes four days after forming, then left on 19 July 1943 to continue its training at Hatston. A further eight Swordfish squadrons passed through; the last, 816 Squadron with Wildcats, left for Machrihanish on 17 April 1944.

Four Albacore squadrons passed through between March 1941 and June 1942. First was 828 Squadron from Campbeltown, followed by 827, 817 and finally 822 from Crail. None stayed for more than a few weeks. With the end of the war in Europe, the amount of aircraft movements declined. 782 Squadron continued its flights, with only the airfield's Station Flight in residence.

Two Royal Navy officers stand in front of Flamingo BT312, Merlin VI, *of 782 Squadron at Donibristle.* Via the late R. C. Sturtivant

Some carrier-based units came and went, but the airfield was restricted to piston types, which often struggled to land on the short runway. Twelve squadrons were briefly based at the airfield during its final years. The last, 1830A Squadron, was formed here on 1 October 1952 with Fireflies and Harvards. By 1 November the unit had left for Abbotsinch, leaving 782 Squadron as the only survivor. This was disbanded on 9 October 1953, and HMS *Merlin* was finally run down and civilianised. The old 782 Squadron was re-formed immediately as the Northern Communication Squadron; now in civilian hands, the aircraft were flown by Airwork pilots and it remained active until 1958.

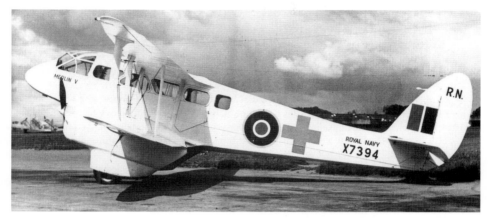

Domine Air Ambulance X7394 Merlin V *of 782 Squadron crashed on 30 August 1946. During a flight from Abbotsinch to Stretton, it flew into Broad Crag, Scafell Pike, killing all six on board.* Via the late R. C. Sturtivant

Airwork had also taken over control of the repair yard, which was now overhauling all current FAA types. By the late 1950s defence cuts started to take their toll and Donibristle was earmarked for closure. The last aircraft to be reconditioned here was Skyraider AEW.1 WT950, which left for 849 HQ Flight Culdrose in January 1959. Three months later the airfield was closed down.

Industry and housing have now obliterated the airfield, although the industrial area has incorporated many of the original buildings into its infrastructure. A row of 1920s barrack blocks, neatly lined along Ridge Way, is a nice reminder of those peaceful interwar years when biplanes came and went. Roads in the area offer some memories, with names such as Beech, Fulmar, Taxi and Bellman Way.

Main features:
Tarmac runways: QDM 277 970 yards, 261 800 yards. *Hangars:* four Bellman, three Bessoneau. *Accommodation:* RN: 1,122; WRNS: 577.

The Donibristle Memorial was unveiled on 3 April 2004 in memory of all who served at HMS Merlin *from 1917 to 1959.*

DORNOCH, Highland

57°52'19"N/04°01'35"W. Half a mile S of Dornoch, on Dornoch Links

The sandy plain south of Dornoch was already in use as a golf course and a small grass strip had been in place since the 1930s. Level pieces of ground were in short supply in Scotland, so the links attracted the attention of the Air Ministry. Preparation began in early 1941, for the use of 45 MU, which was expanding way beyond its capacity. There was no natural cover for dispersed aircraft, and the work, to keep costs to a minimum, only involved levelling the site.

Few buildings were constructed and personnel lucky enough to serve here were accommodated in the Royal Golf Hotel, Dornoch. Opened on 10 August 1941, it was designated as 40 SLG and taken over by 45 MU on 1 September.

The camouflage issue resulted in Dornoch being placed under C&M from 30 September 1943, although it was brought back into use the following year. 45 MU made use of it from mid-1943, but after 41 Group gave up Leanach to FTC, 46 MU needed another SLG. It also used Dornoch from 9 September 1943, for the storage of Beaufighters, ninety of which were on the small SLG in May 1944, and 108 were recorded on site in July 1944, not including the aircraft belonging to 45 MU. In March 1944 Dornoch also gained its one and only hangar when a Super Robin was moved from Lossiemouth.

By early 1945 aircraft were being serviced here rather than stored, although with the end of the war an increasing number left on the scrapman's lorry rather than under their own steam. The last aircraft left on 27 September 1945, just three days before 40 SLG was closed.

Loganair re-established Dornoch in 1967 as part of its service. Flying the Islander, Dornoch became a stop-off on the Inverness to Wick route, which continued until 1972. Today, light aircraft come and go from Dornoch's 800-yard grass runway on a regular basis.

DOWNHILL (BENONE STRAND/COLERAINE), Londonderry

55°10'00"N/06°51'33"W. 6 miles NW of Coleraine off A2 near Downhill

Civilian gliders have been operating from or near Downhill since the 1930s, but not long after the end of the war so did the military. 203 GS moved in from Newtownards in July 1947 flying the Cadet, but by 20 June 1949 it had moved to Aldergrove, leaving Downhill in civilian hands.

DOUNREAY (THURSO), Caithness

58°35'02"N/03°43'36"W; NC995675. 7 miles W of Thurso off A836

Passed from pillar to post even before it was completed, Dounreay turned out to be little more than a folly that played no significant part in the war.

Originally intended for the use of Coastal Command, work began in 1942. By April 1944 the airfield was complete, but with no interest being shown it was placed under C&M. All three runways were then obstructed without a thought to any aircraft that may be lost or in distress. Dounreay's most significant and only aviation incident came on 3 June 1944. Lt J. M. Hyland, in B-24H 42-51190, was being ferried from Labrador to Prestwick, but after straying off course the crew found themselves over the northern coast of Scotland. They only spotted the obstacles on the runway at the last moment and were lucky, after coming to halt, that only minor damage was caused. With no injuries on board, spare parts were flown in by a B-17, and by 12 June the B-24 had left.

It was now the turn of the Royal Navy to look at Dounreay with different requirements. The senior service was on the hunt for a location to house a Repair Yard with an airfield to maintain and store aircraft from carriers arriving at Scapa Flow. Despite Hatston being chosen instead, Dounreay was still transferred to the Royal Navy on 15 May 1944. It was planned to commission Dounreay as HMS *Tern II* as a satellite to Twatt, but once again nothing came of it.

On 1 August 1945 the airfield was transferred to the charge of Flag Officer Carrier Training. During this period of Royal Navy control little changed, with the airfield remaining under C&M until it was transferred on 1 October 1954 to the Air Ministry.

At a similar time the site was chosen by the UK Atomic Energy Authority to house a new nuclear power station, beginning with the DMTR, which was running by May 1958. The DFR, with its familiar dome, was operational by late 1959 and was exporting energy to the national grid by 1962. In the meantime the Admiralty Research Test Establishment had been opened, and by 1972 this had been commissioned as HMS *Vulcan*. Its role was to test prototype nuclear reactors for the Royal Navy's submarines, and by 1981 it was renamed Vulcan NRTE, and continues that work today. The DFR was taken offline in 1977 while another, the PFR, was taken offline in 1994. The decommissioning process for these two reactors will take until 2036!

The airfield's original control tower survived until 2007, possibly as part of the site's decommissioning. A large section of the main runway remains in good condition thanks to its use until recent years, while large sections of perimeter track cling on.

Main features:
Runways: QDM 048-228 2,000 yards, 170-350 1,100 yards, 110-290 1,100. *Accommodation:* RAF: 738; WAAF: 254.

An unused Dounreay in June 1946 under Royal Navy control.

At Dounreay in 2005 the former HMS Vulcan, *now the Vulcan NRTE, is at the top left and the now decommissioned nuclear power station part-covers the airfield.*

DREM (WEST FENTON/GULLANE), East Lothian

56°01'09"N/02°48'01"W; NT505810. 2 miles S of Dirleton off B1345

First opened in late 1916 as one of many LGs for 77(HD) Squadron, the small airfield was originally known as West Fenton and only the most basic of facilities existed. It was later surveyed for further development, becoming home to 2 TDS, which was formed at West Fenton on 15 April 1918.

By now known as Gullane, the only operational unit to serve here was the 41st Aero Squadron, with Camels and Spads. By August 1918 the 41st had left for France, and on 21 November 1919 Gullane was closed.

The site was surveyed in 1938 and seen fit for the operation of 13 FTS, which was formed here with Oxfords and Masters on 17 March 1939. By now the airfield was named Drem, and the first course arrived on 15 April 1939. On 3 September the unit was redesignated 13 SFTS, now flying Harts and Ansons.

After arriving at Acklington on 10 October the Gladiators of 607 Squadron flew several detached defensive patrols from here. On the 13th the Spitfires of 602 Squadron became the first operational squadron to be based here. Fighter Command now staked its claim to Drem, and 13 SFTS had no choice but to disband on 30 October.

On 16 October 1939 at 1400hrs the order to scramble was received and sections from 602 and 603 Squadrons took to the air. Flt Lt G. Pinkerton led Blue Section and was ordered to patrol the Forth Bridge and Rosyth area. He was the first to spot an enemy aircraft, a Ju 88 beginning its bomb run over the Forth. Pinkerton put the enemy in his sights, opened fire and the Ju 88 crashed into the sea off Crail. Only minutes earlier 603 Squadron had claimed the prize for shooting down the first enemy aircraft. However, to this day 602 Squadron will always claim that its bomber hit the sea quicker than 603 Squadron's!

602 Squadron was in action again on 28 October. Red Section, led by Fg Off A. A. McKellar, was scrambled to intercept an intruder approaching the East Lothian coast. While at 10,000 feet over Tranent, McKellar spotted anti-aircraft fire at 16,000 feet north of their position. A single aircraft was seen heading south-east, but McKellar doubted that it was the enemy. Turnhouse Sector control told him to continue his pursuit, and McKellar put his section into line astern and quickly realised that the aircraft was an He 111. Two of the three Spitfires in the section, including McKellar's, managed to attack the bomber, which desperately tried to escape into cloud. Both 602 and 603 Squadron's Spitfires continued to pursue the bomber until they managed to fire sufficient rounds to disable the port engine, which was smoking heavily. The aircraft started to descend and eventually crash-landed east of Humbie near Kidlaw. Scotland was proud that it was her pilots who had brought down the first enemy aircraft on British soil during the Second World War.

King George VI presents the DFC to Sqn Ldr A. D. Farquhar at Drem in 1940 for his part in bringing down two Heinkel He 111s.

The Hurricane made an appearance for the first time at Drem on 7 December 1939, when 111 Squadron, the first unit to be equipped with it, arrived from Acklington. The unit flew mainly convoy patrols during its stay at Drem and was also often scrambled to intercept intruders.

609 Squadron returned from Kinloss on 10 January 1940, still without coming into contact with the enemy. This changed on 29 January, when Red Section was ordered to intercept an enemy aircraft attacking a trawler in the mouth of the River Tay. An He 111 was sighted at a range of 400 yards and the Spitfire pilots opened fire, provoking a quick response from the bomber's rear gunner before disappearing into clouds. The section returned without making a claim for a kill, but later the same day Wick reported that an He 111 had crash-landed there.

111 Squadron left for Wick on 27 February and Drem now entered a quiet period when the resident squadrons were either scrambled or flying most days but contact with the enemy was rare.

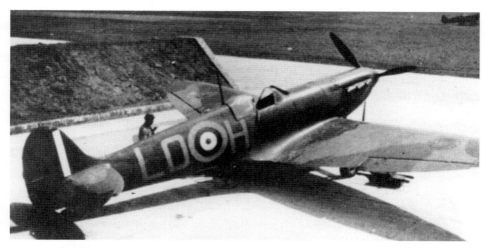

A Spitfire I of 602 (City of Glasgow) Squadron rests between sorties in one of Drem's fighter pens, circa 1940.

The airfield hosted its first night-fighter squadron on 4 April 1940. 29 Squadron was on temporary attachment from Debden for operational duties, and returned to Debden on 10 May, where it achieved its first kill not long after.

602 Squadron left on 13 August 1940, and a tired 145 Squadron took its place on the 14th. 'A' Flight from 605 Squadron moved to Tangmere the same day for a short detachment. 145 Squadron had been equipped with the Hurricane since March 1940, and on 31 August, after a well-earned rest, it moved further north with 'A' Flight to Montrose and 'B' Flight to Dyce.

263 Squadron returned on 2 September 1940, now equipped with the Whirlwind and the Hurricane. After detachments to Macmerry and Prestwick, the squadron moved south to Exeter, without its trusty Hurricanes, on 28 November.

Having arrived in March 1941 on its second tour at Drem, 43 Squadron began scoring again on 7 May when two Ju 88s were shot down, followed three days later by a third. Before the month was over two more Ju 88s had been shot down into the sea. During June and July all of the squadron's successes were achieved by its CO, Sqn Ldr T. F. D. Morgan. He shot down a Ju 88 on 9 June and an He 111 on 11 July, and shared another Ju 88 with Plt Off Bourne on 25 July. During the latter combat, Morgan's Hurricane was hit by return fire, forcing him to ditch in the sea, from where he was later rescued by the Royal Navy. One more enemy kill was scored on 3 October when a Ju 88 was claimed before 43 Squadron left for Acklington on the 4th.

141 Squadron made a third visit from Ayr during May and June 1941. Another Spitfire squadron joined it on 20 May when 64 Squadron arrived from Turnhouse; it returned on 6 August, having claimed a probable He 115 during its tour. The same day, 123 Squadron changed places with 64 Squadron but left for Castletown on 22 September without an enemy kill.

Another unit that claimed a victory was 242 Squadron, whose Spitfires arrived from Ouston on 1 June 1941. Only two days later the squadron intercepted a Ju 88 64 miles east of Drem. The unit claimed the bomber as probably destroyed, and so began the squadron's enemy tally. This was the last significant combat with the enemy by a squadron based at Drem during the war, and by 11 August the squadron moved to North Weald.

The first of several FAA units, 784 Squadron, arrived on 18 October 1942, as a Night Fighter Training Squadron equipped with Chesapeakes and Fulmars. Drem's increasing role as a night-fighter station suited the needs of 784 Squadron, and from October 1943 several FAA-trained crews were attached to RAF night-fighter units.

During September 1944 784 Squadron received its first Firefly with US AI Radar, known as the Firefly INF. The last of the Fulmars left in November 1944 after 2½ years of service. 784 Squadron continued to operate long after the end of the war, receiving the Hellcat and Harvard by November 1945. On 15 January 1946 Drem's longest-serving unit left for Dale.

A 96 Squadron Beaufighter VIF being rearmed at Drem in late 1943.

Typhoons arrived at Drem for the first time when 197 Squadron was formed on 21 November 1942. By the end of January 1943 a second Typhoon squadron had arrived from Charmy Down. 245 Squadron was converting from the Hurricane to the Typhoon and, together with 197 Squadron, became operational in February. 197 Squadron left Drem for Tangmere on 28 March, followed by 245 Squadron two days later to Gravesend.

During February 1945 a large Royal Navy contingent arrived with a view to taking control of the airfield, and further meetings were held in April to discuss the finer details of a transfer to Royal Navy control. After much indecision, Drem was handed to the Royal Navy on 21 April, and was eventually commissioned as HMS *Nighthawk* on 21 June.

With the war nearly over, 603 Squadron arrived from Turnhouse on 7 May 1945 for a special operation. On the 11th twenty-eight Spitfires were tasked with patrolling an area between May Island and Dunbar from 1554hrs. The objective was to intercept three Ju 52s carrying surrender delegates of the German Navy, Army and Air Force, travelling from Norway. At 1940hrs the aircraft were intercepted 3 miles south of Crail and guided to Drem, where they landed 13 minutes later. The Naval delegates were taken to a warship anchored in the Forth while the remainder were taken to Edinburgh for interrogation. Two days later, two of the Junkers returned to Norway, complete with the signed surrender papers. This was the most significant event to occur at Drem for 603 Squadron, which left for Skeabrae on 14 June.

It was the task of 603 Squadron to intercept and escort three Junkers Ju 52s carrying German surrender delegates into Drem on 11 May 1945.

Following the war Drem, now solely occupied by FAA units, was to host the re-formation of another on 15 May 1945. 732 Squadron was equipped with Hellcats, Harvards, Fireflies and Ansons, the latter being used as flying classrooms. The squadron was joined at various times during 1945 by 1791, 892 and 1792 Squadrons before it was disbanded into long-term resident 784 Squadron in November. Despite this flurry of naval activity, 784 Squadron left for Dale on 15 January 1946, becoming the last FAA unit to operate from the airfield.

Back under RAF control by 15 March 1946, the airfield stood silent, with no use being found for this once busy facility. The honour of being the last unit to operate from Drem fell to 3 GS, which arrived from Macmerry in April and operated its gliders from the airfield until it was disbanded on 1 September 1947.

This was the end for Drem, which was closed down in late 1952, although much of the land, including dispersed sites, had already been derequisitioned. Today the airfield is virtually intact despite the fact that its grass runways were returned to agriculture more than sixty years ago. The public can access the perimeter track and three Bellman hangars remain, all in use. Of the buildings

One of three surviving Bellman hangars at Drem. Author

that remain, the majority have been put to good use, especially at Fenton Barnes. Drem is a superb example of a Second World War fighter station built for the defence of Great Britain. It will also remain one of the most significant of Scotland's fighter airfields.

Main features:
Grass runways: QDM E-W 1,850 yards, NW-SE 1,400 yards, NE-SW 1,400 yards.
Hangars: three Bellman, ten over blister, four EO blister. *Hardstandings:* seven SE.
Accommodation: RAF: 1,807; WAAF: 374.

DUMFRIES (HEATHHALL/TINWALD DOWNS), Dumfries and Galloway
55°05'38"N/03°34'24"W; NX998788. 3 miles NE of Dumfries off A701

Today, this airfield has been swallowed up by the need for more new houses and light industry under the name of Heathhall. However, despite more than half of the original site now being covered, a surprisingly large amount of the airfield's buildings, including eight of the original thirty-six hangars built here, still remain standing in good condition.

Dumfries's future was mapped out very early. The plan was to make it into an ASU controlled by 40 MU with the hope that it would be opened by 1 November 1939. Work began on clearing the site, originally known as Tinwald Downs, in late 1938. In the meantime, the seeds of the airfield's first occupant began to germinate with the re-formation of 'H' Temporary MU at Heath Hall Works (formerly Arrol Johnston Co workshops) in Dumfries on 20 March 1939. It was this unit that was supposed to form 40 MU, but a change of plan saw a lengthy delay. Just to add to the confusion a second new unit, 18 MU, also an ASU, was formed on 6 March 1940 at a site described only as 2 miles north-east of Dumfries.

With its two grass runways obstructed owing to a lack of defence personnel, Dumfries was opened with 18 MU destined to become its longest-serving occupant.

10 B&GS arrived from Warmwell on 13 July 1940 with Harrows, Battles, Seals and Henleys. 18 MU, despite growing in size, was now a lodger unit, while 10 B&GS restarted its training on 22 July.

Despite being the summer months, Dumfries's grass runways were not coping with the traffic from 10 B&GS and 18 MU; the latter alone had 141 aircraft here by August 1940, and all had taken their toll on the runways. To relieve the pressure an RLG was opened at Winterseugh.

10 B&GS reverted to 10 AOS on 13 September 1941, and with this change the Botha began to arrive. The establishment was no fewer than seventy-eight Bothas, together with the introduction of a few Ansons and Henleys.

Botha I L6264 briefly served with 10 AOS at Dumfries until it was lost on a NAVEX on 27 October 1941.

As part of 18 MU, an Aircraft Packing Section was formed at Locharbriggs/Tinwald Downs from 24 February 1941. The MU as a whole continued to grow and, as types such as the Blenheim and Wellington began to arrive, the need for SLGs became paramount. Annan and Kayshill had already been used briefly during late 1940 and early 1941, but a more permanent solution was needed. From 1 May 1941 the MU controlled 27 SLG and 36 SLG; 11 SLG followed on 1 July, followed by 9 SLG by December 1941.

225 Squadron brought its Lysanders from Thruxton in late 1941, together with 614 Squadron from Grangemouth. As if the airfield was not busy enough, the Armament Synthetic Development Unit was also formed in 1941, but had moved to Jurby by 1942.

Another MU was formed here on 21 March 1942, which would expand the Locharbriggs site on the edge of the airfield. 215 MU was another Packing Unit, which would prepare aircraft for shipment overseas, a tasked that continued until 24 September 1945.

On 1st May 1942 10 AOS was renamed 10 OAFU and the amount of Ansons on strength had now risen to forty-two. The new OAFU had also gained forty-four Bothas, twenty-one Battles, eleven Dominies and nine Henleys, the latter operated from Annan. The Bothas were being withdrawn by the autumn of 1942, and by 1943 the OAFU had fully re-equipped with Ansons, and the last Bothas had gone by August.

At least two squadrons briefly stayed at Dumfries during 1942 and 1943 in connection with liaison work at the Langholm Ranges, 25 miles west. First was 651 Squadron on 31 July 1942, with Taylorcraft Plus Ds and Plus C.2s from Old Sarum, moving on to Kidsdale twelve days later. 652 Squadron followed from Westley on 1 January 1943, also with Taylorcrafts and Austers. The squadron remained until 20 February before moving to Sawbridgeworth.

When the war came to end, the demand for aircrew training declined and, with more than 400 courses now under its belt, 10 OAFU was redesignated again, this time as 10 ANS, on 11 June 1945. By now Wellingtons were on strength, but the Anson was still prominent although its days at Dumfries were numbered. On 10 July 10 ANS was moved to Chipping Warden, leaving 18 MU as the main unit.

By 21 August 1945, as 18 MU's SLGs were closed, Dumfries began fill with aircraft. To cope, the 1,000-yard runway was closed and used as a giant apron, and by the end of the month 663 aircraft were parked all around. During the war 18 MU had been credited with preparing and despatching 4,688 aircraft before it was closed, and hundreds more for scrapping. There were still 300 aircraft awaiting the axe in 1946, and 18 MU's task was not fully completed until 1 July 1949, when it was disbanded.

The 1950s began with 1 GS moving in from Dungavel, becoming 666 VGS on 1 September 1955. The airfield also hosted an RAF Regiment Training School from 1947 to 1957, whipping the

Until the 1980s Dumfries remained intact and the aircraft museum, in the centre of the photo, appears isolated. An indication of the future is given away by the new access road, which slices through one of the runways; today the site is unrecognisable as an airfield but virtually all of the hangars and tower remain.

National Service recruits into shape. The VGS remained until 15 January 1958, becoming the last RAF unit to serve here when it was moved to Turnhouse, leaving Dumfries to its fate.

Industry quickly took advantage of the airfield's many hangars, which saved many of them from demolition. The three-storey control tower also survives today thanks to the Dumfries and Galloway Aviation Museum, which took over a single hut in 1977. Two years later the tower was theirs and the museum has gone from strength to strength with twenty-one part or complete airframes now on display.

Main features:
Concrete and tarmac runways: QDM 180 1,300 yards, 090 1,000 yards. *Hangars:* thirty-six various. *Accommodation:* RAF: 1,346; WAAF: 445.

DUNDEE (STANNERGATE), Tayside

56°28'N/02°56'W. 2 miles E of Dundee off A930

Stannergate can trace its roots back to 1914 when a seaplane station was built for the RNAS. The first significant activity took place on 30 May 1918 with the formation of 318 and 319(FB) Flights, 400 and 401 (Seaplane) Flights and 450 (Baby) Seaplane Flight. These flights were equipped with the F.2a, H.16, 184, Sopwith Baby and Hamble Baby.

Now occupying more than 24 acres, the station's original two hangars, which may have been moved from Port Laing, were joined by a third in April 1918, and two slipways and a large apron were also built.

Stannergate's transition continued when 78 Wing was formed on 8 August. 'G' Boat Seaplane Training Flight was also formed on 15 August. This small flight only existed until 25 November, when it was disbanded into the Dundee Seaplane Station, which appears to have been Stannergate's own 'station flight'. Status increased again when, just three days later, 249 and 257 Squadrons were formed on the same day. Rather than creating completely new units, 249 Squadron was formed by absorbing 400, 401, 419 and 450 Flights. In similar fashion, 257 Squadron's foundation was its absorption of 318 and 319 Flights, taking over the F.2as and H.16s.

No 2 Marine Acceptance Depot was here from August to October while its new station at Brough was being built. As it departed another unit, 419 Flight, brought a few 184s from Strathbeg, making the torpedo-bomber the most common type here. Even more aircraft arrived when 306 Flight brought H.16s and F.3s from Houton Bay in November and December 1918. Finally, with 1918 drawing to a close, another six 184s arrived when the RAF unit HMS *Pegasus* was formed in December.

78 Wing was disbanded in September 1918, reducing the operations that 249 and 257 Squadrons had been flying. 249 Squadron was the first to go when it moved to Killingholme on 3 March 1919. 257 Squadron was also reduced to a cadre in April 1918, but was not disbanded until 30 June 1919, together with 419 Flight, which was closed down the same month. Going against the grain, yet another unit was formed here under the guise of Delivery Station (Storage) and was destined to remain until September 1919. This left the HMS *Pegasus* force of 184s, which were due to sail for the Mediterranean on 6 March 1920, by which time Stannergate was closed.

Such a useful facility did not escape the attentions of the FAA at the beginning of the next war. After an inspection in late 1940, Stannergate was brought back to life, this time being commissioned as HMS *Condor II* on 15 July 1941. Established as a satellite to Arbroath, 751 Squadron's Walruses moved in on 13 August. The First World War hangars were all still intact and still offered protection from the elements. Under the control of 2 OS at Arbroath, the station also hosted catapult crews, who stayed for three weeks of their ten-week training course. 703 Squadron also used Dundee from early 1942, bringing its Kingfisher, Seafox and Swordfish seaplanes with it.

On 2 May 1944 751 Squadron was disbanded, which resulted in Dundee being paid off on 15 June and remaining under C&M until the end of the war.

Today very little remains, although a Type 'F' shed managed to survive well into the mid-1980s. The area is now lost to industrial development and even the slipways, which often survive, have been built over. The site is now known as the Caledon East Wharf and Prince Charles Wharf, and you are more likely to see an oil tanker undergoing repairs than a flying boat.

DUNDONALD (GAILES), Strathclyde

55°35'07"N/04°36'24"W; NS360355. 4 miles NE of Troon off A759

Starting life as an RLG, Dundonald contributed a great deal to the war effort, especially during the build-up to D-Day.

Sandwiched between a main railway line to the north-west and a major road to south, Dundonald was established from March 1940 when it became an RLG for 12 EFTS. It was used for approximately a year, as 12 EFTS was disbanded on 22 March 1941. The airfield then languished until May 1942, when 3201SC camped here from Redhill as part of a local exercise. A similar exercise saw Dundonald brought back to life when 18 Squadron brought its Blenheims here in July.

Limited development began to take place with the arrival of 1441 Flight from Abbotsinch on 19 October 1942, equipped with a variety of types including Lysanders and Hurricanes. The flight was the nucleus for 516 Squadron, which was formed here on 28 April 1943. The squadron was involved in a host of elaborate and realistic exercises, mostly involving live rounds. The Mustangs and Hurricanes were always in demand, especially for ground attack exercises, which were being planned all along the north-western coast of Scotland. Very low flying for all of 516 Squadron was usually the order of the day, and the risk of striking something on the ground or water was a constant hazard, not to mention regular collisions with seagulls.

Late 1943 saw the airfield undergoing repairs, and during this time 516 Squadron moved to Ayr but had returned by Christmas. Several operational squadrons arrived to take part in exercises, especially during the lead-up to D-Day, when low-level tactical flying and bombardment spotting would be called upon. 414 Squadron's Mustangs arrived from Odiham on 29 February 1944 only to be replaced on 11 March by more Mustangs from 2 Squadron at Sawbridgeworth. A detachment from 63 Squadron also arrived from Turnhouse during March, but had returned by the end of the month.

Exercises involving the shadowing of Royal Navy carriers, known as 'Sleuths', were carried out during April/May 1944. Three FAA fighter squadrons also practised Exercise 'Sleuth', beginning with 808 and 885 Squadrons, which both arrived from Henstridge with their Seafires on 22 April. Both squadrons departed for Ayr on 6 May, to be replaced by 897 Squadron the same day, flying Spitfires. With all focus now being diverted to events on mainland Europe, 897 Squadron was the last operational squadron to visit Dundonald, leaving for Lee-on-Solent on 21 May 1944.

Following D-Day, 516 Squadron's workload dropped, but it managed to survive here until disbandment beckoned on 2 December 1944 and the airfield was placed under C&M.

The Royal Navy carried out a towed target trial from here in March 1945, and the 22nd Beach Signal's Unit lodged here in May. Various services, including the USAAF, visited during the post-war period but none of them showed any serious interest in taking over the airfield. On 1 August 1945 Dundonald was closed, but remained in military hands until it was finally disposed of in 1952.

The airfield quickly returned to agriculture and remained virtually untouched for many years before the large Olympic Business Park was established at the northern end of the old site. The business park has its own helicopter pad close to the B730 and a wartime hangar sits behind the complex; this was either relocated here or shipped in from another airfield long after the war ended.

Main features:
Steel matting runways: QDM 230 1,480 yards, 285 900 yards. *Hangars:* two over blister. *Hardstandings:* five concrete. *Accommodation:* RAF: 204.

DUNDRUM (MURLOUGH), Down

54°14'67"N/05°50'66"W; J405350. 1 mile S of Dundrum at Keel Point

From the late 1920s through the 1930s the owners of Murlough House operated their own aircraft from a grass strip. It is possible that this same strip formed the core of a second airfield, which was surveyed in 1940 for the use of 23 MU.

A test landing by a Blenheim was made on 11 March 1941, and within days the new SLG was ready. However, it was not opened as 19 SLG until 1 May, but would remain under 23 MU control until its closure. As the SLG began to fill with aircraft, it played host to the Battles of 88 Squadron; 'A' Flight arrived on 26 May, leaving for its Sydenham home on 23 June.

19 SLG closed for the winter but reopened in May 1942 ready for another influx of aircraft. Wellingtons made up the numbers, together with a host of smaller types all picketed out in the open. The Austers of 'A' Flight, 615 Squadron, also made use of Murlough during the summer.

Little has changed from Murlough's days as 19 SLG thanks to the area now being a protected nature reserve. The shape of the runway can still be made out running diagonally across the centre of this photograph.

23 MU continued to use 19 SLG until 14 February 1945, when the site was closed, and those aircraft that were still airworthy were moved to 101 SLG at Maghaberry. At least four Wellingtons remained on the site before being broken up by Mullusk-based 226 MU.

Murlough is also associated with other military units. RAF Murlough Bay was a radar station, while the requisitioned house was taken over by the United States Army. From 1942 it was home to the 1st Battalion, 13th Armour of the US 1st Armoured Division and the 818th Tank Destroyer Battalion of the 15th Corp until 29 April 1944.

Now a protected area, only the remains of one building, possibly a tractor shed, survive.

DUNGAVEL, East Ayrshire

55°36'28"N/04°08'40"W

The Duke of Hamilton had a private landing strip at Dungavel during the 1930s. It was claimed that, when Rudolph Hess made his flight to Scotland in May 1941, it was here that he was heading for.

1 GS from Strathaven moved here in March 1944 and remained until April 1950 before moving to Dumfries. In the meantime, the Hamilton family home was sold to the NCB in 1947 and today is a refugee detention centre.

Dungavel House, home of the Hamilton family until 1947.

DUNINO, Fife

56°17'35"N/02°42'15"W. 1 mile W of Kingsbarns

Despite a faltering start, this airfield was developed throughout the war years. Dunino was first recognised as a satellite in October 1940, but it was still several months before aircraft would arrive. When Crail opened on 1 October as HMS *Jackdaw*, the RAF at the time claimed Dunino as a satellite but activity was limited.

The first aircraft to make use of Dunino were the Lysanders of 614 Squadron from Macmerry in April 1941. 309 Squadron followed on the 8 May, from Renfrew. The squadron's main work was to support the many Polish army units based in Scotland, and this involved several detachments. 309 Squadron's stay at Dunino was only planned to be a temporary one and this was reflected in the poor facilities that faced the Poles on their arrival: not a permanent building was to be seen and all personnel were billeted under canvas.

Aircrew of 309 Squadron at Dunino in 1941.

By April 1942 the squadron prepared to receive the Mustang and conversion would begin the following month. 'B' Flight became the new Mustang section of the unit, receiving its first aircraft on 7 June. 'C' Flight was formed in June, and after a gunnery course at Inverness in July the squadron was declared fully operational on the Mustang.

By late 1942 Findo Gask's upgrade from a mere SLG was complete. Almost 18 months overdue, 309 Squadron began to leave in late October. Advance parties left for Findo in October and 'B' Flight departed on 15 November, destined to become part of 35 Reconnaissance Wing based at Gatwick. By 26 November all Polish personnel had left.

Knowing that 309 Squadron was not destined to stay here for very long, the Royal Navy first enquired into the airfield's future in August 1941. The Air Ministry made a verbal offer to the Royal Navy in July 1942, which was accepted the following month, but full control would not happen until the RAF had left. When this finally happened, an advance party arrived from Crail on 1 December, and on the 15th Dunino became HMS *Jackdaw II*. The first FAA unit arrived on 3 February 1943 when 825 Squadron brought its Swordfishes from Worthy Down.

Swordfishes returned on 25 February 1943 when three from 837 Squadron 'A' Flight arrived from Crail. This element of the squadron had been operating from HMS *Argus* on A/S duties off Gibraltar, and was joined by more Swordfishes on 29 March from 'D' Flight of the same squadron from Hatston. All remaining sections of 837 Squadron were reunited here before departing for Machrihanish on 14 April and returning to HMS *Argus*.

Feeding time for 309 Squadron on a summer's day in 1941.

827 Squadron's Barracudas arrived on 24 April 1943 and the unit spent its time here carrying out operational training including night-flying. The squadron had left by 12 August, once again departing to Machrihanish. Its place was taken three days later by the Swordfish-equipped 860 Squadron from Hatston.

The last Swordfish unit to serve here was 838 Squadron; equipped with just four aircraft, the fledgling squadron spent most of its time working with HMS *Nairana* in the Firth of Clyde. Arriving here on 16 January 1944, the squadron was moved to Inskip on 6 February.

By early 1944 Crail was becoming increasingly overcrowded. To alleviate this, 770 Squadron was moved to Dunino on 29 January. The squadron operated nearly twenty different aircraft types during its 4½-year existence. During March 770 Squadron's aircraft strength increased with the arrival of several Blenheims; this was the largest aircraft to operate from Dunino and it seemed to cope quite well with the airfield's poor runways. Hurricanes arrived in June, replacing the troublesome Chesapeakes, and on 25 July the squadron was moved to Drem.

By this stage of the war, aircraft had become plentiful and Dunino's main task was to hold Barracudas. Additional blisters and a large ARS were constructed, and by the end of the war more than 200 Barracudas were picketed out in the open, side by side, all destined to be scrapped.

By 1 October 1945 Dunino was under the control of HMS *Merlin*. Briefly commissioned as HMS *Merlin III* by late 1946, the storage role of the airfield had diminished and the Royal Navy began to lease out the land and buildings. Despite deciding very early on not to retain the airfield, Dunino remained in naval hands until 1957.

The most notable surviving building at Dunino is the unusual control tower.

Having long ago returned to agriculture, the layout of the airfield is still intact, and although traces of the runways have gone, remnants of the perimeter track remain. A two-storey control tower still defiantly stands and the frames of several blisters are extant. Wartime buildings can be found all around in various stages of decay within the surrounding woods and on the airfield site itself.

Main features:
Steel matting runways: QDM 090-270 1,400 yards, 090-270 1,284 yards, 156-336 900 yards. *Grass runway:* 051-231 1,200 yards. *Hangars:* one ARS, eight super blister, four 60 x 70 feet, four storage. *Accommodation:* RAF/RN: 735; WAAF/WRNS: 140.

DYCE, Aberdeenshire/Grampian

57°12'15"N/02°12'01"W; NO879126. 6 miles NW of Aberdeen off A947

One of Scotland's great aviation success stories, Dyce, more familiarly known as Aberdeen Airport, still flourishes today. Now in its 80th year of continuous flying operations, the airport has enjoyed the same prosperity that has been bestowed on the area thanks to the North Sea oil fields.

Dyce was opened on 28 July 1934 thanks to Aberdeen Airways, owned by Mr E. L. Gandar-Dower, which was the first to operate from here. In 1937 the company name was changed to Allied Airways, and would go on to become one of the forerunners of Scottish Airlines.

The airfield gained a military element when, on 1 June 1937, 612 (City of Aberdeen) Squadron was formed. On the outbreak of the war the squadron began to fly coastal patrols on a daily basis with Ansons, but it was not until 16 October 1939 that Dyce became an RAF station and the unit began to be tasked with operations. On that day 'A' Flight flew its first convoy escort sortie from here, providing cover for MVs travelling to Bergen.

A second auxiliary unit was posted here when Spitfires of 603 Squadron arrived from Prestwick on 17 January 1940. The squadron spent the next few weeks operating a detachment at Montrose, from where at least one enemy reconnaissance flight was shot down into the sea. 603 Squadron's stay at Dyce looked like it could become permanent when the unit's HQ moved in on 13 March, but instead the squadron moved to Drem on 14 April.

Aircraft movements were high during this period and the grass runways were suffering the effects. On 16 March 1940 the AOC of 13 Group arrived to discuss Dyce being upgraded to a sector airfield, but this could not happen while it was in such a poor condition. Only weeks later, on 23 May, Dyce was sufficiently improved to become a Fighter Sector airfield. The new sector consisted of an HQ and one flight of Blenheims of 248 Squadron, which arrived from Gosport the previous day.

603 Squadron returned on 30 June when 'A' Flight arrived from Turnhouse. Once again, a second flight was operating from Montrose, and on 3 July both achieved success against the enemy. 'A' Flight intercepted an He 111 many miles off Peterhead and, despite a search by RAF HSL, no survivors were found.

'A' Flight was in action again on 12 July 1940 when it shot down another He 111, which crashed into a part-built ice-rink in Anderson Drive, Aberdeen. The bomber had been taking part in Aberdeen's first major air raid of the war (known as 'Black Friday'). Before falling to 603 Squadron, the He 111 had managed to drop its bombs on the city's shipyard, killing several workers in a canteen. When the bomber hit Anderson Street, it bounced back into the air, striking the ice-rink and bursting into flames, killing all four crew.

After a brief excursion away from serving with Coastal Command, 248 Squadron returned when it began to move to Sumburgh on 20 July 1940. It exchanged places with 254 Squadron, which was also flying the Blenheim, and the first of six aircraft arrived here on 22 July.

A short tour of duty by 'A' Flight of 3 Squadron's Hurricanes during early October 1940 was followed by the more permanent arrival of 111 Squadron from Drem on the 12th. The squadron, also flying the Hurricane, divided itself into two flights, one operating from Montrose and the other from Dyce, and began the first of many regular sector patrols not long after. Combat finally came

Hurricane I V7462 of 111 Squadron on a sortie out of Dyce.

on 3 November when an He 111 was attacked 30 miles east of Rock Point. A brief fight took place only 100 feet above the sea, and one of the Hurricanes was hit by return fire and crashed into the sea followed by the German bomber only seconds later.

During late 1940 612 Squadron had been re-equipping with the Whitley. Conversion training was taking place with 19 OTU, and the first Whitley arrived here in November 1940; its greater capability was welcomed by the squadron. The first action came during March when an Fw 200 was driven away from a convoy and bombs were dropped on a submerged U-boat. 612 Squadron left its ancestral home for Wick on 1 April 1941 and would not return until 1946.

Meanwhile, 248 Squadron returned from Sumburgh on 6 January 1941. Several anti-shipping patrols were flown, quite a few of them venturing as far as the Danish coast, before the squadron moved to Bircham Newton on 21 June. Its duties were exchanged with 235 Squadron, which flew its Blenheims up from Bircham Newton the same day.

During April 111 Squadron began to receive Spitfires, and on 20 July 1941 it returned to the South of England when it moved into North Weald.

A group of 235 Squadron aircrew stand in front of a pair of their Blenheims at Dyce in late 1941.

Two more units arrived on 20 July. The first was 310 Squadron, which was taking over from 111 Squadron. Equipped with the Hurricane, the Czech-manned squadron was very keen to get at the enemy in an area where encounters were rare. It got off the mark on 13 August when a Ju 88 was spotted and engaged off Aberdeen. Firing from 500 yards, the pilot was awarded a 'probable' although the Junkers escaped.

The other unit to arrive was 143 Squadron from Thornaby. It had re-formed the previous month but, as its formation included the absorption of most of 252 Squadron, it quickly became operational. Equipped with Beaufighters, it was tasked as a long-range fighter squadron and its arrival here gave a strike wing feel to the station. The unit was also welcomed by 235 Squadron, as it was suffering without any kind of fighter escort, especially while operating off Norway. Three Blenheims had been shot down with the loss of all nine crew before 143 Squadron's arrival.

404 Squadron also joined the Norwegian operations, being based here from 9 October 1941. However, its Blenheims spent most of their time operating from Sumburgh, and it was posted back there on a permanent basis from 3 December.

603 Squadron, now with Spitfires, returned from Fairlop on 15 December 1941. Poor weather and a multitude of false alarms frustrated its pilots but, on 9 February 1942, the enemy was finally encountered when Red Section damaged a Ju 88 off Aberdeen. The squadron moved to Peterhead on 14 March, destined to move overseas not long after. Its place was taken the same day with 416 Squadron, also flying the Spitfire. By 3 April the squadron had returned to Peterhead.

540 Squadron, which had already been detached from Benson earlier in the year, returned again in late 1944. Flying the Mosquito, the squadron was busy carrying out photographic sorties over Norway. One of the most significant flown from here was on 12 November, just 2 hours after 9 and 617 Squadrons attacked the *Tirpitz* for the final time.

8 COTU was moved to Haverfordwest on 3 January 1945, becoming the last significant unit to have been housed here during the war. The airfield was offered to the Admiralty to house a fighter school but, deemed not suitable, Dyce lay dormant until April 1945, when it became a springboard for several fighter squadrons preparing to operate in Norway.

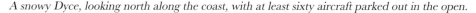

A snowy Dyce, looking north along the coast, with at least sixty aircraft parked out in the open.

Both 331 and 332 Squadrons, flying Spitfires, arrived on 22 April 1945, and both left a month later for Gardermoen. On 24 May 130 Squadron Spitfires moved here from North Weald, leaving for Kristiansand/Kjevik on 20 June. The final two squadrons heading for Norway arrived from Bentwaters on 26 and 29 May respectively; 129 Squadron, flying Spitfires, left for Vaernes on 10 June, and ten days later 165 Squadron's Spitfires left for the same location.

A military presence remained here when 91 Squadron's Spitfires arrived from Fairwood Common on 18 August 1945, moving to Duxford on 1 March 1946. This made way for the homecoming of 612 Squadron, which was re-formed as part of the new RAAF on 10 May 1946. Now equipped with the Spitfire F.14, these were progressively replaced by the Spitfire LF.XVIe from November 1948. The jet age arrived when 612 Squadron was re-equipped with the Vampire from June 1951. Apart from a brief move to Edzell a few months later, the squadron was disbanded for the final time at Dyce, together with the rest of the RAAF, on 10 March 1957.

612 (City of Aberdeen) Squadron flies over the 'Granite City' in 1947 with its Spitfire F.14s.

Civilian operations had resumed at Dyce, which was more commonly referred to as Aberdeen Airport following the end of the war. Nationalised in 1947, the airport steadily grew, with international flights being introduced during the late 1960s. It was the discovery of oil in the North Sea that saw Aberdeen become a very useful departure point for helicopters flying to the new oil rigs. It was not long before Dyce became the world's largest commercial heliport, handling more than 37,000 rotary movements, carrying between them nearly half a million passengers per year.

Main features:
Tarmac-covered concrete runways: QDM 193 1,330 yards, 334 1,330 yards, 241 1,230 yards. *Hangars:* four Bellman, ten EO and two twin EO blister, two twin T3. *Hardstandings:* thirty-seven 80-foot. *Accommodation:* RAF: 1,342; WAAF: 534.

EAST FINGASK, Aberdeenshire

57°20'15"N/02°22'07"W. 2 miles W of Oldmeldrum

An ELG had been established here at the start of the war for the use of 612 Squadron. Facilities were limited, with only a few huts, all located near East Fingask Farm. Which way the runway was laid is debatable, but an estimated take-off run of 800 yards would have been possible.

The small LG has changed little over the years and today can even boast the existence of an original wartime hut just north of the farm.

EAST FORTUNE, East Lothian

56°00'02"N/02°44'03"W; NT555786. 3 miles NE of Haddington

With its origins firmly established during the First World War, East Fortune has steadily raised its own profile with every passing year. Its Second World War history is often overshadowed by the previous conflict and its current role as Scotland's Museum of Flight.

The small LG first saw aircraft in September 1915. It was commissioned as RNAS East Fortune on 23 August 1916 and development of the airfield continued into 1917. 208 TDS was formed here in June 1918 with a host of aircraft including the Camel, 1½ Strutter and Pup. This unit was disbanded a few weeks later to form the Fleet Aerial Gunnery School and 1 TTS, the latter created to train crews on the new Cuckoo. 1 TTS only existed for a few weeks, and the result was the formation of 185 Squadron, which would go on to operate from HMS *Argus*.

The aircraft of 208 TDS are dwarfed by the R.29 at East Fortune in 1918. H. A. Vasse via A. P. Ferguson

With the war at an end, the airfield began to run down with mass demobilisation of personnel. Aircraft were either flown out elsewhere or dismantled on site. This situation did not stop the R.34 from arriving at East Fortune on 30 May 1919.

By mid-1920 the airfield was under C&M, and by 1922 the site was virtually clear of buildings, including three large airship sheds built in 1916. Not long afterwards a tuberculosis hospital was established in the majority of the former airfield buildings.

Very little aviation activity took place during the 1920s and 1930s, other than the odd aircraft using the old flying field as an emergency landing strip from nearby Macmerry or Drem. It was the latter that was immediately in the thick of the action at the start of the Second World War, prompting East Fortune's revival. In June 1940 the original airfield site was requisitioned by the Air Ministry together with considerably more land to the south towards Gilmerton House. Its first role was as a satellite airfield for Drem, but it seems that very little use was made of it.

Despite the lack of use, East Fortune gained Macmerry as its own satellite and further development of the airfield began in early 1941. It was now ready to receive its first unit, and 60 OTU, based at Leconfield, prepared to move to its new home. The unit's task was to train night-fighter crews on Blenheims and Defiants, and the first personnel and equipment began to arrive on 4 June 1941. The aircraft on strength fell well short of the establishment of fifty-five, and only a handful were actually serviceable, including a single Blenheim, which, together with the Defiant, was supposed to be the main training aircraft.

The pace began to quicken by August, with 2,476 hours flown by only a handful of aircraft. Aircraft were badly needed to replace and complement those being wrecked on and around the airfield; ten Defiants were involved in several serious incidents, including the first fatality on 15 August.

60 OTU continued to operate the Defiant throughout 1941, and by September the number of Blenheims on strength had reached more than thirty. This increase brought about a new role for 60 OTU as a twin-engined night-fighter training unit. It was also hoped that the shift towards training crews on the Blenheim would reduce the casualty rate, especially with regard to the Defiant. By the year's end more than thirty-five Defiants had been involved in accidents, ranging from minor taxiing incidents to fatal crashes. On average, during 1941, every course of twenty to twenty-five pupils that passed through 60 OTU lost three to fatal accidents.

When the OTU was redesignated, the intention was not to operate solely the Blenheim, but also the Beaufighter, although 60 OTU had to wait until June 1942 before the first of many arrived. The Beaufighter was equipped with radar, which brought new challenges to the OTU; to deal with this an AI Flight was formed.

132 OTU trained aircrew from all over the world to fly the Beaufighter, including the Australians seen here at East Fortune in 1944. Museum of Flight

60 OTU was chosen for disbandment in late October 1942 as part of a major reshuffle of training units. On 24 November it was closed, but re-formed the same day as 132 (Coastal) OTU. All personnel and aircraft were moved to the new unit, with the exception of eighteen Beaufighters and their groundcrew, who were transferred to 51 OTU at Cranfield. The main task for 132 OTU was to undertake long-range fighter and strike training for Coastal Command squadrons using the Blenheim and Beaufighter.

Four WAAFs see a 132 OTU Beaufort on its way in this publicity photo. Museum of Flight

A sign of a change in the training programme came on 27 July 1943 when ten pilots and ten navigators arrived together. The change in status from a conversion unit to a full crew operational training unit for long-range torpedo-fighters had begun. The navigators did not join their pilots until the fifteenth day of the course; during that time they were employed by the Navigation and Signals Section. The Blenheims were withdrawn and the Beaufort took their place.

On 22 April 1944 the airfield began an association with a new aircraft, the Mosquito. These were segregated into their own unit on the airfield, simply known as 5 Squadron. With the new Mosquito element in place, it was now the task of 132 OTU to produce no fewer than twenty-one Beaufighter and six Mosquito crews per month.

132 OTU began to be broken up on 5 February 1945; it was decided to separate 5 Squadron and transfer it to the Mosquito specialist unit of 8 (Coastal) OTU based at Haverfordwest, and on 6 February the Mosquitoes began to leave for their new Welsh home.

With the war in Europe drawing to a close, a more relaxed atmosphere began to descend upon the airfield, although this was not reflected in the amount of flying that 132 OTU was achieving. During April 1945 the unit's aircraft still managed to total 1,658 flying hours by day and a further 250 hours by night.

Sixty-six courses had passed through 132 OTU since its formation. This equated to approximately 1,300 aircrew trained here, although this does not include those who passed out from the original 60 OTU. The amount of pupils arriving after VE Day declined, but courses continued and would do so for at least a further twelve months.

The early signs of 132 OTU's decline occurred on 8 June when several Beauforts were flown out, followed by a few Beaufighters. The OTU's strength increased again on 13 June when 5 Mosquito Training Squadron returned. All aircraft and personnel were back from Haverfordwest by 17 June, and before the year was over the Mosquito was the most common type here. Seventy aircraft were still on strength by December 1945, forty-one of them Mosquitoes. By now the plan was to replace all of the OTU's Beaufighters with the Buckmaster. It may have been that the end of 132 OTU was foreseen, which may explain why only two Buckmasters ever arrived.

This is RAF East Fortune in late 1941 or early 1942 looking south, with 60 OTU in residence. The old hospital is in the foreground. Museum of Flight

132 OTU was disbanded on 15 May 1946, bringing to an end all major military flying operations from the airfield. A transfer to Fighter Command on 30 September brought no aircraft and no significant use. By the end of the year the RAF had moved out and some land and buildings were returned to their original owners. East Fortune's future was looking distinctly bleak.

The start of the Cold War brought further activity when the airfield was allocated to the USAF in early 1950, and a lot of money was spent upgrading it to take military jets. The main task was to relay and extend the main runway and reinforce the perimeter track. However, not one American jet ever arrived, and the airfield was handed back to the Air Ministry in December 1955.

East Fortune's three runways and perimeter track appear to be intact in this shot taken in the mid-1990s. The Museum of Flight occupies the area at the bottom, with three Callender Hamilton hangars and a T2 housing the collection's aircraft.

A reprieve came in 1961 when the airfield was used while Turnhouse had its runway resurfaced. Between April and August of that year the airfield handled 2,640 civil aircraft movements, carrying more than 96,000 passengers. On the last flight out of East Fortune, two passengers of a Viscount were the surviving members of the transatlantic R.34 crew that had left here on 2 July 1919.

The airfield closed to flying not long after this, and the site was sold off. Some of the hangars were used by the DOE and one of these would prove useful almost a decade after the airfield's closure. On 7 July 1975 the Museum of Flight opened its doors to the public for a two-week period. More than 10,000 visitors arrived, encouraging the museum staff to expand further and arrange more open days. From 1977 the museum was virtually open full-time, as it is today.

Eventually the museum spread itself through all three surviving Callender Hamilton hangars, and today the T2 Mosquito hangar also houses Concorde G-BOAA. Other larger aircraft, stored outside, include a Comet, a Vulcan and a One Eleven. In total, thirty-three aircraft are housed at the Museum of Flight, which is superbly laid out with great encouragement given to educating the young in all aspects of flight.

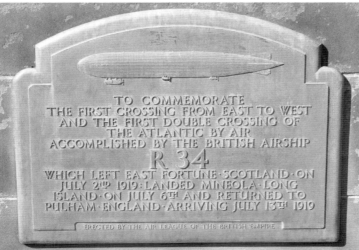

The Museum of Flight's entrance, with the refurbished T2 hangar behind, which now contains the collection's star exhibit, Concorde. Author

The overlooked achievements of the R.34 are commemorated by a very nice memorial near the museum's entrance. Author

Main features:
Hardcore and tarmac runways: QDM 252 1,710 yards, 293 1,560 yards, 192 1,100 yards. *Hangars:* three Callender Hamilton, two over blister 65-foot, six EO blister 69-foot, one T1. *Hardstandings:* forty TE hardcore, six concrete on hardcore. *Accommodation:* RAF: 1,501; WAAF: 704.

EAST HAVEN, Tayside

56°31'41"N/02°39'21"W. Between Arbroath and Carnoustie, S of A92

Built specifically for the use of the FAA, this compact and well-equipped airfield had a short but useful career. Planned to become HMS *Dotterel*, it was opened as HMS *Peewit* instead on 1 May 1943. The first unit, 767 Squadron, with Swordfishes and Albacores, moved in from Arbroath on 5 May; it was a DLT squadron, which made full use of several training carriers as well as East Haven's deck-like runways.

767 Squadron was joined by 769 Squadron, also from Arbroath, and another DLT unit with the Swordfish; however, after only a few days the squadron began to receive Barracudas, although the Swordfish would remain until early 1944. 769 Squadron also carried the additional task of training DLCOs, and several courses were passed out before the task was handed over to a brand new squadron.

731 Squadron was formed here on 5 December 1943 to continue training the DLCOs, which were better known as 'batsmen'; to gain experience the circuit was rarely empty of aircraft as pilots carried out dummy deck landings. It was from this type of training that the term 'Clockwork Mice' was invented, referring to the pilots carrying out endless landings and take-offs. Whether it was through boredom or a genuine order to test the batsmen, many pilots used to carry out what can only be described as 'eccentric' flying to make the task as difficult as possible for the DLCO pupil.

731 Squadron's tasking came to an end on 1 November 1945 when it was absorbed into 768 Squadron. The latter unit had arrived from Ballyhalbert on 25 October 1945, equipped with Seafires and Corsairs. It carried out DLT training offshore with detachments on HMS *Ravager* and HMS *Premier* before disbanding on 16 April 1946.

During this period of activity, East Haven had also been home to an Aircraft Handling training unit and a Fire Fighting School before it was paid off on 14 August 1946. It was not long before the land was returned to its original owners and to agriculture.

Most of the concrete surfaces at East Haven found a second use as hardcore for the A92. However, from the air the airfield reveals itself more clearly.

Surviving buildings are now congregated around Hatton House and Farm, including three S Type aircraft sheds, all now employed by the farmer. Only a small section of one runway remains, thanks to the majority being lifted as hardcore for the A92.

Main features:
Tarmac runways: QDM 055-235 1,220 yards, 009-189 1,060 yards, 099-279 1,015 yards, 145-325 1,000 yards. *Hangars:* twelve 60 x 70 feet, twelve storage. *Hardstandings:* four. *Accommodation:* RN: 1,166; WRNS: 378.

ECCLES TOFTS, Borders

NT759452. 3 miles ESE of Greenlaw off A697 at Eccles Tofts

A basic LG, Eccles Tofts had a brief existence during the First World War, and was one of many used by 77(HD) Squadron between late 1916 and early 1918.

EDZELL, Tayside/Angus

WW1: NO630705. N of Denstrath Farm off minor road

WW2: 56°48'42"N/02°36'20"W; NO630690. At Bridgend 2 miles NW of A94

Three airfields were associated with the name Edzell during the 20th century, and it continued in military hands well into the 1990s.

On 15 July 1918 26 TDS was established here following the dissolving of 36 and 74 TS. Fighter training was its main task, using the Camel, Pup and SE.5a. After an initial flurry of activity, the end of the Great War saw a decline in the TDS, which did well to last as long as 25 April 1919, when the site was closed down.

Several years passed before aviation returned, with a private strip located here (56°48'27"N/02°39'41"W) in 1932 and registered on that year's AA list. Not much more is known about this strip, but it would certainly have been a key factor in drawing the Air Ministry surveyors to the site as the next war approached.

A Camel of 26 TDS at Edzell in late 1918.

Work began on upgrading the airfield for an MU after the outbreak of the war. Before it was completed, aircraft from 8 FTS began using Edzell as an RLG from 3 July 1940. Many basic amenities and services were still lacking when 44 MU was formed on 1 August. The first aircraft, a Hurricane, arrived on 13 August, and was placed in the only hangar, a Type K, which was still not finished. By the war's end there would be thirty-six hangars on the airfield of various designs.

By the end of the year a steady flow of aircraft arrived, including Oxfords, Wellingtons and Proctors, and it was clear that Edzell was going to need SLGs to cope with them. The first was 26 SLG in May 1941, followed by 24 SLG in July and 25 SLG in November. Only 24 SLG at Methven would serve the MU throughout the war years, but others would be needed during peacetime.

By early 1941 hangars were springing up all around, and to keep pace with CRO commitments three major companies moved into the airfield. First was Cunliffe-Owen, which arrived in February and was tasked with assembling the Hudson; later, repair work was also carried out. Cunliffe-Owen remained here until 30 June 1944, by which time the SMT Co Ltd had also moved in. This company arrived on 4 June and its first task was also to carry out repair work on the Hudson. Specialising in American-built types, Corsairs, Hellcats and Venturas were all worked on here until early 1946. Finally, SAL also had a hangar here, but it is not clear which types the company was tasked to work on, such was the wide range that it was able to handle.

8 FTS relinquished its use on 25 March 1942, during which time the first of two concrete runways were being laid; the first was open by April. Earlier in the year 2 FIS had been formed at Montrose, and 8 FTS was dissolved into it. The new school continued to use Edzell as an RLG despite it being such a busy place, and 2 FIS continued to use it until June 1945. A stock-take in July 1945 revealed that 44 MU had 819 aircraft on its books; it would take years to dispose of these, which were still being added to only months before 44 MU was finally disbanded on 31 May 1949.

It was not long before aircraft returned, and it would be the first and last time the airfield received jets when 612 Squadron moved in from Leuchars on 14 October 1951 with its Vampires. The auxiliaries left for Dyce on 12 November 1952 to be replaced by a more sedate unit: 5 GS moved in from Dyce and continued under this title until it was disbanded into 662 VGS on 1 September 1955. The gliders left for Arbroath on 10 May 1958 to become the last RAF flying unit to serve here.

Edzell was brought back to life again in 1960 when it became part of the USN worldwide HFDF network, which was capable of listening to multiple targets all around the planet. Another American unit, the 17th SSS, was reactivated here on 1 August 1982, tasked with operating sensors for the LASSS. Nearly 3,000 personnel served here at its peak, but with the end of the Cold War technology had advanced and in the mid-1990s the network was declared obsolete. The HFDF network was shut down, the 17th SSS was disbanded and USN Edzell was closed in October 1997.

Edzell still remains a very delicate site and is still in the hands of the MoD; thus many of its wartime buildings are in a good state of preservation. It is a station that appears to be of more use to countries further afield, which may mean that its future is slightly more secure than if it was being operated solely by the British.

Main features:
Concrete runways: QDM 334 1,600 yards, 243 1,600 yards. *Hangars:* thirty-six various. *Hardstandings:* thirty 'Y' type, fifty concrete, sixteen tarmacadam. *Accommodation:* RAF: 722; WAAF: 335.

Thanks to continued military occupation, most of Edzell's original wartime infrastructure still remains.

EGLINTON (LONDONDERRY EGLINTON/CITY OF DERRY AIRPORT), Londonderry

55°02'34"N/07°09'39"W; C540220. 1 mile NE of Eglinton off A2

Eglinton's military aviation history is quite remarkable, not just because it spanned twenty years of continuous service but also because, during that time, more than 160 flying units passed through it, nearly ninety of them in peacetime.

Planned for Coastal Command, Eglinton was opened prematurely in April 1941. 53 Squadron's Hudsons arrived in August but only remained for two weeks before Eglinton's purpose was changed.

The airfield was now tasked with the defence of Londonderry, which was one of the most important ports in the British Isles at the time. Hurricanes of 504 Squadron from Ballyhalbert were the first fighters to begin the daily routine of patrols and convoy escorts. The task was then taken over by 133 Squadron's Hurricanes from Fowlmere, which arrived on 8 October 1941. Unfortunately, four pilots were killed en route when they flew into mountains in bad weather, and two more were lost in accidents within two weeks of arriving. Three weeks later, the Hurricanes were replaced with Spitfires, which were scrambled on many occasions but saw no action.

One of Eglinton's successes came thanks to 504 Squadron, which shot down this Ju 88 near the airfield.

134 Squadron took over in December, followed by 152 Squadron from Coltishall on 17 January 1942. The latter squadron's tour was extended so that it could introduce the 52nd FG to operations. The 52nd was equipped with Spitfires on arrival on 13 July, and the RAF pilots passed on their experience to their American counterparts. On 8 August the 52nd FG was declared operational after flying a combined sortie on a convoy escort duty. After building up more flying time, the 52nd moved to Goxhill on 25 August; meanwhile 152 Squadron had moved to Angle on the 16th.

Fighter cover returned with 41 Squadron's Spitfires moving from Llanbedr on 22 September 1942, and Mustangs of 4 Squadron from Clifton for Army exercises. All had gone by the end of the month to make way for another American unit, the 82nd FG, which arrived on 4 October with the P-38G and, later, several Spitfires. Made up of three squadrons, the 95th and 96th FS established themselves while the 97th FS set up at Maydown. Several long-range practice missions were flown with B-17s from Eglinton before the unit was operational in mid-December. On 3 January 1943 forty-three P-38s of the 82nd FG departed for St Eval. Before the end of 1942 485 Squadron served here from Kirkistown before moving to King's Cliffe, and both 501 and 153 Squadrons were detached in November and December.

On 1 May 1943 Eglinton was transferred to the Royal Navy together with its satellite at Maydown. By 15 May it was commissioned as HMS *Gannet*, with the first of many squadrons arriving on the 30th. The first FAA aircraft were the Swordfishes of 834 and 835 Squadrons and 837D Flight, none of which would stay for very long. Scores of squadrons would pass through, but the airfield's primary role was to house front-line fighter squadrons during their working-up period. Several second-line squadrons would also serve. The first, 725 Squadron, was formed with Rocs on 27 August 1943. This FRU unit received more Rocs in October, followed by Martinets in December; at least two were detached to Ballykelly in August 1944 to provide target-towing facilities for 3 NFW. Four more Martinets were detached to Ronaldsway, but these were moved to Ballyhalbert by November and back here by early 1945. 725 Squadron was typically equipped with a variety of aircraft, including the Anson, Hellcat, Reliant and Traveller; it moved to St Merryn on 4 August 1945.

Many squadrons of American-built fighters passed through here during late 1944 and early 1945, the majority being prepared for the final showdown in the Far East. Hellcats, Corsairs and Wildcats were a common sight right up to VJ Day.

It was 794 Squadron from St Merryn that carried Eglinton into a more peaceful period, arriving on 9 August 1945. The unit was created from three second-line squadrons to provide a school of air firing training. Equipped with the Firefly, Corsair, Seafire, Spitfire, Wildcat, Harvard and Martinet, while serving here the squadron also provided ground attack, air combat and photo reconnaissance instruction. By the end of October the squadron had become 3 NAFS, complete with its own ADDLs Flight at Maydown. During February 1946 794 Squadron continued to grow after absorbing 1 NAFS (759 Squadron), and was also incorporated into the 52nd TAG in August. Later in the year this unit began DLT training on HMS *Theseus* and HMS *Implacable* before disbanding on 26 February 1947.

Other second-line units that provided a vast range of courses included 719 and 744 Squadrons, which provided A/S training. Both served here during the late 1940s and both also returned to carry out the same task together with 744X Flight during the 1950s. Refresher and conversion training was another of Eglinton's many tasks during the immediate post-war period. DLCO training was also carried out during late 1948 and 1949 by 768 Squadron.

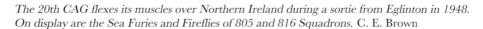

The 20th CAG flexes its muscles over Northern Ireland during a sortie from Eglinton in 1948. On display are the Sea Furies and Fireflies of 805 and 816 Squadrons. C. E. Brown

815 Squadron's Barracuda III RJ921 at Eglinton in 1950.

Several squadrons for the Canadian and Australian navies were worked up during 1947 to 1950. 803, 806 and 825 Squadrons with Sea Furies, Fireflies and Hornets were all dispatched to HMCS *Magnificent* by May 1948. 803 and 825 Squadrons returned, together with 883 Squadron from HMCS *Magnificent*, in mid-1950 for further training. Both 805 and 816 Squadrons, with Sea Furies and Fireflies, were re-formed here on 28 August 1948, and both joined HMAS *Sydney* on 8 February 1949.

HMS *Gannet* was paid off on 31 May 1959, but was reactivated in May 1960 as HMS *Sea Eagle*. 719 Squadron was re-formed here with Whirlwinds on 17 May 1960, followed by 819 Squadron with the same type on 5 October 1961. The latter unit left for HMS *Centaur* on 4 February 1963, and four days later Eglinton's long military history came to an end.

It was not long before the airfield was under the control of Londonderry City Council, and the first civilian operations were carried by the original Emerald Airways. A limited service to and from Glasgow was not successful, and by the early 1970s the only resident was the Eglinton Flying Club, which is still active today. By 1978 the Council had purchased the entire site from the MoD and developed it, and Loganair began services from 1979, once again to Glasgow. The airport was redeveloped throughout the late 1980s and early 1990s, and within ten years Ryanair was flying its Boeing 737s from here. British Airways followed, and today the airport handles nearly 4,000 movements and almost 340,000 passengers per year.

City of Derry Airport is seen in 2011, with an Airbus on the apron. Niall Hartley

Eglinton is now a subtle mix of old and new, with a modern terminal and new tower combined with the original layout and a few wartime Pentards and S sheds still being used by aircraft.

Main features:
Tarmac runways: QDM 088-268 1,600 yards, 032-212 1,100 yards, 153-333 1,100 yards. *Hangars:* ten 70 x 90 feet, seven blister, five storage. *Hardstandings:* ten A/C standings, twelve pens, 340 x 120 feet aprons, one 600 x 80 feet apron. *Accommodation:* RN: 1,944; WRNS: 365.

ELGIN (BOGS O'MAYNE/MILTONDUFF), Grampian

57°37'22"N/03°20'27"W. 3 miles SW of Elgin off B9010

In 1934 Highland Airways submitted an application to build an aerodrome at Wester Manbeen. With civil flying at its peak during the 1930s, it was surprising that nothing more was made of the proposal, which would have been a stopping-off point for the Aberdeen to Inverness route.

Lossiemouth was opened in the spring of 1939 and its new OTU would need at least one SLG to operate effectively. The original 1934 plans were looked at again, and the Wester Manbeen site was visited; it was found that, with considerable expansion, it would be suitable for the construction of an SLG.

The work was completed by the summer of 1940 and, with no unit allocated, the airfield was obstructed. 20 OTU was formed in May, and this large Wellington-equipped unit left very little room at Lossiemouth. 57 Squadron, operating Blenheims, had been at Lossiemouth since June, but as 20 OTU continued to grow it was decided to move the squadron to Elgin to continue its anti-shipping operations. On 14 August it duly moved, Elgin having been opened on 30 June with Lossiemouth as the parent unit.

57 Squadron continued its sweeps over the North Sea and, thanks to the Blenheim's range, could carry out attacks on enemy targets in Norway. The squadron moved to Wyton on 6 November 1940 and was replaced by 21 Squadron, which also flew Blenheims on anti-shipping duties and operated from here during the late summer of 1940 before leaving for Watton in October.

A detachment of 614 Squadron Lysanders from Grangemouth arrived in 1940 and possibly visited again while stationed at Macmerry. However, despite Elgin being under 20 OTU control, it was a fighter squadron that would arrive next. The Luftwaffe had shown an interest in the activities at Lossiemouth, and to combat this it was decided to move 232 Squadron down from Skitten on 4 December; it flew defensive patrols from Elgin until 29 April 1941, when it moved to Montrose.

From 18 April 1941 Elgin was finally brought into use by 'A' Flight of 20 OTU, bringing at least a dozen Wellingtons and several Ansons. 242 Squadron's duties were taken over by 17 Squadron, which moved in from Castletown on 16 June. Like 242 Squadron before it, encounters with the enemy, if any, were few and far between. On 17 September the squadron took its Hurricanes to Tain.

During May 1942 all Bomber Command OTUs were called upon to supply aircraft for the first batch of 1,000-bomber raids into Germany. Several aircraft from Elgin departed for English bases on the first raid to Cologne; they flew to Stanton Harcourt on 26 May and carried out the Cologne raid on the 30th/31st, then attacked Essen two nights later. 20 OTU also took part in a raid to Bremen on 25/26 June and a 479-strong attack on Dusseldorf on 10/11 September.

A second unit took up residence here from May 1943. 19 PAFU needed RLGs to keep pace with its own flying training programme and, equipped with Oxfords, operated from Elgin until 31 July, moving on to Leanach and Brackla before it was prematurely disbanded in February 1944.

20 OTU's activities at Elgin came to an end on 24 June 1945, having trained hundreds of bomber crews. The same day this once busy airfield was placed under C&M.

However, it was not long before aircraft returned and in even greater quantities than it had ever received during the war. On 28 July the airfield was taken over as a satellite for 44 MU. The same day Elgin also became 105 SSS under 46 MU control, and rapidly filled with war-surplus Lancasters

Two-dozen 20 OTU Wellingtons can been dispersed around Elgin in this Second World War aerial view.

and Harvards. By 1947 the aircraft holding had significantly reduced, and the MU's task was coming to an end. 45 MU took over control on 15 February, steadily winding down its own duties as the year progressed. On 15 December all had left, and by early 1948 the Air Ministry had no further use for the airfield.

The very impressive 20 OTU memorial at Elgin is maintained by RAF personal from Lossiemouth.
Author

One relic of 20 OTU's time at Elgin survives as a permanent memorial to those who lived, and died serving with it. In 1943 the station commander of Lossiemouth commissioned a large 20 OTU badge; moulded from a plaster cast, it was made from reinforced concrete before being painted and put on display outside Lossiemouth's main gate. Thanks to the enthusiasm of local people, the memorial was looked after and is today, once again, the responsibility of Lossiemouth.

Main features:
Grass runways: QDM N-S 1,400 yards, E-W 1,250 yards, SE-NW 1,100 yards. *Hangars:* one T1, one B1. *Hardstandings:* nineteen Heavy Bomber. *Accommodation:* RAF: 1,087; WAAF: 234.

ERROL, Perthshire/Tayside

56°24'18"N/03°10'54"W. 2 miles NE of Errol off B958

Errol enjoyed a short but intensive career. Its first occupant was 9 (P)AFU from Hullavington on 1 August 1942, with Masters and Hurricanes. Despite being an RAF unit, a large proportion of its time was spent training Navy pilots, and this introduced several Swordfishes and Albacores.

Military servicemen from all over the Commonwealth passed through Errol, introducing a vast range of languages. However, from December 1942 Russian was introduced thanks to Britain agreeing to supply 100 Albemarles to the Soviet Union. To cope with this operation, 305 FTU was formed on 14 December to train Russian ferry crews to fly the Albemarle. The first crew, comprising three pilots and three engineers, arrived on 11 January 1943 and began training two weeks later. By May at least twenty crews had been trained and several Albemarles had made it to the USSR. No more than fourteen Albemarles actually ever made it, but 305 FTU continued to operate until it was disbanded on 20 April 1944.

Meanwhile, 9 PAFU was expanding and RLGs would be needed. The first of four, Findo Gask, was used from 12 July 1943, but was closed during the winter for improvements. Open again by March 1944, 9 PAFU was then reorganised. 1 Group Fighter Training, consisting of 'A' and 'B' Flights, remained at Errol and 2 Group TBR Training, made up of 'C' and 'D' Flights, moved to Findo. By now the unit's establishment had swelled to more than 125 Masters, but by August these had been replaced by nearly 100 Harvards, and in October the Swordfishes and Albacores were removed.

Errol's useful position was also taken advantage of by 1680 Flight, which first arrived from Prestwick on 22 April 1944. The flight operated various aircraft for ferrying VIPs to the Hebrides, Orkneys and Shetlands, and continued to operate on and off through 1944; a final detachment was flown from here in January 1945.

During May 1945 9 GS was formed with the Cadet, which was soon to become the only military aircraft operating from Errol. On 21 June 9 PAFU was disbanded and the final course was posted to Ternhill. The GS only lasted a few more months before being moved to Scone.

260 MU was formed here as a GED, later an EDD, in June. With various sub-sites under its control, the MU was wound up in July 1948, becoming the last RAF unit to be active at Errol.

Prior to its closure, the airfield was listed in a Hansard report as one of many that had the potential for further use, but nothing came of it. Hardly changed since its closure, nearly all concrete surfaces remain intact, one T1 hangar is in use, and the Type 12779 control tower just remains. The technical site has now been taken over by several businesses, which have certainly played their part in preserving a deceivingly large number of buildings. Light aircraft have also been flying from here for many years, and since the early 1990s Errol has also been the home to Gannet T.5 XG882.

Main features:
Tarmac and wood chippings runways: QDM 230 1,600 yards, 290 1,180 yards, 350 1,170 yards. *Hangars:* six T1, thirteen blister 69 feet. *Hardstandings:* seventeen circular concrete. *Accommodation:* RAF: 1,865; WAAF: 430.

EVANTON (NOVAR), Highland

57°39'56"N/04°18'39"W; NH625664. 1 mile NE of Evanton off A9

Thanks to a lack of room to expand Delny after the end of the First World War, the Admiralty searched for another site close by. The Navy needed areas that could handle large numbers of aircraft while its Home Fleet was at anchor at Invergordon; it chose a site near the village of Evanton, and named it Novar after the estate that owned the land.

Blackburn N9588 of 450 Flight at Novar in 1930.

Novar was ready for its first aircraft from 1922 and was at its most active between April and October. On arrival aircraft were serviced, mainly by RAF personnel, who were detached from Leuchars. It was the IIIFs of 820 Squadron from HMS *Courageous* that were the first to arrive on 12 May 1933. On 24 September of that same year, 821 Squadron, also flying the IIIF, flew in from Catfoss before leaving for Manston in late October. During June and July of the following year, 820 Squadron returned, now with Seals, and 823 Squadron's IIIFs staged through from Leuchars to embark on HMS *Courageous* by 26 October 1934.

Numerous squadrons and flights from the FAA passed through Novar/ Evanton during the 1930s. Blackburn S1052 of 449 Flight was there in 1932.

From 1937 the airfield was renamed Evanton and a great deal of expansion work began. Hangars were erected and FAA squadrons were on the increase. 801 Squadron returned from HMS *Furious* in May and 810 Squadron carried out an APC here from HMS *Courageous* in June. Two more squadrons from HMS *Furious*, 822 with Sharks and 811 with Swordfishes, arrived in June and July before the airfield's long-term purpose began.

Despite being a Royal Navy airfield, it was an RAF unit that would form the backbone of the station when 8 ATC was formed on 1 September 1937. Its job was to train air observers and air gunners in air-to-air firing, and from 1 October the range at Tain was brought into use. Aircraft used were the Audaxes, Tutors, Gordons and Hart Trainers.

On 1 April 1938 8 ATC was renamed 8 ATS, still using Gordons and Henleys. The Swordfishes of 820 and 821 Squadron were the first to make use of the ATS's facilities from HMS *Courageous* on 2 May. Both left on 4 June after sharing the airfield with 810 Squadron's Swordfishes and later 800 Squadron's Nimrods and Ospreys. The RAF arrived that year when Heyfords of 7 and 99 Squadrons from Finningley and Mildenhall stayed. The ATS was also well subscribed with aircraft from 6 FTS and 8 FTS.

One of the big events at Evanton in 1939 was the Empire Day air show on 24 May, which attracted more than 9,000 spectators. All roads leading to the airfield were blocked by cars, such was the enthusiasm generated for these events. The previous month the RAF had arrived again with 83 Squadron's Hampdens from Scampton. 106 Squadron followed in June with Ansons and Hampdens from Thornaby as part of the increasing number of exercises that were occurring as the war beckoned.

The FAA returned in July, with X Flight of 771 Squadron bringing Swordfishes from Lee-on-Solent until August. Also in August HMS *Ark Royal* arrived at Invergordon and its two squadrons, 803 with Skuas and Rocs and 820 with Swordfishes, disembarked on the 22nd. These two squadrons would become the last peacetime units to visit Evanton, 820 Squadron returning to *Ark Royal* just two days before war broke out.

818 Squadron was the only FAA unit ever formed here, on 24 August 1939. Its Swordfishes did not stay for long, and by the 31st 818 Squadron had embarked on HMS *Ark Royal* in Scapa Flow.

On the first day of the war, 8 ATS was redesignated 8 AOS, only to be renamed again on 1 November as 8 B&GS with Harrows and Henleys.

The task of fighter defence of the Fleet was given to the Blenheims of 64 Squadron, which arrived from Church Fenton on 4 December. However, no enemy aircraft were encountered during the tour, which came to an end on 8 January 1940.

The Skuas of 801 Squadron stayed for a few weeks from February to April 1940 from Donibristle, and moved on to Hatston. HMS *Ark Royal*'s aircraft returned again in April and May 1940, with both 820 and 821 Squadrons bringing their Swordfishes ashore. 823 Squadron also made use of Evanton at the same time with its Swordfishes, which detached themselves on two occasions to HMS *Glorious* until they returned to their Orkney home in mid-May.

The Lysanders of B Flight, 614 Squadron, arrived on 11 June 1940 from Grangemouth, and the departure of 825 Squadron back to Lee-on-Solent on 31 January 1941 marked the last FAA flying unit to visit for the remainder of the war. Evanton was now the domain of 8 B&GS, which from April saw its Harrows replaced by Bothas. A further reshuffling of RAF training units saw a name change on 9 June when 8 B&GS became 8 AGS. The new school was now expanding as the demand for air gunners for Bomber Command increased. By July the Botha, Harrow and Battle were on strength and the unit continued to grow further as another year passed.

The Bothas began to be replaced by Ansons from July 1943, although thirty-one remained until the last of them left in November. The demand for air gunners declined during the summer of 1944 and the RAF again began to restructure its training establishments. The members of the very last 8 AGS course, No 138, were awarded their brevets on 18 August 1944 as part of a station parade. The AGS's days were now numbered and the school was disbanded on the 26th, despite the war being far from over.

Airspeed Oxford I PH453 rests near one of Evanton's many hangars during the late 1940s.

The same day the airfield was placed under C&M, although this state was not to last long. It was still of use to the Royal Navy, and by 1 September 1944 was taken over and allocated as a reserve storage airfield for Fearn. This scenario was to be short-lived, a raise in status seeing Evanton commissioned as HMS *Fieldfare* on 9 October.

HMS *Fieldfare* was rapidly expanded into a busy Royal Navy Air Maintenance Yard at great expense to the public purse. It had a capacity of 250 aircraft and this total was reached on many occasions during late 1945. Only one FAA flying unit is recorded as having served at the airfield during the Navy's tenure: 771 Squadron arrived on detachment from Gosport briefly in late August 1946, but only stayed for a few weeks. Despite a total of £2 million being spent on the airfield by the Royal Navy, HMS *Fieldfare* was paid off on 24 March 1948. Remaining in military hands, the airfield served as an RLG for 8 FTS, whose Oxfords were seen up to 30 September 1953, when the site was finally closed to flying.

By the 1970s the majority of the technical and hangar area had become an industrial estate, with various businesses moving in. Steel scrap processing, fence-making, textiles and several oil-related companies took over the site; the latter area in particular also saw a expansion in the size of the town.

The runways have survived, with the west end of the east-west strip being partly built over by an oil pipeline construction frame, which extends on to a causeway running out into the Cromarty Firth. Most of the land between the runways has reverted to farmland.

Main features:
Tarmac runways: QDM 043-223 1,233 yards, 095-275 970 yards. *Hangars:* two B&P, four Bellman, one F, one S, six EO blister. *Hardstandings:* hangar apron 190 x 280 feet. *Accommodation:* RN: 383; WRNS: 128.

FAIR ISLE, Shetland

59°32'06"N/01°37'43"W. Centre of Fair Isle

Halfway between the Shetland and Orkney islands, it made sense that an ELG was established on Fair Isle during the war, although the island itself could have easily served as an emergency airfield without any kind of official reference.

Very little is recorded about its use, although a Spitfire from 8 OTU did crash-land on 22 July 1941 after setting out from Wick. Flown by Flt Lt M. Hood, the aircraft was returning from Norway and whether it actually crash-landed on the ELG or just somewhere on the island is open to debate.

The current 1,640-foot airstrip in the centre of the island may have been the position of this wartime ELG. Popular with private flyers, this important lifeline also receives a scheduled Loganair flight linking it to the mainland, and averages more than 700 movements per year.

FEARN (BALINTORE/CLAYS OF ALLAN), Highland

57°45'29"N/03°56'35"W; NH845760. Between Fearn and Balintore, SW of B9165

Several of Scotland's remote airfields have stood the test of time very well, and Fearn is no exception. Originally designed to be used by the RAF, its operational days were under FAA control, and this produced an airfield with a diverse mix of buildings, many of which survive today.

Opened in late 1941, Fearn saw very little activity with only the odd aircraft making use of it. By early 1942 the RAF had no use for the airfield, but the Royal Navy did.

On 15 July 1942 Fearn was transferred to the Admiralty, and became a satellite for Donibristle on 1 August. The Navy built a three-storey control tower next to the RAF one and the original technical site was expanded. Hangars were brought in by the lorry-load, and thirty-three were on site by the end of the war.

The first units to arrive were 819 and 825 Squadrons, both with Swordfishes, on 30 September 1942 from Hatston. During the squadron's stay Fearn was commissioned as HMS *Owl* on 11 October, no longer under Donibristle's control.

825 Squadron left for Thorney Island on 9 December, followed by 819 Squadron, which departed for Machrihanish on 21 January 1943. One more front-line Swordfish unit, 824 Squadron, arrived two days later from Machrihanish and returned on 11 March, leaving Fearn poised to begin its main war role as a torpedo training school.

HMS *Owl* was now ready to receive several TBR squadrons, which were working up to operational status. To help achieve this a resident TBR Pool Squadron was formed with Swordfishes, Barracudas, Ansons and Albacores.

747 Squadron was formed on 22 March 1943 as an OTU, with Ansons being used for radar training and the Swordfishes added later. Tain range was used by Fearn's squadrons, and the surrounding Dornoch Firth was a good area for dropping torpedoes. With its basic training now complete, 747 Squadron was moved to Inskip on 9 June to become part of 1 Naval OTU. 747 Squadron would return within months, bringing 1 OTU back with it.

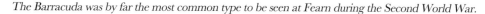

The Barracuda was by far the most common type to be seen at Fearn during the Second World War.

Before the first of thirteen Barracuda units passed through the torpedo school, 816 Squadron arrived from Exeter on 25 June 1943. Equipped with the Seafire, this unit had left for Machrihanish by 8 July. The same day saw the arrival of 847 Squadron's Barracudas from Lee-on-Solent. This was to be Fearn's first course, and each crew would carry out an average of 30 hours of training. By 13 July the entire squadron was here and its course was completed on 14 August. The same day 847 Squadron left for Machrihanish, then the process would start again, this time with 823 Squadron, also flying the Barracuda, from Lee-on-Solent. This unit stayed until January 1944 before moving on to Burscough. 822 Squadron followed from Tain on 16 January but moved early to Crail on 1 February.

747 Squadron was back on 26 January 1944, bringing No 1 Naval OTU with it. During 1944 five more Barracuda squadrons arrived and two more TBR training squadrons were also formed. The first, 717 Squadron with Barracudas, formed on 1 July, was joined by 714 Squadron, which was re-formed one month later. Both squadrons worked closely together receiving aircrew from their specialist training and assembling them into crews. Both of these units moved to Rattray on 30 October. 747 Squadron had also already departed for the final time, this time to Ronaldsway on 14 July.

TBR training continued into 1945 with 816, 821, 817 and 818 Squadrons all arriving before VJ Day. Two more Barracuda units, 815 and 826 Squadrons, carried out part of their operational training here into late 1945. 826 Squadron was disbanded here before becoming operational on 28 February 1946.

Something different arrived on 5 December 1945, in the shape of the Firebrand TTU, aka 708 Squadron. Supported by various marks of Seafire, several practice combat sorties were flown from here by the unit's Firebrands. Even at this early stage of the aircraft's development, it was obvious that the Firebrand was not going to be the easiest aircraft to bring into service, and on 8 January 1946 the unit moved to Rattray to continue its trials.

719 Squadron was re-formed on 1 March 1946 as a Strike Training Squadron. Using the Barracuda, the squadron moved to Eglinton on 14 May. 860 Squadron, with Fireflies, was to be the last FAA unit to operate from Fearn. Arriving from Ayr on 19 April, it had left for St Merryn by May. With no further role to play, the airfield fell silent on 2 July when it was paid off by the Royal Navy and placed under C&M. Remaining in the hands of the MoD, the airfield, now under RAF control again, became an RLG for 8 FTS from 12 May 1952 until 30 September 1953.

The Standard naval four-storey control tower dominates the airfield today, having been sold as a private dwelling. Only 100 metres from this, the original RAF single-storey watch office also remains, not to mention one hangar, the decontamination block, bomb stores and a host of other technical and domestic buildings in varying states of repair. On the south side of the airfield a modern grass strip has been established for many years, maintaining an aviation connection with this once busy airfield.

Main features:
Tarmac runways: QDM 052-232 1,475 yards, 115-295 1,260 yards, 176-356 1,180 yards. *Hangars:* two squadron, fourteen 60 x 70 feet, sixteen storage, one 125 x 185 feet. *Hardstandings:* seven, plus six pens. *Accommodation:* RAF: 1,214; WAAF: 347.

FERMOY (CARRIGNAGROGHER), Cork

52°09'06"N/08°17'61"W; W80419 99941. Three-quarters of a mile N of Fermoy bridge

Fermoy was constructed on open land west of the Dublin road and south of Ballyarthur road. The area was used by the British Army as an exercise ground and a racecourse.

Work began in mid-1917 and by December its first unit, 19 TS, had moved in from Hounslow. The TS brought a range of aircraft here, representing virtually every service type of the day.

The airfield was fairly basic during its early days, with just a pair of Bessoneau hangars, a few wooden technical buildings and virtually all accommodation under canvas. There were two grass runways marked out, one 'long' at 1,000 yards and one 'short' at 600 yards.

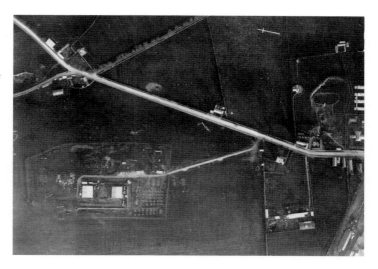

Two Bessoneaus and three 106 Squadron RE.8s give away Fermoy's position in the bottom left of this photograph taken on 9 December 1918.

The first unit to arrive was 106 Squadron from Ayr with RE.8s. It had the airfield to itself from 27 June 1918 as 19 TS moved to The Curragh. The RE.8s were replaced by F.2bs from January 1919, but on 8 October 106 Squadron was disbanded.

105 Squadron brought its F.2bs on detachment from Oranmore in November, and 2 Squadron did the same in April 1920. 2 Squadron had made Fermoy its home by July, bringing its F.2bs from Oranmore, only to return a few weeks later on detachment. 2 Squadron was to become the last RAF squadron to serve here, leaving for Digby on 13 February 1922.

FIFTEEN ACRES (PHOENIX PARK), Dublin

53°21'59"N/06°20'41"W; O10621 35218. 2½ miles W of O'Connell Street Bridge

An ELG was located here from 26 April 1917, although it is possible that it was in civilian use prior to this. It was used by the RAF from 1918 to 1921, by which time it had returned to civilian hands, or its original owner, and continued in use until 1938.

FINDO GASK, Tayside

56°22'31"N/03°36'22"W; NO010215. 2 miles N of Dalreoch Bridge off A9

From small beginnings as an SLG that was not needed, Findo Gask was developed throughout the war years. Constructed for the use of 44 MU, 25 SLG was opened on 1 May 1941, and within days was transferred to 309 Squadron's Lysanders.

During its construction 309 Squadron operated from Dunino until 26 November 1942, when it made Findo its home. By this time the squadron had also gained several Mustangs. The Lysanders served the unit until March 1943, and at the same time Findo's runways were beginning to deteriorate. On 10 March the squadron was moved to Kirknewton to give the runways a chance to recover and for repairs to be carried out. Only the squadron's HQ made a brief appearance in June of that year as operational requirements had resulted in 309 Squadron moving south to Snailwell.

Change of ownership came again on 12 July 1943 when Findo was offered to 9 PAFU. With the main unit based at Errol, Findo was relegated to RLG duties but remained lifeless until late March 1944. Two flights, 'C' and 'D', with Masters, moved here with the task of training mainly FAA pilots for TBR squadrons. This naval influence resulted in the airfield's control tower being upgraded into a three-storey standard.

By 2 November 1944 9 PAFU had left Findo and its poorly drained runways for the concrete at Tealing. Now under yet another owner, the War Department, the airfield was used for training the local Polish Army units until the end of the war. During peacetime it was Maintenance Command's turn, when on 6 November 1945 the airfield became a satellite for 44 MU and a sub-site for 260 MU. By 16 May 1946 44 MU had left, and by the end of 1948 260 MU had also gone.

This late 1940s view of Findo Gask shows a deserted but complete wartime airfield.

Very little remains at Findo today and, following the removal of the Sommerfeld Track, not even a trace of the runways is evident. Only a section of the northern perimeter track remains and, thanks to some executive-style house, any features that remained up until a few years ago have been wiped away. One feature, however, remains defiant: the three-storey naval-type control tower. Despite being close to the new estate, it will possibly be converted to residential use.

Main features:
Steel matting runways: QDM 070 1,950 yards, 110 1,250 yards, 010 1,100 yards. *Hangars:* one half T2, seven blister 69 feet. *Hardstandings:* sixteen circular. *Accommodation:* RAF: 667; WAAF: 196.

FORDOUN, Aberdeenshire/Grampian

56°53'09"N/02°24'24"W. 4 miles NE of Laurencekirk, crossed by B966

This site was surveyed in 1941 on land surrounded by the rising Grampian Hills. Construction began not long after, north of Fordoun, with the main Dundee to Aberdeen railway and Old Aberdeen Road restricting the eastern border.

Oxfords from 2 FIS became the first to make use of Fordoun on 2 November 1942, leaving on 26 May 1943. On 9 September 2 FIS returned, but by mid-1944 the runways had begun to deteriorate, and by 13 September the FIS had to abandon Fordoun. Repairs were considered, but with the end of war in sight and no significant unit needing the airfield, Fordoun was closed to flying. However, this did not stop 5 GS being formed during October, operating Cadets. In the hands of the War Department from December, the GS remained until 1946.

From 21 August 1945 Fordoun became a satellite of 98 MU at Mawcarse in Kinross-shire. 98 MU disbanded on 7 August 1947, closing its satellite here the same day. Six days earlier, a second unit, 243 MU, had established a sub-site here handling ordnance. It remained here until 30 September 1950, becoming the last RAF unit to make use of the airfield.

Seen from the Old Aberdeen Road is one of two surviving 65-foot blister hangars at Fordoun in 2009.

The airfield was disposed of in 1956 and in the early 1960s the runways were used for several karting events. Despite the condition of the runways, flying returned to Fordoun in May 1965 with several private aircraft taking up residence. In 1967 the Fordoun Flying Club was formed, which later re-formed as the Bon Accord Flying Group. It continued to operate from the airfield until April 1994 when it relocated to Aberdeen.

Flying returned to Fordoun in 1967 with the Bon Accord Flying Club, which remained until 1994. Keith Grinstead

In 1995 the site was purchased by Hunting, which now runs a North Sea pipe management centre from it. The runways are covered by large pipes and industrial buildings, but the main shape of the airfield remains, although recent expansion has moved the operation beyond the runways. The perimeter track is complete and the remains of some of the fighter pens also remain. Two blister hangars are still standing; one has been reclad while the other is in need of attention.

Main features:
Concrete runways: QDM 060 1,500 yards, 170 1,100 yards. *Hangars:* four blister 65 feet. *Hardstandings:* six double fighter. *Accommodation:* RAF: 474; WAAF: 61.

FORRES, Grampian (Moray)

57°36'05"N/03°38'29"W. 1 mile W of Forres off A96

Once 19 OTU was formed at Kinloss in May 1940, it was clear that this large unit needed at least two satellites to operate effectively.

Forres SLG was ready for Whitleys of 'D' Flight, 19 OTU, on 21 January 1941. Almost all of the Whitleys that served with the OTU in the early years had already seen service with at least one front-line bomber squadron, so a strict servicing schedule was essential to keep these aircraft in the air. To speed up this process a Minor Inspection Unit was established here. 'C' Flight had also arrived by 13 May, taking over dispersals close to the River Findhorn Bridge.

Whitley V N1349 served for many years with 19 OTU at Forres.

While other OTUs were re-equipping with or had already received Wellingtons, 19 OTU saw out 1943 still operating its Whitleys. Eleven had been lost by the end of 1943, three of them in October, making that the worst month on record at Forres for losses.

By late 1944 Forres's usefulness was coming to an end and 19 OTU began to reorganise. Wellingtons had finally begun to arrive at Kinloss, but were never destined to be used here.

Hundreds of aircrew from all over the Commonwealth passed through Forres, the majority going on to serve with a front-line squadron. Losses were high, however; twenty-six Whitleys were lost, resulting in fifty-five aircrew killed and many more injured.

During mid-October 1944 'C' Flight moved back to Kinloss, leaving 'D' Flight behind. On 22 October 'D' Flight was ready to leave, and in traditional style the Whitleys were flown out of Forres. The airfield was now under the control of the War Department, which made very little use of it. Its final military purpose was to billet members of the Polish Army Forces from 1945 to 1947. Not long after, the land was returned to its original owners.

An empty Forres was photographed immediately after the end of the Second World War.

Aviation did return in 1960 when a section of the dispersal road was extended along the eastern bank of the Findhorn, south-west of Mundole. The strip was 870 yards long with turning circles at both ends, and was used by a director of United Biscuits Ltd flying an Aztec. A local distillery also operated Aztecs, and later the larger King Air was flown from the short strip until at least the mid-1970s.

Today a few huts and dispersals remain but, more importantly, a memorial cairn has been erected on the side of the A96. Forres has slowly encroached on the north-eastern side of the old site, but the vast majority of the flying field remains. Forres, like so many other purpose-built SLGs, was a small but important cog in the machine that was training aircrews for Bomber Command.

Main features:

Grass runways: QDM NE-SW 1,700 yards, NW-SE 1,100 yards. *Hangar:* one T2. *Hardstandings:* twenty-two frying pan. *Accommodation:* RAF: 834; WAAF: 173.

FORT GEORGE, Highland

NH761566

On the outbreak of the First World War there were only two active RNAS stations, both operating seaplanes; they were Dundee and Fort George, which had been in operation since 1913.

Fort George came about following the ending of seaplane operations from Cromarty in late 1913. At least one hangar was dismantled at Cromarty and transported by tug to Fort George in October. On the 27th the tug *Resource* was used to deliver the advance party and stores, and it took the remainder of the year to move all the equipment, aggravated by poor weather conditions. Under the command of Lt Cdr A. Longmore, potential LGs at Ardesier and Carse of Delnies were inspected but considered to be unsuitable.

No specific unit was ever based here, but the most common type seen was the Wright Navy Seaplane. These flimsy-looking pusher biplanes continued to fly from the Moray Firth until 1916, with only one being recorded as lost during this period. Wright No 155 was wrecked during a gale on 8 April 1915, becoming Fort George's only recorded casualty.

At least one 70 x 70 feet shed was constructed here during the First World War, but was removed to Smoogroo on 25 June 1918.

FRASERBURGH (INVERALLOCHY/CAIRNBLUG), Grampian

57°40'09"N/01°56'04"W. Due S of Inverallochy off B9107 and B9033

A Short 184 built by Sage of Peterborough is prepared for a lift onto the harbour wall at Fraserburgh. Never officially referred to as a seaplane base, this image proves that some aviation-related activities took place here during the First World War. Stuart Leslie

Work began on Fraserburgh during the winter of 1940/41 as a satellite for the fighter squadrons that were passing through Peterhead. Opened on 6 December 1941, the first unit, 823 Squadron with Swordfishes, arrived the same day. Poor weather restricted the squadron's flying, and on 30 January 1942 it moved out to Machrihanish. Two days earlier 883 Squadron's Sea Hurricanes had arrived from Peterhead, staying until 15 February. While the odd convoy patrol was flown, no enemy interceptions were made.

Seen from the air in early 1942, Fraserburgh is open for business, but this view indicates that there was still a great deal work to be done.

Devoid of any flying units, only the odd visitor arrived from February to May. A permanent unit did not arrive until 13 May, when 3 SGR moved in from Squires Gate. The PRU Conversion Flight, also from Squires Gate, provided the nucleus to form a new unit. 8 (Coastal) OTU was formed on 18 May to train PR pilots, for which the Mosquito was used from October. 8 OTU continued to gain in strength, and with more Mosquitoes arriving it was decided to move it to a larger airfield. On 8 February 1943 the OTU moved to Dyce, and Fraserburgh was placed under C&M until another use could be found.

Just like the previous year, the airfield lay dormant from February to May. It was not until 25 May that the Oxfords of 14 PAFU moved in. With the main unit operating from Banff, Fraserburgh served as an RLG to help accommodate the 160-plus aircraft on strength. Training sorties mainly consisted of local flying and very few days passed without at least one Oxford in the circuit. 14 PAFU was disbanded on 1 September 1944 and, for the third time in its short career, Fraserburgh fell silent.

With the formation of the Banff and Dallachy Strike Wings, the need for ASR support was never higher. 279 and 281 Squadrons, both based at Banff and Dallachy, had been providing regular ASR since September 1944. With Banff becoming busier, it was decided to move 279 Squadron to Fraserburgh. On 26 December four Warwicks fitted with airborne lifeboats arrived, one of them setting off immediately in support of an attack on Leirvik.

Without fail a Warwick would accompany the strike aircraft towards Norway. On 11 January 1945 Warwick 'B' HG209 responded to a faint 'urgent assistance required' message that had been sent by a 143 Squadron Mosquito, forced into the sea by a Bf 109. A dogfight was still raging overhead when Flt Lt J. Moreton and his crew located the wreckage of the Mosquito and a man climbing into a dinghy. Flying at 500 feet, Moreton began his run to drop a lifeboat near the

A 279 Squadron Vickers Warwick ASR.I, complete with airborne lifeboat, stands at a Fraserburgh dispersal in early 1945.

dinghy, but as he did so a Bf 109 closed in. The Warwick's gunners tried to fend off the fighter, but it found its mark and HG209 plunged into the sea. The six crew had no chance as the Warwick sank within 10 seconds. A second Warwick left to look for survivors, but no trace was found.

From early January the airfield was used to carry out Mosquito modifications and prepare new aircraft, which were mainly for 235 and 248 Squadrons at Banff, having been delivered from MU airfields in England by ATA pilots.

The town of Fraserburgh was a dumping ground for bombs as the Luftwaffe returned to Norway. With the war drawing to a close, one German bomber had planned a one-way trip. On 2 May a Ju 188 landed here and the crew surrendered. This was one of only two Ju 188s to be captured by the RAF during the war.

279 Squadron flew its last ASR operation on 31 May when a Hurricane failed to find a ditched B-17. On 10 June Fraserburgh's short career came to an end. The same day the Warwicks departed for Keflavik and the Hurricanes relocated to Banff.

Flying returned in the 1950s with the Aberdeen Gliding Club, but since then Fraserburgh has slowly deteriorated to a few sections of runway and several buildings. The majority are at Tershinty, which would have been a dispersed communal site.

Main features:
Tarmac runways: QDM 236 1,350 yards, 170 1,100 yards, 304 1,000 yards.
Hangars: one T1, six double blister. *Hardstandings:* three loop, eighteen frying pan.
Accommodation: RAF: 987; WAAF: 227.

GANAVAN SANDS (OBAN), Argyllshire

56°26'20"N/05°28'20"W; NM862328. 2 miles N of Oban in Ganavan Bay

The satellite at Ganavan Sands is often overlooked and can usually be found in the history of Oban. Opened in 1940, it had a slipway and one hangar together with a few technical buildings, and was established to carry out minor servicing and maintenance when Oban-based flying boats required it. It was first referred to as an FBSU, but later became 4 FBSU from 25 September 1942; this unit was disbanded in April 1944.

This beautiful spot is now being developed into a holiday village. The slipway is still in place and until recently the runners of the hangar doors could still be seen. This small station's memory will live on, though, as there is an RAF Oban memorial on the site, reading 'To the memory of all air and ground personnel of 18 Group Coastal Command who served at RAF Oban'.

GIFFORD (TOWNHEAD), Lothian

55°54'59"N/02°43', 06"W; NT545695

Established for 77(HD) Squadron in 1918, this LG was classified as a 3rd Class LG. This basically meant that approaches were allowed along a single axis, and it could only be used when there was no better local alternative.

GILMERTON, Edinburgh City

55°53'50"/N03°07'38"W; NT297678. S of Gilmerton Station Road, with A720 passing through site

This was another LG for the use of 77(HD) Squadron, and was in use between 1916 and 1918.

GORMANSTON, Meath

53°38'05"N/06°13'84"W; O17038 67631. 2½ miles NW of Balbriggan

Gormanston can trace its history back to 1917 when work began on a substantial TDS. Nine hangars were built and at least forty technical buildings and ample accommodation for all who served here. The airfield extended towards the Irish Sea coast and was only halted by a railway line.

Its first occupant was 22 TDS, which was formed on 1 August 1918 from 26 and 69 TS. A wide range of aircraft were flown, but by 13 April 1919 22 TDS had become 22 TS, and although training continued it was on a reduced scale.

The home of 22 TDS, Gormanston is captured on 3 November 1918 with hangars completed but building work still carrying on behind.

Viewed from the roof of a hangar, once again the quality of the building work is evident, trimmed off with white-painted stones and neat grass.

117 Squadron became the only operational unit to serve here, arriving from Tallaght on 24 April 1919 with DH.9s; it was later absorbed into 141 Squadron on 6 October. In the meantime 22 TS was disbanded in September, leaving a detachment of 141 Squadron at Baldonnel to become the last RAF unit stationed here in December 1919.

GRANGEMOUTH, Falkirk (Central Region)

56°00'36"N/03°42'05"W. E of centre of Grangemouth, with hangars off Abbotsinch Road

This new airport in the centre of Scotland was opened in May 1939. Sadly, it could not realise its full potential before the outbreak of the war.

Work began on 9 February 1939 and within a short space of time Grangemouth was ready. Opened by AM Viscount Trenchard on 1 July, two giant aircraft sheds fronted by a beautiful terminal building dominated the new airport. At the front of the terminal was the control tower, which looked out onto a large apron and the runways beyond.

35 E&RFTS was formed on 1 May with Tiger Moths, Ansons, Hinds and Audaxes, joined by 10 CANS, both under the control of SAL. On the outbreak of the war, 35 E&RFTS was disbanded and most of its aircraft were transferred to 10 CANS. Grangemouth was now used as a satellite for 603 Squadron's Spitfires from Turnhouse, which flew here every day.

On 1 November 1939 10 CANS was redesignated as 10 AONS, with twelve Ansons on strength. However, the unit was not destined to stay much longer, moving to Prestwick on 27 November.

Less than three weeks earlier 614 Squadron had moved in from Odiham with Lysanders. The squadron took part in many defensive patrols, covering the East Coast from Berwick to Inverness.

58 OTU was formed on 21 October 1940 with the intention of training night-fighter crews. It relied heavily on 614 Squadron for basic equipment, and received its first aircraft on 2 November when a Master arrived. With only five officers and 224 airmen on strength, due to lack of accommodation, no more personnel were being posted here. Later, 13 Group HQ was informed

A lone 35 E&RFTS Tiger Moth is the only aircraft visible at Grangemouth only weeks before the new airport was officially declared open in July 1939.

that no more aircraft or personnel for the OTU could be accepted owing to the lack of facilities. Perth was inspected as an alternative but was found to be no better, so 58 OTU was disbanded.

Since the OTU's formation in October work had continued on upgrading Grangemouth with concrete runways. The new 58 OTU was formed here again on 2 December, this time as a day-fighter training unit with Spitfires. Poor weather now hindered the OTU's early training, but by 20 January 1941 the first pupil had gone solo. More aircraft arrived and, with additional instructors, the pace began to increase. The first pupils passed out as Spitfire pilots from No 1 Course on 17 February, having spent a mere six weeks training.

614 Squadron, which had just returned from Tangmere flying ASR operations over the Channel, was getting ready to leave for the final time. On 4 March the squadron, which had helped 58 OTU so much during its early days, moved to Macmerry.

News came on 30 June that 58 OTU was to get its own satellite at Balado Bridge, the plan being for pupil pilots to receive their ground training and the final stages of their flying training under operational conditions at the satellite. Pupils from No 17 Course first arrived at Balado on 23 March 1942 and it was hoped that more flying hours could be achieved here.

58 OTU was redesignated 2 CTW on 5 October 1943. The objective of the new unit was to deliver further training in air warfare to those pilots who had graduated from an OTU. At first all pupils who passed through the CTW had no combat experience, but as the unit matured more advanced training was given to pilots who had already served in squadrons. On 15 October the CTW was renamed again as 2 TEU, becoming a specialist unit to provide operational training for both fighter and fighter-bomber pilots. On 25 June 1944 2 TEU was disbanded and Grangemouth fell silent.

141 Squadron brought its Defiant night-fighters to Grangemouth during the summer of 1940.

58 OTU Spitfires and Masters are scattered across Grangemouth in early 1942. Via A. P. Ferguson

Many Poles passed through 58 OTU, including this motley crew in front of a Master at Grangemouth in 1942.

The airfield was reduced to C&M on 3 July 1944, with just a few personnel resident. By early October it was placed under Maintenance Command, then on 12 October it became one of many 243 MU sub-sites, and the unit was destined to remain here until 31 August 1947.

Military flying returned before the end of the war. 6 GS was formed in February 1945, but by January 1946 it had moved to Turnhouse, only to return in 1951 to disband. 2 GS was also formed here on 1 November 1947, flying a diverse collection of aircraft, and grew further still when it took over 6 GS's gliders as well.

The most significant post-war flying unit, 13 RFS, was formed on 1 April 1948 with Tiger Moths. A sign of the future brought about the unit's closure when the local authorities acquired part of the airfield for the expanding Shell oil refinery. The RFS was disbanded on 19 April 1949 and absorbed into 11 RFS at Perth.

4 GS was the last flying unit to arrive here, during November 1951. The following year 243 MU no longer needed the airfield and left on 7 January 1952. Not long after, 4 GS was disbanded, leaving 2 GS as the only flying unit left on the airfield. The latter was by now one of the biggest glider schools in the country, and was busy until its closure was announced in July 1954.

By now the local council was buying up large sections of the airfield, and if it did not get the land, the oil refinery would. The old terminal building was being used by 2 GS when, on 3 October 1953, this once beautiful building was gutted by fire. By the summer of 1955 2 GS was winding down and was disbanded on 1 September 1955, although RAF personnel remained until 1956.

Housing spread itself across Grangemouth from the west while the oil refinery extended from the banks of the Forth south towards the eastern side of the site. Eventually the two met and the airfield was gone. The original large pre-war hangars remain, and in a open area at Inchyra Park a small piece of the runway is in place. Grangemouth was elevated to the important role of training fighter pilots only to be swept away as if it had never existed. Thankfully, though, a memorial cairn was erected in 1994 in memory of the airfield's wartime role and the sacrifice made by those young pilots.

Main features:
Tarmac runways: QDM 278 1,400 yards, 222 1,100 yards. *Hangars:* two civil airport type, eight blister. *Hardstandings:* twenty. *Accommodation:* RAF: 388; WAAF: 206.

GRANTON HARBOUR, Edinburgh

NT240775

A detachment of seaplanes had been operating from Granton Harbour since 1914. This continued into 1915, but began to tail off by the end of the year. The occasional Beardmore-built seaplane also used Granton, but by 1916 the site was closed.

The name Granton is also associated with another of 77(HD) Squadron's LGs. If there was space available, this small LG would have been active between 1916 and 1918.

GREENCASTLE (CRANFIELD), Down

54°02'40"N/01°32'51"W; J285115. 2 miles SW of Kilkeel on unclassified road

Nestled below the Mourne Mountains close to the Republic should not the most ideal location for an airfield. However, this area of agricultural land was the location for a major airfield built to an A Class standard. This would warrant a minimum of 400 acres of land, which, despite a lot of hostility from the local people, began to be requisitioned from late 1941. Inadequate compensation was offered but proudly refused, and for those people affected in the area of Derryoge, Dunavil, Ballynahatten, Grange and Cranfield it was to be a grim time indeed. With no obligation to find them alternative accommodation, the Air Ministry gave people affected by the construction just three days to leave their homes before work began. There were cases of bulldozers demolishing homes as people tried to carry furniture out of the front door.

Construction began on 1 January 1942 and involved up to 1,300 workers. The airfield was set to become the home of a bomber OTU, but only days before it was due to open it was allocated to the USAAF. It was opened on 30 July, but it would be more than a year before the USAAF finally arrived on 3 August 1943, and Greencastle was designated as Station 237.

Now under control of the 8th AFCC, the first units to arrive were the 42nd DRS and the 42nd DSS. The latter only stayed a few weeks before moving to Langford Lodge on 30 August. The 42nd ADG HQ and HQ Squadron arrived not long after and both units remained here until they moved to Warton on 13 October 1943.

It was always the intention of the USAAF to house a CCRC here; there was already one operating in the province. The 2nd CCRC was already training air gunners but, with the activation of the 5th CCRC here in December, ground-to-air training could also be offered. The 5th CCRC specialised in training for the crews of the B-24, and many hundreds, possibly thousands, of gunners were destined to pass through here. The CCRC taught the skills needed for all gunnery and bombing techniques and, as its name suggests, also made up replacement crews for those lost in action, which, in the case of the 8th AF, were numerous. Greencastle was also a location where new crews could meet those who had already completed a full tour of operations, passing on their experience before continuing home to the United States.

On 26 February 1944 the 5th CCRC moved to Cheddington, but the same day the 4th Replacement & Training Squadron (Bomb) was formed to carry out the same task. This was joined by the 4th Gunnery & TTF, which was activated as an element of the 8th AFSC on 9 March. This flight added an aerial dimension to the training programme, which until now had been carried out on other airfields. The flight flew a variety of aircraft including the A-20, Lysander, A-35 and A-28, together with several P-47s for fighter affiliation exercises. Gunnery practice was carried out near Dundrum Bay, while bombing and air-to-air firing practice took place off Annalong and Ballymartin.

Following D-Day, Greencastle began a long and steady run-down, but this did not stop the 4th CCRC Group HQ and HQ Squadron being formed here on 15 August 1944. Gunnery training came to an end on 15 September when the gunnery flight moved to Chipping Ongar, and the 4th CCRC HQ and training squadron departed for Boreham.

Only a handful of 'Y'-type bomber dispersals and frying pan dispersals give away Greencastle's existence in 1992. Even less is visible today.

By this time Greencastle had become a satellite for Langford Lodge. Construction had been continuing to build more than 100 'Y'-type bomber standings on top of the dispersals already in place. Throughout the year a steady influx of B-17s and B-24s flew in to be prepared as replacements for those lost serving with the 8th AF. However, long-term open storage was out of the question owing to the airfield's proximity to the sea – aircraft and sea salt did not mix. The airfield was taken over by the 5th Airdrome Squadron in February 1945, by which time there were at least 320 aircraft dispersed here. These were all flown out by the time the war in Europe was over, and on 31 May Station 237 became RAF Greencastle again, but was closed not long after.

From this point Greencastle as an airfield was quickly eradicated from the history books, almost in retaliation for the hardships that it had caused to the local people. The fact that it trained thousands of American aircrew to fight above the clouds seems almost irrelevant. The control tower survived into the 21st century but has since been demolished. The only firm evidence of the airfield's existence today is a few 'Y'-type dispersals straddling Grange Road, while a few hundred yards north a handful of military buildings have been incorporated into a farm at the Lurganconary road junction.

Main features:
Concrete and wood chippings runways: QDM 080 2,000 yards, 140 1,400 yards, 030 1,400 yards. *Hangars:* four T2. *Hardstandings:* thirty loop, 100 'Y'-type for bombers. *Accommodation:* USAAF: 2,512.

GREENOCK (CAIRD'S YARD AND GOUROCK BAY), Renfrewshire

Caird's Yard: 55°57'02"N/04°45'24"W; NS285765. Greenock Docks

Gourock Bay: 55°57'34"N/04°48'00"W. E side of Gourock Bay, S of Ironotter Point

One of the busiest wartime ports in Scotland at the time, Greenock would not have seemed a natural location for a flying boat station. However, this is what was established here on 10 October 1940 when RAF Greenock was created as an FBSU.

Stranraers were the first customers, followed by Lerwicks from November 1940. Others, such as the Singapore, were also maintained here, and by December a 228 Squadron Sunderland became the first of this type to be seen here. A Catalina made an appearance in early 1941, followed by one of 'G' Flight's 'C' Class flying boats, which was being modified by Short Brothers.

The first flying boat to arrive at Greenock was Stranraer K7295 in November 1940.

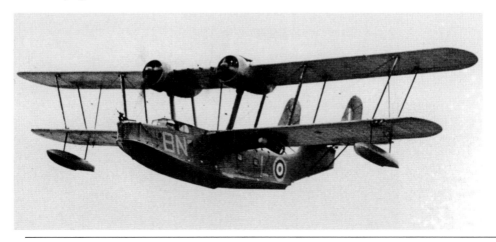

The flying boat station did not escape being damaged during the two nights of the Greenock Blitz on 6/7 May 1941. The Luftwaffe's main targets were the ships and shipyards, but it was the civilian population, thanks to some very erratic bombing, that took the brunt, with 280 people killed and more than 1,200 injured. RAF Greenock suffered a direct hit on a hangar and storage yard, destroying two Catalinas, a Sunderland and a Swordfish. A second slipway had been constructed further along the coast within the shelter of Gourock Bay, and not long after all aircraft were stored here in case of a further attack, which thankfully never came. Located south of Ironotter Point, several civilian flying boats continued to use Gourock into the early 1950s.

The CRO also operated from Greenock, with SAL carrying out the work. During 1941 this mainly consisted of preparing Catalinas for squadrons, a task that continued until 1944. By this time it was mainly Sunderlands being handled, one of the jobs being to convert the Mk III to Mk V standard.

Another unit created here was 2 FBSU on 25 September 1942. It was tasked with the maintenance of Catalinas from 190, 202 and 210 Squadrons, 1477 Flight, 302 FTU and 4 and 131 OTUs until it was disbanded in June 1945. Space was created for another unit, 8330 SE, which was detached from Oban in June 1943 to service 330 Squadron's Sunderlands at Greenock.

Sunderland conversions continued until 25 July 1945, when the last, ML819, left for Calshot. After only a few weeks the station was taken over by Maintenance Command, with 97 MU moving in from Ferryside on 15 August. This MCRU was disbanded into 213 MU on 1 October, which moved in from Dumbarton the same day. By 30 November 1947 213 MU had also disbanded, and RAF Greenock was closed not long after.

HATSTON, Orkney

58°57'29"N/02°54'18"W; HY435125. 1 mile NW of Kirkwall off A965

Hatston was another airfield that owed its existence to Capt Fresson, but unlike all the others this time it was chosen because of his advice. Fresson was approached in early 1939 by staff from the Admiralty who were looking for the best place to position an airfield on the Orkneys. Not only did he give them details of the area, but he also recommended that any runways laid should be made of tarmac. The reason for this was simply the weather: the winter rain would quickly render a grass airfield unserviceable.

Construction began in February 1939, and by the summer Hatston was ready to receive its first unit. On 26 August a Swordfish of X Flight from Evanton, flown by Lt Cdr Mortimer and TAG H. Davison, became the first of thousands of aircraft to land here. The flight was dissolved into 771 Squadron by late September and would continue to serve here until July 1942. On 27 August 800 Squadron with Skuas arrived from HMS *Ark Royal* to begin the first of many visits, being the first of sixty-five squadrons to fly from here.

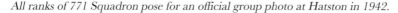

All ranks of 771 Squadron pose for an official group photo at Hatston in 1942.

By early October 1939 the Naval Co-Operation Unit was formed, and on 2 October the airfield was commissioned as HMS *Sparrowhawk*. Its main role throughout the entire war was to offer a shore base to front-line squadrons that were disembarking from ships moored in Scapa Flow.

The airfield was already into the routine of squadrons coming and going, so 803 Squadron's arrival from Wick on 10 February 1940 was nothing unusual. Five days later it was joined by 800 Squadron, which had embarked from HMS *Ark Royal* with Skuas and Rocs. Both units had already taken part in action over Norway, and as the German assault gained momentum against that country further contact with the enemy would occur. By April Germany was making great advances, and as part of Operation 'Weserübung' used its Navy to transport large numbers of soldiers from Wilhelmshaven to Bergen. Two of the ships involved were the *Bremse* and the light cruiser *Königsberg*, both of which had been damaged by Norwegian coastal guns on 9 April, causing them to remain in Bergen for repairs. News of the two ships' positions was reported back to the Admiralty, and by the early hours of the following morning both 800 and 803 Squadrons were prepared for an attack. Seven Skuas of 800 Squadron, led by Capt R. T. Partridge, and nine more from 803 Squadron, led by Lt Cdr W. P. Lucy, took off before dawn from Hatston and set course for Bergen harbour. Brimming with fuel and each carrying a single 500lb armour-piercing bomb, the Skuas struggled into the air before setting course for the 300-mile flight. The Norwegian coast was reached as planned and within just 1 minute of the ETA. The *Königsberg* was attacked by all sixteen Skuas, resulting in three direct hits that set the cruiser ablaze before it capsized into Bergen Harbour. The Skuas returned to Hatston after their 4½-hour flight having only lost one aircraft on their return trip. Both squadrons had earned themselves the distinction of becoming the first aircraft to sink a significant warship during the Second World War.

800 and 803 Squadrons left for HMS *Ark Royal* and HMS *Glorious* respectively on 22 April 1940, but both would return here many times. Another success story for Hatston occurred on 22 May thanks to Lt N. E. Goddard, CO of 771 Squadron. Close attention was being paid to the *Bismarck* at this time, and current intelligence had her moored in a fjord south of Bergen. Several squadrons, including one with Albacores loaded with torpedoes, were poised to attack the battleship as soon as news of her departure from the fjord was reported. Poor weather was keeping the RAF reconnaissance crews on the ground, but the FAA crews were impatient for news of the ship's whereabouts, so Lt Goddard and crew volunteered to fly one of the squadron's unarmed Marylands to look for it. The weather was so poor that Goddard was forced to make the flight only a few feet above the waves, but thanks to some excellent navigation he made landfall over the fjord where the *Bismarck* should be. However, the fjord was empty, as were the surrounding ones, and after a look in Bergen Harbour, followed by some unwelcome flak, it was clear that the battleship was now at sea. The news was too important to maintain radio silence, so the Maryland's TAG tried to contact Coastal Command, without success. Not to be deterred, the TAG called on a 771 Squadron frequency and made contact with another wireless operator, who was completely unaware of how important the signal was, but sent it on to the Fleet. Thanks to Goddard's flight, the Fleet was at sea and within days the *Bismarck* was sunk.

823 Squadron moved in from Evanton on 14 May 1940, following one of several detachments on HMS *Glorious*. The squadron returned to *Glorious* on 3 June, but their stay came to a premature end with her sinking at the hands of the *Scharnhorst* and *Gneisenau* on the 8th. Half of 823 Squadron was on board at the time, leaving just nine aircraft at Hatston. The suggestion of inflicting the same fate upon the *Scharnhorst* was probably received with enthusiasm, and on 21 June both 821 and 823 Squadrons prepared to carry out the first ever torpedo attack on a capital ship at sea. Intelligence had been received that the *Scharnhorst* was heading south, and a small strike force consisting of three Swordfishes from each squadron left Hatston to attack her. In clear weather, without a cloud in the sky, the Swordfishes found the *Scharnhorst* screened by several destroyers, which put up a barrage of anti-aircraft fire. The clear visibility had removed any element of surprise, but all pressed home their attacks although none of them struck the battleship, and all of the Swordfishes were hit by enemy fire. Two of them were shot down while the remaining four landed at Sumburgh to refuel and carry out temporary repairs before returning to Hatston.

Another glimpse of a Maryland in FAA service, once again with 771 Squadron. King George VI is carrying out an inspection of the squadron at Hatston.

Several training squadrons were based here during the war. 700 Squadron was formed on 21 January 1940 when the 700 series of Catapult squadrons were amalgamated. At first the squadron had more than forty Walruses and several Seafox and Swordfish floatplanes. The squadron acted as a pool and HQ for all catapult aircraft that embarked on battleships and cruisers, so there was never a quiet moment for the unit. By May 1942 there were more than sixty Walruses operating from Hatston and the squadron had by now outgrown it. 'A' Flight, which was made up of the squadron HQ and Training Flight, was moved to Twatt on 22 June 1942, but retained a presence at Hatston until the end of the war.

In a typical scene in Scapa Flow, Fulmars disembark from HMS Victorious *in October 1941 for some shore leave via Hatston.*

Another second-line unit that served here was 712 Squadron, which was re-formed on 2 August 1944. Created from 'B' Flight of 771 Squadron as a Communications Squadron, the unit flew a host of different types.

'A' Flight of 746 Squadron brought its Fireflies here from Ford for ADDLs and a pre-embarkation exercise prior to embarking on several different escort carriers. The latter included HMS *Smiter*, *Ravager*, *Premier* and *Searcher*, and only days before end of the war in Europe the flight became operational before returning to Ford on 10 May 1945.

The Meteorological Office at Hatston in 1943, with an Avenger poking its nose in on the right.

On 1 August the airfield was paid off, but the same day became HMS *Tern II*, now serving as a satellite to Twatt. Only 712 Squadron was serving here, and had been disbanded by 23 August 1945. Hatston's satellite days were destined to be short, and on 15 September the airfield was reduced to C&M and was paid off again.

Before the end of 1945 civilian flying had taken over and Hatston was now Kirkwall's new airport, with routes now under BEA control. The airline's Dakotas found Hatston a bit of squeeze, so in 1948 it moved its operations to the other side of the town. Hatston languished for several years before the Orkney Flying Club operated from here between 1953 and 1957, when flying ended, and it was not long before industry moved into the hangars, which still remain today. By comparison, only a handful of the many technical buildings survive.

Main features:
Runways: QDM 071-250 1,310 yards, 101-281 1,240 yards, 154-334 970 yards. *Hangars:* six squadron, one 185 x 105 feet, seven storage. *Accommodation:* RN: 435; WRNS: 174.

HAWKCRAIG, Fife

NT198838. SE of Aberdour

Positioned at the bottom of the cliffs on the western side of Hawkcraig Point, no unit was ever allocated to this seaplane station. Operations began as early as 1913 with the Baby and later the 184. A large tent-type hangar was constructed on the shoreline with its own slipway together with a few buildings behind it. One 184, N1650, served at Hawkcraig from 1918 and was still there by January 1919.

HELENSBURGH (RHU), Strathclyde

56°00'47"N/04°46'24"W; NS272834. Rhu Marina, 1½ miles SE of Rhu on A814

Located nearer to Rhu than Helensburgh, this flying boat station was established on the outbreak of war. It was created at short notice for the use of the MAEE, whose activities at Felixstowe were seen as far too close to the front line. The MAEE moved here on 21 September 1939.

On the day of the MAEE's arrival, a new flight was formed, the SD Flight, which would carry out trials in close co-operation with the MAEE. It operated the 'C' Class flying boat, which was impressed into RAF service at the outbreak of the war. Detached to Invergordon briefly in March 1940, the SD Flight moved to Bowmore on 25 December.

Thanks to the MAEE, Helensburgh saw a wide variety of flying boats during the war, including this Saro A.37 Shrimp moored in Gare Loch.

The MAEE was tasked with carrying out trials of new types of aircraft. The RAF's main flying boats, the Sunderland and Catalina, had long been evaluated, but as they were developed later marks flew their trials from Helensburgh. Both were seen on a regular basis, and a Lerwick was also trialled here in 1940. Slightly more exotic was a Bv 138, which was captured at Trondheim in 1940. Four Norwegian Navy He 115s were given the same treatment after their crews had escaped the fall of their country. As the war progressed and more US-built machines entered the war, single examples of a Mariner and a Coronado were here in 1943.

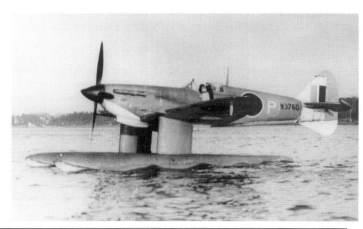

Another interesting trial carried out by the MAEE was the idea of putting floats on a Spitfire. W3760 is seen under test at Helensburgh in late 1942.

Every mark of Sunderland passed through the MAEE at Helensburgh during the Second World War. This is Mk V PP105 on Gare Loch, off Rhu in November 1944.

Exactly one year after the MAEE arrived, another new unit was formed in the shape of 'G' Flight. It was created to operate three S.26 'G' Class flying boats on patrols over the Atlantic. These once graceful peacetime passenger-carrying aircraft were now drably painted in camouflage and modified with gun turrets. By 26 November 1940 'G' Flight had moved to Stranraer.

During 1940 the flying boat station was transferred to the MAP. This did not affect the activities of the MAEE, which was a law unto itself. With the war at an end, the MAEE returned to Felixstowe on 1 August 1945, but Helensburgh remained under MAP control. On 24 August 62 MU moved in from Dumbarton to carry out the maintenance and storage of RAF craft. The unit remained at Helensburgh until 30 November 1947, and not long after this important station was closed.

HOPRIG MAINS (PENSTON/TRANENT), East Lothian

55°56'07"N/02°,52'49"W; NT446736. W of B6363 near Butterdean Wood

During the First World War an LG at Penston served 77(HD) Squadron between late 1916 and 1918. The site was viewed again during the late 1920s for potential use as an airfield. The Edinburgh Flying Club eventually settled for an area of land slightly north, referring to the new airfield as Tranent. The small grass airfield, which was located approximately 14 miles east of Edinburgh, opened in 1929 and, while known as Macmerry, was also referred to as Tranent or Penston throughout its history.

HOUTON BAY (including ORPHIR), Orkney

58°55'01"N/03°11'03"W. E and W of Houton Bay, 10 miles SW of Kirkwall off A964

Houton Bay was the largest Seaplane and Kite Balloon Station constructed on the Orkney mainland during the Great War. It covered from Quoy of Houton in the west through the Houths to Midland Ness in the east, surrounding the Bay of Houton. The harbour was perfect for seaplane operations, with the protection of the Holm of Houton.

Construction began in 1916 and buildings included three seaplane sheds, two slipways and its own jetty. It also had an engineer's workshop, a carpenter, tinsmith and blacksmith. It even had its own meteorological section, engine store, test house, butcher and tailor for the 350-plus personnel that served here.

By late 1917 various aircraft, including the H.16, F.2 and F.3, were stationed here on the hunt for enemy U-boats, which were now forced to travel around Scotland because huge nets had been strung across the English Channel.

Felixstowe F.3 N4403 of 306 Flight at Houton Bay in late 1918.

The first of several seaplane and flying boat flights was formed on 30 May 1918; this was 430 Flight, which was created from the station's 'War Flight' flying the 184. 306 Flight followed on 31 July with a variety of aircraft.

'F' Boat STF was another unit formed here on 15 August 1918, with the F.3. It was intended to move to Calshot as part of 210 TDS, but this never happened and its personnel and aircraft were disbanded into Houton's own strength by 25 November.

Even after the war, units continued to be formed, including Orkney Wing, which only lasted from June to 27 October 1919. The previous month, both 306 and 430 Flights had been disbanded, leaving Houton in a temporary state of flux. This lasted until 16 March 1920 when the station was retitled as RAF Practice Base (Houton Bay), using aircraft that had been on Houton's establishment. By 1921 this once busy seaplane station had no further purpose or role to play in peacetime, and was closed by September.

One of many Felixstowe F.2As that served at Houton Bay was N4517, pictured in late 1918.

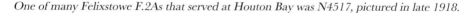

INCHINNAN, Strathclyde/Renfrewshire

55°53'01"M/04°26'22"W; NS476684. 1 mile NW of Renfrew off A8

In late 1915 Beardmore's won a contract to build a large naval airship, and to carry out this work a new airship shed was built south of the Dalmuir shipyard at Inchinnan. Work began on the building in January 1916 and was completed by September. At the time it was one of Scotland's largest buildings, measuring 720 feet in length, 230 feet across and 122 feet high, covering 320 acres. The shed was steel-framed and clad with galvanised steel sheeting. Its massive sliding doors were counter-balanced with hundreds of tons of concrete to prevent from being blown over. The first airship built here was the R.24, followed by the R.27 and the more famous R.34.

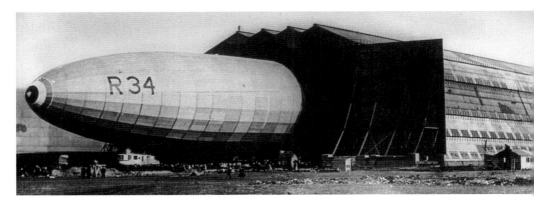

The 643-foot-long R 34 emerges from the giant 720-foot-long airship shed at Inchinnan for the first time in March 1919.

In 1917 No 6 AAP was moved here, having been formed as the Glasgow AAP for the acceptance of locally built aircraft, including Cuckoos built by Fairfield and DH.9s and FE.2bs built by W. & J. Weir. Beardmore-built aircraft were also here, but were test-flown at Dalmuir. On 12 October 1917 the unit was renamed No 6 (Glasgow) AAP until it moved to Renfrew on 10 March 1918.

With the AAP gone and no more orders for new airships, the site was closed down just after the end of the war. The giant shed lingered on for a few years, but in 1923 was sold off and reduced to scrap.

INVERKEITHING BAY, Fife

During the 1930s the RAF established a seaplane station east of Inverkeithing Bay, probably in connection with Donibristle. Built with six mooring places, it was not in use a great deal, but 948 (Balloon) Squadron was here from October 1939 to early 1942. The site was later soaked up by the sprawl of Donibristle, whose dispersals extended all the way down to the bay.

JOHNSTON CASTLE (WEXFORD), County Wexford

52°17'44"N/06° 30'29"W; T020165. 4 miles SW of Wexford town

Located in the grounds of Johnston Castle, the peace was occasionally shattered by the drone of airship engines.

Operational from January 1916, an area positioned west of the Castle's lake was used as a Mooring Out Station by the USN, with Pembroke as the parent. It remained in this role until the end of the war and was not decommissioned until July 1920.

KAYSHILL, Ayrshire

55°29'N/04°27'W

Originally intended as an SLG for 18 MU, work was abandoned in 1941. However, it must have reached an advanced stage, as it was used by the MU for dispersal of several aircraft in 1942.

KIDSDALE (BURROW HEAD), Dumfries and Galloway/Wigtownshire

LG: 54°42'7"N/04°25'4"W; NX44303687. E of Kidsdale approached via Arbrack off A747

AAPC: 54°41'00"N/04°24'15"W. Due S of Cutcloy, 2 miles SW of Isle of Whitehorn

This small aerodrome was located at the southern tip of The Machars peninsula and was split into two camps, one known as Kidsdale, the other Burrow Head. The latter was not really an airfield but a launching area for Queen Bee target aircraft. The camp extended from Cutloy down to the cliff edge between Castle Feather and Ducker Rock, and was developed into a maze of roadways with several technical buildings and positions for anti-aircraft guns.

Opened on 8 May 1939, Burrow Head's first occupant was 'W' Flight of 1 AACU from Henlow, with the Queen Bee. The resident unit at Burrow Head was 2 HAAPC, whose main role was the training of anti-aircraft crews. The HQ of 'W' Flight was moved to Kidsdale on 1 December, where the sight of Battle and Henley target tugs was a regular occurrence.

De Havilland Queen Bee N1837 is on its launcher at Kidsdale in early 1939. The aircraft crashed off Burrow Head on 20 July 1939.

By late March 1942 the number of serviceable Queen Bees had reached a critical level; the vast majority of 'W' Flight's stock had by now either crashed or been shot down into the sea. On 18 April 'W' Flight was disbanded, and 2 HAAPC at Burrow Head was closed down not long after.

Only one RAF squadron was recorded as making Kidsdale its home during its short history. This was 651 Squadron, with Taylorcrafts and Austers, which arrived from Dumfries on 11 August 1942; by 30 October it had left via Gourock for North Africa.

Offered to the Admiralty in late 1942, Kidsdale was briefly considered for expansion into fighter or TBR training. Expansion was possible but costly, and its proximity to existing aerial and bombing ranges was enough to put off the Royal Navy.

Kidsdale came under the charge of the War Department from 25 November 1943 and no further flying took place. The technical site at Kidsdale was converted into one of two DECTRA stations in the UK, with a 600-foot mast. When DECTRA was shut down, the giant mast was re-used and Kidsdale became the DECCA North British master station.

Today, thanks to Kidsdale's post-war use, a large proportion of the site is still preserved, while Burrow Head is now a caravan park. The vast majority of the latter's road network, together with several original buildings, is also still in place.

KILCONQUHAR, Fife

56°12'28"N/02°50'23"W; NO478020. Due S of Kilconquhar Loch

Kilconquhar was a 3rd Class LG for 77(HD) Squadron from May 1918 to May 1919. Facilities were sparse on this level piece of land, south-east of Broomlees Farm.

KILKENNY, Kilkenny

S5??5??

This small LG was used by the RAF from April 1921. By 1922 it was either closed down or most likely was passed to IAAC control.

KILLADEAS, Fermanagh

54°25'23"N/07°41'05"W; H205525. 5 miles N of Enniskillen off B82 at Gusblusk Bay

A new flying boat station on the shores of Lough Erne had been in the planning since May 1941. Despite this, 240 Squadron is credited with serving at Killadeas from 28 March to 23 August with its Catalinas, several months before the station was supposed to have been commissioned by the USN. 240 Squadron then moved to Lough Erne (the former Castle Archdale).

This shoreline flying boat station then stood empty, awaiting the arrival of the USN. However, it never came and the station was taken over by the RAF in June 1942, while the remaining buildings were taken over by the US Army.

Coastal Command took over in late June, and on 20 July a new unit, 131 (C)OTU, was formed to train crews on the Catalina. The unit's SHQ was located at St Angelo and the OTU's target tugs and later its fighters were also based there. The OTU's strength increased in September 1943, when the Catalina element from 4 (C)OTU at Alness was taken over, centralising the type's training to just Killadeas.

The Sunderland was introduced from May 1944, and to help cope a satellite mooring area was established at Boa Island on the 31st. This proved very useful for the larger aircraft and remained in use until 1 March 1945.

On 1 May 1944 12 (Operational) FIS was established at St Angelo to train former operational pilots for instructor duties. Part of this task involved the Catalina and Sunderland, and 131 OTU's aircraft were used. 12 (O)FIS was renamed the CCFIS in February 1945, by now only flying Sunderlands.

Peak establishment for 131 OTU was reached in early 1945 with twenty-nine Catalinas and twenty-two Sunderlands. The Sunderland commitment was transferred to 4 (C)OTU on 13 February 1945 and, with their departure, the pace at Killadeas began to slow.

Before the end of the war 302 FTU from Oban made Killadeas its home from 15 April. Tasked with training crews to ferry flying boats overseas, the FTU operated the Catalina and Sunderland, and its ground personnel were accommodated during their tenure at Killadeas.

With the war over in Europe, the Catalina was taken out of service, and with that 131 (C)OTU was disbanded on 28 June. The activities of the CCFIS came to an end here simultaneously and, to bring the station to a clinical end, 302 FTU left for Alness on 1 July.

This excellent view of the shoreline flying boat station at Killadeas in 1944 includes a 131 OTU Sunderland for scale.

Sunderland III W6066 sits on a cold Lough Erne in 1944. This aircraft had already served with 246 and 422 Squadrons, so was no stranger to the lough.

On an even colder Lough Erne groundcrew battle to stop the thick ice from crushed the hulls of the comparatively fragile Sunderland.

A 302 FTU Sunderland V rests after a sortie on Lough Erne in early 1945. Via Bill McConnell

It was not quite the end, however, as 272 MU was formed here on 1 August, its role being a Flying Boat Long Term Storage Unit with a sub-site at St Angelo. There was very little storage carried out, but rather disposal, before the unit's duty was completed on 28 February 1947, bringing Killadeas's military history to an end.

By 1950 the Lough Erne Yacht Club had taken over the site, making use of the slipways, moorings and a single hangar, all of which remain today. The nearby Manor House, which was requisitioned as the SHQ, also remains, now operating as a hotel. Other details, such as the original flagstaff with a 131 OTU memorial stone at its base and a pair of flying boat mooring blocks, add the final touches to the memory of Killadeas.

KINLOSS, Moray/Grampian

57°38'57"N/03°33'38"W; NH070630. 3 miles NE of Forres off B9089

Kinloss was one of the busiest airfields in the UK. Although earmarked at an early stage for a training unit, the designers had the foresight to lay out the airfield as per a bomber station.

Kinloss was opened on 1 April 1939 and 14 FTS was formed the same day with Oxfords. Training was in full swing by the summer, with other types such as the Harvard, Anson, Hart and Audax also being used.

14 FTS flew several Harts during its time at Kinloss, including K6417 '18'.

With the beginning of the war, 14 FTS was renamed 14 SFTS, and during October and November, and again in January 1940, it flew armament training detachments at 8 APC. A pair of RLGs at Rose Valley and Waterside were planned but not built before a decision on the future and location of 14 SFTS was made. With the invasion of Norway in April 1940, the SFTS was moved to Cranfield, and on 19 April Kinloss belonged to Bomber Command.

Bomber squadrons, in particular 10, 51, 77 and 102, all flying the Whitley, had already been using Kinloss for detachments and exercises. The detachments continued after the war, beginning with 49 Squadron's Hampdens from Scampton and 50 Squadron from Waddington, flying from here on operations from late 1939.

On 6 April 1940 Kinloss gained another unit that grew into the largest on the airfield and continued to operate for many years after the end of the war. 45 MU was formed primarily for the preparation of new aircraft direct from the manufacturer. It was not until May that the first of thousands of aircraft began to arrive, starting with a batch of Oxfords. During June 45 MU's presence here was already having an impact, not only with the increase in personnel but also with the construction of extra hangars and buildings. By early 1941 the MU had grown even more, eventually occupying eleven hangars. Extended dispersals and perimeter tracks were built and more fields were requisitioned. Even with all this additional space, 45 MU needed SLGs to cope. The first was 41 SLG in August, followed by 40 SLG in September. A third at Brackla was inspected in late 1944 but not taken over until February 1945. During the post-war period 45 MU was by far the busiest unit here, with emphasis now on disposal. During 1946 there were more than 1,000 surplus aircraft awaiting the axe, but the unit's original task would be reinstated when it began to receive and prepare Lincolns for squadron service. The Canberra followed in 1951 and the Hunter and Sabre in 1952. After handling thousands of aircraft, 45 MU was disbanded on 15 January 1957.

Another long-term resident was 19 OTU. Established on 27 May 1940, it was formed to train night-bomber crews on the Whitley. Course No 1 began on 15 June and was completed on 29 July, with the first crews being posted to 78 Squadron at Dishforth.

Whitley V Z6665 had along association with Kinloss, beginning with a detachment from 51 Squadron in 1939 in which it incurred this damage. The Whitley was then transferred to 19 OTU before being transferred to 42 OTU, only to be written off after a taxiing accident in February 1945.

The New Year also brought expansion for 19 OTU when it gained a satellite at Forres in January 1941. The unit was now split into four flights, 'A' and 'B' operating from here and 'C' and 'D' from Forres. The SLG came in very useful only days after it opened because poor weather had rendered Kinloss's runways almost useless and the majority of flights were carried out from Forres over the following weeks.

The OTU could grow again when a second SLG was made available at Brackla in January 1942. Whitley strength remained well above fifty and, despite Bomber Command flying its last operation over Ostend in April with the type, it did not look like the OTU would be giving up its examples for the foreseeable future.

The airfield played host to another heavy bomber operation in early 1942 when the Halifaxes of 35 Squadron arrived from Linton-on-Ouse on 30 March. The target was the *Tirpitz* and, of the thirty-four Halifaxes taking part in the raid, twelve would depart from Kinloss, joining with 10 Squadron flying from Lossiemouth and 76 Squadron from Tain. The *Tirpitz* was supposed to be located in a fjord near Trondheim at the time, but the force failed to find her and only three aircraft managed to bomb a few flak positions. Six aircraft failed to return, claiming the lives of all forty-two aircrew. Three of the aircraft belonged to 35 Squadron.

35 Squadron returned for a second attack on the *Tirpitz* and other German warships that were believed to have congregated in Trondheim fjord on 27 April 1942. On this occasion thirty-one Halifaxes took part, joined by twelve Lancasters flying from Lossiemouth. This time the *Tirpitz* was found but, despite all forty-three aircraft dropping their bombs, no hits were scored. Five bombers were lost, including two more from 35 Squadron. The squadron took part in its final attack on the *Tirpitz* on 28/29 April. This time hits were claimed, but not confirmed, much to the frustration of a unit that had sacrificed a great deal on this target.

19 OTU played its own small part in Bomber Command operations when it was called to arms to help make up the numbers for the third and final '1,000-bomber' raid. In fact, only 960 aircraft in total were made available for the attack on Bremen on 25/26 June 1942, twelve of them from 19 OTU. Operating from Abingdon, only one of Kinloss's aircraft failed to return.

By mid-1944 19 OTU had expected to begin a steady wind-down in a similar vein to other training units of this type. However, instead of facing disbandment the OTU's Whitleys were to be replaced by Wellingtons. The first are thought to have arrived as early as June, but it was not until August that they appeared here in numbers. Most were in no better condition than the Whitleys, but the OTU soldiered on regardless, flying both types until at least October. In fact, it was while serving here that the last Whitley in Bomber Command was lost, on 17 October, when AD685 broke up over Seaham harbour. This was also the last of 111 Whitleys lost by 19 OTU since May 1940. To put this figure in context, the unit lost a total of 124 aircraft, the others made up of Lysanders, Ansons and finally Wellingtons.

A very busy Kinloss, with at least 200 aircraft visible, in shown in this late war aerial view. 19 OTU's Wellingtons appear to be concentrated in front of the main hangar line, while the aircraft of 45 MU are scattered all around the perimeter.

By early 1945 the pace had slowed and the final course passed out on 25 May, the majority of the crews joining 4 Group. The last daylight exercise flown by the unit took place on 1 May and the last night cross-country on 13 June. In typical clinical fashion, 19 OTU was disbanded three days later. No more profound slogan than 'Survive OTU and you will survive the war' could be applied to those who passed through Kinloss.

A visiting 210 Squadron Neptune MR.1 at Kinloss in 1954.

Another training unit was installed from 18 July 1945 when 6 COTU moved in from Thornaby. Initially the unit was training crews on the Warwick, but from July 1946 the Lancaster ASR began to arrive. Twelve months later the unit was redesignated 236 OCU, going on to train crews on the Neptune and Shackleton. By 1956 the OCU was combined with 1 MRS to form the MOTU, which continued to train on the Shackleton and introduce the Nimrod.

120 Squadron served at Kinloss with the Shackleton MR.3 from the late 1950s, later converting to the Nimrod from 1970. The squadron disbanded at Kinloss in April 2010 pending the arrival of the Nimrod MRA.4 – unfortunately the project was cancelled.

A Nimrod MR.2 of the Kinloss Wing flies over the station in the early 1990s.

120 Squadron, which first arrived in late 1949, had been permanently established here since April 1959 and was preparing to operate the Nimrod MRA.4. Another long-serving Kinloss resident was 201 Squadron, which first arrived in March 1965, operating the Shackleton MR.3. Two marks of Nimrods followed and, like 120 Squadron, it was also preparing for the MRA.4. However, infamously harsh defence cuts saw the cancellation of the MRA.4 only weeks before it was due to arrive here.

All flying operations are due to cease here in the summer of 2011, and closure of Kinloss as an RAF station will follow on 31 March 2013.

Main features:
Concrete and tarmac runways: QDM 263 2,000 yards, 208 1,400 yards, 321 1,400 yards. *Hangars:* nine L, two K, two Bellman. *Hardstandings:* forty-two heavy bomber. *Accommodation:* RAF: 2,385; WAAF: 554.

Kinloss in the mid-1990s still had a reasonably secure future, although even by this stage the resident Nimrods were ready for replacement.

KINNELL, Tayside

56°39'06"N/02°38'17"W. 1 mile NE of Friockheim, due N of Kinnell

Construction of a satellite for Tealing began in mid-1941 and was ready by early 1942. Built with fighters in mind, the airfield had two runways and limited facilities.

Flying began on 29 March 1942 when four Lysanders from 56 OTU were based here. This unit was tasked with training fighter pilots on the Hurricane, and as the training course developed Kinnell was increasingly used. The final three weeks of the course was now used for exercises, all of which were flown from here. Because of its proximity to hills, night-flying practice could not be carried out at Tealing, so from 16 September this part of the syllabus was flown here, and later on at least five hours in the circuit would be needed to complete the course.

56 OTU was redesignated as 1 CTW on 5 October 1943 and initially very little changed here. Reorganised into squadrons, 1 Squadron was to serve at Kinnell, specialising in air-to-air firing and evasive manoeuvre training. It was during the CTW period that Spitfires were seen for the first time here, although the original Hurricanes still soldiered on.

Another redesignation came on 1 January 1944 when the CTW became 1 TEU and a fighter-bomber element was introduced. 1 Squadron's original tasking remained the same, though, until the TEU was disbanded on 31 July after many of its pupil pilots had served during the Allied invasion of Europe the previous month.

Kinnell lay quiet for a few weeks, awaiting its next resident. It was another training role for the airfield, as it was allocated to 9 PAFU at Errol on 1 September as an RLG. Whether the PAFU found the airfield unsuitable is not clear, but by 13 September ownership had been transferred to 'G' Flight of 2 FIS, flying the Oxford. Making very little demand of what Kinnell had to offer, 'G' left on 11 July 1945 and the airfield's brief flying days were over.

Maintenance Command took over on 21 August 1945 when Kinnell became a satellite for 44 MU. The ASU used Kinnell until May 1946, although it also became a sub-site for 260 MU. The date of the unit's departure is unclear, but by the end of July 1948 it had disbanded at Errol so it can be presumed that Kinnell was closed not long after.

The unusual Type 3156/41 watch office is all that gives away Kinnell's aviation past today. A minor road that now dissects the site is a good viewpoint and, although difficult to see at ground level, both runways remain intact albeit covered in sheds and farming paraphernalia.

Main features:
Asphalt runways: QDM 153 1,400 yards, 108 1,100 yards. *Hangars:* four EO blister. *Accommodation:* RAF: 667; WAAF: 65.

KIRKANDREWS, Dumfries and Galloway

55°03'N/03°01'W

It is very difficult to position where this small SLG was thanks to the terrain in this area. It would not have been large, as its only customer was the Tiger Moths of 15 EFTS.

KIRKCOLM (CORSEWALL), Dumfries and Galloway

54°57'11"N/05°04'05"W

Loch Ryan was a busy flying boat harbour. The slipway here, for major engineering work, is huge, and dwarfs the modest yacht club that now uses it. There are remains of camp buildings along the shore.

KIRKISTOWN, Down

54°27'20N/05°28'09"W. At Kirkistown off B173

Only 5 miles south of its parent, Kirkistown was opened as a satellite to Ballyhalbert in July 1941. Intended to house fighter squadrons, it would be another six months before this would occur. It was 12 January 1942 when the first Spitfires arrived from Ballyhalbert with 504 Squadron. Flying convoy patrols, mixed with the odd scramble, the squadron returned on 19 June without making contact with the enemy.

On 28 February 1942 the airfield it was offered to the USAAF, and allocated to the 8th AF as a fighter station from 4 June. No significant activity took place, and by April 1943 the lease had expired and the airfield was back under RAF control. Once again it was allocated as a tactical fighter base from 12 July, but was never used. By 1944 USAAF visitors were prevalent and several aircraft, ranging from C-47s to B-24s, passed through either to check where they were or make an emergency landing.

Spitfires returned on 24 October 1942 with 485 Squadron from King's Cliffe. The squadron still took part in several convoy patrols but had been moved to Eglinton by 5 November. Little did it know, even in this stage of the war, they it already become the last RAF flying unit to serve here.

It was now the turn of the FAA, which arrived with 887 Squadron on 4 November 1942. Flying the Fulmar, the squadron was joined by another FAA fighter unit, 'B' 881 Squadron from Donibristle operating the Martlet. During the following month both squadrons flew several convoy patrols, but by 19 December both had left, 887 Squadron to Lee-on-Solent and 811 back to Donibristle. Clearly both squadrons preferred to spend Christmas at more comfortable stations!

The first of two Swordfish squadrons, 818, arrived on 2 December 1942 from Machrihanish, but like its fighter colleagues it was off back before the festive season began. This left just 835 Squadron, which also arrived from Machrihanish on 18 December. It remained here with its Swordfishes until 29 January 1943, when it returned to Machrihanish.

881 Squadron returned briefly on 30 December, only to return to Donibristle six days later. After this brief flurry of FAA activity, Kirkistown fell silent for several months before a completely different role was found for it.

The FAA did return when 808 and 885 Squadrons, both flying Seafires, arrived on 21 August 1944. They were here to practice ADDLs and it is assumed that a simulated aircraft carrier deck was painted onto one of the runways while the Seafires carried out circuits and bumps in 'Clockwork Mouse' fashion. A bombing target was also built on the airfield, but the FAA was encouraged to use the local Gransha Point range instead after a few wayward bombs started punching holes in a runway. Both Seafire squadrons left on 1 September for Hawarden.

The RAF Regiment training continued until 11 May 1945 when it was moved to Newtownards. Once again dormant, the airfield was transferred to Admiralty charge on 14 July and commissioned three days later as HMS *Corncrake II*, again as a satellite for Ballyhalbert. This was

Race School Ireland's circuit is clear in this aerial view of Kirkistown taken in 1992.

to be short-lived, though, as the airfield was paid off on 15 January 1946 and placed under RAF control until it was closed, having seen no more activity, in 1952.

Kirkistown is now home to Race School Ireland and is licensed to host events for bikes, cars and karts, making use of almost a third of the airfield on the northern side. This unintentionally preserves the section while the remainder is extant, but has been steadily reclaimed. Numerous buildings still survive scattered around, from the ubiquitous pillbox to the officers' toilet block! I wonder if the junior ranks' toilets were not as well built.

Main features:
Tarmac runways: QDM 222 1,300 yards, 280 1,160 yards, 341 1,000 yards. *Hangars:* four blister. *Hardstandings:* thirty-four frying pan (fighter), six double dispersal pens. *Accommodation:* RAF: 1,319.

KIRKNEWTON, West Lothian

55°52'27"N/03°24'05"W. 2 miles SW of Balerno between B7031 and A70

Kirknewton was brought into use as an LG in late 1940 and, at 652 feet above sea level, was one of the highest airfields in Scotland. Work began in early 1941 and by October the airfield was ready. Kirknewton was then placed under the control of 32 Wing, whose role was to control all Army Co-operation units in Scotland, including those destined to be posted here.

During October 1940 13 Group AACF arrived from Dalcross with Blenheims, Lysanders and Hurricanes. On 17 November the unit became 289 Squadron, while still retaining its original aircraft. By March 1942 the squadron only operated the Hurricanes, but also gained Oxfords and Defiants. It worked with various Army units and anti-aircraft batteries throughout southern Scotland and northern England. On 20 May 289 Squadron moved to Turnhouse, but the airfield was not quiet for long.

Three days later 32 Wing relinquished control to FTC, and 1 RFTS arrived from Moreton Valence operating Oxfords, Masters and Tutors. The school's lifespan was short, however, as the training policy changed and it was disbanded on 31 October 1942.

The airfield, after only being open for seven months, was placed under C&M until 6 March 1943. Two days later it became a satellite for Findo Gask, and on the same day 309 Squadron arrived with Lysanders and Mustangs. With three fully operational flights of Mustangs available, the squadron departed on 3 June for Snailwell, and the airfield reverted to C&M, still under FTC control, despite the earlier activities of 309 Squadron.

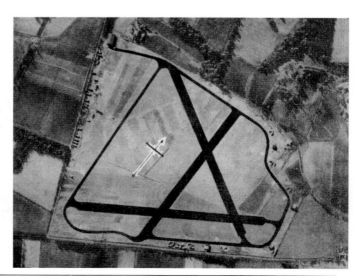

The aerial view of Kirknewton in July 1943 shows its compact layout and few technical buildings, the majority located on the western edge. Via A. P. Ferguson

Air Ministry officials arrived on 18 August 1943 to investigate whether the airfield could be expanded, but any plans were quickly shelved. It was not until 13 December that a more serious investigation took place into the future of the airfield, when staff from 42 Group inspected it to investigate whether it was suitable for the storage of explosive and non-explosive stores.

The survey must have been favourable because on 10 February 1944 243 MU was formed as an AAP and, over a short period of time, the amount of stores here rose rapidly. Despite there being more than 100 RAF personnel working at the MU, by the beginning of May more were needed, and they arrived from an unexpected source – 195 Italian 'Co-operators' arrived from the RAF Italian Holding Unit based at Hednesford.

Grangemouth became a satellite on 1 November 1944 with a view to expanding 243 MU's storage capability. After the war the MU gained a second sub-site at Fordoun, from 1 August 1947 to 30 September 1950. The Grangemouth site, together with 243 MU, closed on 7 January 1952.

Control of the airfield was passed to the USAF not long after 243 MU's departure. From May 1952 it became the home of the 37th RSM. Aerials of various types were erected, all tasked with intercepting Morse signals with emphasis being placed on Soviet radar and air operations. The 37th RSM later became the 6952nd RSM, all under the control of USAFSS, until the units closed in August 1966. The airfield was also home to the 7535th Air Base Squadron, which used it for storage.

Passed back to the Air Ministry, one unit returned on 2 April 1967 when 661 VGS was re-formed. Originally the unit operated the Cadet, but today it is equipped with the Viking.

It always comes as a pleasant surprise to see that the RAF still has a presence in the most unusual of places. RAF Kirknewton is still very much active today thanks to the presence of 661 VGS. Author

Still firmly in the hands of the MoD, Kirknewton remains the home of 661 VGS and will be for the foreseeable future. Very few original wartime buildings remain, the most significant exceptions being a pair of blister hangars and a Bellman, which protects 661 VGS's aircraft from the elements.

Main features:
Tarmac runways: QDM 182 1,100 yards, 060 1,100 yards, 002 945 yards. *Hangars:* one Bellman, four blister. *Accommodation:* RAF: 168.

KIRKPATRICK, Dumfries and Galloway

55°01'11"N/03°10'17"W; NY250700. 1 mile SW of Kirkpatrick-Fleming, N of Flosh

The small RLG near Kirkpatrick was born from the needs of 15 EFTS, whose home at Carlisle (Kingstown) was not ideal; it suffered from poor drainage, and the EFTS's workload could only be fulfilled with at least two extra LGs.

The first at Burnfoot was opened in July 1940, and Kirkpatrick was brought into use on 24 November. Initially 15 EFTS flew the Magister, which was later replaced by the Tiger Moth. Night-flying was implemented here from July 1941 and continued until it closed on 9 July 1945.

A 15 EFTS Magister prepares for a training sortie in a scene that would have been commonplace at Kirkpatrick.

Several wooden huts, including the original Flight Office, survived into the early 1980s, but sadly today there is nothing to indicate the airfield's aviation past.

Main features:
Grass runways: QDM NW-SE 1,200 yards, SW-NE 1,200 yards. *Hangars:* 3 Standard Blister, 2 EO Blister. *Accommodation:* 126 RAF.

KIRKTON (GOLSPIE), Highland

NH805985. 2 miles S of Golspie, E of A9 near Kirkton

Kirkton was 45 MU's most northerly SLG, located on open land, exposed to the sea on its eastern border, and hemmed in by the Mound and Silver Rock to the west. Despite these natural hazards, work began in early 1941. There was very little natural cover, other than Balbalir Wood to the south, which would serve as a useful dispersal area.

Probably owing to its distance from the parent unit, more buildings than usual were constructed at Kirkton in an effort to make life a little more bearable for those who served here. Accommodation was mainly centred on Kirkton House next to the A9, although more huts were constructed not too far from the beach, which were used by the RAF Regiment detachment that defended the SLG.

Designated as 41 SLG, it was inspected in May 1941 by 45 MU, which found it satisfactory, taking over on 1 September. The first aircraft were Whitleys and Spitfires, followed by Wellingtons and Havocs in June 1942.

By late 1942 through to early 1943 the SLG began storing four-engined types. From March 1943 the Halifax began to be stored here and Kirkton's capacity rose from fifty to seventy aircraft. By 1944 Kirkton was storing Harvards, and by early 1945 also several Warwicks.

During January 1945 the more conveniently positioned Brackla was also taken over by 45 MU for open storage of its aircraft. From February arrivals at Kirkton virtually stopped, and for the remainder of the war all traffic was now departing. Replaced by 102 SLG at Brackla on 14 March, Kirkton was derequisitioned on 7 May.

Kirkton lay empty for a short period before it became a camp for Italian POWs. German POWs followed, and many of them worked on local farms and later stayed in the area. Golspie football team had at least three German players in its line-up, one of them later marrying a local girl.

Only a single-track concrete road, with the odd enlarged dispersal branching from it, gives away Kirkton's position today. Recently a bungalow-type watch office, which was made of red brick, rather than local stone, was demolished.

KIRKWALL (GRIMSETTER), Orkney

58°57'29"N/02°54'18"W; HY480085. 2½ miles SE of Kirkwall off A960

Kirkwall started its days as a Fighter Sector Station, and despite opening on 17 October 1940 it would be more than eighteen months before a squadron would move in. The operations room that was built for this purpose was known locally as the 'Black Building', and still remains a landmark today.

Unlike most sector stations, Kirkwall served as a satellite for Skeabrae until the arrival of 132 Squadron on 11 June 1942, which operated Spitfires on convoy escorts before leaving for Martlesham Heath on 23 September. Two days later the task was taken over by 129 Squadron's Spitfires from Thorney Island. The squadron's duties involved a detachment to Sumburgh and Skeabrae, before leaving for the latter on 19 January 1943. The same day 234 Squadron's Spitfires moved in from Perranporth.

234 Squadron was the last RAF fighter unit to serve at Kirkwall in 1943.

In the meantime the first of many FAA units had arrived; 800 Squadron brought its Sea Hurricanes from Machrihanish, only to return on 12 March 1943. 234 Squadron became the last RAF fighter unit, moving to Skeabrae on 24 April. 884 Squadron passed through on 5 May with its Seafires before heading to Turnhouse one week later. Already earmarked for use by the Admiralty, the final RAF unit to use Kirkwall was 1476 Flight with its Ansons, between 7 and 25 June.

On 6 July 1943 Kirkwall was transferred to the Royal Navy, and on 15 August became HMS *Robin*. Avengers then began arriving with 846 Squadron from Hatston. Two more Avenger-equipped units followed, 848 Squadron from Ayr and 849 Squadron from Speke; the latter had left for Maydown by mid-February 1944. Sixteen FAA squadrons passed through during 1944, equipped with the full range of Royal Navy types including the Swordfish, Firefly, Corsair, Seafire, Wildcat, Hellcat and Barracuda. Arrivals declined from early 1945 onwards, with just a pair of Seafire squadrons and two Wildcat units passing through; the last, 882 Squadron, left for HMS *Searcher* on 27 April. Kirkwall remained under Royal Navy control until it was paid off and transferred to 13 Group on 31 July.

Prior to this, the RAF had already laid claim to Kirkwall, establishing Fighter Sector HQ, 13 Group, here on 1 July 1944. By November the unit was renamed as Orkney's Sector HQ, but it was to be short-lived as it was disbanded on 8 April 1946.

A Loganair Islander on the pan at Kirkwall in 2002.

Not long afterwards the RAF departed, and the airfield became Kirkwall Airport, mainly thanks to the lack of room at Hatston, which was closer to the town. Services expanded over the years and the DC-3 was by far the most common type right through to the 1960s. The main runway was extended and aircraft as large as the Viscount could now operate from Kirkwall. Now under the control of HIAL, Kirkwall can boast a new tower and modern terminal, and is used by the Flybe franchise operated by Loganair.

Main features:
Runways: QDM 071-250 1,310 yards, 101-281 1,240 yards, 154-334 970 yards. *Hangars:* six squadron, one 185 x 105 feet, seven storage. *Accommodation:* RN: 435; WRNS: 174.

KIRKWALL BAY, Orkney

HY442115

A Seaplane Station was located on the edge of the bay during 1913.

LANGFORD LODGE, Antrim

54°37'23"N/06°18'00"W; J100760. 3 miles E of Crumlin

'Mighty oaks from little acorns grow' is a good phrase to describe Langford Lodge, which expanded from an SLG into one of the biggest USAAF depots in the British Isles.

Surveyed in early 1941, land belonging to the Packenham family was selected for another SLG for 23 MU. It was opened on 1 June, but it is not clear how much use 23 MU made of it before it was closed in early 1942. The reason for its closure was a request by the US Government for a site to establish a large depot for the repair and servicing of all USAAF aircraft passing through Northern Ireland.

Probably seen as the least disruptive option to the RAF's own building programme in the country, the Americans were offered Langford. Under the 'lend-lease' scheme, construction of the airfield would fall to the UK Government at cost of £1¼ million, while the US Government would pay the bill for all specialised equipment. Work began on 20 February 1942, involving the construction of multiple hangars, several workshops and five large domestic accommodation sites that could cater for up to 2,600 civilian staff. Because of the site's remoteness, a single-track railway was built from Crumlin.

Construction was due to be completed in just six months, but failed to hit this target. This did not stop HQ Langford Lodge and the AAU opening on 15 August. The AAU was created under the 'Y' Scheme for the assembly of USAAF aircraft by the LOC. It later became HQ 1st Service Area, and by late 1942 Langford became Station 597. Despite this title, and thanks to contracts already signed across the Atlantic, the airfield was under the control of Lockheed, but this did not stop the 7th ADG from moving in during September. Of the four air depots that would be established across the British Isles, Langford was the only one under civilian control, although it was working under the supervision of the 8th AFSC. The ADG was moved to Warton in January 1943.

The first aircraft, a P-38, arrived at Sydenham on 11 November 1942 and was forwarded to Langford. Many more would follow, and by early 1943 P-38 conversions were the specialism of the newly named 3rd BAD. Many of the P-38s that left went on to serve with the 12th and 15th AFs operating in North Africa and later Italy. B-17s were also modified, and by March 1943 the first of several batches of P-39s arrived. During that month 125 aircraft were handled, including a batch of Bermudas that had been assembled for the RAF.

Rows of P-38 Lightnings are seen at the 3rd BAD, Langford Lodge, in 1943.

The number of aircraft reached its peak during the summer of 1943 and Langford was struggling to cope. To help, Greencastle became a satellite for the depot and aircraft movements were carried out by ferrying squadrons. The 325th FS served here from mid-1943 through to May 1944, when it was moved to Heston. Its work was taken over by the 311th and 312th FS, which moved in from Maghaberry the same month.

The work carried out at the 3rd BAD was vast and diverse, and covered all spectrums of aircraft engineering. Between November 1942 and April 1944 more than 3,300 aircraft were reassembled, modified, repaired or overhauled, while another 11,000 were serviced. By January 1944 the LOC recorded that 555 engines had been rebuilt. Additionally 274,000 spark plugs had also been refurbished between July 1943 and April 1944. From January 1944 the BAD started to repair electric propellers, an item that the base was no stranger to as 11,500 of them were adjusted, cleaned and reassembled.

The employment figures are no less impressive, and a survey carried out on 1 January 1944 revealed that 6,900 personnel were serving here; 1,104 were US servicemen, 2,883 were employed by the LOC, and a further 2,913 were local workers.

Throughout the BAD's tenure, the LOC had been working under six-month renewable contracts; in the summer of 1944 the USAAF did not renew, and the 3rd BAD was closed down on 7 August. Langford's role was now to receive war-weary surplus aircraft, many of which had passed through here in the first place. Numbers began to climb rapidly during late 1944, with more than 300 B-24s lined up on every available piece of hardstanding. The number of aircraft peaked at almost 600 by the end of the war, mainly made up of A-20s, B-17s and B-24s.

It was not until March 1946 that the airfield became RAF Langford Lodge again, and 257 MU used it as a sub-site until early 1947. By the early 1950s the airfield had come alive again, although it appears to have been little more than a paper exercise. 4 ANS was formed here on 22 September 1952, only to be renamed 5 ANS in November before any aircraft arrived. In turn, 5 ANS was not destined to receive any aircraft either, and was disbanded in January 1953.

Langford Lodge remains in a reasonable condition today. The Martin-Baker rocket sled run can be seen on the left of the main runway.

Not long afterwards the airfield was taken over by Martin-Baker for testing ejection seats. Until recent years aircraft, mainly Meteors, have also been flying here from Chalgrove to take part in flight testing. The company constructed a 6,200-foot-long rocket sled to test ground ejections, which was in use from 1971. While still maintaining a foothold here, it appears that Martin-Baker is now served by the Langford Lodge Engineering Company Ltd, which also supports Goodrich, Bombardier, Airbus and Randox. Security is still reasonably tight, but if you can get on site the unique control tower still stands together with several hangars, and runways are all serviceable.

Main features:
Asphalt and tarmac runways: QDM 022 2,000 yards, 066 1,530 yards. *Hangars:* nine T2, providing 232,328 square feet of storage. *Hardstandings:* 126 cement. *Accommodation:* USAAF: 3,500; civilian: 1,500.

LARGS CHANNEL, Strathclyde

55°48'00"N/04°52'16"W; NS200595. N of town centre

While not a military 'action station', Largs was under the control of SAL for the reception of all kinds of flying boats. These would predominantly be military aircraft from the RAF and USN, the latter often having traversed the Atlantic.

A new terminal was opened in December 1942 as well as slipways and moorings located near Great Cumbrae Island. The most common visitors were Catalinas, operated by the RAF and to a lesser extent by the USN. RAF Mariners also called, and from June 1944 the Coronados of 231 Squadron began a regular service to and from Newfoundland.

A brief service by an Icelandic Airways Catalina saw a temporary civilian use from July 1945, but it was short-lived. The last flight out of Largs was made by Coronado JX498 on 25 September 1945, bringing this flying boat station's short career to an end.

LEANACH (CULLODEN MOOR), Inverness-shire

57°28'50"N/04°4'36"W. Half a mile E of Battle of Culloden visitor centre, S of Newlands off B9006

This small airfield can trace its roots back to 1921 when it was brought into use as an ELG for Longman, whenever the latter was closed by fog. That same year, a Highlands Airways biplane was recorded as having used it.

The site was visited in early 1941 in response to 46 MU's need for space to disperse its aircraft. Leanach was deemed fit for use, despite the planned runway, described as 'grass and moorland', being perched at the top of a hill that dropped towards the River Nairn. All sides of the airfield were restricted for expansion owing to roads, except the eastern perimeter; this was bounded by the Inverness to Perth railway line, which used Culloden Viaduct across the River Nairn.

Opened as 43 SLG on 10 May 1941, the first aircraft were Defiants, Hurricanes and Spitfires. Despite efforts to disperse and camouflage the SLG, visiting aircraft would often compromise the site. Strict rules were in place that dictated that pilots should only use the SLG in an emergency. However, there were several occasions when aircraft were diverted from both Dalcross and Longman, giving away Leanach's true use.

During its early existence, aircraft were stored under frames that supported camouflage nets and were picketed down with large concrete blocks.

From early 1942 larger types were considered for the SLG. On 22 April a Wellington was landed with little margin for error; clearance was given for Wellingtons to operate here, but only specialist pilots were selected. In fact Wellingtons never arrived, but Beaufighters did, and this was to be the main type stored here for the remainder of 46 MU's tenure.

The Oxfords of 19 PAFU made use of Leanach from 6 June 1943, but had left by November. The sudden influx of aircraft operating on and around the SLG did not go down well with 46 MU, and despite 19 PAFU's earlier-than-expected departure, an alternative site was sought. The MU concentrated its dispersal operations at 40 SLG from 11 October, retaining Leanach in reserve until early 1945. There was very little flying here during 1944, and by early 1946 the site had been derequisitioned.

Permanent buildings on the SLG during its existence were few and far between, but a handful can still be found today. A crew hut and ancillary building still stand north of the B851 at Cumberland's Stone, and further out into the field a pair of sorry-looking huts just cling on before nature gets the better of them.

LENNOXLOVE (HADDINGTON), East Lothian

55°56'03"N/02°45'42"W. 1 mile S of Haddington

During the Great War 77(HD) Squadron operated from an LG near Gifford, only 3 miles away from Lennoxlove. During the 1930s the Marquis of Douglas and Clydesdale also operated a light aircraft from a strip near Lennoxlove House.

The site's use was not decided until mid-1940, when representatives arrived from 18 MU. Insufficient land was available for a large-scale airfield, but as an SLG it was ideal. Work began on preparing the LG in January 1941, and it was named 27 SLG. The only land needed was owned by the Lennoxlove estate, but it was soon clear that more would be needed from the Colstoun estate, located to the immediate south of the LG.

After an inspection in March, the runway was found to be too short and a minor road that crossed the site would have to be closed. Before work began a Battle made a trial landing on 24 April 1941, and not long afterwards Hurricanes began to be stored here. Once the work was completed on the runway extension, Blenheims also arrived, and were to be the main type stored here during the summer of 1941, although others would follow.

Capacity at the SLG was increased and test flights were carried out during December 1941, using Wellingtons, followed by the first being delivered on the 10th. The first Halifax arrived in late July 1944; all were dispersed in Colstoun fields.

Up to October 1944 every aircraft that was allocated to 18 MU was flown to Dumfries by the ATA and prepared for service or dispersed to an SLG. To reduce the amount of aircraft movements at Dumfries, arrangements were made to deliver those aircraft not destined for front-line service direct to the SLG. This quickly raised the holdings of all of 18 MU's SLGs. By the end of October the unit held 109 aircraft, increasing to 119 by November, the majority of which were Wellingtons.

With the war over, aircraft movements began to decline, but not before another type arrived for dispersal. The majority of the seventy-five Welkins built ended their days dispersed here. This was to be the last flying at Lennoxlove, and in August 1945 the SLG was closed. All aircraft that could be made airworthy returned to Dumfries, while the remainder were dismantled on site by 63 MU based at Carluke, south-west of Motherwell.

The site has changed very little and it is quite easy to imagine aircraft landing and taking off. The line of the landing strip, which runs parallel with the B6369 as it turns north for Haddington, is now farmed, but virtually no trace of the RAF occupation remains.

LERWICK, Shetland

60°09'32"N/01°08'56"W; HU465433. 2 miles N of Lerwick on shore of Bressa Sound

Occupying 15 acres of land, construction of a Kite Balloon Station began in late 1917. Facilities included twelve sheds, a hydrogen production plant and five piers positioned along the shoreline. It was at these piers that Royal Navy ships berthed to collect the balloons.

By the end of the war the site was still occupied, but its use was limited and it was probably closed by 1919. Today the landscape has completed changed with modern roads straddling the site and a large marina now occupying the original shoreline.

LEUCHARS, Fife

56°22'23"N/02°52'06"W. 5 miles NW of St Andrews off A919

Leuchars can trace its roots back to 1911 when the Royal Engineers conducted balloon experiments very near to the present site. By 10 November 1918 the airfield was occupied by FSoAFG from East Fortune, and it was still expanding when the war ended, including the construction of seven Belfast Truss hangars, four of which remain in use today. Renamed RAF Base Leuchars on 6 March 1920, several RAF squadrons passed through during the early 1920s.

Avro 504N J9428 taxies across the grass at Leuchars for a training sortie over Fife.

This oblique aerial view of Leuchars taken on 28 June 1928 shows the seven original Belfast Truss hangars. Via A. P. Ferguson

From 1925 the airfield was known as RAF Training Base Leuchars, then became 1 FTS on 1 April 1935. Prior to this several FAA squadrons served here, including 810 and 811, both with Ripons, 802 with the Nimrod and Osprey, and 822 with the IIIF. 1 FTS moved to Netheravon in August 1938 and Leuchars then became a Temporary Armament Training Station, hosting many detachments with a gunnery range at Tentsmuir.

The first operational squadron to arrive was 224 Squadron with Ansons from Thornaby on 20 August 1938. Two days later a second unit, 233 Squadron, also arrived from Thornaby with Ansons in the same role. Both squadrons would take Leuchars into the war, but not before they had both re-equipped with the Hudson.

A Fairey IIIF undergoes trials at Leuchars from a E.IIH Catapult designed for ship operations.

Hawker Nimrod I S1618 of the Base Training Squadron is captured on a sortie out of Leuchars.

A Nightjar of 401 Flight comes to grief at Leuchars.

Five Hudsons were returning from a routine patrol near Rattray Head on the day war was declared. The following day nine 233 Squadron Hudsons were on patrol again, and it was not long before there was contact with the enemy. Hudson 'T' was attacked by a Do 18 and hit several times in the fuselage and fuel tank, but still managed to make it safely home. The same day the Hudsons of 224 Squadron were on patrol and several reported seeing Do 18s flying their own reconnaissance sorties.

After a month of trying to engage the enemy, on 8 October 1939 three 224 Squadron Hudsons flew a reconnaissance sortie that developed into an offensive patrol. While over Jutland all reported attacking a Do 18 and shot the flying boat down into the sea. Two of the Hudsons received slight damage from return fire, but this success raised the spirits of all in the squadron. Very little is made of this engagement, but it was actually the first enemy aircraft to be shot down by the RAF during the Second World War. Credit for the kill was given to Flt Lt A. L. Womersley and crew in N7217.

Two U-boats were attacked during February 1940, the first by 224 Squadron on the 12th and the other by 233 Squadron on the 21st. A Hudson from 224 Squadron, together with another from 220 Squadron at Thornaby, intercepted the German prison ship *Altmark* on 16 February. HMS *Cossack* later secured the release of 299 prisoners, many of whom were merchant seaman.

Raids on Stavanger took place during April and May 1940 and persistent visits finally paid off during a raid on 17 May. Three Hudsons of 224 Squadron dropped a total of fifteen 250lb GP bombs and thirty-five 25lb IBs onto the airfield. Numerous bombs fell within the airfield boundary, starting at least four fires. Incendiaries also fell onto the nearby seaplane base and the slipway was also damaged. 233 Squadron left for Aldergrove on 8 December and the Aldergrove detachment of 224 Squadron returned the same day.

The Blenheim was no stranger to Leuchars – a few had operated with 233 Squadron. The first of many fully Blenheim squadrons arrived on 2 February 1941 with 86 Squadron from Gosport, which left for Wattisham on 3 March.

224 Squadron's Hudsons were in the thick of the action again throughout February. Six Hudsons attacked the dockyard and shipping at Kristiansand without loss, although every aircraft was damaged by flak. On 15 April 224 Squadron moved to Limavady.

Beauforts of 42 Squadron arrived from Wick on 1 March 1941. The following day, three Beauforts took part in the first of many shipping strikes by the squadron. Two MVs were successfully torpedoed and machined-gunned.

Blenheims returned on 3 March with 107 Squadron from Wattisham. Two days later four Blenheims went into action on patrol followed by regular attacks on Norwegian coastal targets.

While on convoy patrol, 42 Squadron was in action on 11 March when an He 111 attempted to bomb the vessels. An anti-aircraft barrage was fired at the bomber, which quickly tried to make its escape. One Beaufort of 42 Squadron had other ideas, shooting the bomber down into the sea off Tentsmuir. Two days later, six Beauforts carried out a sweep off the Norwegian coast. Several enemy destroyers were spotted and the Beauforts descended to sea level to carry out a torpedo attack. A destroyer received a direct hit in the stern, causing a huge explosion and leaving the ship in flames.

A Beaufort I of 42 Squadron at Leuchars in early 1941.

144 Squadron's Hampdens arrived from North Luffenham on 17 April 1942, and spent most of its time here training for its new role of torpedo-bombing. On 4 September the squadron was ordered to fly to North Russia, from where its main task was to protect the many Arctic convoys passing through the region.

During January 1943 144 Squadron began converting to the Beaufighter, and on the 21st another Beaufighter unit, 235 Squadron, arrived from Chivenor. Eight days later the squadron flew as fighter escort for four Hampdens of 489 Squadron and seven from 455 Squadron. The shipping strike was a great success, with 489 Squadron sinking an MV and 455 Squadron sinking at least two other ships. The presence of the Beaufighters with their 20mm cannons certainly helped the Hampdens concentrate on the target.

On 30 January 1943 235 Squadron went hunting on its own, coming across a convoy of one MV with at least five armed trawlers. The Beaufighters were fitted with a pair of 250lb bombs, rather than a torpedo, although they often caused just as much damage with their 20mm cannon. From the beginning of March the squadron began to detach to various airfields, but by late July it had regrouped here, only to move to Portreath on 29 August 1943.

455 Squadron was operational with its Beaufighters by March 1944, but plans for an ANZAC Wing were under way. On 6 March an operation was flown from Leuchars involving four 489 Squadron Beaufighters fitted with torpedoes; the Australians of 455 Squadron provided fighter protection with eight Beaufighters. An MV was sunk during the strike, while the cannon-armed Beaufighters scored numerous hits on other ships. The operation was a great success and marked the beginning of a partnership that would last to the end of the war. By April the ANZAC Wing was at Langham.

OC 455 Squadron, Wg Cdr J. N. Davenport (centre), talks with OC 'A' Flight, Sqn Ldr A. L. Wiggins (left) and OC 'B' Flight, C. G. Milson.

Since 1941 BOAC had been operating a service from Leuchars to Sweden, flying Hudsons, but from 1943 the Mosquito proved to be the better aircraft for the job. It obviously could not carry a huge amount of cargo, but mail and even engineering items such as ball-bearings were usually carried. By 1945 Dakotas and Lodestars had begun to fly the route as the chances of encountering an enemy fighter began to diminish. On 17 May 1945 the service was moved to Northolt, the Mosquitoes by this time having completed 520 round trips from Leuchars.

BOAC Mosquitoes flew 520 round trips from Leuchars to Norway and Sweden from 1941 to 1945.

The Liberators of 206 Squadron arrived on 11 July 1944, and it was not long before the squadron could claim its first U-boat destroyed; sadly it was at the cost of the ten-man crew. A second Liberator unit, 547 Squadron, arrived on 28 September from St Eval. Two days later three aircraft flew their first patrols from Leuchars, and by 12 October the squadron was to see its first action.

With the war drawing to a close and more U-boats trying to make it back to Germany, several were being sunk in air attacks; 5 May 1945 was no exception, with five U-boats sunk, three of them attacked from the air. One of them was U-579, sailing with U-733 and a steamer. Fg Off A. A. Bruneau and crew, of 547 Squadron, singled out the U-boat, bombing it with depth charges and sinking it with the loss of twenty-four hands.

This visiting 5 Squadron Lightning F.6 is on detachment at Leuchars in the early 1970s.

The most demanding job now for 206 and 547 Squadrons was to escort the large number of U-boats and German warships that had surrendered. 547 Squadron was disbanded on 4 June 1945 and 206 Squadron was moved to Oakington on 31 July, disbanding in April 1946.

After the war Leuchars remained with Coastal Command until 1950, when it was transferred to Fighter Command. The usual array of Cold War jet fighters passed through, including the Meteor, Vampire, Hunter and Javelin. The Lightning first arrived in 1964 with 74 Squadron, and was replaced by the Phantom. By the late 1980s the Cold War was coming to an end and the Phantom was withdrawn from RAF service, the Tornado F.3 taking over the UK Air Defence role with 43(F) and 111(F) Squadrons. By April 2003 the Tornado F.3 OCU and 56 (Reserve) Squadron were also established here but, with the Typhoon now in service, changes were afoot. By April 2008 56 Squadron was merged with 43 Squadron, but by July 2009 the latter had disbanded here. This now left 111 Squadron, which was formally disbanded in March 2010 to make way for the next generation of air defence fighters to be based here. 6 Squadron became the first Typhoon unit to be based in Scotland when it was re-formed here on 6 September 2010, to continue the role of QRA covering the north of the United Kingdom. Unfortunately, it was announced in July 2011 that Leuchars was to close and the Typhoon force would be transferred to Lossiemouth. By 2015, Leuchars will be in the hands of the army.

228 OCU trained Phantom crews at Leuchars from 1968 to 1991.

Leuchars's Type C hangars dominate the flight line while the First World War vintage aircraft sheds still remain in use.

This remarkable airfield's history is so rich that this account has only skimmed the surface of what has taken place here over the years. The Leuchars story could easily fill this book on its own, and more!

Main features:
Concrete and wood chippings runways: QDM 275 2,020 yards, 228 2,000 yards. *Hangars:* four C, two Bellman, four aircraft sheds, nine EO blister. *Hardstandings:* six 100-foot diameter concrete, forty-four BRC fabric. *Accommodation:* RAF: 1,470; WAAF: 381.

LEVEN, Fife

NO382003. On beach near Leven on edge of Largo Bay

A temporary seaplane base occupied the beach near Leven in the summer of 1913. Several aircraft used it, including a Borel Seaplane, to take part in a naval exercise. The site was meant to have been cleared away, but instead provided a stepping stone while more suitable stations were being built. It was certainly active twelve months later, but whether it still existed by 1915 is doubtful.

LIMAVADY (AGHANLOO), Londonderry

55°04'23"N/06°56'22"W; C675255. 2 miles N of Limavady off A2

Limavady was the first of four airfields built on the north coast of Northern Ireland after surveys in 1938. It was planned as an ATS, but by the time it opened in late 1940 it was allocated to Coastal Command and would remain so throughout the war years.

Its first unit was 'A' Flight, 502 Squadron, with Whitleys from Aldergrove. The squadron moved on 27 January 1941 and the airfield supported several other Aldergrove detachments during late 1940 and early 1941. These included Blenheims of 272 Squadron and Hurricanes of 245 Squadron, which served on several occasions. 48 Squadron was also attached here from Hooton Park with Beauforts during January and February.

A 502 Squadron Whitley V on patrol out of Limavady in 1941.

A/S patrols were flown by 224 Squadron, which arrived from Leuchars with its Hudsons on 15 April 1941. Its area of operations was around the mouths of the Clyde and Mersey, from where the vital convoys were coming and going. It was joined by 221 Squadron, which flew long-range patrols over the Atlantic with Wellingtons before moving to Reykjavik on 29 September.

Four squadrons were detached here from May to October 1941, including 612 Squadron from Wick, 48 Squadron from Stornoway and 500 Squadron from Bircham Newton. 224 Squadron left for St Eval on 20 December, its duties being taken over by 53 Squadron's Hudsons three days earlier. This task was taken over by 224 Squadron again from 19 February 1942, with 53 Squadron leaving for North Coates the previous day. 224 Squadron carried out one detachment to Stornoway during its second tour here before leaving for good on 16 April.

After 224 Squadron's departure, Limavady was non-operational, thanks to the reformation of 7 (Coastal) OTU on 1 April 1942, which was tasked with carrying out operational and torpedo training for Wellington crews. It took a while for the aircraft to arrive and training did not begin until mid-May.

245 Squadron was on detachment at Limavady in late 1941.

A planned satellite airfield at Ballymoney would never come to fruition, but facilities were made available at Mullaghmore from December 1942 to January 1944. Early in March 1943 a TTF was formed within 7 OTU, but within days it was absorbed into 1 TTU at Turnberry. Mid-1943 saw a reduction in torpedo training and the unit decrease in size. Aircraft numbers continued to decline towards the end of that year before the TTU moved to Haverfordwest on 8 January 1944.

It was not long before Limavady was operational again, ready for 612 Squadron to arrive from Chivenor on 26 January, joined by 407 Squadron, also from Chivenor, three days later. Both squadrons flew Wellingtons fitted with Leigh Lights. 612 Squadron achieved success on 10 February when Plt Off M. H. Paynter and crew caught U-545 on the surface west of the Hebrides. The four depth charges dropped caused crippling damage, but only one of the fifty-six crew was killed in the attack; the survivors were rescued by U-714. 612 Squadron returned to Chivenor on 1 March, followed by 407 Squadron on 28 April.

With all focus now being applied to events leading up to D-Day, Limavady lay empty for several months. The Royal Navy moved two Wildcat squadrons here on 10/11 June 1944, but both 811 and 846 Squadrons had gone by mid-July, and 850 Squadron moved in from Perranporth with Avengers on 1 August. While here, a flight of four Wildcats was added, and several A/S patrols were flown by the Avengers. More Wildcats arrived with 811 Squadron, returning from HMS *Biter* on 25 August, but these had left by late September to HMS *Vindex*. 825 Squadron also served here from 9 September with Swordfishes from Machrihanish. 825 and 850 Squadrons moved to Mullaghmore on 6/7 November, bringing an end to FAA activity.

Operational RAF squadrons returned on 1 September 1944. First was 172 Squadron with its Wellingtons, joined by 612 Squadron, which returned on 9 September. 304 Squadron's Wellingtons were also detached here from Benbecula during October and November. Neither unit achieved success during their tours, which, for 612 Squadron, came to an end when it moved to Langham on 19 December. 172 Squadron stayed until it was disbanded here on 4 June 1945.

The sole occupant during this period was 281 Squadron, which had moved from Mullaghmore with Warwicks and Sea Otters on 31 March 1945. Detachments were carried out at Tiree and Valley until 13 August, when the unit moved to Ballykelly.

Another unit that moved in from Mullaghmore was the LTU on 3 April with Wellingtons. On 20 April the LTU was changed to the Coastal Command Anti-U-boat Devices School until it was disbanded on 25 August. 22 ACHU was re-formed on 1 June, but was moved to Aldergrove on 18 August, bringing all RAF occupancy to an end.

Limavady today reveals a site that does not hide its aviation past. As can be seen in this view looking south, many dispersals still remain in place with large sections of runway beyond. Niall Hartley

Limavady was transferred to the Admiralty on 1 December 1945, but, unlike 1944, no FAA units ever used it. The airfield now lay empty until it was sold off in 1958. Today, several large sections of runway and perimeter track remain, together with some frying pan dispersals in good condition. The control tower and at least three hangars, which have been re-clad, also survive, as well as the control tower and a rare Gun Trainer Dome.

Main features:
Concrete and tarmac runways: QDM 178 1,690 yards, 269 1,530 yards, 313 1,370 yards. *Hangars:* two T2, three Bellman, six blister. *Hardstandings:* twenty-four 125-foot-diameter concrete, one 100-foot tarmac, twenty-four 75-foot tarmac, four 60-foot tarmac, three double standing. *Accommodation:* RAF: 2,115; WAAF: 354.

LIMERICK, County Limerick
There have been several airfields and LGs around Limerick over the years, but the one to which 2 Squadron was detached in March 1913 is a bit of a mystery. The squadron brought its BE.2As from Montrose and probably stayed for just a few weeks.

LOCH BAGHASDAIL (LOCHBOISDALE), South Uist
NF795185. 5 miles E of Dalabrog

The loch was allocated for the use of 10 Squadron RAAF flying Sunderlands from Oban during 1941. There is no reason why this 'emergency' status was not continued with other squadrons; however, records suggest that it was not used by any other unit.

LOCH DOON, Strathclyde

55°15'29"N/04°23'18"W. On shore of Loch Doon

Located in one of the most beautiful parts of Scotland, Loch Doon was no more than an expensive attempt to provide an aerial gunnery school. The idea was the brainchild of Brig Sefton Brancker, who, having returned from France, saw the importance of thorough training in aerial fighting. There was no doubting his philosophy; however, on this occasion it was applied to the wrong site.

Despite being offered alternative sites all over the British Isles, work began on the school here in mid-1916. An elaborate moving target range was also built at the north-eastern corner of Loch Doon. By spring 1917 more than 3,000 men were working here, but despite thousands of yards of pipe being laid, the marshy soil could not be drained and the site was abandoned in favour of Dalmellington, a few miles north.

LONG KESH, Down

54°29'22"N/06°06'33"W; J230615. 3 miles SW of Lisburn off A3

The history of Long Kesh as a busy airfield has long been clouded by the fact that the site was once the home to one of the most infamous prisons in British history.

Ready by November 1941, the airfield's first unit arrived on 11 December when 231 Squadron moved in from Newtownards with Lysanders and Tomahawks. Another Lysander unit was formed on 18 December to provide air gunnery refresher training; 1494 TTF also provided extra training to visiting units, including 88 Squadron's Bostons from Attlebridge on 15 January 1942.

On opening, Long Kesh gained Maghaberry as a satellite, and it was to here that 231 Squadron moved on 6 January 1942. Fighters arrived with 74 Squadron from Llanbedr on 24 January to carry out patrols over Belfast; this was a quiet duty for the squadron, which left for Atcham on 25 March. 1494 Flight left for Sydenham on 13 April, and the peace was only disrupted by the arrival of three Taylorcrafts on 6 May; these belonged to 'A' Flight of 651 Squadron from Old Sarum, which remained until mid-June.

231 Squadron returned from Maghaberry on 20 November 1942, but this was short-lived as Coastal Command wanted to use Long Kesh to house an OTU. On 29 December the airfield was transferred, and the same day 5 OTU moved in from Turnberry, its task being to train and convert crews, generally from Blenheims to Beauforts and Hampdens. 231 Squadron made room for the OTU's aircraft when it moved to Nutt's Corner on 2 January 1943. The OTU retained the use of Maghaberry from 2 February and would continue to use it until it was taken over by the USAAF.

Nearly sixty serious accidents involving the Beaufort alone were recorded, and this only began to decline from November onwards, when training on the type was reduced by two-thirds following success in the Mediterranean. The same month the Hampden was replaced by the Ventura and Hudson, although much of the latter's training was taken over by 1 OTU at Silloth. With a depleted number of Beauforts, 5 OTU returned to Turnberry on 15 February 1944.

Activity returned on 20 March with the arrival of the first FAA unit, 801 Squadron's Seafires from HMS *Dale*, joined four days later by 807 Squadron from Grimsetter and 879 Squadron from HMS *Attacker*, both with Seafires. The following day 290 Squadron moved in from Newtownards with its Hurricanes, Oxfords and Martinets to carry out Army Co-operation work. This gathering of aircraft would be used for local exercises around Lough Beg, and the FAA squadrons remained until the end of April and early May, while 290 Squadron left for Turnhouse on 25 August.

Long Kesh continued to be used by the FAA during 1944. Three of the units, 899, 882 and 800 Squadrons, remained here from October until the end of February 1945.

From this point only 22 RC, which had been here since 25 March 1944, remained, until it moved to Aldergrove on 23 June 1947. With the war over, the task of demobilising thousands of RAF personnel began, handled by many centres throughout the British Isles. One of these was 103 PDC, which was formed on 15 May 1945 and continued processing servicemen until 7 March 1946.

Two hangars were used by Miles during 1945/46 for the final assembly of Messengers. 201 GS moved in from Newtownards in May 1946, but only remained a couple of months before disbanding. It was then the turn of 63 MU from Aldergrove to make use of the airfield before it left for Montrose in the late 1940s.

Several years passed, but Long Kesh remained in MoD hands. Gliding returned in mid-1955 when 203 GS moved in from Aldergrove. The school was renamed 671 VGS on 1 September, but by 1956 had returned to Aldergrove, becoming the last military unit to use the airfield. Civilian gliding was also carried out from the early 1960s when the Ulster and Short Gliding Club was here, before being forced to move out in 1968.

This view of Long Kesh was taken in the early 1990s, when aerial photography of prisons was still very sensitive. The two hangars have been dismantled together with many of the original wartime buildings that appear in this image.

By now the site was being cleared to house a new prison, which would be known as 'The Maze'. Opened in 1971, the prison housed paramilitary prisoners until it was closed in 2000, and since late 2006 the majority of The Maze has now been razed. While construction of the prison erased virtually the entire airfield, some sections of runway, perimeter track and the odd dispersal can still be found. Two hangars remain and are now occupied by the Ulster Aviation Society, which moved here in 2006.

Main features:
Tarmac runways: QDM 270 1,550 yards, 340 1,190 yards, 020 1,100 yards. *Hangars:* two T2, two Bellman, five blister. *Hardstandings:* twenty-nine 150-foot circular, two 125-foot circular. *Accommodation:* RAF: 3,580; WAAF: 389.

LONGMAN (INVERNESS), Highland

57°29'21"N/04°13'13"W. 1 mile N of Inverness city centre

Opened on 17 June 1933 by the Duke and Duchess of Sutherland as Inverness Municipal Airport, Longman was first used by Highland Airways. Routes to Wick and Kirkwall were established, and later Renfrew, Perth and Sumburgh. Scottish Airways continued services up to the start of the war.

Unlike many requisitioned airfields, it was many months before any military activity occurred. 14 Group's CF was the first when it was formed here on 20 July 1940; it only operated a Magister and an Oxford and would continue to do so until it was disbanded into 13 Group CF on 15 July 1943.

241 Squadron, which was re-formed here on 25 September 1940, was a busier unit, taking part in many exercises while still flying operational coastal patrols. The Roc Flight was also attached to 241 Squadron from 4 November to carry out dive-bombing exhibitions for Army units.

When 1 RSS moved into Bunchrew House in Inverness on 1 November 1940, its calibration flight began operating from here. Aircraft included a few Blenheims, two Hornet Moths and a C.30A. Redesignated as 70 (Signals) Wing on 17 February 1941, this unit operated from here until 25 August 1945, when it moved to Tealing.

241 Squadron was moved to Bury St Edmunds on 11 April 1941, and it was not until July that a few Lysanders returned with 13 Group AACF from Turnhouse. More Lysanders returned in August when 309 Squadron from Dunino was here for a few weeks.

One of the Royal Navy's largest communications squadrons was detached here from 22 January 1942; 782 Squadron, based at Donibristle, used Longman as a stepping stone for its operations further north, continuing until 24 August.

Early 1942 was a busy period thanks to Dalcross being flooded by heavy rain. At least six aircraft from 2 AGS operated from here until late spring, together with 289 Squadron from Kirknewton; the latter had left by the end of May. 56 MU, which had its main base at 46 Strothers Lane, Inverness, also began to overspill some of its salvage work from this period onwards.

The calibration flight of 70 Wing helped to form the nucleus of a new squadron on 15 June 1943. 526 Squadron was equipped with Blenheims but also took over the flight's Hornet Moths and an Oxford. The squadron continued radar calibration work for both RAF and Royal Navy units, and from August had a Dominie, which flew communication flights across Northern Scotland. 526 Squadron operated solely from here during its existence until it was disbanded into 527 Squadron on 1 May 1945. 527 Squadron was also detached here in the early summer of 1944.

With civilian flying restrictions now lifted, Longman looked to the future, but air transport had moved on since the pre-war days and the airfield's size was against it. BEA operated Ju 52s from here for a short period, followed by Dakotas. Despite aircraft as large as B-24s and B-17s arriving here during the war, Longman was too small for the safe operation of a fully laden Dakota. By 1947 Dalcross had won the brief battle to become Inverness Airport, and Longman was closed.

The prime land on the edge of Inverness was sold off and today is covered in every conceivable form of industrial and commercial business. The A9 also slices through the northern side of the site before it crosses the Kessock Bridge, which traverses the entrances to the Beauly and Moray Firth.

Main features:
Grass runways: QDM E-W 1,468 yards, NE-SW 1,260 yards. *Hangars:* two Bessoneau, one T1, one Bellman, one Super Robin, one blister, one civil airport. *Accommodation:* RAF: 2,115; WAAF: 354.

LONGSIDE (LENABO/PETERHEAD), Aberdeenshire

57°28'25"N/01°57'05"W. 6 miles WSW of Peterhead in Lenabo Woods

RNAS Longside was established in 1915. It was built as an airship station with giant sheds, dominating the skyline for miles around. It was operational by 1917, becoming the home to

An artist's impression of Longside Airship Station, showing a single large shed protected by a pair of smaller SS-type sheds, to help reduce crosswinds.

more than 1,500 personnel operating three different classes of coastal patrol airships. Their task was to escort convoys and deter the enemy's U-boats. This massive base, which cost a fortune to build, was abandoned by the Air Ministry in 1920 and its once grand buildings sold off for a pittance.

A very nice memorial marks the spot within the wood where some ruined buildings, concrete foundations and anchoring blocks still remain.

LOSSIEMOUTH, Grampian

57°42'19"N/03°20'21"W. 4 miles N of Elgin, 1 mile W of Lossiemouth

Lossiemouth remains one of the United Kingdom's busiest military airfields, despite recent stinging defence cuts. Since opening, the airfield has seen continuous flying activity far beyond the end of the war. Since the departure of the RAF's long-serving Jaguar, it is the Tornado that now dominates, together with regular visits by aircraft from NATO and the rest of the world.

It was December 1937 when surveyors paid a visit to land west of Lossiemouth. By early 1939 a few huts marked the site, and these were followed by the foundations and steel frames of several Type C hangars. Despite being unfinished, Lossiemouth was ready for its first unit, and 15 FTS was formed on 1 May with Oxfords and Harvards. With very few staff and even fewer aircraft, the new unit did not start training until 12 June.

46 MU was formed on 15 April 1940 and extra hangars were built to accommodate the amount of aircraft that would pass through this new unit. Its task was to accept new aircraft and bring them up to RAF standard by fitting additional military equipment. The first aircraft were seventeen Hurricanes on 17 April, followed by a variety of types including Masters, Beaufighters and later Lancasters. Despite expanding, 46 MU found that it still needed more space, and began searching for suitable SLGs of its own. By September 1941 the MU had been allocated 42 and 43 SLG, both of which served until well into 1945. A third dispersal area, 40 SLG, also came into use

A 50 Squadron Hampden I on detachment at Lossiemouth, in January 1940.

from September 1943 and September 1945. During the post-war period 46 MU was allocated Elgin from 28 July 1945, until it disbanded on 15 February 1947.

107 and 110 Squadrons, both from Wattisham, arrived on 15 and 19 April 1940 to carry out operations over Norway, the majority of sorties being flown to Stavanger, with particular attention being paid to the airfield. On 17 April twelve Blenheims left to bomb the airfield, but two failed to return, both lost without trace. Nine more attempted to bomb Stavanger again two days later, but seven had to return early owing to foul weather. On 2 May both squadrons returned to Wattisham with very little to show for their efforts other than a high casualty rate.

Bomber Command's original plan was shelved during May and Lossiemouth would become home to a training unit instead. 20 OTU was formed on 27 May, tasked with training night-bomber crews on the Wellington.

Meanwhile, the Blenheim squadrons continued to arrive, 57 Squadron from Wyton on 23 June 1940 and 21 Squadron from Watton the following day. Both were sent here to carry out anti-shipping sweeps off the Norwegian coast. On 9 July twenty-six Blenheims set course for Norway on various tasks. Twelve of them attacked Stavanger again, but it is not known if any of them managed to bomb the airfield before they were attacked by several Bf 109s. The Blenheims stood no chance as six – four from 21 and two from 57 Squadron – were shot down with the loss of all eighteen aircrew. 57 Squadron moved to Elgin on 14 August while 21 Squadron continued to fly sweeps, staying clear of Stavanger for the remainder of its stay.

During a routine training sortie over the Moray Firth, a trainee air gunner, Sgt G. Pryor,

20 OTU, first formed in April 1940, was equipped with Wellingtons from the start. This is a Wellington X in 1944 being prepared, despite the weather, for another training sortie.

spotted an aircraft diving from cloud towards him. The aircraft turned out to be a Ju 88, and without hesitation Pryor fired a quick burst from his guns, sending the machine diving into the sea. Several witnesses in another Wellington flying nearby confirmed Pryor's first kill. This was the only occasion when an OTU bomber shot down an enemy aircraft.

21 Squadron returned again on 27 May 1941. On 4 June the squadron took part in an extensive sweep, which involved fifty-four Blenheims attacking shipping and airfields from Norway down to Belgium; at least one ship was claimed hit. All of 21 Squadron returned to Lossiemouth before leaving on 14 June back to Norfolk. Back again on 7 September to continue its attacks on shipping, no further success was achieved before the squadron left Lossiemouth for good on 21 September.

Before 1941 was out, there was one final operation that involved the Blenheims of 2 Group moving north to Lossiemouth again. Operation 'Archery' was a combined operation to test German forces in Norway and convince them than an invasion of the country was always feasible. Planned for 27 December, the Blenheims of 110 Squadron from Wattisham and 114 Squadron from West Raynham arrived the previous day. The objective was Vågsøy Island, and six Blenheims from 110 Squadron and thirteen from 114 Squadron would take part. As the operation began, 110 Squadron attacked shipping in the Oberstad area to draw away German fighters from the main assault. This they did successfully, but found a convoy that attacked, causing the loss of four aircraft, either shot down by ships' defences or brought down by the fighters. 114 Squadron's job was to attack, at low level, the Luftwaffe airfield at Herdla. This was skilfully carried out but was marred when two Blenheims collided and crashed onto the airfield. The operation was classed as a success, but not for 110 and 114 Squadrons. Six aircraft failed to return, with the loss of eighteen aircrew. Both squadrons returned to their respective airfields the following day, bringing an end to Blenheim operations from Lossiemouth.

The condition of the airfield, which was still grass, was causing concern to 20 OTU. The disruption was becoming so bad that, for several weeks during the winter of 1941/42, a large proportion of the unit was detached to Lakenheath while the runways recovered.

During late 1942 the overdue construction of concrete runways began. These made 20 OTU's task much easier, now being able to operate in conditions that would have closed the airfield months earlier. The loss rate was only marginally improved, with twenty-three Wellingtons being written off in various accidents compared with the twenty-six aircraft lost during 1942.

Bomber Command, having tried to sink the *Tirpitz* from here on several occasions, returned on 15 September 1944 with 9 and 617 Squadrons gathering again in Scotland for another attempt. Thirty Lancasters and a 463 Squadron camera aircraft took off from Lossiemouth, Kinloss and Milltown on 12 November, and in clear conditions the *Tirpitz* was ripped apart by at least two direct hits and many more close enough to cause even more damage. The vessel capsized, claiming the lives of approximately 1,000 of the 1,900 sailors on board.

Unlike several bomber OTUs, which had disbanded before the end of the war, 20 OTU continued to operate until it was disbanded on 17 July 1945, having prepared hundreds of aircrew for operations with Bomber Command. However, as always with a unit of this type, it came at a cost, and during its time here 20 OTU lost 385 aircrew and 135 aircraft.

It was not long before Lossiemouth was taken over by another unit; 111 (Coastal) OTU with Liberators and Wellingtons was re-formed here on 1 August, being joined by 1674 HCU on 14 November from Milltown, only for it to disband here days later. A detachment by 280 Squadron and its Warwicks followed in early 1946, and in May of that year 111 COTU was also disbanded.

From 2 July 1946 Lossiemouth belonged to the Royal Navy and was renamed HMS *Fulmar*. It became the largest RNAS station in Scotland, and between 1946 and 1972 every single type of fixed-wing and rotary FAA type passed through. On 29 September 1972 Lossiemouth was back in RAF hands, although the Navy retained a presence with 849 Squadron's Gannets until 1978. The Wessexes of 'D' Flight, 202 Squadron, were the first to take up residence and remain here today, now with Sea King HAR.3/3As. 8 Squadron's Shackleton AEW.2s moved in on 25 August 1973, being at that time the largest squadron in the RAF. 226 OCU was re-formed with the Jaguar on 20 January 1974 and two Jaguar squadrons followed, with both 6 and 54 Squadrons serving here during that year.

While 20 OTU's Wellingtons huddle around the main hangars, the rest of the airfield and surrounding fields are covered in aircraft under the charge of 46 MU.

The sight of 8 Squadron's Shackleton AEW.2s is still missed, not only by many who served at Lossiemouth, but also the locals.

With HASs, extended and upgraded runways, a larger bomb dump and a host of other modern buildings, Lossiemouth would have been a step too far for the latest defence cuts.

The Buccaneer, which was last seen at Lossiemouth flying with the Royal Navy, returned with 12 Squadron from Honington in 1980. 208 Squadron, also flying the Buccaneer, moved in during July 1984, followed by 237 OCU, also from Honington, in 1984. During the 1991 Gulf War, and having never seen combat during their long career, the Buccaneers proved their worth, only to be removed from RAF service in 1994.

Now an all-Tornado station, Lossiemouth is the home to 12, 14, 15[R] and 617 Squadrons, all flying the Tornado GR.4A. Lossiemouth's future looks brighter than most, and it is hoped that it remains a fast jet base for many years to come.

Main features:
Concrete and tarmac runways: QDM 236 2,000 yards, 268 1,500 yards, 190 1,400 yards. *Hangars:* three C, one J, seven L, four K. *Hardstandings:* forty-two heavy bomber. *Accommodation:* RAF: 3,316; WAAF: 831.

LOW ELDRIG, Dumfries and Galloway

54°44'31"N/04°56'04"W.6 miles N of Drummore off A716

If an airfield at Low Eldrig had been surveyed during peacetime it would have been apparent that the site was totally unsuitable. Allocated to 18 MU, it was in December 1940 that site was inspected, and a few buildings were marked out for the contractors. Six months later the site was visited again, and despite a reasonably dry spring the southern third of the runway was found to be soft. This was the first area of peat discovered, but to make things worse a second area was found in the middle of the runway; both areas were dug out and refilled with stones and earth.

Despite talk of abandoning the SLG, Low Eldrig was reprieved, but any aircraft stored here would be restricted to types no bigger than a Blenheim. On 3 June 1941 the first landing was made, and Low Eldrig, now known as 11 SLG, was brought into use on 1 July.

With a capacity of forty-five aircraft, the SLG filled with Blenheims, Battles and the odd Hurricane, but with the end of the summer the drainage and peat problems returned. Further excavation work was carried out, but despite the efforts of the contractors no further landings were allowed from October onwards. All aircraft stored at 11 SLG were flown back to Dumfries, and Low Eldrig was closed for the winter.

Re-opened in May 1942, the same problems continued to plague the site, and only nineteen aircraft were recorded here by July. 11 SLG struggled on for a few more months, but on 30 September the site was closed. Low Eldrig remained in military hands until 13 November 1944, when it was handed back to the original landowners.

LUCE BAY, Dumfries and Galloway

54°51'17"N/04°55'46"W. E of East Galdenoch off the B7077, now covered by West Freugh

Construction of an airship station and aerodrome began in early 1915 on ground close to the long dunes at the head of Luce Bay. The site was 444 acres in size, although only 6 of them were covered in buildings, the largest by far being a single airship shed.

Luce Bay was opened as a Class B Airship Station for non-rigid RNAS airships on 15 July 1915. Sub-stations were located at Ballyliffan, Larne, Machrihanish and Ramsey, and its 'SS' Class airships saw a great deal of action while patrolling off the Scottish coast.

This is Luce Bay Airship Station in late 1917, showing its massive single shed and an 'SS' airship moored in the open to the right.

By June 1918 the station was under RAF control, and on the 5th 523(SD) and 524(SD) Flights were formed here within 255 Squadron. The latter was already detached with DH.6s, and remained until the end of the year. The two SD flights became part of 258 Squadron when it was formed here on 25 July. After re-equipping with Fairey IIIAs the unit disbanded in March 1919.

25 Group was formed here on 12 August 1918 to control the North Western Area, 258 and 278 Squadrons, Luce Bay and Larne. Three days later 529 Flight was formed within 258 Squadron with the DH.6, but was also disbanded by March 1919. 244 Squadron was detached from Bangor with DH.6s in late 1918, leaving 25 Group as the last unit, which disbanded on 12 June 1919.

The site has now been swept away thanks to the area being developed into West Freugh during the next war. The general location of the airship shed is now the bomb dump, although the taxiways and access roads that surround it seem to follow the same alignment as the First World War access roads.

MACHRIHANISH (STRABANE/CAMPBELTOWN AIRPORT), Strathclyde

WW1: NR682201. 1 mile W of Stewarton, N of B843

WW2/current: 55°26'11"N/05°40'48"W; NR660233. 3¼ miles W of Campbeltown

The first airfield to bear the name Machrihanish was established in 1917 as a sub-station for Luce Bay. The site was a combined aerodrome and airship sub-station, which provided a place to land when the weather prevented a return to Luce Bay. No more than 600 yards by 550 yards in size and spread across 65 acres, the site was located north of Strath Farm and hemmed in by the Campbeltown to Machrihanish light railway to the north.

272 Squadron was formed here on 25 July 1918 from 531, 532 and 533 Flights, flying the DH.6 on 'scarecrow' A/S patrols. From November 1918 the Fairey IIIA arrived, before the squadron disbanded on 5 March 1919. The airfield was then closed down, but enjoyed a second existence as Campbeltown from the 1930s, before being overshadowed by its larger neighbour.

Construction of the second airfield to be known as Machrihanish began in 1940, although it was known as Strabane until August 1941. The site was in a new position north of Machrihanish Water occupying land up to the dunes on the edge of the bay. On 15 June 1941 the airfield was commissioned as HMS *Landrail*.

The first of more than 100 FAA units to serve here did not have to move very far. 772 Squadron made the short hop from Campbeltown with Swordfishes and Skuas the same day that the airfield was commissioned. Its role was varied with duties that included target-towing, height-finding exercises, aerial photography and radar calibration. From May 1942 the squadron received the Walrus, which it used for ASR duties, committing one aircraft on alert every day. June 1942 saw the arrival of Chesapeakes, Fulmars and Defiants; the latter were used for target-towing until replaced by Martinets from September 1943. Swordfishes returned in October 1942, followed by Hurricanes and Blenheims in mid-1944. 772 Squadron contributed several aircraft for a dummy invasion exercise with the Fleet on 27 May 1944 in preparation for the forthcoming real invasion. 772 Squadron's long tour came to an end on 2 July when it moved to Ayr.

There is not enough space here to record all the FAA squadrons that passed through Machrihanish, but the majority were fighter units equipped with the Sea Hurricane, Seafire and Wildcat, to name a few. The Swordfish, Barracuda and Avenger were also prevalent, and there was no let-up during the post-war period. However, activity came to an abrupt end in early 1946, and the Royal Navy, seeing no further use for Machrihanish, paid off the site on 16 April.

The airfield languished under C&M until 1 December 1951, when it was recommissioned as HMS *Landrail* again. Its task was now to provide training for Firefly crews, and 799 Squadron was moved in from Yeovilton on 3 December; under the title RFTU, it worked with crews until it was disbanded here on 12 August 1952. Pondering whether to retain the airfield, the Admiralty decided against it and it was paid off for a second time on 30 September 1952.

Machrihanish in June 1979 is a far cry from the original wartime design. The original runways can just still be traced at the western end of the airfield while the new main runway dominates at just under 10,000 feet in length. At the extreme bottom right-hand corner is Bleachfield Farm, which is on the northern edge of Campbeltown airfield.

The airfield then entered a new phase of its career when it underwent a massive reconstruction period from 1960 to 1962. It would now serve NATO as a diversion airfield and would become home to the USN for the next thirty years as a weapons facility. The original four runways were swept aside to make way for a single 10,000-foot runway, and up to the 1990s a host of NATO aircraft came and went. In the meantime BEA and later BA flew from here during the 1970s, followed by Loganair from 1977. The long runway was put to good use on several occasions for Concorde pilot training. By 1995 the USN had relinquished Machrihanish and handed it back to the MoD. While some intriguing military activity still takes place from here, flying is now mainly civilian thanks to Campbeltown Airport being another HIAL airfield.

Main features:
WW2: *hard surface runways:* QDM 119-299 1,190 yards, 030-210 1,030 yards, 075-255 1,030 yards, 165-345 1,000 yards. *Hangars:* seventeen 60 x 70 feet squadron, eight storage, three 185 x 105 feet workshop. *Hardstandings:* six TE. *Accommodation:* RN: 1,836; WRNS: 692.

MACMERRY, Lothian

55°56'55"N/02°53'36"W. Due N of Macmerry, 2 miles E of Tranent

A de Havilland Moth and a Fox Moth of the Edinburgh Flying Club stand at Macmerry/Tranent in the 1930s. Via A. P. Ferguson

Taken over by the Air Ministry at the start of the war, Macmerry was quiet until a small RAF contingent arrived during the summer of 1940. It was joined in September until November by a detachment of Hurricanes of 263 Squadron from Drem. Another Hurricane unit, 607 Squadron, arrived from Usworth on 16 January 1941 and stayed until 2 March when it moved to Drem, followed by 614 Squadron, which arrived from Grangemouth two days later. Equipped with the Lysander and later the Blenheim, the squadron's role was Army Co-operation.

A Blenheim IV of 614 Squadron at Macmerry in 1941.

During 1941 Cunliffe-Owen set up a factory to the east of the airfield. Closer to Galdsmuir than Macmerry, its employees worked mainly on the Hudson. Cunliffe-Owen's work was taken over by SMT later in the war, and SAL is also thought to have carried out work here.

After a visit by staff from 58 OTU on 8 December 1941, it was agreed that Macmerry should house a single flight. Two days later, 'F' Flight, with six Spitfires, arrived from Grangemouth, and remained until 3 April 1942.

While 614 Squadron went on detachment to York, 225 Squadron took its place, its Mustangs arriving from Thruxton for a low-level tactical reconnaissance exercise. The squadron returned to prepare for its first operation against the enemy since its formation and, after taking part in several raids from West Raynham, it moved to Odiham on 26 August.

This 614 Squadron Blenheim IV was most likely heading in the opposite direction towards the Nissen hut before the pilot managed to bring the aircraft to a halt, minus its undercarriage.

63 Squadron was another tactical reconnaissance unit that settled here on 20 November 1942 with Mustangs. On 6 December the squadron began the first of many detachments, moving to Lossiemouth; it returned eleven days later, then moved to Odiham on the last day of 1942. The airfield also hosted the formation of a new unit in December, 1497 TTF, equipped with Lysanders, which would operate from here until 22 June 1943, when it moved to Ayr.

63 Squadron returned on 19 February 1943, and was were joined four days later by Lysanders of 309 Squadron from Findo Gask for exercises, only to return there on the 25th. By the end of July the squadron had moved to Turnhouse.

Instructions were received from 13 Group on 7 September 1943 to reduce Macmerry to C&M. While aircraft may have deserted the airfield, the RAF Regiment was still here, and on 5 October a signal was received that 200 USAAF personnel would be arriving on the 15th. Visits by senior RAF and USAAF officers inspected before an advance party arrived on the 13th from Northern Ireland. Two days later, as planned, the main party arrived and Macmerry effectively became a holding unit for this group, whose members were all posted around the United Kingdom by early 1944.

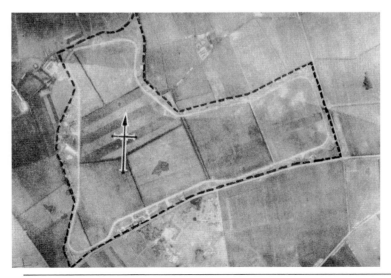

This aerial view of Macmerry in 1944 shows the perimeter highlighted by the broken line. The First World War airfield site is at the bottom centre of the picture. Via A. P. Ferguson

Flying operations from late 1944 to early 1945 were limited to occasional use by the Beaufighters of 132 OTU. The situation did not change a great deal until, on 21 April 1945, Macmerry was loaned to the Navy, and was commissioned as HMS *Nighthawk II* on 1 June.

Halifaxes of 644 Squadron from Tarrant Rushton made use of Macmerry on 4 October 1945. The squadron had arrived at East Fortune the day before to participate in a para-dropping demonstration, and Macmerry was used as the drop zone before the squadron returned to East Fortune and home to Dorset. By early 1946 the sight of Beaufighters and Mosquitoes of 132 OTU had virtually gone. Without making any use of the airfield whatsoever, the Admiralty returned Macmerry to the RAF on 15 March 1946. This signalled the end of military use for the airfield, and on 31 August Macmerry was back under the control of the Edinburgh Flying Club. Between the club arriving and the RAF abandoning the site, much of the flying field had been ploughed up. The landing facilities were very poor, and by 1953 Macmerry was returned to the farming community.

The A1 has now crept further onto the flying area, and very little is left of hangars and dispersals. The exception is a pair of fighter pens sandwiched between the A1 and the A199. Pillboxes and remnants of hutments can be found on and around the various domestic sites, but the bulk of the technical area is now under an industrial estate. The old Cunliffe-Owen site is virtually complete; all of the hangars have been re-clad and today belong to grain merchant W. N. Lindsay Ltd.

Main features:
Grass runways: QDM WSW-ENE 1,500 yards, NW-SE 1,200 yards, NNW-SSE 1,200 yards. *Hangars:* one T1, one civil, eight blister. *Hardstandings:* six Blenheim. *Accommodation:* RAF: 887; WAAF: 178.

MAGHABERRY, Antrim

54°30'50"N/06°10'54"W. 3 miles NE of Moira off A26

Maghaberry was active for five years, but always served under the shadow of its parent at Long Kesh. Opened as a satellite on 15 November 1941, it was first used by Lysanders and Tomahawks of 231 Squadron from Long Kesh. The squadron moved in permanently on 6 January 1942 to carry out Army Co-operation duties with local Army units until it was forced to return on 20 November.

A pair of T2 hangars would serve until early 1945 for the assembly of Stirlings; by the end of 1942 at least two aircraft had been completed and test flown. The fuselage and wings were built at Long Kesh and delicately transported by road to Maghaberry for final assembly. The sight of an 87-foot-long Stirling fuselage perched on top of a 'Queen Mary' must have been an image to behold!

The reason for 231 Squadron's sudden departure was to make way for 5 OTU, although the unit's Hampden Flight and a pair of Martlets did not arrive until 2 February 1943. The Hampdens would later give way to Venturas and Hudsons until 5 OTU moved to Turnberry in February 1944.

The OTU was briefly joined by Beauforts and Beaufighters of 306 FTU from 15 June 1943, which moved to Melton Mowbray from 13 August, making way for 'A' Flight, 104 OTU, which arrived from Nutt's Corner on 7 September. The unit's Wellingtons remained until January 1944, following the reopening of Nutt's Corner.

While 104 OTU was settling in, plans were already in place to turn Maghaberry into a fighter CCRC for the USAAF. From mid-October 1943 hundreds of USAAF personnel arrived to establish four ferrying squadrons instead, under the control of the 27th ATG based at Grove. The advance party of the 311th FS was the first to arrive only days before Maghaberry was redesignated as Station 239.

By 9 December 1943 four ferry squadrons, the 311th, 312th, 321st and 325th FS, had been formed. All of the pilots and their crews who served under the 27th ATG were very experienced; several pilots had flown with the ATA, including the CO of the 311th FS. Aircraft ferrying covered every type from fighters through to bombers and transports. Maghaberry quickly became one of the busiest airfields in Northern Ireland, with aircraft constantly being shuttled from Langford Lodge, then on to operational airfields throughout Britain.

This period of activity began to come to an end when the 311th FS moved to Langford. The remaining squadrons left not long after and, on 6 June 1944, the airfield was in RAF hands. It was placed under C&M but was still used by Short's and the runways remained opened for emergencies.

It was more than six months before another use for Maghaberry was found. On 11 January 1945 it became 101 SLG under 23 MU control, replacing 16 and 19 SLGs. Ironically, after providing Short Brothers with a site to assemble Stirlings for many years, Maghaberry would become a dispersal centre for them. Hundreds arrived, all falling to the scrapman's axe. This task took until mid-1947 to complete, and on 1 June of that year 101 SLG was closed down.

This view of Maghaberry in May 1992 shows that the areas not obliterated by the HMP remain in reasonable condition, including the two Stirling assembly hangars on the northern side.

Maghaberry was later used as motorbike circuit, and in 1969 future World Champion Joey Dunlop won his first race here. Still in the hands of the MoD, by 1974 the land was purchased by the NI Office for the site of a new prison. HMP Maghaberry opened in 1986 and remains a high-security prison capable of holding up to 850 inmates. The building of the prison meant that huge swathes of the airfield were lost, but the two T2s used for Stirling assembly still stand on the northern side, one of them having been re-clad.

Main features:
Concrete runways: QDM 106 1,500 yards, 032 1,100 yards, 156 1,070 yards.
Hangars: two T2. *Hardstandings:* seventeen frying pan, fourteen spectacle.
Accommodation: RAF: 1,959; WAAF: 328.

MALAHIDE, Dublin

53°26'62"N/06°10'09"W; O220453. Three-quarters of a mile SW of Malahide railway station

Malahide was a Class B Airship Patrol Station that offered tethering facilities. It was a sub-station for Anglesey (Llangfni) from 26 September 1915 and was active until 1919. The active airship area was 400 metres west of the castle, within a clearing in the woods.

MAYDOWN, Londonderry

55°02'00"N/07°14'23"W; C485210. 4 miles NE of Londonderry off A2

From humble beginnings, Maydown grew into one of the Navy's busiest airfields and is credited with being occupied by the largest squadron in the FAA.

On 1 May 1941 Maydown was opened as 17 SLG for 23 MU. It was not used to any extent but its potential was recognised and it was closed for redevelopment on 15 September. By the summer of 1942 it was reopened as a satellite for Eglinton, and on 7 August its first occupants were the Spitfires of the 2nd FS, 52nd FG. Several convoy escorts were flown before the unit moved to Goxhill on 24 August. The 82nd FG moved into Eglinton in late September, and by 6 October one of its squadrons, the 97th FS, moved its P-38s here. It was training missions that were flown during this time, which came to an end when the 82nd FG moved to St Eval in late December 1942. By 3 January 1943 the airfield was closed for further expansion.

Reopened on 1 May 1943, it was now in the hands of the Royal Navy serving as a satellite for Eglinton. An RAF presence was retained, first to support any fighter squadrons that might arrive on a lodger basis, and second to run the CASTS, which was formed on 16 June. Run by both RAF and Royal Navy personnel, the school remained here until July 1944.

One of hundreds of Swordfishes that passed through 836 Squadron at Maydown during the Second World War.

The first FAA unit was 838 Squadron with Swordfishes from Machrihanish on 13 June 1943, only to leave for DLT on HMS *Argus* on 9 July. The squadron left permanently for HMS *Activity* on 18 July, and this would be quite typical of how the FAA used Maydown for the remainder of the war. However, it was the arrival of the second unit on 17 June that would dominate flying operations.

836 Squadron moved in from Machrihanish to become an Operational Pool for Swordfishes operating from MAC ships being built to help protect the Atlantic convoys. With its HQ firmly repositioned here by 13 August 1943, the squadron had twenty-seven Swordfishes and briefly two Walruses on strength after absorbing 838 and 840 Squadrons, 700W Flight and detachments of 833 and 834 Squadrons. It was not long before the squadron was given the responsibility for all MAC-ship flights, consisting of three or four Swordfishes each.

The airfield became HMS *Shrike* on 1 January 1944 with a capacity of 105 aircraft. Most of the space was filled by 836 Squadron and a second pool unit, 860 Squadron, which had arrived from Machrihanish on 6 December 1943. The two squadrons controlled eighty-three aircraft between them, operating from nineteen MAC ships.

As the U-boat threat subsided, 836 Squadron was run down, and by February 1945 only had thirty aircraft. With VE Day approaching, its role was now surplus to requirements; its aircraft were also surplus, and by May were leaving for Barton to be broken up. One aircraft that served with 836 Squadron was saved; LS326, coded 'L2', which served with 'L' Flight on MV *Rapana*, survives today as part of the RNHF. 836 Squadron was disbanded at Maydown on 29 July 1945.

860 Squadron's fate was more positive, probably because its formation was rooted in the Royal Netherlands Navy. Its tasking in the MAC ship role also came to an end after VE Day, but after losing its Swordfishes it was re-equipped with Barracudas acquired from 822 Squadron on 30 June. 860 Squadron remained until 3 September, when it was moved to Ayr to continue working up. Unlike many of our country's FAA units, this squadron still exists as part of the Royal Netherlands Navy, now flying the Lynx.

During this busy period Maydown also played host to at least twenty-six other FAA squadrons; the vast majority came and went via Machrihanish, using Maydown as part of their work-up period.

Another of Maydown's Swordfishes was LS326, which was coded 'L2' and served with 'L' Flight on MV Rapana. *The 'Stringbag' survives today as part of the RNHF.*

HMS *Shrike* was paid off on 13 September 1945, only to be re-commissioned as HMS *Gannet II*, once again as a satellite to Eglinton. Despite the parent airfield remaining consistently busy, only two further squadrons made use of Maydown. First was 744 Squadron from Eglinton, with Barracudas, on 1 May 1946; it worked with the Sonobuoy Tracking School, which was also here. 804 Squadron's Seafires also made an appearance from Donibristle on 6 January 1947. On 27 January the Barracudas left, and 804 Squadron moved on to HMS *Theseus* on 7 February 1947 to become the last flying unit to operate from here. Maydown was completely closed to flying by January 1949, having already been reduced to C&M status.

Looking north-east across Maydown, the last significant section of runway can be seen towards the Dupont plant, which produces Kevlar fibre. Niall Hartley

The airfield is now completely swallowed by industry, with the exception of the two sections of runway that are only truly revealed when viewed from above. Aviation tenuously continues here thanks to Maydown Precision Engineering, whose customers include Bombardier.

Main features:
Concrete runways: QDM 069-249 1,650 yards, 002-182 1,350 yards. *Hangars:* nine super blister, one T1. *Hardstandings:* thirty-seven aircraft standings, six double pens. *Accommodation:* RAF: 1,321; WAAF: 351.

METHVEN, Tayside

56°24'41"N/03°31'59"W. 1½ miles E of Methven off A85

Another SLG for 44 MU was surveyed in early 1941 and was ready by 1 July. Designated as 24 SLG, the first aircraft to arrive were Ansons and Wellingtons. On 30 July 1942 a Stirling was landed and the SLG was cleared for the bomber, although it was not until the end of the year that Stirlings arrived, by which time the Defiant and Hurricane were also stored here. It also went on to become a specialist ATA dispersal area for Beauforts.

Methven's location was not overlooked by the nearby Royal Navy depot at Almondbank. After a visit by personnel from Donibristle it was agreed that Methven could be used for the delivery of stores to the nearby naval base.

Various RAF Auster squadrons passed through, but only one has been recorded. This was 652 Squadron, which arrived from Sawbridgeworth on 28 March 1943. By 2 July the squadron had moved to Ayr to continue its training with several army units.

24 SLG's wartime career was brought to an abrupt end when 44 MU abandoned the site in September 1944. It remained under Air Ministry control until the end of the war, but beyond that is doubtful.

While Methven faded into history, the military retained a presence at Almondbank and, under DARA control, was a major employer in the area. A complex site grew up during the post-war years and helicopter movements were commonplace. Whirlwind HAS.7 XM660 was on the gate for many years but has since been removed to the NEAM at Usworth. Today the site is in civilian hands under Vector Aerospace, and its future is uncertain.

MILLISLE, Down

54°36'22"M/05°35'07"W; J560755. 2 miles W of Millisle on B172

Millisle was intended for use by a USAAF CCRC, but work was brought to a halt when it was at an advanced stage. Two other airfields in the region, Kells Point and Ballymoney, were also planned, but never left the drawing board. Of the three runways, the main, straddling the Moss Road, was virtually completed while a second was part-finished before work stopped. Many technical buildings had also gone up, as well as a large section of perimeter track.

The AAC made use of one of the runway sections up to the late 1980s, while virtually every technical building survives, now in the hands of several light industry businesses.

MILLTOWN, Grampian

57°40'31"N/03°14'13"W. 3 miles NE of Elgin

In late 1939 Lossiemouth had two decoys in an effort to divert an attack by the Luftwaffe. One was at Kingston, west of Spey Bay, and the other, at Milltown, served in this role until 1941, when it was decided to expand it into a much larger airfield.

On 27 October 1941 the decoy was closed and construction began on a three-runway airfield for Coastal Command. A dual role as an advanced base for Bomber Command was also planned.

By the time it was completed, in August 1943, its original role had changed. On 14 June it became a satellite for 20 OTU, and the same day 'D' Flight's Wellingtons became the first occupants.

The OTU was here throughout the summer of 1944, but a requirement by Coastal Command resulted in the unit returning to Lossiemouth on 1 September. The U-boat threat had diminished around the French coast and Bay of Biscay, but there was still a need for A/S squadrons to operate over the North Sea and along the Norwegian and Danish coasts. In response, 224 Squadron's Liberators were moved up from St Eval on 11 September.

A 224 Squadron Liberator VI out of Milltown in early 1945.

It was not long before 224 Squadron tasted success with an attack on U-867 by Fg Off H. J. Rayner and crew on 19 September. The U-boat was found on the surface 90 miles west of Stadtlande. A stick of well-aimed depth charges left the U-boat in a crippled state and the sixty-man crew had no choice but to man the lifeboats. No rescue was forthcoming for them and they all perished in the icy waters.

One of the airfield's intended uses came to fruition on 29 October 1944 when several Lancasters left in the early hours to attack the *Tirpitz*. The weather saved the warship this time, and one aircraft that had taken off from Milltown had to crash-land in Sweden because of flak damage. Lancasters also used Milltown for the last, successful attack on the *Tirpitz* on 12 November.

20 OTU returned in February 1945 while repairs were carried out at Lossiemouth. This move was a temporary one, and the Wellingtons stayed only until June.

As the war drew to a close, the area in which the U-boats could operate was shrinking rapidly, and by May 1945 all had withdrawn to bases in northern Germany, Denmark and Norway. With so many U-boat targets in the same area, there was a great deal of confusion as to who sank the final vessels of the war. 224 Squadron's last is open to debate and, once again, was either shared with or claimed instead by 86 Squadron's Liberators. On 6 May U-3523 was the target, attacked by Flt T. H. Gouldie and his crew. After being forced to surface, the U-boat was then seen to rapidly sink, taking fifty-seven crewmen with her. Some sources claim that the U-boat was sunk by 86 Squadron.

With the war now over, much of the squadron's time was taken up flying patrols looking for U-boats that had surrendered; the last of these was carried out by Flt Lt Pretlove and crew on 2 June. On 20 July 224 Squadron left for St Eval, having destroyed eleven U-boats and at least three more shared.

111 (Coastal) OTU arrived on 1 August 1945 with Liberators and Wellingtons. It was joined by another Liberator training unit on 10 August when 1674 HCU arrived from Aldergrove. These would be the last permanent RAF units to fly from here; the HCU went first to Lossiemouth on 14 November, followed by 111 COTU, which was disbanded on 21 May 1946.

224 Squadron's Liberators cover Milltown in this post-war aerial view.

From 15 July Milltown was under Royal Navy control and was renamed HMS *Fulmar II*. 767 Squadron, with Seafires, was the first FAA unit to arrive from East Haven. 766 Squadron also made use of Milltown as a satellite, as later did the Attackers from 890 Squadron. The long-serving 764 Squadron also operated a variety of jets here from 1957 until the Royal Navy relinquished control in July 1972. 663 VGS was the only permanent RAF flying unit, operating between 1973 and 1978. Up until then the runways were in a good enough condition for a Harrier and Hercules detachment in 1973.

Closed to flying from March 1977, Milltown became the home of 81 SU, and more than fifty aerials were erected, providing HF communications up to a distance of 1,500 miles from the coast. A recent and costly technological upgrade took place, and it looks as though Milltown's role as a communications base is over. The airfield remains in MoD hands and access to the site is restricted.

Because of its use during the post-war years, the original airfield has stood up well to the test of time. All three runways, the perimeter track and the dispersal areas remain in good condition. However, only a single original hangar remains standing, and the chance of any original wartime buildings still existing is remote, but while Milltown remains tenuously in military hands its preservation is better than most.

Main features:
Concrete and tarmac runways: QDM 054 1,900 yards, 114 1,540 yards, 175 1,400 yards. *Hangars:* two T2, one B1. *Hardstandings:* twenty-seven spectacle. *Accommodation:* RAF: 1,638; WAAF: 145.

MONTROSE (BROOMFIELD), Tayside

56°43'50"N/02°27'03"W. 1 mile N of Montrose off A92

The history of Montrose spans both of the World Wars, and its establishment in early 1914 makes it one of the oldest military airfields in Scotland.

The airfield came about when the CO of 2 Squadron, Major J. Burke, began a local search for an alternative to Upper Dysart Farm. He discovered the Broomfield site in the summer of 1913, and later in the year kit-form wooden hangars that had been intended for Dysart were diverted to Broomfield. Before it was completed, 2 Squadron moved to the second oldest military airfield in Scotland on 1 January 1914, but only enjoyed its new surroundings for a few months before taking its BE.2Cs to Netheravon on 11 May.

A pair of Bleriot XIs formed the CPF here in August 1914, but it had disbanded by the end of year. A period of quiet then followed and it was during this time that the airfield began to expand. Several large side-opening aeroplane sheds were built, together with an extensive technical and domestic area in preparation for Montrose becoming a training station.

A 2 Squadron BE.2C at Montrose in May 1914, only days before the unit left for Netheravon.

On 17 July 1915 6 TS was formed, but was held in limbo for several months before becoming the nucleus for 25 Squadron, which was formed on 25 September. The squadron moved to Thetford on 31 December to continue its training, and by February 1916 was fighting in France.

1916 saw the formation of 18 TS, which provided the nucleus for another fighter squadron on 15 April, but 43 Squadron did not stay here for long, moving to Stirling four days later. 39 TS was formed on 29 August, and by the end of the year had at least eighteen Maurice Farmans. 18 TS was responsible for the formation of 83 Squadron on 7 January 1917 and 82 (Canadian) TS on 9 February, although neither unit stayed here for very long. 39 TS was no less busy, and provided the core of 85 (Canadian) TS, which moved to Canada on 2 April.

A BE.2C of 18 TS at Montrose in late 1916.

80 Squadron arrived from Thetford on 10 August 1917 and would train here until 27 November, when it moved to Beverley. 52 TS moved in from Beverley on 1 September to replace 39 TS, which moved to South Carlton two days later. 52 TS left for Catterick on 24 November, replaced three days later by 36 TS from Beverley until it was disbanded into 26 TDS at Edzell on 15 July 1918. The Americans showed their faces briefly during March 1918 when the 41st Aero Squadron brought its Spads for one month before leaving for Gullane.

The formation of the RAF brought many changes, and by 15 July Montrose's TSs were dissolved into a TDS. 32 TDS introduced several new fighters, but by 30 May 1919 had been disbanded, and not long afterwards Montrose was abandoned.

Sixteen years later Montrose was lucky enough to be one of many chosen as part of the RAF's mid-1930s expansion scheme. After the land was repurchased a great deal of time and effort was spent on repairing the runways, which were in a poor state. While this work was still being carried out, 8 FTS was formed on 1 January 1936, flying Harts followed by Audaxes and Oxfords.

On the first day of the war, 8 FTS was redesignated as 8 SFTS. By late June 1940 the SFTS was changed to a single-engined school, and the Oxfords were dispersed to other training units. Up to the end of the Battle of Britain more than 800 pilots had been trained by the SFTS, many of them fighting in the conflict. Late 1940 saw more than 100 Masters, and additional airfields, especially for FLP work, were essential. Thanks to 42 SFTS opening in Canada, 8 SFTS's workload was transferred overseas, but the school lived on here until it was disbanded into 2 FIS.

On a sortie from Montrose in 1940 are 8 FTS Hawker Furies in training colours with camouflaged upper surfaces and yellow lower.

Montrose provided an FOB for fighter squadrons from early 1940 through to late 1941. First to arrive were the Spitfires of 603 Squadron from Dyce in January, remaining until May when they were joined by 'A' Flight, 602 Squadron, in April. The Blenheims of 248 Squadron were here in June as the airfield prepared itself for the first of many air raids. While Montrose bolstered its airfield defences and airmen were training to deal with enemy paratroopers, the first raid came at 0942hrs on 18 July 1940. An He 111 dived down and at 500 feet dropped its bombs. Two RAF personnel were killed, several more were injured, and a dozen aircraft were damaged by splinters. A single enemy aircraft also dropped one bomb on 23 July, this time without causing any serious damage. It was not until 25 October that Montrose was singled out again. At 1920hrs three Ju 88s approached at 50 feet and, with all guns blazing, dropped twenty-four bombs across the airfield. Six airmen were killed and more than twenty seriously injured. Two hangars were destroyed and the officers' mess was set ablaze.

2 FIS was re-formed on 5 January 1942 to train instructors for FTSs and PAFUs on both single- and multi-engined types, using Tutors, Masters, Magisters and Oxfords. By 14 April this huge unit also absorbed 8 SFTS, a week later taking over all the various satellites and FLPs used by it. 2 FIS continued to serve here until it was disbanded on 11 July 1945, having trained hundreds of instructors for the RAF.

416 Squadron carried out the last fighter 'air defence' detachment here in April 1942, and it was not until 4 May 1943 that another unit joined 2 FIS. 8 AAPC TTF was formed with Lysanders to support local anti-aircraft units, changing its name to 1632 Flight by 17 June, only to disband into 598 Squadron by December. 598 Squadron then maintained a detachment here until it rejoined the main unit at Peterhead in March 1945.

2 FIS was the last RAF flying unit to serve at Montrose, but it was not long before the airfield found a final use with Maintenance Command. 260 MU established a sub-site here from August 1945 through to 15 January 1947, then 63 MU moved in from Woolsington on 24 March 1946, later moving to Edzell on 31 March 1950.

This aerial view of Montrose in 1993 shows an airfield, from a distance, in a remarkable state of preservation. Despite the efforts of the Luftwaffe during the Second World War the original First World War hangars remain as well as a host of later buildings. The original grass runways and perimeter track can be clearly seen.

Limited civilian flying occurred only briefly, although Montrose was used by British Airways for night-flying training during 1977/78. This exercise resulted in the Second World War control tower having its first floor demolished so as to reduce obstacles; it has since been completely demolished. Generally the airfield is in a good state of preservation and three of the First World War hangars, now re-clad, still survive, as do two 'modern' Bellmans. The Montrose Air Station Heritage Centre is also located here, helping to keep the spirit of this wonderful airfield alive.

Main features:
WW2: *Steel matting runways:* QDM 040 1,325 yards, 070 1,000 yards, 170 766 yards. *Hangars:* four Bellman, three Bessoneau, three WW1, one 73 x 82 x 24 feet, two 211 x 65 x 22 feet. *Hardstandings:* forty-five Sommerfeld track. *Accommodation:* RAF: 1,544; WAAF: 251.

MONTROSE (UPPER DYSART), Angus

NO685545. 3 miles S of Montrose

Scotland's oldest military airfield was created on 26 February 1913 with the arrival of 2 Squadron after an epic 360-mile flight from Farnborough with its BE.2As. The first aircraft missed the small aerodrome and landed at Sunnyside Royal Hospital before continuing to Upper Dysart Farm. An advance party had travelled to the site in January to erect several canvas hangars, while the majority of the squadron's 130 personnel were accommodated in a barracks in the town.

BE.2A 218 is about to set out from Farnborough via several stops en route for Upper Dysart Farm in February 1913.

From the start, 2 Squadron was not happy with its new location, but thanks to several detachments it did not operate from here for a great deal of the time. Six aircraft departed for a detachment to Limerick in March 1913, and in November Capt Longcroft flew 650 miles non-stop from Montrose, via Portsmouth, finishing at Farnborough.

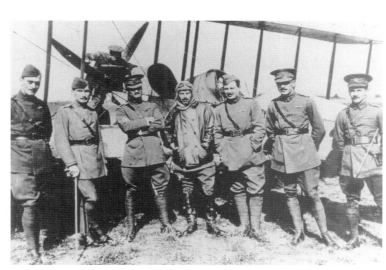

Officers of 2 Squadron, with a BE.2A behind, pose for the camera at Upper Dysart Farm in 1913.

A temporary camp was also set up on St Andrews beach during 2 Squadron's stay, to practise take-offs and landings. Tents were erected on Bruce Embankment and the flying drew a large crowd. ELGs were also made available to the unit at Muirhouses, Kirriemuir and Edzell; the latter was more often than not covered in sheep. Various aircraft types passed through the squadron during its tour here before it moved to Broomfield on 1 January 1914. The hangars were dismantled and moved to the new airfield, leaving behind no trace of this historic site.

MULLAGHMORE, Londonderry

55°01'53"N/06°35'46". 4½ miles NE of Garvag, 7 miles S of Coleraine on A54

Nestling between the River Bann to the east and the River Agivey to the west, the designers of this airfield did well to squeeze it into the space available. Work began in November 1941 and Mullaghmore was ready by the summer of 1942; it opened on 17 August. A few weeks later an American party visited from the 8th AF, indicating that Mullaghmore had a part to play in the arrival of thousands of servicemen from 'across the pond'.

The weeks rolled by until finally, in October 1942, the airfield was prepared for flying. Several buildings were demolished by the Royal Engineers as they were considered obstructions; these included the school in Droghed and a mill chimney. Obstruction lights were also fitted to a house and tall trees at Glenkeen and Claggan.

On 28 December 1942 the airfield became a satellite for 7 OTU, tasked with carrying out operational training for Wellington crews of Coastal Command. A detachment from 104 OTU made Mullaghmore an all-Wellington affair from 2 March 1943, and both would operate from here until January 1944.

The advance party of US personnel began to arrive on 21 November 1943, and they would go on to form the 6th Replacement and Training Squadron (Bombardment) HQ and HQ squadron, which were activated on 16 December. Under the control of the 6th CRCC, Mullaghmore was handed over to the USAAF on 20 December, becoming Station 240.

During late February 1944 the 6th CCRC departed for Cheddington, leaving behind a few HQ personnel and ground staff. Station 240 was then informed that it should prepare for up to eighty aircraft for short-term storage, the first of which, a B-26, arrived on 28 February. Twenty-five C-47s and C-53s also arrived the same day, bringing freight and passengers from Stansted. A further twenty-five transports arrived from Earls Colne and Fersfield via Andreas on 11 March 1944.

This was the largest and only serious aviation activity carried out here. The airfield reverted to RAF Mullaghmore on 1 May 1944, and plans were put into place to prepare it to receive two Coastal Command squadrons, but this never happened. It was not until 29 September that 4 RFU arrived from Haverfordwest with Wellingtons, Halifaxes and Liberators. As well as flying long-range navigational sorties, the RFU doubled as an ASR unit, a task it continued until January 1945. By 5 October the RFU had been disbanded, but re-formed the same day as the LORAN TU, tasked with training navigators to use LORAN, until it moved to Limavady on 3 April 1945.

In the meantime several operational FAA squadrons arrived, starting with the Swordfishes of 842 Squadron from Benbecula in early November 1944. 850 Squadron's Avengers moved in from Limavady to carry out A/S patrols from 6 November, joined by the Wildcats of 825 Squadron the following day from the same station. By 11 December 825 Squadron had moved to HMS *Vindex*, while 850 Squadron was disbanded here on Christmas Eve.

New Year 1945 saw the Fireflies of 1771 Squadron move in from Hatston, but they only remained a month before moving to Ayr. Before they left, 815 Squadron's Barracudas arrived from Ayr on 26 January, and on two occasions during early March carried out depth-charge attacks on two U-boats. Neither could be confirmed, and the last operational squadron to serve here left on 20 April 1945. 281 Squadron, which had relieved the LORAN TU of its ASR role, operated its Warwick from here on detachment in January, and on 7 February moved in permanently from Tiree. It was to be a short tour; like so many other units that had served here, it moved to Limavady on 31 March 1945.

Mullaghmore, seen here in the early 1990s, has not deteriorated a great deal since, with large sections of the original airfield still in place.

The airfield's runways now provide a solid base for many local businesses, and both are complete, as is a third, which was never quite completed. At the southern end of the airfield a section of perimeter track provides a 400-yard runway for several light aircraft now based here. Wartime buildings still remain on all sides of the airfield, and the Type 12779 control tower is now a private dwelling.

Main features:

Concrete/asphalt runways: QDM 190 2,000 yards, 270 1,421 yards. *Hangars:* four T2. *Hardstandings:* three 150-foot circular, twenty-seven 125-foot, fifty 40-foot-wide 'fingers'. *Accommodation:* RAF: 3,304.

MUSGRAVE CHANNEL (BELFAST HARBOUR), Belfast City

53°37'00"N/05°53'30"W; J365765. One-third of a mile W of Belfast City Airport

Flying boats made use of the Channel from 1928 to 1949. Civilian aircraft also used it before and after the war, with the RAF and quite possibly occasional USN machines using it during wartime.

Sunderland V PP151 is moored in Belfast Harbour during the late 1940s, having been returned to Short's following service with 302 FTU, 209 Squadron and the MAEE.

MYRESIDE, Edinburgh

NT235715

This is another First World War LG located on the edge of Edinburgh that was used by 77(HD) Squadron.

NEWTOWNARDS (ARDS), Down

54°34'51"N/05°41'40"W. 1 mile SW of Newtownards

Described as 'Ulster's First Airport' when it opened as Ards Airport on 31 August 1934, technically it was Northern Ireland's first dedicated airport, taking over from the limited civilian facilities that had been offered by Aldergrove up to this date. The site was created thanks to Lord Londonderry, who gave up 50 acres of his estate. Conveniently, the Lord was a pilot himself and also the Secretary of State for Air from 1931 to 1935.

The small but busy airport was operated as a private venture by Airwork Ltd, and drew in many small airlines including Blackpool & West Coast, Olley Air Services and Northern & Scottish Railway Air Services, flying a host of different types including the DH.84 and 86. This booming period was brought to a halt when Sydenham was opened in March 1938, and all the airlines moved there. Only the Northern Ireland Flying Club remained, but with the beginning of the war all civilian flying was brought to a close.

Ulster's first airport is seen on its official opening day, 31 August 1934.

Ards, which was now referred to as Newtownards, was requisitioned by the military, which wasted no time in expanding it. It became an RLG for 24 EFTS from 13 November 1939, but, by the summer 1940 the Tiger Moths and Battles had moved to Luton. They were replaced by 416 Flight's Lysanders, which arrived from Aldergrove on 27 June. While serving there, the flight was redesignated as 231 Squadron, which moved here permanently on 15 July, only to leave for Long Kesh on 11 December 1941.

Its place was taken by 1480 AACF from December, also equipped with the Lysander. This unit was joined by 82 Group CF on 5 January 1942 and 1493 TTF the following day, both from Ballyhalbert. 'S' Flight, 1 AACU, was also formed here on 26 January with Henleys for target-towing duties with 17 LAAPC at St John's Point.

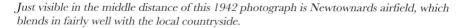

Just visible in the middle distance of this 1942 photograph is Newtownards airfield, which blends in fairly well with the local countryside.

By April Defiants began to arrive for 1480 Flight, with Hurricanes following in June, and by 1943 Oxfords and Martinets were also added. The flight spent most of the spring and summer detached at Eglinton, from where it worked with 501 Squadron from Ballykelly. Renamed 1493 Flight, it moved to Ballyhalbert on 26 January 1943.

1480 Flight was detached to Sydenham during September 1942 and, despite having a wide of range of types, it was the Lysanders that were still carrying out most of the work. 'S' Flight, 1 AACU, was redesignated 1617 AACF on 1 November and was now working with 18 HAAPC, also at St John's Point. 1480 Flight joined 1617 Flight on 17 September 1943, and on 1 December, together with 1617 Flight, was dissolved to create 290 Squadron. The new squadron's role was still anti-aircraft co-operation, but by now its aircraft were just the Hurricane, Oxford and Martinet. Newtownards's association with this role came to an end on 25 March 1944 when 290 Squadron moved to Long Kesh. A lack of hangars and rapidly deteriorating runways had forced the move, and the only military aircraft to operate from here from now on were gliders.

The runway layout has barely changed over the years, although the main one has since been extended. Remnants of wartime occupation can still be found.

With the airfield now relegated to C&M, under the control of Long Kesh, 201 GS was next to arrive from Lisburn in April 1944. It was joined by 203 GS, which was formed here in early 1945, and they operated side-by-side until 201 GS moved to Long Kesh in December. By now the airfield had been passed back to the Londonderry estate, but 203 GS remained until mid-1947, by which time it was operating from Downhill. The GS returned briefly in November 1952 before moving on to Toome on 3 July 1953.

Miles aircraft built Messengers in the 1950s, and Silver City also flew Type 170s to West Freugh from here. However, both fell by the wayside and it is thanks to the formation of the Ulster Flying Club in 1961 that Newtownards still thrives today. Limited military activity made a comeback on 1 November 1995 when 664 VGS was re-formed with the Vigilant.

Newtownards's wartime past can still be revealed thanks to pillboxes, a seagull trench, gun butts and air raid shelters, which still remain around the edge of the airfield. The pole for the wind-sock on the top of a pillbox, which is actually a Miles Aerovan tail-boom, also still survives.

Main features:
Concrete and tarmac runways with grass extensions: QDM 040 1,287+50 yards, 160 667+50 yards, 090 364+550 yards. *Hangars:* four blister, one airport. *Accommodation:* RAF: 1,171.

NIGG, Highland

NH790690

A seaplane station was located here from 1913, but was not used a great deal and was not developed. During the Second World War there was an MTB base on the same site near the Nigg ferry.

NORTH QUEENSFERRY, Fife

56°00'01"N/03°24'00"W; NT125807

Opened in the summer of 1917, North Queensferry was a Kite Balloon Station. It housed eight balloons and worked closely with the Grand Fleet. Personnel were accommodated in wooden huts on the site, while the officers enjoyed the Ferry Gate House.

NUTT'S CORNER, Antrim

54°37'54"N/06°09'46"W; J190775. 2 miles E of Crumlin off A52

This busy airfield and no less busy post-war civilian airport is a good example of what could have been. Its location, facilities and access all indicated that this would be Belfast's international airport, but alas it was not to be.

Flying began from here in the early 1930s, when it was little more than a small grass airfield. The province's first flying service to London began in 1934, and this factor would not have been overlooked when sites for expansion were surveyed at the beginning of the war. In the summer of 1940 Nutt's Corner was selected, and within weeks construction of a large airfield for the use of Coastal Command was under way.

The first unit was 120 Squadron, which re-formed on 3 June 1941. Five days later Liberators began to arrive to equip the unit and the process of working up to operational status began. On 20 September the first operation was flown, followed by the first convoy patrols, which began a few days later. Contact with the enemy came on 4 October with a long combat with an Fw 200, resulting in both aircraft being damaged. A similar combat took placed on 22 October when Flt Lt T. M. Bulloch and crew tackled an Fw 200 head-on, scoring several hits. While the Fw 200 escaped into cloud, a U-boat was also spotted, staying visible long enough for Bulloch to straddle it with three depth charges.

A Liberator III of 120 Squadron is being prepared for another long-range Atlantic sortie from Nutt's Corner.

While 120 Squadron continued flying over the Atlantic hunting for U-boats, 220 Squadron moved in from Wick on 9 January 1942. Equipped with the Fortress I, the squadron spent the next three months working up, flying its first operational sortie on 29 April. Very few were flown and 220 Squadron moved to Ballykelly on 20 June.

1445 Flight arrived from Lyneham on 7 May 1942 with Liberators, which were flown by 159 and 160 Squadron crews. The same day 160 Squadron arrived, also from Lyneham, with its Liberators, to gain A/S experience before it left for the Middle East. The same month Lancasters from 44 Squadron from Waddington arrived to carry out A/S training, returning on 19 July. Two days later 120 Squadron moved to Ballykelly.

Nutt's Corner then became very quiet and the opportunity to upgrade the airfield was taken. The main runways were extended following criticism from Liberator captains who were always on the edge of safety margins when taking off fully loaded. By the end of 1942 the contractors were still occupied, not only with the runways but also with fifty spectacle dispersals, and it was not until 2 January 1943 that another unit arrived. 231 Squadron brought its Tomahawks and Lysanders from Long Kesh, only to disappear to Ballyhalbert on detachment for a few weeks. After returning, the Army Co-operation squadron departed to Clifton.

On 12 March 1943 Nutt's Corner became the home of 104 (Transport) OTU, equipped with Wellingtons. With workmen still all around, the OTU did the best it could until 10 July, when 'A' Flight was moved to Maghaberry. The flight was later moved to Mullaghmore on 2 October, eventually returning here on 18 January 1944 when all groundwork had been completed. The newly combined 104 OTU was to be short-lived, and was disbanded on 5 February. Aldergrove was going through a period of disruption of its own during early 1944, and 1674 HCU moved in with its Fortresses and Liberators until the work was completed on 18 March.

On 7 October 1944 1332 CU arrived from Longtown with Stirlings, Liberators, a C-87 and Yorks. With fewer aircraft in the circuit, Nutt's Corner's workload entered a downward trend in early 1945. 1332 CU departed for Riccall on 27 April, leaving the airfield to celebrate the end of the war with only a few RAF personnel in residence.

Weeks passed before the airfield's future took another turn in June when the Royal Navy arrived. By 9 July the airfield was under Admiralty control, and two days later was commissioned as HMS *Pintail*. The first FAA units arrived on 31 July with 1837 Squadron's Corsairs from Eglinton. The unit was disbanded here in August, together with three others, 891, 1835 and 1852 Squadrons. 803 Squadron, the first of several Seafire units to pass through, arrived from Arbroath on 23 September 1945, and 801, 802, 807, 883 and 879 Squadrons followed. The last of them was gone by February 1946; this left just a detachment from 772 Squadron, which left for Burscough in March.

On 31 March 1946 HMS *Pintail* was paid off and handed back to RAF Transport Command. Back in 1944 44 Group had established a Transport Diversion Terminal Unit here, which was probably still active during the Royal Navy's tenure as it was not fully disbanded until 25 April 1946.

The scene was now set for a new role, and thanks to BEA threatening to withdraw its services from Northern Ireland due to lack of space at Sydenham, Nutt's Corner was offered as an alternative. On 1 November 1946 the airfield became to new Belfast Airport by quickly modifying existing buildings into a presentable terminal befitting a regional airport. Alas, its tenure as an airport was as temporary as its buildings, and the role was lost to Aldergrove on 26 September 1963.

Limited light aircraft operated from here until the end of the 1960s, and thanks to a lack of development the airfield's runways and dispersals are virtually complete. The A26 Moira Road now follows a straight course down one of the runways, and Nutt's Corner Road follows the northern perimeter track.

Main features:
Tarmac runways: QDM 260 1,600 yards (extended to 2,000 yards in 1943), 222 1,600 yards, 158 1,200 yards. *Hangars:* two T1, two T2. *Hardstandings:* fifty loop. *Accommodation:* RAF: 2,093; WAAF: 318.

Nutt's Corner is seen in near pristine condition on 23 January 1968, photographed by a Canberra PR.7 from 18,000 feet.

OBAN, Strathclyde

56°24'23"N/05°29'59"W; NM855300. In Oban Bay off Kerrera Island

Conveniently sheltered by Kerrera Island, the waters of Oban Bay first attracted flying boats in 1933. British Flying Boats Ltd, using the Saro Cloud, brought fare-paying passengers for special events such as the Lochaber Games.

The RAF spotted Oban's use as a flying boat station, but at first only used it as a refuelling stop. However, once the war began service personnel began to arrive and contractors started to expand the site. Moorings were established in the bay and a bomb dump was built at the north-eastern end of Kerrera Island. Accommodation was provided by hostels in Oban, and by 1940 Ganavan Sands was opened to provide maintenance facilities. From 7 October 1939 Oban was a fully functioning RAF station, and the same day the Stranraers of 209 Squadron moved in from Invergordon.

Blackburn Perth flying boats of 209 Squadron at Oban in the 1930s.

The old but reliable Stranraers carried out many patrols over the Atlantic, but unfortunately for 209 Squadron it was earmarked to receive the Lerwick from December onwards. This flying boat immediately struggled with serviceability problems, and the squadron wisely held on to its Stranraers during the transition to the Lerwick.

By April 1940 the squadron's Stranraers had gone and the unit struggled on. The whole squadron was grounded on at least two occasions for modifications, and another aircraft was lost on 29 June. The squadron continued to operate from here until 12 July, when it moved to Pembroke Dock. During its tour two U-boats were attacked by Lerwicks, causing no damage to either.

The next day 210 Squadron's Sunderlands took over from Pembroke Dock. Following detachments to Reykjavik, Sullom Voe and Stranraer, the Sunderlands were replaced by Catalinas in April 1941, and after working up on the Catalina the squadron moved to Sullom Voe on 28 February 1942.

Sunderlands returned on 10 March 1942 when 228 Squadron arrived from Stranraer. Oban began to get very busy when 423 Squadron was formed here on 18 May; it spent the majority of its time working up before moving to Lough Erne on 2 November. It was replaced by 422 Squadron, equipped with Catalinas, which arrived from Long Kesh the same day.

422 Squadron exchanged its Catalinas only days after arriving and, like the squadron before it, spent most of the tour here preparing for operations. The rest was spent on detachment at Jui in Sierra Leone before moving on to Bowmore on 8 May 1943. By early December 228 Squadron also

moved to Lough Erne, and on 23 January 1944 Oban became the home of 330 Squadron from Reykjavik. The squadron maintained a detachment at Reykjavik with a pair of N3P-Bs while it flew the Catalina from here. Detachments continued at Reykjavik and Budayeri until February, when the unit began to convert to Sunderlands. The N3P-Bs were flown from Iceland to Oban, where they were dismantled and stored until the end of the war. By late April the squadron began to fly the Sunderland on operations, later moving to Sullom Voe on 12 July.

302 FTU followed on 21 July, bringing four Catalinas from Stranraer for its crew training. Only one unit was ever formed here, and that was 524 Squadron on 20 October. The squadron was equipped with the Mariner but, unlike the USN, which used the type in great numbers, the aircraft was found to be unsuitable for RAF operations. This was mainly due to its poor single-engine performance, which was not much better than the Lerwick. By 7 December 524 Squadron was disbanded here.

This rare machine in RAF markings is a 524 Squadron Mariner at Oban in 1943.

The FTU expanded on 12 January 1944 when it absorbed 308 FTU and took over its Sunderlands. Detached to Alness from March to 11 June, 302 FTU was destined to be the last RAF unit to operate from Oban, leaving for Killadeas from 15 April 1945.

Less than two weeks later, Oban was reduced to C&M, its usefulness now deemed to be over with full closure following shortly afterwards. Today some remnants can still be seen, including the remains of slipways and the substantial bomb dump, which still defiantly sits on Kerrera Island.

OMAGH (STRAUGHROY), County Tyrone

54°37'16"N/07°19'40"W; H437748. 1½ miles NW of Omagh

This First World War LG was home to 105 Squadron for more than eight months. Its use prior to that is unknown, but on 19 May 1918 the unit's RE.8s arrived from Ayr. The squadron briefly detached to Oranmore in June, and by December had re-equipped with the F.2b. 105 Squadron moved to Oranmore on 28 January 1919, and with that Omagh undoubtedly closed.

ORANGEFIELD, Belfast City

54°35'19"N/05°52'83"W; J370730; 2 miles ESE of Belfast City Hall

A small LG was located here for the use of RAF communications aircraft from July 1922.

ORANMORE, County Galway

53°17'01"N/08°55'15"W. 5 miles E of Galway

Like Omagh, it was 105 Squadron's RE.8s that were the first aircraft to use Oranmore during a detachment in June 1918. On 28 January 1919 the squadron returned, now with the F.2b.

During June, 106 Squadron arrived from Fermoy, only staying a few weeks. 105 Squadron was renumbered 2 Squadron on 1 February, but had moved to Fermoy by July 1920. Finally, the last of the RAF movements here was another detachment; this time by 100 Squadron from Baldonnel.

PAISLEY, Renfrewshire

4 GS, with Cadets, was formed here in November 1943 and remained until May 1945, when it moved to Abbotsinch.

PERTH (SCONE), Tayside

56°26'21"N/03°22'19"W. Off A94 halfway between Scone and Balbeggie

Now in its eighth decade and with a secure future ahead of it, Perth (or Scone) is as busy today as it ever was. While its training establishments are not churning out as many pilots as they did during the war, it still supports up to 70,000 aircraft movements per year.

It was opened on 5 June 1936 by the Secretary of State for Air, Lord Swinton, and managed by Airwork Ltd for Perth Corporation. While civilian aircraft movements would be commonplace before the outbreak of the war, Perth's first military unit was 11 E&RTFS, formed on 27 January 1936.

Airwork was tasked with opening a second unit on 9 January 1939, resulting in the formation of 7 CANS with Rapides and Ansons. On the outbreak of war only one change occurred, with 11 E&RFTS becoming 11 EFTS on 3 September. 'D' Flight of the A&AEE brought its RDF Battles from Martlesham Heath on 15 September, then went through a number of changes, including becoming the Station Flight and being renamed 'A' Flight, SD Flight, before moving to St Athan on 14 November.

7 CANS was the next to change its title by becoming 7 AONS on 1 November 1939, now with observer and navigator training added to its remit. From January 1940 both the EFTS and AONS training sorties were flown by military instructors following orders to mobilise all airmen in that role. Most ground personnel and engineers were still civilian, but this would be diluted as the war progressed. These changes only affected 7 AONS for a short while as it was disbanded on 7 June 1940.

From 4 September 1939 British Airways began a new service to Stavanger. Swedish-registered Ju 52s were also seen at Perth from November 1939 through to April 1940. This joint Norwegian and Swedish service came to an end with the German invasion of Norway.

Perth's flying training ability was expanded again on 8 October 1940 with the formation of 5 FIS from 'E' Flight of 11 EFTS to train flying instructors with Tiger Moths and Magisters. In practice, all of these were shared with 11 EFTS, which by December had its own establishment raised from seventy-two to ninety Tiger Moths. Also operated by Airwork, 5 FIS made good use of Perth's own SLG, which had been established at Whitefield since December 1939. By 23 November 1942 5 FIS had been disbanded.

Hundreds, if not thousands, of pilots passed through 11 EFTS during the war years, the majority going on to serve with Bomber Command after completing their AFU training. Poor weather and accidents attempted to hinder the process, which was carried out twenty-four hours a day. Despite the war approaching its finale, further pre-AFU courses were laid on for those pilots trained in Canada and Africa, and the 'culture shock' of the British weather was quickly taught to these 'fair weather flyers'.

The association with the Tiger Moth continued during the post-war years, and on 18 March 1947 11 EFTS was renamed 11 RFS. Still operated by Airwork, it was not until the early 1950s that Chipmunks began to replace Tiger Moths. This was to be short-lived, though, as Perth's longest-serving military training unit was brought to a close on 20 June 1954. 666 Squadron with Austers was re-formed here in 1949, comprising 1966 and 1967 Flights; both had left by the early 1950s.

Not many of 11 EFTS's aircraft can be seen in this aerial view of RAF Perth/Scone in 1943.

One of the larger aircraft to visit Perth over the years was this Airwork Ltd Viking IB during a late 1940s/early 1950s air show.

By now the airfield was owned by Airwork, and in 1960 the company bought AST, an engineer school, and established it at Perth. The whole training operation was known as AST, which has since gained an enviable reputation and is referred to as Britain's Air University. By 1996 AST no longer carried out pilot training and the business was sold to Morris Leslie Ltd. Regardless, Perth remains the busiest GA airfield in Scotland and has been the home of the Scottish Aero Club since 1927.

Perth is a charming airfield, and manages to retain some of its 1930s heritage thanks to the original pre-war hangars and a host of restored and well-maintained buildings covering the site.

Main features:
Grass runway: QDM NE-SW 1,300 yards. *Hangars:* one 60 x 90 feet civil, one 120 x 110 feet, six EO blister. *Accommodation:* RAF: 391.

PETERHEAD (LONGSIDE), Grampian

57°30'55"N/01°52'23"W. 3 miles W of Peterhead off A950

Peterhead was opened before it was ready and became active from 4 July 1942, when 132 Squadron was re-formed with Spitfires. By 19 July the squadron was operational despite the airfield being far from it. Only two runways and two-thirds of the perimeter were open, with technical and domestic buildings far behind.

A snow-covered Beaufighter IF of 68 Squadron stands at Peterhead in early 1942.

Peterhead gained Fordoun as a satellite from September and a second at Fraserburgh from December. A host of fighter squadrons, both RAF and FAA, served here between 1941 and 1944, all tasked with flying sector and convoy patrols. The Spitfire was the most common type in the RAF inventory, although the Beaufighter was also a regular resident at Peterhead. Fulmars and Sea Hurricanes made their presence felt from the FAA, but encounters with the enemy by any unit up to late 1944 were rare or non-existent.

The first of two Army Co-operation squadrons, both flying the Mustang, passed through on 4 January 1944. 430 Squadron was first, replaced by 414 Squadron on 5 February. Like its predecessor, 414 would carry out vital low-level reconnaissance leading up to and during D-Day. The squadron left for Odiham on 20 February, having shared the airfield with a detachment of 63 Squadron Mustangs from Turnhouse. 63 Squadron returned briefly at the end of March.

This group of pilots of 'B' Flight, 602 Squadron, includes Fg Off J. A. Marryshow (far right), who hailed from Trinidad, one of many from the Caribbean who served this country.

From September 1944 the activities of several airfields in the north-east of Scotland were being affected by the formation of the new strike wings. Losses were mounting on their operations along the Norwegian coast, and despite Mosquitoes providing fighter escort a dedicated fighter unit was needed. Peterhead was destined to provide the home for several more fighter squadrons, the first of which, 65 Squadron with Mustangs, arrived on 3 October from Matlaske to escort a Beaufighter 'Ramrod' being flown the following day.

The first permanent fighter squadron to be based here as a direct result of the formation of the strike wings was 315 Squadron, which arrived from Coltishall on 1 November. It was no stranger to flying long-range operations and its Mustangs would prove to be very useful over Norway.

315 Squadron joined by 309 Squadron on 13 November from Drem, another Polish unit that was no stranger to Peterhead; it had been coming and going for several weeks, having only re-equipped from the Hurricane to the Mustang during the previous October.

One of the first operations flown by 315 Squadron was on 11 November 1944, when six aircraft were detailed to escort seven Liberators. After several successful escort sorties during the remainder of November, the squadron was now into the routine of joining up with Mosquitoes and Beaufighters.

From 7 December the low number of defending German fighters would increase after a large number of Fw 190s and Bf 109s moved into Norway. Mustangs of 315 Squadron escorted a large force of Beaufighters and Mosquitoes for a strike in the Ålesund area, but before they had chance to attack they were pounced upon by several enemy fighters. One Mustang was shot down by a Bf 109, which was also shot down before the German pilot had a chance to celebrate.

309 Squadron left on 12 December followed by 315 Squadron on 16 January 1945, both moving to Andrews Field. They swapped places with 65 Squadron, which arrived here two days later, but before it had chance to settle in it moved to Banff on 28 January, only to return again on 2 February. The following day 65 Squadron carried out its first operation from Peterhead by escorting nineteen Mosquitoes on an anti-shipping patrol successfully and without loss.

This 309 Squadron Mustang III, seen with its Polish pilot, operated from Peterhead on three occasions.

Peterhead's capability was bolstered again on 13 February when more Mustangs from 19 Squadron arrived from Andrews Field. The unit had gained valuable experience flying long-range bomber escorts and armed reconnaissance flights over Germany before moving to Scotland.

65 Squadron was very lucky not to have incurred high losses when it was bounced by at least fourteen Bf 109s on 16 February. Coming out of the sun, the escort was preparing to head for home when the enemy struck, hitting several of the Mustangs. A series of dogfights followed and three of the attacking Bf 109s were shot down, together with a fourth probable victory. All of the Mustangs returned safely, the majority with an extra hole or two.

19 Squadron flew its first escort on 3 March 1945 when it looked after twenty Mosquitoes that were heading for a strike between Bergen and Stavanger. It was not until 12 March that 19 Squadron's tally was on the increase again during an escort in the Skagerrak area. After finding no shipping to attack, the force was just about to set course for home when it was engaged by at least ten Bf 109s. Sqn Ldr Hearne, the OC, ordered his pilots to jettison their drop tanks and, within seconds, a dogfight began. Down below him Hearne spotted a pair of Bf 109s attacking a section of Mustangs and, despite one of the German fighters flying with its undercarriage down, it still managed to turn as tightly as the Mustang. Closing on the tail of one of the Bf 109s, Hearne fired two short bursts, hitting the starboard wing. After a final burst of fire the Bf 109 entered a steep dive before hitting the sea.

More Mustangs arrived on 1 May 1945 when 234 Squadron moved in from Bentwaters, briefly making Peterhead one of the busiest fighter stations in Scotland.

Further combined escorts were flown by 19 and 65 Squadrons on 2 May, and the following day 65 Squadron flew its last operation. On the same day 234 Squadron took part in its first operation when it joined 19 Squadron to escorted Mosquitoes on a shipping strike. The two squadrons flew together again on 4 May, which was to be the last anti-shipping escort operation of the war from Peterhead. While the strike was reasonably successful for the Mosquitoes, it was a disaster for the Mustangs. Light flak over the targets brought down three 234 Squadron aircraft and, while manoeuvring low over the sea, two from 19 Squadron collided.

122 Squadron's Mustangs arrived from Andrews Field on 5 May, while 65 Squadron left on the 6th for Andrews Field. The final squadron to arrive here was 611 Squadron from Hunsdon the following day.

The four Mustang squadrons that remained were now tasked with the odd ASR sortie while they awaited their own and the airfield's fate. 19 Squadron was the first to go when it was posted to Acklington on 23 May 1945. On 3 July 122 and 234 Squadrons left for Dyce and Molesworth respectively., leaving just 611 Squadron, which, together with the other AAF squadron, was disbanded here on 15 August.

This brought an end to military flying at the airfield, which remained Air Ministry land until September 1959. Aviation made a comeback in 1975 when North Scottish Helicopters began operations; setting up on the northern side of the airfield, the company built a pair of new hangars and supporting buildings, flying from a section of the original shorter 1,465-yard east-west runway. A subsidiary of Management Aviation, the company flew the Sikorsky S-76 from Peterhead out to the oil rings for many years from what is now more commonly known as Longside Heliport. Still very much in use, the heliport is also visited by Bond and Bristow helicopters, usually as a refuelling point for operations from Aberdeen.

This 1990s aerial view shows the Peterhead heliport positioned on the north-eastern edge, making use of the centre of the runway just to the south of it. A short 350-yard fixed-wing grass runway is also marked out alongside the original concrete one.

The remains of the airfield are now fenced off but easily accessible. All three runways remain intact as well as the perimeter track, hangar and blister bases and dispersals. The control tower was knocked down many years ago, but many other buildings can still be found around the site.

On 14 September 2003 a memorial cairn was unveiled just off the A950 on the Buthlaw turn-off. Erected by the Longside branch of the Royal British Legion (Scotland), the memorial is a fitting tribute to all who served at Peterhead during the Second World War.

Main features:
Tarmac runways: QDM 171 1,772 yards, 231 1,500 yards, 290 1,465 yards. *Hangars:* five Teesside, eight over blister. *Hardstandings:* four SE, five TE. *Accommodation:* RAF: 1,576; WAAF: 389.

PETERHEAD BAY, Grampian/Aberdeenshire

NK130447

A seaplane repair and store base was opened here in 1918, but is likely to have existed only until 1919 at the latest.

PIEROWALL (WESTRAY), Orkney

59°21'03"N/02°57'00"W; HY440482. Bay of Pierowall, Westray, Orkney Islands

A seaplane station was here by early 1917 in a very good position, 30 miles north of Scapa Flow. Babies were the first aircraft to make use of it during the summer, and a detachment of two F.3s of 306 Flight from Houton Bay stayed from 10 August 1918. One of these aircraft, N4411, flown by Capt P. Bend, attacked a U-boat on 29 August.

Beyond this, very little is known about Pierowall, and it is surprising that it was not used more. Operating from here cut down the flying time to the Fair Island Channel, where most of the opportunities for attacking U-boats existed.

This is one of just two Felixstowe F.3s of 306 Flight that saw service at Pierowall during the last few months of the Second World War.

PORT ELLEN (ISLAY/GLENEGEDALE), Strathclyde

55°40'54"N/06°15'24"W; NR325515. 4 miles NNW of Port Ellen on A486, Isle of Islay

Compressed between a local major road and the edge of Laggan Bay, Port Ellen was also known as Glenegedale, which was a hamlet on the opposite side of the main road and the site for a large communal area.

Port Ellen was opened in August 1940 and one of the first aircraft to arrive was a 48 Squadron Anson from Aldergrove. The squadron returned on detachment after re-equipping with the Beaufort in early 1941, then after a few weeks it left for Hooton Park, becoming the only RAF front-line squadron to stay here during the war. 3 (C)OTU carried out night-flying practice from August 1941 until the end of the year.

Visitors were on the increase during 1942, especially FAA types such as Swordfishes and Rocs from Machrihanish. Although never designated as such, Port Ellen found itself steadily becoming an ELG, especially for the USAAF, which was now beginning to cross the Atlantic in numbers. One example was B-24D 41-11874, which developed an oil leak and landed on 9 September; the six 20th FG P-38s escorting the bomber also landed.

Port Ellen finally gained its own unit on 31 December 1942 when 304 FTU was formed, tasked with training Beaufighter and Boston crews to fly long-distance ferry flights for overseas destinations. Very few Bostons ever arrived, but the Beaufighter served here in generous numbers, and as a consequence suffered a high accident rate.

On 18 October 1943 lodger facilities were offered to a pair of FAA squadrons, 878 and 890 with Martlets, which arrived from HMS *Illustrious*. A few days later these were replaced by Wildcats and both squadrons remained as part of their working period before leaving for Eglinton on 13 December. Their brief stay may have brought Port Ellen to the attention of the Admiralty, which looked at the possibility of making it an FOB for Eglinton. Unfortunately it never happened, despite several FAA fighters making good use of the airfield before the end of the war.

By late 1943 the airfield was still being extended and now had a bomb dump and permanent control tower. Despite this, 304 FTU was moved to Melton Mowbray from 3 January 1944.

Only waifs and strays descended throughout 1944, and it was not until June 1945 that aircraft intentionally arrived. The first of several detachments by Mosquitoes of the MAEE carried out weapons trials from here, the last leaving on 21 September.

By 1947 the airfield was under the control of the MoA, and not long afterwards BEA began scheduled services. By the late 1970s Loganair was in charge and, as with most of Scotland's regional airports, Port Ellen (now known as Islay Airport) is under the control of HIAL. Various scheduled services to the mainland and air ambulance flights are the airport's main workload today, and annual movements total more than 2,500, while passenger numbers are approaching 30,000. It was at Islay that Prince Charles overshot the runway in a 32 Squadron BAe 146 on 29 June 1994.

Main features:
Bitumen and sand runways: QDM 226 1,760 yards, 135 1,630 yards, 266 1,366 yards. *Hangars:* five half T2, one Callender Hamilton. *Accommodation:* RAF: 1,113; WAAF: 266.

PORT LAING (CARLINGNOSE), Fife

56°00'56"N/03°23'27"W. Near beach at Port Laing, half a mile N of North Queensferry

Established in 1912, this seaplane base was not busy until just before the start of the First World War, when Longhorn Seaplane No 71 and Borel No 86 were flying from here until early 1914. However, on 28 February 1914 the station had to be moved and dispersed due to the expiry of the lease. The station's hanger was later moved to Stannergate.

The site is now occupied by 'executive'-type houses.

PORTOBELLO BARRACKS (CATHAL BRUGHA BARRACKS), Dublin

53°19'65"N/06°16'15"W; O153322. 1¼ miles S of O'Connell Street Bridge

This was the location of one of the British Army's early forays into aviation. From 22 July 1817 the barracks was used as an Army balloon launch site.

PRESTWICK (PRESTWICK AYR/GLASGOW PRESTWICK), Strathclyde

55°30'28"N/04°35'12"W. Immediately NE and E of Prestwick town

When the small airfield at Prestwick was opened on 17 February 1936, those present could have had no idea that it would grow to be one of the busiest in Scotland during the war and beyond.

On the day of its opening 12 E&RFTS was formed with a wide range of aircraft, and was not joined until 15 August 1938 when 1 CANS arrived; both were operated by SAL. On the outbreak of war, 12 E&RFTS became 12 EFTS, and by 1 November 1 CANS had become 1 AONS. The EFTS was flying Tiger Moths while the new AONS had Ansons and three ex-KLM Fokker airliners. On 2 December 10 AONS from Grangemouth was absorbed, making 1 AOS the largest of its kind with a capacity to train up to 300 pilots at a time.

From December 1939 onwards, SAL began to gain a large amount of aircraft modification, assembly and preparation for service work, beginning with Wellesley modifications. Many minor contracts were to follow, and before the war was over SAL was running large factories, not only at Prestwick but also at eight other sites across the country. Types handled ranged from gliders through to Liberators. SAL worked as part of the CRO until 1946, and the experience and, more importantly, the wealth gained secured the future of the company.

Pending the completion of Ayr, several fighter squadrons moved in during late 1939 and 1940. As Prestwick's traffic increased, 12 EFTS gained Dundonald as an RLG from 21 March 1940. September saw the arrival of 102 Squadron's Whitleys from Leeming to carry out convoy escort duties for Coastal Command; five weeks later the unit was moved to Linton-on-Ouse.

263 Squadron was detached with Hurricanes in October and, later the same month, the AI/ASV School was formed with Blenheims. By the end of the year the school became 3 RS, now with Blenheims for AI training and Bothas for ASV training. Before the end of 1941 Ansons were being used, and on 1 June a separate AI Flight was formed, which moved to Usworth where it formed the nucleus for 62 (AI)OTU that was established there. On 19 August 1942 the unit changed its name again, this time to 3 RDFS, and moved to Hooton Park in December.

602 Squadron's Spitfires arrived from Westhampnett on 17 December 1940 and were joined by a detachment of 600 Squadron with Beaufighters from Catterick in January 1941. Having served during the Battle of Britain, 602 Squadron's pilots were very amused by the commotion caused when the air-raid siren was sounded for the first time; the 'enemy' turned out to be a Blenheim and a Manchester. 602 Squadron moved to Ayr on 15 April and, thanks to Prestwick's neighbour finally opening, fighter squadrons became a rarity.

In March 1941 the foundations for Prestwick becoming the largest transatlantic ferry base in the country were laid. The RAF Delivery Flight Reception Party was formed to accept aircraft arriving from North America and to welcome, feed and accommodate aircrews and passengers.

By now 12 EFTS had been disbanded, and on 19 July 1941 1 AONS was part-absorbed into other units and part-emigrated to Queenstown, Cape Province, being renamed 47 Air School, SAAF. The latter departure was to make way for the establishment of the ATFERO, which was created by MAP and run by BOAC. The first aircraft had been crossing the Atlantic since late 1940, terminating in Northern Ireland; from now on they would head direct for Prestwick. To help control the large amount of traffic, a TAC was formed at Powbank Mill to look after local airways; by October it had moved to Redbrae House, where it would remain until the end of the war.

Hudsons were the first aircraft to arrive in bulk, and to keep the flow moving a Return Ferry Service was formed with Liberators to fly crews back for more aircraft. Initially the service operated

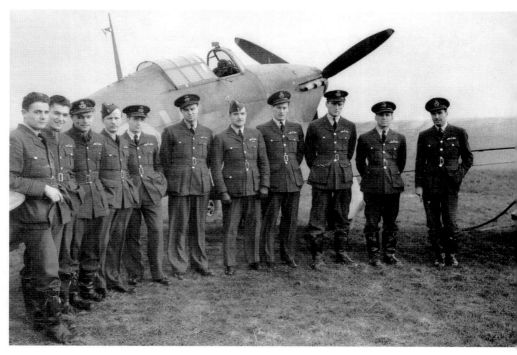

Pilots of 1 Squadron RCAF pose at Prestwick during its early wartime days when it served as a stepping stone prior to the opening of Ayr.

A 120 Squadron Liberator III is undergoing maintenance in Scottish Aviation's giant 'Palace of Engineering' hangar at Prestwick in 1941.

A Catalina arrives at Prestwick after crossing 'the pond' via Iceland in 1941.

from Ayr, which was no quieter than Prestwick. Ferry Command took control of the operation until March 1943, when it was superseded by Transport Command. The opening of the Atlantic Ferry route accelerated the delivery time of American and Canadian-built aircraft by months.

Liberators, Dakotas, Mitchells and Canadian-built Lancasters arrived throughout 1942. A B-17 for delivery to the 97th BG at Polebrook arrived on 1 July, the first of 12,357 B-17s that would pass through Prestwick. Canadian-built Mosquitoes followed en masse from 8 August 1943, the first aircraft flying from Gander to Prestwick in a record time of 5hr 37min.

By early 1944 the ferry workload was so high that the 311th FS moved in from Cluntoe to help with the onward delivery to the four BADs. More American support units arrived during the year and in August 1944 7,847 aircraft movements were logged here. Prior to this the RAF had formed its own Air Despatch and Reception Unit to handle the aircraft for its own use.

Several regular services were flown, starting with Trans-Canada Airlines flying Lancasters from Dorval via Montreal and on to Prestwick, loaded with mail for its Canadian servicemen. The USAAF flew scheduled services with C-54s, and the RCAF's 168 Heavy Transport Squadron flew mail runs using B-17s.

Prestwick begins to sprawl across the countryside as dispersals and any spare concrete fill with B-17s and B-24s.

By the end of the war more than 37,000 aircraft had been delivered to Prestwick, and it was not until late August 1945 that the last flew across the Atlantic. During September the Americans began to withdraw and military movements now made way for civilian ones. On 22 October a Skymaster of American Export Airlines became the first post-war commercial flight, travelling from New York, via Labrador, Reykjavik and on to Prestwick. An array of wartime aircraft converted to airliners, such as Liberators and Lancasters, were replaced by DC-4s and Constellations, flown by airlines such as BOAC, KLM, SAS and TLA.

From 1 April 1946 Prestwick was under state ownership, and one month later control of TAC, Approach and Tower (located in the roof of Orangefield House) was handed over to the MoCA. The same day the ACC, Prestwick, was opened and continued under this guise until it was renamed the Scottish ATC Centre (Military) on 22 January 1974.

SAL had created a great deal of wealth for itself during the war and it rode on this success during the post-war period, gaining large contracts to convert ex-military C-47s and C-54s into civilian airliners. All of the work was carried in several large hangars, including the company's own 'Palace of Engineering', built for the Empire Exhibition, which was moved from Bellahouston in 1941. SAL went on to design and build the Pioneer and Twin Pioneer from 1952 to 1962, when production came to an end. Later, SAL would build the Bulldog and Jetstream here and win

The largest commercial airfield in Scotland, Prestwick remains busier but now lags behind Edinburgh and Glasgow.

overhaul contracts for RCAF CF-100s, CF-104s and T-33s. SAL ceased to exist from 1977 when it was dissolved into Hawker Siddeley, but still lives on with Spirit AeroSystems at Prestwick following BAe Systems' sale of its aerostructures business. The company now supplies Airbus, Boeing and Raytheon and has an average annual turnover of $3.28 billion.

The USAF returned in 1951 with the 1631st ABS to support the growing number of MATS flights that used Prestwick as a bridgehead. The 67th ARS also served here with HU-16s to provide ASR over the Atlantic until it moved to Spain in 1966, when the USAF element was closed down. Despite the units' departure, the USAF continues to use Prestwick as a staging point.

The same site that was occupied by the Americans was taken over by the Admiralty in 1971 and commissioned as HMS *Gannet* on 23 November. Prior to this 819 Squadron moved in its Sea Kings from Culdrose on 27 October. The squadron was in the A/S role and was here to support Clyde-based submarines and take part in exercises. During the 1970s 820 and 845 Squadrons, both with Sea Kings, also served here. 814 Squadron was re-formed at HMS *Gannet* in the A/S and Commando role on 20 March 1973. Its Sea Kings flew innumerable detachments to ships such as HMS *Bulwark* and *Hermes*, and left on the latter for Luqa on 7 February 1974. The early 1980s saw further detachments by 810, 814 and 826 Squadrons, leaving 819 Squadron to continue serving here ever since. However, its role has now changed and as from 31 October 2001 it was disbanded but renamed the same day as HMS *Gannet* SAR Flight of 771 Squadron, now operating the Sea King HAS.6. The unit is the only Royal Navy SAR in Scotland, and covers and area from southern Scotland to Edinburgh, 200 nautical miles west of the Irish coast, as far north as Ben Nevis, and south to the Lake District.

Prestwick's future as an airport is not quite so clear-cut as others in Scotland; it has seen a steady decline of passenger numbers since 2007, although approximately 1.6 million still pass through its gates. The reduction is partly due to several airlines focussing their operations on Edinburgh, which has been able to receive more flights from across the Atlantic.

Military movements still pass through, mainly from the USAF, but these are also in a steady decline, possibly a reflection of the world climate or the fact that modern transport no longer needs staging posts. Regardless, Prestwick's future is brighter than most.

Main features:
Concrete runways: QDM 315 2,200 yards (extended to 2,987 yards), 256 1,500 yards. *Hangars:* three Bellman, two B1, two 150 x 50 feet freight. *Hardstandings:* loops for three- and four-engined aircraft, aprons of 227,500, 68,444 and 59,200 square yards. *Accommodation:* RAF: 551; WAAF: 316.

QUEENSTOWN (COBH/AGHADA), Cork

51°50'38"N/08°12'37"W; W85088 65690. 2 miles NE of Whitegate

Queenstown was home to a USN seaplane station from 22 February 1918 to 10 April 1919. It was also used as an assembly and repair depot, and for training and seaplane patrols.

RAEBURNFOOT, Dumfries and Galloway

55°02'N/03°06'W

This was credited as an ELG or RLG during the Second World War.

RATHBANE HOUSE (BANEMORE OR BAWNMORE), Limerick

53°38'52"N/08°36'25"W; R591547

A small private LG was located here in September 1913, and was used by the RFC during the post-war period until returned to civilian hands and remaining in use until 1936.

RATHMULLAN (LOUGH SWILLY), Donegal

55°05'79"N/07°31'99"W; C298278; NW of Rathmullan Pier

Rathmullan was the home of 13 BB from 15 April 1918 until it was disbanded on 12 March 1919. Prior to this it is possible that the site was a Royal Navy Kite Balloon Station.

RATTRAY (CRIMOND), Aberdeenshire

57°36'46"N/01°53'13"W. 1 mile NE of Crimond off A90

In mid-1942 the Royal Navy was trying to find a new airfield at which to locate an OS. Dallachy was under construction and, after being turned down by Coastal Command, was offered to the Navy. With only two runways it was unsuitable for training, so the Navy decided to find its own airfield and turned down the offer in September 1942.

Looking west beyond Rattray Head in 1941, the land west of Strathbeg Loch will become one of the busiest airfields in the FAA's inventory.

A suitable location was found near Crimond, on the edge of the Loch of Strathbeg. The plan was to have the airfield completed by September 1943 but, due to trouble finding a contractor, work did not begin until March.

Construction took longer than planned and the need to move 2 OS had passed by the time the airfield was open. However, by July 1944 it was ready and the first unit, a detachment of 774 Squadron from St Merryn, brought its Barracudas here. It carried out TAG training while contractors still worked around it. Finally completed on 3 October, Rattray was commissioned as HMS *Merganser*.

By 24 October 1944 the rest of 774 Squadron arrived and the airfield began to come alive. Two more units, 714 and 717 Squadrons, moved in on 30 October, both from Fearn with Barracudas. With its three squadrons now in place, the task of training aircrew from being able to fly a Barracuda to being able to fight in one began. The courses covered a wide range, from formation flying, dive-bombing, low-level bombing and navigation exercises (both day and night) to night-landing training.

714 and 717 Squadrons were both TBR training squadrons and, working side-by-side, they received aircrew from their specialist training and assembled them into crews. 774 Squadron was responsible for armament training for observers and TAGs, hence the training earlier in the year. Using its own Barracudas, the squadron's Defiants were used as target tugs and the Hurricanes would give fighter affiliation experience.

The airfield was renamed RNAS Rattray Head on 1 July 1945, after the peninsula to the east of the airfield on the Aberdeenshire coast. The same day another Barracuda (ASH) unit was re-formed, this time 825 Squadron. By 31 August, like its predecessors, it had moved to Fearn.

Although the war in Europe was now over, TBR training did not slow down, as the Admiralty saw that there was still a need for torpedo-dropping aircraft in the Far East. The airfield became even busier on 28 July 1945 when 769 Squadron, another TBR training unit, arrived from East Haven.

The number of aircraft stationed here during 1945 was never less than 100. However, this could not last as the conflict in the Far East was drawing to a close. The first unit to disband was the first to arrive, namely 774 Squadron, which was disbanded on 1 August. 714 and 769 Squadrons were both disbanded on 29 October; the former was dissolved into 717 Squadron.

The Barracuda served with every FAA unit that passed through Rattray from July 1944 to March 1946.

In the meantime, more units arrived before the year was out, including 821, 815 and 753 Squadrons, all flying the Barracuda. On 4 January 1946 708 Squadron arrived with Firebrands, followed by 766 Squadron on the 20th with Harvards and Fireflies.

From January 1946 all of Rattray's units were disbanded, the last being the Martinet Flight of 766 Squadron on 2 September, when it departed for Lossiemouth. In no time at all this busy airfield was paid off on 30 September and reduced to C&M.

Despite the run-down, the airfield stayed in MoD hands and remains so today. Its use from the late 1940s through to the 1970s is unknown, if indeed it was used at all. The Royal Navy did return in 1978 to establish a Wireless Telegraphy Station; a control building was constructed and aerials now cover the airfield. The majority of the runways and perimeter tracks can be seen from the air and many wartime buildings remain. A £200 million upgrade of the now tri-national transmitter station has just taken place, ensuring that the MoD will be at Crimond for many years to come.

During the 1950s Crimond Raceway was established using the original perimeter track and runways as part of the circuit, and on 16 June 1956 Jim Clark took part in his first competitive race. The circuit was relocated several times before settling in its current position in the early 1970s.

Main features:
Runways: QDM 300 1,200 yards, 255 1,200 yards, 344 1,000 yards, 206 1,000 yards. *Hangars:* five large squadron, six Fromson, eight storage. *Accommodation:* RN: 2,285; WRNS: 637.

RENFREW (MOORPARK), Strathclyde

55°52'00"N/04°23'26"W. M8 motorway follows line of runway

It was local manufacturer W. & J. Weir that flew its aircraft from Renfrew in late 1915. Contracts for the production of the BE.2C/E and FE.2b saw the establishment of the AI, Glasgow, from April 1916. On 10 March 1918 6 AAP moved in from Inchinnan and the AI was dissolved into it. The unit was renamed 6 (Renfrew) AAP before closing down on 31 May 1919. In the meantime, 55 Squadron arrived from St Andre-aux-Bois and 6 (Scottish) ARD was formed on 31 May. The ARD only lasted until 29 September 1919, and 55 Squadron was moved to Shotwick on 1 January 1920, bringing this first phase of Renfrew's history to an abrupt end.

A visiting North Sea Aerial Navigation Blackburn Kangaroo generates a lot of interest at Moorpark.

It was not long before aircraft returned with Renfrew, when it was used as a stop for the first King's Cup Air Race on 22 September 1920. Private aircraft continued to operate throughout the 1920s and the military returned on 12 September 1925 when 602 (City of Glasgow) Squadron was formed here. It operated the DH.9A until January 1928, by which time Renfrew was the home of the Scottish Flying Club. 602 Squadron remained here until 20 January 1933, when it made the short hop to Abbotsinch; it would be another nineteen years before it would return.

Beardmore WB.X G-EAQJ at Renfrew in 1920.

The Scottish Flying Club was now in charge of operating Renfrew for the local council. Developed throughout the 1930s, regional airlines began to include Renfrew as part of their services. The Scottish Air Ambulance Service was inaugurated here in 1933, thanks to a rescue flight from Renfrew to Islay.

Following the outbreak of war it was more than a year before the Lysanders of 309 Squadron moved in from Abbotsinch on 6 November 1940. The Lysander was ideal for such a small field, hemmed in by high ground, industry and barrage balloons. It was not until December that the first sorties were flown, and the Polish pilots struggled within the restricted space. A detachment to Perth helped the squadron work up, but on 8 May 1941 309 Squadron moved to Dunino.

By July 1940 Airwork and SAL were working for the CRO on various contracts. At first work was carried out on the Blenheim, but as the war progressed the Avenger became the most common type seen here. Both companies stayed until their contracts were fulfilled on 20 June 1945, but SAL would keep a presence for many years to come. They were joined by LOC, which built an assembly factory from late 1943. Before this happened, a pair of concrete runways were laid to cope with the increased activity that the American company would bring. LOC mainly reassembled P-38s and P-51s, all of which arrived at the nearby King George V dock at Shieldhall.

BEA was now in charge of all flying services including the additional hangars constructed during the war. SAL retained its own corner of the airfield, and later used it for CF-100 and F-86 overhauls, which it carried out from 1954 to 1960. BEA carried out all of its maintenance here for its Scottish Division aircraft during the immediate post-war period.

A military presence returned on 2 July 1949 when both 33 and 80 Squadrons' Tempests and Spitfires flew in from Gütersloh. Both units were prepared for the Far East, and on 14 July they both left for Hong Kong on HMS *Ocean*.

A pair of AOP units were formed here on 1 December 1951, 666 Squadron with Auster AOP.6s and 1967 AOP Flight created within it. Recruiting for the latter was held at the Renfrew Drill Hall, and after a slow start the flight moved to Abbotsinch on 5 December 1952 with AOP.6s.

In the meantime, 602 Squadron was also re-formed here, bringing Renfrew briefly into the jet age with its Vampires. Once again, however, Abbotsinch was deemed more suitable and the squadron was moved on 18 June 1954, probably to make way for Renfrew's upgrade as an airport. This came on 26 November when a state-of-the-art, beautifully designed terminal building, incorporating a parabola arch and new control tower, was opened. However, the state-funded terminal was not enough to see Renfrew through the 1960s, when there was a massive increase in both domestic and international air travel. Only a mile separated Renfrew from Abbotsinch, and on 2 May 1966 the last departure was made, only to land at the new Glasgow Airport a few minutes later.

Everything looks rosy at Renfrew in 1960 as a BEA Viscount disgorges its passengers. Six years later the airport was closed.

The land was quickly swallowed up by housing and development while the main runway formed the first urban section of the M8 motorway. By 1978 the terminal and the vast majority of buildings were demolished, and two years later the parabolic wonder was replaced by a Tesco supermarket.

Main features:
Concrete runways: QDM 008 2,000 yards, 003 1,350 yards. *Hangars:* minimum of one J Type, one LOC.

RERRIN (BEAR OR BERE ISLAND), Cork

51°37'96"N/09°49'26"W; V73932 43858. S of Rerrin pier, S of road

The RAF made use of an LG of 300 yards by 40 yards from 1918 until 1921. It is believed to have existed in private hands for several more years.

RIVER BANN (SOUTH LANDAGIVEY), Derry

55°01'73"N/06°34'42"W; C912211. 1 mile E of Mullaghmore airfield

Although it seems hard to believe, considering the amount of open water in Northern Ireland, the RAF established a small flying boat station on the River Bann. It is possible that the river was used as a quick way to access Mullaghmore following arrival by flying boat. The river flowed fairly straight in several positions and a landing run of 1,000 yards by 100 yards is achievable. The site was active from 1941 and was used by private flying boats during the post-war period.

RIVER FOYLE, Derry

55°00'66"N/07°18'07"W; C447184. Three-quarters of a mile N of Foyle Bridge

The Royal Navy established a flying boat station on the River Foyle from 16 September 1931. Facilities were quite sparse but 2,000 yards of water was available for take-offs and landings.

ROSYTH, Fife

56°01'18"N/03°25'45"W

By late 1912 a small Hydro-Aeroplane Station was at Rosyth. However, by early 1914 what little had been built here was moved to Dundee. Not to be confused with Port Laing, the Rosyth Seaplane Station was developed and located within the Naval Base. It consisted of a pair of seaplane sheds, one of which was used as a store. The station's main role was to service naval aircraft, a task that it carried out until its closure in 1918, following transfer of the work to Donibristle.

ROYAL BARRACKS (COLLINS BARRACKS), Dublin

53°20'90"N/06°17'55"W; O114345. 1¼ miles W of O'Connell Street Bridge

By far the earliest 'action station' in this book, the barracks was a British Army balloon-launching site, first used in 1785.

ST ANGELO (ENNISKILLEN AIPORT), Fermanagh

54°23'56"N/07°39'07". 3 miles N of Enniskillen straddled by B82

Surveyed in 1940, this beautifully located airfield was earmarked for the use of 23 MU and, despite the undulating terrain, two runways were laid at right angles to each other in an 'L' shape – very unusual for an SLG.

It was opened on 6 June 1941 as 18 SLG, but was never used by 23 MU. A site as well-built as this did not escape the Air Ministry's notice for long, and Fighter Command in particular was in need of extra airfields in Northern Ireland.

Work continued to raise it to the standard of a sector fighter station, and a satellite close to the border with the Republic at Lisnaskea was planned but not built. Reopened on 15 September 1941, it was only ever occupied by small flights of fighters, which tended to be the Spitfires from 133 and 134 Squadrons from Eglinton. The reason for using St Angelo was to intercept any reconnaissance flights that approached along the west coast of Ireland. None were ever intercepted, however, and by early 1942 both squadrons had moved to English airfields. A pair of Defiants from 153 Squadron were detached from Ballyhalbert from 28 March for a while, and St Angelo remained a sector airfield until October.

The airfield's accommodation saw an influx of personnel from 131 OTU in July 1942. While construction continued at Killadeas, the HQ could not be established, so operated from here for several weeks. This was the beginning of a lengthy association with the flying boat station and, as 131 OTU found its feet, the unit's TTF of Lysanders and later Martinets flew from here. By mid-1943 St Angelo was transferred to Coastal Command, becoming a satellite for Killadeas from 4 August.

Personnel from 422 Squadron made use of the accommodation while their Sunderlands operated from Lough Erne, remaining until 13 April 1944. The Beaufighters of 235 Squadron from Portreath also briefly operated here during February and March before returning to Cornwall.

It was not until 1 May 1944 that St Angelo gained its own unit when 12 (O)FIS was formed to train former operational pilots in instructor duties for service with Coastal Command OTUs. Over the next few weeks, Mosquitoes, Wellingtons and Beauforts arrived, and the first instructors' course began in mid-June with seventeen pilots. By the following month the FIS was given the additional work of training instructors on Catalinas and Sunderlands, which were shared with 131 OTU.

On 23 February 1945 the FIS became the CCFIS without any change to its training or aircraft. Buckmasters began to arrive here as replacement for the Beauforts before the war's end, but had barely settled in when the FIS was moved to Turnberry on 9 June. St Angelo came under Maintenance Command from 1 August, housing a sub-site 272 MU and 106 SSS; the latter provided additional storage for Ansons, which would be scrapped here. This task was completed on 28 February 1947 when 106 SSS was closed, and the airfield was abandoned not long afterwards.

In the mid-1960s Fermanagh District Council reopened the airfield using just the shorter runway, as the main one was now bisected by the B82. The small, picturesque airport operated successfully for several decades, but by the end of the century was in decline and was becoming a financial drain on the council and, more importantly, the tax payer. St Angelo was therefore 'mothballed', but by 2003 the council realised that the airport had commercial potential that should benefit the local economy if it was professionally run. Before the year was out a consortium presented its business proposal to the council and Enniskillen Airport Ltd was established.

Businesses here now include Corporate Air Ltd and Unique Helicopters, which offers training, hire and pleasure flights. A new terminal and modern tower have freshened the airport no end following the demolition of the original tower in 2002.

St Angelo is seen here in the early 1990s, prior to its recent incarnation as Enniskillen Airport. The Army helicopter base is positioned within the compound on the original main runways at the bottom of the picture.

On the eastern side of the B32, within a high fenced compound on the runway, was an Army helicopter base, active from 1976 to 1996. The hospitality was excellent – you can take my word for it!

Main features:
Concrete runways: QDM 056 1,860 yards, 336 1,460 yards. *Hangars:* three T1, eight blister. *Hardstandings:* sixty 26-foot diameter. *Accommodation:* RAF: 3,144.

SANDY BAY (LOUGH NEAGH), Antrim

54°34'76"N/06°16'52"W; J115715. 4 miles SW of Crumlin

A large RNAS airship station was planned here in 1916 but was never built. Sandy Bay was also associated with the military prior to the Second World War, when a 3-square-mile area north of Sandy Bay served as a range for 2 ATS between April 1938 and April 1939.

Another use for Sandy Bay during the Second World War was for the USNTS, flying Coronados to and from the USA. Sheltered by Rams Island, twelve moorings were built, together with a few buildings on the shoreline. Remains of a Nissen hut and jetty are extant.

SCAPA, Orkney

58°57'42"N/02°58'12"W; HY441090. 1 mile S of Kirkwall, at Nether Scapa

Some of the earliest patrols of the First World War were flown from Scapa. Opened around August 1914 as a seaplane station, Henry Farman pusher-type seaplanes were patrolling from September.

Temporary structures were built to protect the two seaplanes serving here. By the end of September these were replaced by the slightly more substantial Bessoneau and a pair of Piggot tents. It was not long before the weather got the better of the hangars, and on 21 November one collapsed in a gale; a Sopwith Boat pusher amphibian, one of only two serving with the RNAS at the time, was destroyed.

A solid pair of 69 feet by 69 feet hangars were later added, together with additional technical buildings such as an engineering workshop and a variety of tradesmen's huts. Only two accommodation huts and a separate officers' quarters were built. Expansion steadily continued as the war progressed, and by 1918 a Fleet Aircraft Repair Base and Stores Depot was established here. All military occupation came to end the following year.

SCATSTA, Shetland

60°25'58"N/01°17'45"W; NU385725. 20 miles N of Lerwick, SW of oil terminal off B9076

Scatsta is a good example of a 'strip airfield', which had enough room between the undulating terrain for two runways. This was no open-plan design with connecting perimeter tracks and a complex system of dispersals – it was the most practical form of military airfield you could get and was born from a distinct lack of fighter stations in the Shetland Islands at the very beginning of the Second World War.

Work began on the most northerly airfield in the British Isles in late 1939, which was shoe-horned between hills rising to 800 feet on the edge of Sullom Voe. At first the airfield served Coastal Command for nearby RAF Sullom Voe. By the spring of 1940 work began on three runways, the first of which was completed by April 1941. The work was carried out by Zetland County Council, but by the time work for the third runway was about to begin the task was abandoned due to a labour shortage.

Communications aircraft constantly used the airfield, and it also provided a safe haven for several bombers low on fuel from operations over Norway. Up to mid-1942 no resident unit had served here, but a pair of Spitfires were detached to deal with enemy reconnaissance aircraft; none were ever encountered and they had gone by early 1943. During the same year at least one Anson and a Walrus of 282 Squadron were detached here to provide ASR cover. A Martinet from 3 APC at Leuchars was also here from September 1944 to June 1945 to provide air-firing practice for local units.

Scatsta's one wartime claim to fame was acting as a diversionary airfield for Lancasters returning from attacking the *Tirpitz* on 29 October 1944. Two of 617 Squadron's bombers arrived for extra fuel before heading south; one landed with its 12,000lb 'Tallboy' still on board and, despite the extra fuel, had no trouble leaving. Scatsta also provided a refuelling stop for PR Mosquitoes supporting the *Tirpitz* attacks.

Early in 1946 Scatsta was reduced to C&M, but opened again in 1952 for Operation 'Mainbrace', the first large-scale naval exercise performed by ACLANT. While the RAF was not a major player in 'Mainbrace', Scatsta was used by Dakotas of 18 Group CF on mail runs from Kinloss, Sullom Voe and Norway from 14 to 25 September. This was to Scatsta's last military role, and it was subsequently abandoned.

Apart from a flurry of activity on 24 May 1969, when a USCG C-130 arrived in connection with a LORAN station, the airfield lay dormant until 1978. It was thanks to the Shetland oil industry and, in particular, the Sullom Voe oil terminal that Scatsta is now one of Scotland's busiest airports, mainly due to helicopter movements from oil rigs in the Norwegian and Faroes sectors together with a seven-to-eight-times-daily shuttle to and from Aberdeen. The latter ferries offshore workers to Scatsta for onward travel by helicopter to the oil rigs.

Only the longer of the two runways is in use today, while the shorter one serves as a parking area with a modern terminal, hangars and control tower alongside.

Main features:
Tarmac runways: QDM 250 1,510 yards, 130 1,400 yards. *Hangar:* one 10-bay T1. *Hardstandings:* floor and aprons for hangars T1 and T2. *Accommodation:* RAF: 362.

SCONE PARK, Perthshire

An ELG at Scone Park was allocated to 11 EFTS during the First World War. It is most likely that the location was the racecourse, which would have been ideal for the Perth-based Tiger Moths.

SKATERAW (INNERWICK), East Lothian

NT737753. Above Skateraw harbour near Torness nuclear power station

Described as 'on cliffs of sea coast', that was literally where Skateraw was. This small 3rd Class LG served as such for 77(HD) Squadron.

SKEABRAE, Orkney

59°03'50"N/03°16'23"W; HY275205. Off A967, 7 miles N of Stromness

The construction and eventual rise to becoming operational was a long and often confusing affair for Skeabrae. Intended for the use of the Admiralty, when still far from complete Skeabrae was handed over to the Air Ministry on 2 May 1940. The plan was to house two RAF fighter squadrons, but events developing in the south of the country were destined to intervene.

RAF personnel arrived on 15 August to find Skeabrae part-built, and, thanks to heavy rain, all level ground was a sea of mud. The situation was aggravated by a lack of local workmen, and those that were on site had no incentive to finish the jobs they had been given. Eventually some order descended upon Skeabrae and on 15 September a Whitney Straight became the first aircraft to land here.

The expected squadrons never arrived; instead, the first unit was 804 Squadron from Hatston with Sea Gladiators. The squadron received Martlets in September and proceeded to fly air defence patrols with them. A flight of Martlets was on patrol over Scapa Flow on 27 November 1940 when a Ju 88A-4 was intercepted by Lt Carver and Sub Lt Parke, forcing it to crash-land near Kirkwall; Carver and Parke had scored the first American-built fighter success of the war. No further success was achieved before the unit moved to Skitten on 7 January 1941.

The same day the first RAF squadron arrived when 3 Squadron's Hurricanes moved in from Castletown, returning one month later. 253 Squadron, also with Hurricanes, arrived from Leconfield on 10 February and stayed a lot longer, leaving for Hibaldstow on 21 September.

Hurricanes of 253 Squadron on duty at Skeabrae in 1941.

The RAF and FAA flew side-by-side from November 1941 when 801 Squadron joined 331 Squadron, which had arrived from Castletown on 21 September. No enemy aircraft were encountered by either squadron, and during 1942 tours of duty here were carried out by 132, 164, 602 and 129 Squadrons from the RAF, and 882 and 884 Squadrons of the FAA.

602 Squadron returned from Detling on 17 January after a hectic period of operations. Arriving with Spitfire IXBs, the squadron had to give them up for some tired Spitfire VBs, which the pilots described as 'clipped and clapped'. Despite the 'new' aircrafts' apparent weariness, the older mark of Spitfire was put to good use on 20 February 1944. Two were on patrol 50 miles east of the Orkneys when a Bf 109 fitted with long-range tanks was spotted cruising along at 32,000 feet. After a long chase it was caught and, after a few bursts of fire, it was spiralling down into the sea. In early March a Ju 88 was shot down over Scapa before the squadron left for Detling on the 12th.

Barracudas came for the first time in October 1944 when 841 Squadron carried out the first of four detachments from Hatston. Only 882 Squadron followed on 28 January 1945 with its Wildcats from Grimsetter, becoming the last FAA unit when it left for Hatston on 2 March. In the meantime the air defence of Scapa never dropped and the RAF squadrons continued to serve here right to the bitter end. 441 Squadron took over from 611 Squadron in December 1944, remaining here until April 1945, when it moved to Hawkinge. The same day 329 Squadron began patrolling over Scapa Flow after moving from Turnhouse with its Spitfires. Before it left for Harrowbeer on 25 May, 451 Squadron was posted in from Hawkinge a week earlier; it left for Lasham on 12 June, and it was appropriate that a Scottish auxiliary unit, 603 Squadron, was the last RAF squadron to serve at Skeabrae; it stayed until 28 July, when it moved to Turnhouse.

Skeabrae was transferred to the Admiralty as a satellite for Twatt and was one of three airfields given the name HMS *Tern II*. However, before the end of 1945 it was under C&M until it was paid off in 1957.

There were several proposals for uses for Skeabrae during the 1960s and 1970s but none ever came to fruition. Thanks to its remote location, the airfield is reasonably well preserved, but buildings that were only designed for a few years' use are now, seventy years after they were built, beginning to decay. The elements are winning the battle, and one of their victims was the Type 518/40 control, which was demolished a few years ago; I fear the remainder will not be far behind.

Main features:
Tarmac runways: QDM 064 1,000 yards, 204 1,000 yards, 294 1,000 yards, 334 1,000 yards. *Hangars:* twelve Teesside, one Callender Hamilton. *Hardstandings:* more than twelve double fighter pens. *Accommodation:* RAF: 1,610; WAAF: 174.

SKITTEN, Caithness

58°29'45"N/03°09'53"W. 1½ miles E of Stornoway off A866

Often overshadowed by its neighbour at Wick, which would become its parent station, Skitten enjoyed a very busy wartime career. Ready by late September 1940, the first unit was 232 Squadron with Hurricanes from Castletown on 13 October, but by 4 December the squadron moved to Elgin.

With Castletown as its first parent, all units that passed through prior to July 1941 were fighter squadrons. These included 260 Squadron with its Hurricanes from Castletown, the Martlets of 804 Squadron, and finally 607 Squadron from Drem in April. The latter converted to Hurricanes and had left for Castletown by 27 July. The same day, patrols were taken over by Blenheims of 404 Squadron; still not operational, as part of its work-up it took part in Exercise 'Leapfrog', a tri-service affair that replicated an enemy invasion of the Orkney Islands. It was not until 22 September that the squadron flew its first operations with a convoy escort and reconnaissance off Norway; the squadron moved to Dyce on 9 October.

By now Wick was interested in taking over Skitten as a satellite, its location being perfect from a liaison and administration point of view. Designed as a fighter station, the arrival of 48 Squadron Hudsons from Stornoway on 20 October put a great deal strain of the airfield's facilities. The squadron carried out several anti-shipping strikes before moving to Wick on 6 January 1942.

489 Squadron's Hampdens arrived on 5 August 1942 from Thorney Island, and flew many 'Rovers' off Norway looking for ships. A small enemy convoy was sighted off Obersted on 17 September; two of the three Hampdens managed to drop their torpedoes directly into the side of an MV while a third torpedo missed the larger ship and was last seen heading towards a steamer. The three Hampdens did not wait around to see the results as enemy fighters closed in. 489 Squadron continued its operations from Wick from 24 September.

The torpedo-carrying Hampdens of 489 Squadron are seen over the Scottish coast between sorties from Skitten.

A 172 Squadron Wellington VIII, with its Leigh Light retracted, over the North Sea during a long-range sortie from Skitten.

Skitten hosted 172 Squadron, which was operating the Leigh Light-equipped Wellington. One of the squadron's flights formed the nucleus of 179 Squadron, which was formed on 1 September. By 18 November the squadron were transferred to the Mediterranean to operate from Gibraltar.

Skitten was starting for Operation 'Freshman' on 19 November 1942. Two days earlier a pair of Halifaxes, thirty-four airborne troops and a pair of Horsas arrived here under the code -name 'Washington Party'. Their objective was to destroy the German-controlled Norsk Hydro chemical plant at Vemork in Norway. Sadly, a catalogue of equipment failures resulted in all but one of the combination crashing in Norway and the survivors later being interrogated and murdered by the Gestapo.

By early 1943 Skitten was a reserve airfield for Bomber Command with the means to accommodate up to twenty-four heavy bombers. Coastal Command units operating from here would now have to move at short notice if required, but this did not stop 407 Squadron's Hudsons from arriving on 16 February. Within days of arriving, the unit was declared non-operational and began re-equipping with the Wellington. Without flying a single operational sortie from here, the unit left for Chivenor on 1 April to continue flying A/S patrols.

Traces of the runways at Skitten still remain, but their existence is tenuous thanks to the quarrying on site.

Another unit formed here in 1943 was 1693 Flight, on 8 September, with Ansons. The small unit was tasked with providing A/S cover for aircraft on courses and exercises in the Home Fleet Exercise Area. Independent A/S and ASR followed before the unit moved to Wick on 11 December. The day before, 519 Squadron moved in from Wick with Spitfires and Venturas. The squadron's role was to carry out meteorological reconnaissance flights, using the twins for long distance and the Spitfires for altitude. Hudsons were reintroduced to the squadron by August 1944, and before the squadron returned to Wick on 28 November one or two Fortresses may also have been operating from here. 519 Squadron was the last operational squadron to serve at Skitten during the war, and very few if any aircraft arrived here before the airfield was closed in the summer of 1945.

Several wartime buildings survive in the old technical area while the rest of the airfield is slowly being eaten away by a quarry. One event that has been recognised is Operation 'Freshman', thanks to a memorial unveiled on the edge of the airfield in 1992.

Main features:
Tarmac runways: QDM 188 1,590 yards (extended in 1942 to 2,000 yards), 306 1,350 yards (extended to 1,600 yards), 245 1,120 yards. *Hangars:* one Bellman, six double EO blister, three standard blister. *Accommodation:* RAF: 1,350; WAAF: 80.

SLIDDERYFORD BRIDGE, Down

54°14'31"N/05°51'60"W; J395343. 2 miles NE of Newcastle bus station

Described as a field strip, it was in civilian hands from September 1913 and at some point was taken over by the RFC.

SMOOGROO, Orkney

58°55'09"N/03°07'49"W. 7 miles SW of Kirkwall

In mid-1917 a small piece of land on the northern edge of Scapa Flow found itself becoming the only airfield available to the Grand Fleet while berthed in the Orkney Islands. Smoogroo was used as a safe haven for pilots who were taking part in the first experiments with flying land-based aircraft from ships. After launching, there was no return to the ship other than a ditching, and however rough and ready it was it would have been a welcome place under the wheels of any man's aircraft.

It was from Smoogroo that history was made when Sqn Cdr E. H. Dunning took off in his Camel and successfully landed on the moving deck of HMS *Furious* on 2 August 1917. This was the first time an aircraft had been landed on a moving ship, and from that moment the aircraft carrier was born.

It was from Smoogroo that history was made when Sqn Cdr E. H. Dunning took off in his Camel and successfully landed on the moving deck of HMS Furious *on 2 August 1917.*

*Sadly, despite the efforts
of those on board HMS
Furious, the Camel
slipped over the side of
the ship and Dunning
was drowned.*

Designated a Fleet Practice Station, facilities were limited with shelter provided by three Bessoneaus. Any repairs were carried out at the Houton Bay or Scapa Flow seaplane station and aircraft were transferred by ship via a lengthy jetty on the eastern shore of the site.

Camels, Pups and Strutters were here, although the DH.6 also made an appearance. On 16 March 1920 RAF Practice Base (Smoogroo) was formed out of the old station establishment, the majority of which had been based at Houton Bay. By 1921 this small but useful little airfield had been abandoned. Today the site is still as open as it was nearly 100 years ago, and only the jetty remains, providing a useful berth for small vessels.

SNELSETTER/HOY & LONGHOPE, Orkney

Hoy: 58°46'50"N/03°10'40"W. W end of South Walls, N of Bu' of Aith

S nelsetter was a pre-war civilian aerodrome that was requisitioned as an ELG during the Second World War. Located on the Isle of South Walls and the southern end of Hoy, a private strip was located at Longhope at the western end of South Walls. Both sites remain untouched.

SOLLAS (NORTH UIST), Western Isles

Original location: 57°39'25"N/07°20'47". End of road at Claggan Sollos, between ford and graveyard, N of Loch Sollas

Beach: 57°39'51"N/07°19'32"W. On Tràigh Ear beach, North Uist

A ir services operated from Sollas on North Uist from 1936 to 1945. While not fully requisitioned, the RAF also flew operations from here, and it was designated as an ELG. During the 1950s the airfield became unfit for use and a new site was moved to the beach at Tràigh Ear in front of Machair Leathann Dunes. Flying has continued ever since from the same beach.

*There was not much that got past the eyes of the
Luftwaffe, and despite being just an ELG Sollas
was photographed in December 1940.*

Wartime aerial photographs suggest that at least one half-size T2 was here, but there is very little evidence of its location or military occupation today.

SOUTH BELTON (DUNBAR), Lothian

55°59'11"N/02°33'22"W; NT654775. 2 miles from Dunbar

South Belton was another of 77(HD) Squadron's LGs, open from 1916 to late 1918. It was categorised as a 2nd Class LG by day and 3rd Class by night.

SOUTH KILDUFF (KINROSS), Fife

NO083017. 3 miles W of Kinross

The useful landmark of the nearby Loch Leven may have helped the pilots of 77(HD) Squadron find this LG, which was active between 1916 and 1918.

STENNESS LOCH, Orkney

58°59'18"N/03°13'04"W. 10 miles W of Kirkwall

Only 5 miles north of Houton Bay, another much smaller seaplane station was established on the edge of Stenness Loch, the largest brackish lagoon in Great Britain. 200 personnel were stationed here, the majority accommodated in the Standing Stones Hotel and eleven wooden huts.

Three flights, 309, 310 and 311 Flights, were formed in May and July 1918, and all three operated the F.3 for A/S patrols and operations for the Grand Fleet. The Loch was found to be shallow and exposed for flying boat operations and all flying took place from Houton Bay. All three flights were disbanded here by September 1918. The Standing Stones Hotel continued to play a role, becoming the home of 28 Group (Orkney & Shetland) on 13 July. The group remained under the control of the C-in-C Grand Fleet until it was disbanded into 29 Group on 15 April 1919.

STIRLING (KINCAIRN/GARGUNNOCK), Central

This LG was brought into use for 77(HD) Squadron during 1916. Not in the best of locations, at the foot of the Gargunnock and Touch hills, this, together with its westerly location for Zeppelin defence, probably brought about its premature closure.

STIRLING (RAPLOCH/FALLENINCH FARM), Central

56°07'23"N/03°57'50"W; NS785945. 1 mile NNW of town centre

This First World War aerodrome was located west of Castle Hill and north of the Dumbarton road. A few wooden hangars protected the aircraft while all personnel were accommodated under canvas.

43 Squadron from Montrose was the first resident with FK.3s on 19 April 1916. By June the squadron had received the BE.2C and 504 before it moved to Netheravon on 30 August.

A 43 Squadron Armstrong Whitworth FK.3 at Stirling/Raploch in 1916.

63 Squadron was formed on 5 July from the nucleus of 43 and 61 Squadrons, equipped with DH.4s. With 43 Squadron's departure, 63 squadron inherited the FK.3, BE.2C and 504s, and in October the BE.12 and BE.2E were also added to the inventory. The plan was to mould 63 Squadron into a light bomber unit for operations over the Western Front, but this never came about, and on 31 October the unit left for Cramlington.

Raploch lay silent until 18 March 1917 when 52 TS arrived from Catterick. Equipped with at least ten different aircraft types, the training squadron left for Montrose on 1 September, becoming the last unit to operate here. 77(HD) Squadron also based aircraft here during 1916 and 1917, but its use for Zeppelin defence patrols was limited.

STORNOWAY (including HMS *MENTOR* [LEWS CASTLE]), Western Isles

58°12'48"N/06°19'44"W; NB459932. 1½ miles E of Stornoway off A866

Stornoway was another airfield that had connections with Capt Fresson. In 1934 he landed a Dragon on the Melbost Golf Links to demonstrate that it was possible to construct four 600-yard runways across the links and, by filling in a few bunkers, the eighteen holes could still be retained. Unsurprisingly, the golf club was not keen and it took four years before the idea of a flying service from Inverness to Stornoway was approved. By now the war was approaching and, despite his best efforts, Fresson had to postpone the service. The golf club could not stand in the way of the Air Ministry, which took over the site and obliterated the course with a large Coastal Command airfield.

Work began in early 1940, and by April of the following year an SHQ was established. While construction continued, 701 Squadron's Walruses operated from Stornoway Harbour from 6 November. The squadron's accommodation for all personnel was in Lews Castle, which was commissioned as HMS *Mentor*. A slipway was built at Cuddy Point and the squadron carried out A/S and reconnaissance patrols until moving to Hooton Park on 13 March 1941.

The first operational squadron here was 827 Squadron from Crail with Albacores on 14 March 1941; it carried out regular A/S patrols before moving to Thorney Island on 1 May. It was not until 3 August that an RAF unit arrived in the form of 48 Squadron with Ansons from Hooton Park. Few operations were flown from here and in October the squadron moved to Skitten.

Several months passed before 224 Squadron's Hudsons from Limavady arrived in March 1942. Before they left a second Hudson unit, 500 Squadron, arrived from Bircham Newton on 22 March. Two U-boats were attacked in April and on both occasions the crews reported that the enemy vessel was left with its bows in the air. During July, Fg Off M. A. Ensor and crew caught a U-boat on the surface and, by using broken cloud and diving to sea level, caught the enemy by complete surprise. With guns blazing, the Hudson dropped four depth charges, sinking the U-boat; the conning tower briefly reappeared before the submarine slipped below the waves. 500 Squadron's duties were taken over by the Whitleys of 58 Squadron from St Eval on 20 August, but endless patrols did not yield any success during the squadron's tour before it moved to Holmsley South on 2 December.

It was a new role from 15 December when 303 FTU formed here. Its task was to carry out ferry training of GR crews with Wellingtons, although by 5 March 1943 the unit was moved to Talbenny. 518 Squadron was formed on 6 July with Halifaxes. The unit flew many long-range Met flights deep into the Atlantic before continuing this task from Tiree on 25 September. Yet again, no resident units were based here, this time for almost a year, but USAAF arrivals kept the airfield busy.

The RAF returned on 10 August 1943 when Ansons of 1693 Flight were detached from Sumburgh, before a pair of squadrons that would see out Stornoway's wartime days both arrived from St David's. First was 58 Squadron on 1 September, then 502 Squadron, which flew in two weeks later. Both flew the Halifax, and both, working closely together, began searching for prey along the Norwegian coast and the North Sea. With no targets attacked in October, both units changed to nocturnal anti-shipping patrols, their focus being the Kattegat and Skaggerak around the Danish and southern Norwegian coasts. On 27 October a pair of 502 Squadron Halifaxes shared in the demise of U-1060 off Bronnoysund, the last of many attacks in which the unit had played a hand.

A typically complex Royal Navy airfield, Stornoway is pictured in July 1944. Note the ten half-sized T2s all around the edge of the airfield, two of them almost on the shoreline.

By March 1945 neither squadron relented as the amount of bombs dropped on shipping continued to increase. By the following month the squadrons were so effective that the shipping between Denmark and Norway was almost eliminated. 502 Squadron alone flew for 717 hours during April and dropped 86 tons of bombs. When the war ended, messages of congratulation were sent to both squadrons, thanking them for their efforts. The Admiralty estimated that they could claim to have sunk or damaged more than a million tons of shipping. Two days after VE-Day, four Halifaxes left for a sortie over the Baltic, where the crews reported seeing more than 100 surrendering enemy vessels of all shapes of sizes, flying white flags and heading for Kiel. Both squadrons were disbanded here on 25 May.

The following year Stornoway was under MoA control, and on 14 July 1948 it was the start and finishing point for a record-breaking flight. Six Vampires of 54 Squadron left to become the first jets to cross the Atlantic via Keflavik and Goose Bay, before completing their 3,000-mile journey in Montreal. By the early 1970s the airfield was declared an FOB for Strike Command, and expansion work began, including lengthening the main runway. Throughout the 1970s and 1980s the airfield also hosted several detachments from 841 and 819 Squadrons, both flying the Sea King. At the tail-end of the Cold War the airfield saw further expansion to enable it to support both Nimrods and Tornados, but as the Soviet threat passed the RAF side of Stornoway was closed on 31 March 1998.

Civilian flights have been taking place from here for many years, but since the RAF's tenure came to an end it is now known as Stornoway Airport. Now owned by HIAL, services consist of scheduled passenger flights and Royal Mail deliveries together with a pair of S-92 helicopters flown by HM Coastguard.

Main features:
Tarmac runways: QDM 189 2,000 yards, 254 1,350 yards, 306 1,290 yards, 238 870 yards. *Hangars:* ten half T2. *Hardstandings:* five 100-foot circular, runway 238 used as parking area. *Accommodation:* RAF: 1,993; WAAF: 241.

STRACATHRO, Tayside

56°45'45"N/02°35'02"W; NO645635. NW of Muirton of Ballochy, 4 miles NE of Brechin

Little more than an RLG and satellite during its five-year existence, this airfield was rarely quiet. From June 1940 it became an RLG for 8 FTS, but it does not appeared to be have been seriously used until 16 July 1941, when 'A' Squadron, 8 FTS, was here flying the Master both day and night, remaining until early 1942.

On 2 July Stracathro became a satellite for 2 FIS, which used the airfield until 30 June 1944. The only unit to be formed here was 1541 BATF on 17 May 1943. It was affiliated to 2 FIS but, despite the school leaving, the flight continued at Montrose until it was disbanded on 11 July 1945.

The airfield was taken over by 44 MU in August 1945 to cope with a flood of surplus aircraft, but by November had been transferred to 260 MU. It was now used as a sub-site for equipment disposal from 6 November to at least early 1948, then not long afterwards it was closed down.

A few wartime huts still survive on the southern side of the airfield, and the entire half-perimeter track and several dispersals are still in situ. The flying field is exactly as it was more than seventy years ago.

Main features:
Grass runway: QDM NE-SW 1,300 yards. *Hangars:* eight blister 69 feet. *Accommodation:* RAF: 323.

STRATHAVEN (COUPLAW FARM), South Lanarkshire

55°40'48"N/04°06'20"W. 2 miles W of Strathaven

The current airstrip at Strathhaven was established thanks to Gp Capt G. Pinkerton buying Couplaw Farm in the 1950s. However, prior to this possibly the same site saw the formation of 1 GS in December 1942 with Cadets. The school remained until March 1944, when it moved to Dungavel.

STRATHBEG, Aberdeenshire

57°36'33"N/01°51'45"W; NK130447

Strathbeg was used as a sub-station for Dundee from as early as 1916. The first unit, 401 Flight, arrived in August 1918 with 184s. It was joined by 249 Squadron from September, also flying the 184. By the end of the war both units had returned to Dundee.

STRAVITHIE, Fife

56°18'09"N/02°44'53"W; NO540125. 3 miles SE of St Andrews off A959

Opened on 1 May 1941 for the use of 44 MU as 26 SLG, the first airmen were posted here only two days later, and all were billeted in St Andrews. By 9 May the first aircraft began to arrive, and by the end of the month forty-four Hurricanes and Wellingtons were dispersed here.

Aircraft movements averaged forty per month during the summer, but by August the numbers began to fall. With the onset of winter, the SLG was reduced to C&M and all aircraft were moved to Edzell or other SLGs.

During February 1942 the SLG was upgraded, the work being completed by the beginning of April, with camouflage hedging in place. It had been a hard winter, with much of the airfield being covered by snow throughout it. Despite this, an inspection found that the runway had stood up well to the weather and preparations began to reopen it.

During June thirty-four aircraft were delivered and nineteen were dispatched; this was the highest total for the year. The aircraft holding steadily declined through the summer.

As in the previous year, 26 SLG was closed down for the winter on 30 September. However, on this occasion there is no evidence that it reopened and no record of any aircraft being stored here. It is known that the SLG remained under the control of 44 MU until at least the end of the war. With Dunino being located only 2 miles to the east, it is quite possible that increased activity brought about the early closure of Stravithie. The Lysanders of 309 Squadron based at Dunino did use the SLG, but apart from this very little activity occurred.

The unique watch office at Stravithie is deteriorating and it can only be hoped that a preservation order will be place upon it before it disappears. Author

By the war's end Stravithie was closed down and no further flying would take place. Today, the whole site is farmed and can easily be seen from the B9131. Only a handful of brick buildings were constructed, but one of these, the watch office, defiantly stands very close to the roadside. Converted into a small bungalow during the post-war years, it now stands empty and is semi-derelict so its future looks in doubt.

SULLOM VOE (GARTH'S VOW), Shetland

60°27'21"N/01°16'54"W; HU390740. 25 miles N of Lerwick off B9076, E of Scatsta

The RAF's most northerly station was opened in July 1939. It was crucial that the seas between Iceland and Norway could be covered by aircraft, and Sullom Voe was destined to be a very busy flying boat station.

201 Squadron was the first to arrive on 2 August, bringing its Londons from Invergordon; it flew patrols around the clock until its return on 6 November. Two days before, another London-equipped unit from Invergordon, 240 Squadron, arrived to take over 201's watch.

The Sunderlands of 204 Squadron arrived from Mount Batten on 2 April 1940, and within 24 hours one of them was in the thick of the action. Flt Lt F. Philips and his crew were on convoy escort when they entered into combat with several enemy bombers. Two of them were driven off with the help of fire from the convoy, and another was shot down by the Sunderland's rear gunner. Another enemy aircraft was also attacked before the heavily damaged Sunderland had to limp away, eventually making it safely to Invergordon.

By now 240 Squadron had moved to Pembroke Dock to re-equip with Stranraers on 27 May. The previous day a second Sunderland unit, 201 Squadron, arrived from Invergordon, and both

240 Squadron, with its Londons, was the second unit to operate from Sullom Voe from November 1940.

A 204 Squadron Sunderland I taxies at Sullom Voe after returning from a patrol over the North Sea. This squadron saw a great deal of early action from here.

units flew daily convoy patrols, although the odd U-boat was also attacked, without success. A pair of Sunderlands from 204 Squadron were tasked with shadowing the *Scharnhorst* on 21 June, while another was attacked by Bf 109s on the same day, shooting down one of them. N6133 of 203 Squadron was not so lucky on 9 July, when it was shot down by an Me 110; none of the ten aircrew survived. Some revenge was had on 26 August when Flt Lt Gibbs and crew of 204 Squadron destroyed four He 115s in Tromsø harbour and damaged four others.

700 Squadron, aka Shetlands Flight, also operated here from 16 July 1940 with Walruses and a Swordfish seaplane. Many patrols were flown and at least one U-boat was attacked with depth charges dropped by a Walrus. The flight was disbanded on 28 May 1941.

204 Squadron left for Reykjavik on 5 April 1941, leaving 201 Squadron on its own. The following month a 201 Squadron Sunderland played its part in the demise of the *Bismarck* after spotting it and reporting its position to HMS *Norfolk*. No further success against the enemy befell the squadron during the remainder of its tour, which ended on 9 October when it moved to Lough Erne.

It was now the turn of 413 Squadron, arriving on 1 October 1941 from Stranraer. The unit brought the Catalina here for the first time and, within days of arriving, was flying convoy escorts hundreds of miles away from base. 210 Squadron returned on 5 February 1942, now with the Catalina, while 413 Squadron prepared for service overseas; it left on 4 March, en route for Ceylon. 210 Squadron flew its fair share of patrols from here during 1942 and also managed to serve at Grasnaya, to help protect the Russian convoys. After returning, the squadron only remained a few more weeks before leaving again, this time for Pembroke Dock, on 4 October.

190 Squadron was formed on 17 February 1943 using the nucleus of 210 Squadron with Catalinas. Fully operational by the end of March, it saw its first action on 22 April when U-231 was attacked with depth charges and machine-gun fire south-east of Iceland. The submarine was lucky, escaping any serious damage, but one of its crew was lost overboard during the action. Before the day was over, Catalina 'S' was also in action, attacking U-531 off Iceland but only causing minor damage. A 206 Squadron Fortress also had a go at U-531 and a second 190 Squadron Catalina 'E' also attacked it with depth charges, but the submarine escaped undamaged.

Catalina FP183, being flown by Sqn Ldr J. A. Holmes, was lucky to make it back after an encounter with U-667 on 29 May 1943. Holmes attacked the U-boat between Iceland and the Faroes, but as the aircraft approached it was hit in the port engine by anti-aircraft fire before dropping depth charges astern of the U-boat. Gunfire was then exchanged, resulting in the co-pilot being wounded. U-667 thought better of continuing the fight and dived, leaving FP183 to limp back home.

330 Squadron moved in on 12 July 1943, bringing its Sunderlands from Oban. The squadron began the first Atlantic patrol the following day, but it would be quite some time before a U-boat was attacked.

190 Squadron was in action again on 3 August when Flt Lt B. Crosland and crew in Catalina FP280 were assisting a Fortress in an attack on U-489. After the Fortress left the scene, the U-boat opened fire on the Catalina, unbeknown to the pilot, almost severing the rudder cables. Crosland headed for Iceland while 269 Squadron attacked U-489, causing serious damage and forcing it to dive.

190 Squadron kept up the pressure throughout the rest of 1943 but never achieved the ultimate prize of a U-boat kill. On 1 January 1944 the unit lost its identity and was renumbered as 210 Squadron.

Sunderland JM667, flown by Sub Lt C. T. Johnsen and crew of 330 Squadron, managed to catch U-668 on the surface west-north-west of Ålesund on 16 May 1944. As the Sunderland dived, the U-boat opened up with anti-aircraft fire, causing the flying boat to miss its target. Johnsen went round for a second run, managing to drop four depth charges, but the Sunderland had soaked up an enormous amount of damage. The front gunner was killed and two other aircrew wounded, while the Sunderland's starboard engines were both damaged. The aircraft eventually made it back on three engines.

Success finally came again for 210 Squadron on 24 May when U-476 was so severely damaged north-west of Trondheim that the submarine had to be scuttled the following day. U-396 was attacked by Fg Off J. C. Campbell on 28 June and damaged sufficiently to abort its patrol.

210 Squadron took on another U-boat on 17 July 1944 when Fg Off J. A. Cruickshank and crew attacked U-361 west of Narvik. As Cruickshank dived to attack the submarine, the depth charges failed to release, forcing him to make a second run. As the Catalina approached again, the submarines flak gunners found their mark and a shell smashed into the cockpit, killing the navigator and injuring four others, including Cruickshank. Seconds later the depth charges released, sinking U-361 with the loss of all fifty-two hands. Unaware of his injuries, Cruickshank set course for home, a flight that would take 5 hours. Refusing a morphine injection when the Catalina arrived over the Voe, rather than risk a night landing Cruickshank circled the base for an hour to improve their chances of a safe landing. This was achieved and, as the flying boat taxied, water began pouring in from the flak damage in the hull until it was beached. For his actions that day Cruickshank was awarded the VC, while the second pilot, Flt Sgt J. Garret, received the DFM.

Two days after this action, 330 Squadron managed to damage U-387 off the Norwegian coast, but no more encounters were achieved by the squadron before it left for Stavanger on 15 June 1945. In the meantime 461 Squadron had also served from here with its Sunderlands from 28 September to 29 October 1944. 210 Squadron's outstanding wartime achievements were also brought to a close following its disbandment on 4 June 1945.

210 Squadron was another unit that saw considerable action while serving at Sullom Voe with its Catalinas.

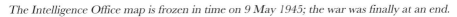

The Intelligence Office map is frozen in time on 9 May 1945; the war was finally at an end.

By 1946 Sullom Voe was under C&M, but flying boats did briefly return for Operation 'Mainbrace' in 1952. 201 Squadron's Sunderlands operated alongside several Mariners of the USN during the exercise, but once they left the old flying boat station was closed down for good.

One slipway remains in place today but, other than a scattering of hut bases near Graven, the Voe has been virtually erased.

SUMBURGH, Shetland

59°52'44"N/01°17'44"W. 25 miles S of Lerwick off A970

Capt Fresson helped to establish Sumburgh back in 1933, but it was not until 1936 that the first Highland Airways scheduled service began, coming to an end with the outbreak of war.

This DH.89A Rapide of Allied Airways (Gandar Dower) Ltd is seen parked at Sumburgh just before the outbreak of war.

Sumburgh's position at the southern tip of the Shetland Islands drew military interest despite a survey describing the airfield as needing improvement if it was to accommodate modern fighters. However, the aircraft that would operate from here were not modern, and began with a detachment of Gladiators from 'B' Flight, 152 Squadron, from Acklington during November and December 1939. A permanent unit was created from the flight when, on 27 December, three Gladiators remained to form the Fighter Flight, Shetlands. The biplanes had a great deal of responsibility placed upon them, yet their strength never grew during the early months of the war. On 5 January 1940 the unit was renamed as Fighter Flight, RAF Sumburgh.

The airfield began to evolve when an SHQ was created on 13 May to look after 254 Squadron, which arrived from Hatston three days later. This Blenheim unit was the first of many squadrons that would take their turn in carrying out air defence and convoy protection all around the islands. While carrying out its duty, the Fighter Flight claimed two enemy aircraft as probably destroyed before it was moved to Roborough on 21 July to become 247 Squadron.

42 Squadron's Beauforts used Sumburgh as an FOB on 21 June 1940 after moving into Wick the same day from Thorney Island. The *Scharnhorst* had been seen off the Norwegian coast and nine Beauforts were detailed to attack it. The crews were not trained to drop torpedoes, and even if they had been none were available at Wick. Instead, a pair of 500lb bombs was fitted and the Beauforts would carry out a dive-bombing attack. The raid was a disaster and the unit lost three aircraft and twelve aircrew.

July saw more Blenheims from 248 Squadron from Dyce on the 14th to carry out anti-shipping patrols. Earlier in the month 'B' Flight of 3 Squadron, with Hurricanes, arrived from Skeabrae. This small flight formed the nucleus of 232 Squadron, which was re-formed here on 17 July and, during its working-up period, flew several convoy patrols and the odd scramble. It was on one of the latter that the squadron scored its first success when, on 3 August, an He 111 was shot down off Fair Isle.

The previous day 254 Squadron left for Dyce, and 232 Squadron departed for Castletown on 18 September. 248 Squadron, which had been operating under Fighter Command control, continued its dangerous operations over the North Sea. Now serving with Coastal Command, the squadron operated from here until 6 January 1941 when it moved to Dyce.

143 Squadron began flying anti-shipping patrols on 27 September 1941. Using the Beaufighter, it roamed the Norwegian coast looking for targets of opportunity many years before dedicated strike wings were formed. Before leaving for Dyce on 5 December, the squadron was joined by 331, 821 and 404 Squadrons on detachments.

1942 began with yet more detached units, 132 Squadron from Skeabrae in February and 48 and 217 Squadrons from Wick and Leuchars in March, followed by the Beauforts of 86 Squadron from Skitten in April. The airfield was expanding and its ability to support more offensive squadrons began from 30 May when 248 Squadron arrived from Dyce. The Beaufighters were joined by 608 Squadron's Hudsons from Wick on 29 July, both units flying anti-shipping and convoy escort duties. Both had left by August to be replaced by 404 Squadron's Blenheims from Dyce on 5 August. The bombers were replaced by Beaufighters from September 1942, and the same month 48 Squadron arrived from Wick to carry out A/S patrols with its Hudsons. 404 Squadron left for Dyce on 24 September followed by 48 Squadron, which moved south to Gosport on 30 November. Before the year was over the Spitfires of 129 and 602 Squadrons were on detachment here.

Pilots and groundcrew of 602 Squadron pose during a detachment to Sumburgh in late 1942.

Fighter detachments continued into 1943 with 234 Squadron taking over the role and achieving success on 24 March when an Me 210 was shot down off Fitful Head. Spitfire squadrons on detachment were prevalent here from March to November, many of them from Castletown and Skeabrae. Beaufighters of 235 and 236 Squadron also served, as well as the Lysanders of 278 Squadron from Coltishall.

307 Squadron brought some action when it moved up from Drem to carry out 'Rhubarbs' over Norway with its Mosquitoes. At least two He 177s and one Ju 88 were shot down during the unit's

time here, as well as a large number of enemy aircraft destroyed on the ground. Many of the latter were claimed on 19 January 1944 when a Luftwaffe seaplane station at Stavanger was strafed, leaving several Bv 138s burning on the water. The squadron returned to Drem a few weeks later.

Fighter detachments reduced during 1944, with only 118, 313 and 611 Squadrons, all from Skeabrae, operating from here in April, August and November. One unit that made Sumburgh its home for the remainder of the war was 1693 Flight, which moved in from Wick on 14 June. Possibly the last operational unit to make use of the Anson, the flight was tasked with carrying out A/S patrols and ASR duties. The flight was detached here in August before leaving for Docking on 31 May 1945.

With the war now over, Sumburgh was rapidly wound down; its operations room was shut by 4 June. Several squadrons transited through to Norway during the month, but by 29 August the airfield was under C&M with Sullom Voe as the parent.

BEA was in charge by 1947 and its Dakotas were employed to fly scheduled services to and from the Islands. The airport gained a slightly longer main runway by the mid-1960s and this opened it up to visits by larger airliners such as the Viscount.

Passenger numbers climbed rapidly during the 1970s thanks to the effect of the oil business; numbers peaked at 685,000 passengers and 51,000 aircraft movements in 1978. A new terminal was built in 1979 and further runway extensions took place in 2005. The latter involved transporting several large rocks from Norway to help protect the runway from the unforgiving elements.

Main features:
Tarmac runways: QDM 155 1,330 yards (extended to 1,560 yards), 100 1,120 yards, 045 980 yards. *Hangars:* three Bellman. *Hardstandings:* area of 500 x 300 feet. *Accommodation:* RAF: 1,321.

SYDENHAM (BELFAST HARBOUR/BELFAST CITY/GEORGE BEST BELFAST CITY AIRPORT), Down

54°36'25"N/05°52'37"W; J375765. 2 miles NE of Belfast city centre off A2

Sydenham owes its existence to the shipbuilding giant Harland & Wolff moving into aircraft manufacture in 1936. The company established itself as a subsidiary company for Short Brothers (Rochester), known as Short & Harland Ltd, on land next to Queens Island, which was deemed fit for a new airfield and centre for aircraft construction. The company was no stranger to aircraft production, having built hundreds during the First World War, test-flying them from Aldergrove. The rest is history; the airfield has been associated with Short's ever since and, despite being absorbed into Bombardier in 1989, the original spirit still lives on.

Opened in 1933, the airfield's surface was far too soft to support passenger aircraft. It was following Harland & Wolff's expansion of the site, by building a new factory in 1936 and setting about improving the airfield, that commercial flying could begin. Sydenham Airport was opened by Neville Chamberlain on 16 March 1938, and it was not long before several airlines moved in, the majority of them from Newtownards, thanks to Sydenham's location, just 5 minutes' drive to Belfast city centre.

Meanwhile, Harland & Wolff gained a contract to build 190 Herefords, which were destined to be the first of many military aircraft that were ordered thanks to events occurring in mainland Europe.

Short Brothers operated 24 E&RFTS here from 1 January 1939, flying a variety of aircraft. 23 E&RFTS moved here from Rochester the day before the war began, and was absorbed into the renamed 24 EFTS. The main type on strength was now the Magister, and by January 1940 thirty-six were on strength. In early June control of Sydenham was taken over by the RAF and it was not long before the first squadrons arrived. First was 88 Squadron from Driffield on 23 June, followed by 226 Squadron from Thirsk on the 27 June, both flying Battles.

88 Squadron re-equipped with Bostons and Blenheims from February 1941 before moving to Swanton Morley, while 226 Squadron had already left for Wattisham on 27 May.

Despite the squadron's departure, Sydenham was already busy with several second-line units already here. HQ RAFNI CF had been formed in October 1940 with a variety of communications aircraft, and the Belfast (Queens) UAS was formed on 8 March 1941. With one Tiger Moth on strength, the UAS, which was renamed Queens UAS in April, later moved to Aldergrove in June 1943; it returned on 31 March 1947 and remained until January 1994.

Thanks to Stirling production gaining pace, 8 FPP was formed in March 1941 to ferry the bombers to the mainland, then onwards to squadrons. This was a task that 8 FPP would do from here until 15 September 1945.

The full-size prototype Stirling N3638 at Sydenham in 1941.

On 27 November 1941 Sydenham was renamed RAF Belfast, and by February 1942 was hosting detachments by the Lysanders of 6 AACU, which remained until 30 May 1943. From 10 May 1942 the first of fifty FAA squadron movements began with the arrival of 702 Squadron's Sea Hurricane Flight from Lee-on-Solent. Lodger facilities were offered by the RAF, and all FAA squadron accounts were controlled by the nearby Battle of Jutland survivor, HMS *Caroline*. The first operational FAA unit to stay here was 808 Squadron with its Fulmars from Yeovilton. It was joined by 804's Sea Hurricanes and the Fulmars of 886 and 887 Squadrons before the end of the year.

The Stirling III prototype R9309 after being rolled out at Sydenham in June 1942.

It was obvious to the Royal Navy that Belfast was ideally situated for handling aircraft from carriers anchored in the harbour. All was fairly quiet here during early 1943 with only 807 and 819 Squadrons passing through prior to the airfield being transferred to Admiralty control. On 21 June it was commissioned as HMS *Gadwall* to handle squadrons leaving carriers and to establish a Royal Navy Maintenance Yard. Located on the opposite side of the airfield, the yard prepared FAA aircraft for overseas operations, later specialising in the Barracuda and Sea Otter. From the late 1940s through to the 1970s the yard was also employed to overhaul and modify all FAA jets, including the Sea Hawk, Sea Vixen (FAW.1 to FAW.2) and finally the Buccaneer.

From June 1943 onwards, the FAA squadrons began to pour in from escort carriers; this was the first time that the Royal Navy had access to an airfield close to a deep-water wharf that could handle carriers. Fireflies from 1772 Squadron passed through in January 1945 to serve with HMS *Ruler*, and a rare formation of a unit occurred on 1 March when 721 Squadron was created; equipped with the Vengeance, the squadron left on HMS *Begum* on 17 April.

The transport variant of the Stirling, the Mk V, prepares for a test flight from Sydenham in 1944.

Ten more squadrons came and went during 1945; the last, 807 Squadron, left for Nutt's Corner with its Seafires on 31 October. These were not the last FAA units to serve here, but it did mark the end of the airfield's most intensive period of operations, which had lasted for almost three years.

HMS *Gadwall* was decommissioned on 20 April 1946, but the same day became HMS *Gannet III*, with Eglinton as the parent. Only 812 and 827 Squadrons passed through during the late 1940s to embark on HMS *Ocean* and *Triumph*, but the Royal Navy was a long way from giving up Belfast.

Short's aircraft kept going during the post-war period thanks to some Seaford to Solent conversion work. However, it was destined to receive healthy sub-contracts from both Bristol and English Electric for the Britannia and Canberra. The company also produced a host of its own designs including the Seamew, Sturgeon and later the SC.1. The Belfast was also built here, but the only orders received for the giant transport were ten for the RAF. Short's then ventured into civilian aircraft with the Skyvan, which first flew from here on 17 January 1963. The SD330 and 360 followed, and the 125 that were produced were all built here between 1974 and 1992. The company also won the early-1980s competition to build a replacement for the Jet Provost fleet; the Tucano won the competition in 1985 and the first licence-built aircraft made its maiden flight on 20 December 1986. In the meantime, Short's became a PLC in 1984, and on 4 October 1989 was sold to Bombardier for just £30 million. Today the company designs and builds various aircraft components and flight control systems not only for its parent company but also for Boeing, Rolls-Royce, General Electric and Pratt & Whitney.

Another Short prototype, this time the Sturgeon TT.2 VR363, during an engine run at Sydenham in 1946.

Short's first serious venture into the civilian aircraft market was a successful one. This is the prototype Skyvan G-ASCN taking to the air for the first time at Sydenham on 17 January 1963.

The airfield was relinquished by the Royal Navy on 2 July 1973 and the RAF took over the old Maintenance Yard until it was closed in April 1978. A flurry of FAA activity returned in 1982 thanks to the Falklands War, when three flights of 845 Squadron embarked on RFA *Fort Austin* and *Tidespring* berthed in the harbour.

By now the airfield was beginning a steady transformation into a successful regional airport and, despite being still under military control, was named Belfast Harbour Airport from the mid-1970s. Commercial flights began to increase and by 1983 the site was fully open to civilian operations, being subsequently renamed Belfast City Airport. Bombardier sold the airport operation in 2003 for £35 million to Ferrovial, which, rather than invest, sold the airport on at a colossal profit to ABN Amro for £132.5 million in September 2008. Passenger numbers reached a record high of 2,740,341 in 2010, but 2011's figures were expected to drop thanks to Ryanair's recent departure. However, the future is still bright for the airport but further expansion will be difficult thanks to the built-up area all around it. Regardless, Belfast will remain an active airport for the foreseeable future.

A lot of airfield crammed into a small space is the best way to describe George Best Belfast City Airport.

The airport changed its name again in 2006 when it was christened the George Best Belfast City Airport on 22 May, which would have been the great footballer's 60th birthday.

Main features:
Concrete runways: QDM 046-226 1,100 yards (extended to 2,800 yards during WW2; currently 1,950 yards), 143-323 1,100 yards. *Hangars:* twenty-nine various. *Accommodation:* RN: 498; WRNS: 131.

TAIN, Highland

57°48'36"N/03°58'23"W; NH830820. 2½ miles E of Tain, N of Loch Eye

Tain was originally a small airfield that served the local ranges. While the strip and wartime airfield have been consigned to history, the ranges are still in use, mainly serving Lossiemouth-based aircraft as well as units further afield.

Opened on 16 September 1941 as a Fighter Section Station, 17 Squadron with its Hurricanes moved in from Elgin the following day. Several 'X' raids were intercepted, but the expected enemy activity never came as each turned out to be a false alarm or friendly. 17 Squadron moved to Catterick on 31 October and its duties were taken over the following day by 'B' Flight, 123 Squadron, with Spitfires, from Castletown. The Spitfires were replaced by 801 Squadron and its Sea Hurricanes from Skeabrae from 15 February 1942. Nine days later the fighter defence was bolstered by the arrival of 417 Squadron from Colerne with Spitfires.

The scene was now set for Tain to become one of three FOBs designated by Bomber Command for attacks on the *Tirpitz*, which was now berthed near Trondheim. 76 Squadron from Middleton St George was earmarked for Tain, and on 27 March 1942 twelve Halifaxes arrived. The first attack took place on 30/31 March, with 76 Squadron joining 10 and 35 operating from Lossiemouth and Kinloss respectively, making a total force of thirty-four bombers. Unfortunately the *Tirpitz* was not found and six Halifaxes were lost, together with all forty-nine aircrew on board. One of the Halifaxes, R9453, being flown by Sqn Ldr A. P. Burdett, came down in the sea 16 miles south of Sumburgh Head. A second attack was attempted on 5 April, but poor weather caused it to be aborted and 76 Squadron returned to its home base the following day.

By now 417 Squadron had left for the Middle East, but 801 Squadron remained in case the Luftwaffe decided to retaliate following the attack on the *Tirpitz*. 76 Squadron returned for another go at the battleship on 27/28 April; thirty-one Halifaxes and twelve Lancasters set out and on this occasion found the *Tirpitz* and several other warships in Trondheim Fjord. Once again, though, no hits were scored, and two Halifaxes failed to return, neither of them from Tain. Twenty-three Halifaxes and eleven Lancasters returned on 28/29 April, and this time several bombers claimed to have hit the *Tirpitz*, but none of the claims were confirmed. Once again, all returned back to safely to Tain before leaving for Middleton St George later in the day, together with 801 Squadron, which left for Turnhouse.

The CCDU, which was working away in the background, was responsible for the creation of a new unit here on 1 January 1943. 1 TRS was one of two schools formed to provide training facilities for torpedo-bomber crews and FAA personnel returning to operations with new equipment. Wellington crews for TB co-operation squadrons were also trained in new bomb sights, ASV and RP attacks.

The TRS did not have any aircraft of its own on strength but taught crews with the aircraft in which they arrived. The first unit to attend a 1 TRS course was 547 Squadron, with its Wellingtons, from Chivenor on 22 January. The FAA took full advantage of the school, especially for those units based at Fearn, although the first to arrive was 822 Squadron, with Barracudas, from Croft on 10 November. 815, 817 and 829 Squadrons, all with Barracudas, were 'refreshed' at Tain, before the school was disbanded on 28 January 1944, the CCDU having left the previous April for Dale.

1944 began with 186 Squadron moving in from Ayr on 7 January to replace its Typhoons with Spitfires. 817 Squadron's Barracudas also served here from Machrihanish in February before embarking on HMS *Begum* by the end of the month. 186 Squadron took its new Spitfires to Lympne on 1 March before becoming operational.

The first of two new 'heavy' units to arrive was 86 Squadron, with Liberators, from Reykjavik on 1 July 1944. Before the end of the month the squadron was in action against U-865, which was caught on the surface. The U-boat put up a stern defence with its flak guns but this did not stop the Liberator dropping several depth charges. The U-boat and Liberator were damaged, but both managed to limp away to their respective bases.

Tain's role for the remainder of the war was complete when a second Liberator unit, 311 Squadron, arrived from Predannack on 7 August. Both squadrons roamed the North and Norwegian Seas in the hunt for U-boats. Despite the submarines' area of operations being shut down, successes against them were still proving difficult, and it was not until May 1945 that 86 Squadron could claim any more; U-534 was sunk by ten depth charges on the 5th, although forty-nine of the fifty-four crew managed to escape. The following day U-3523 was sunk off Skagen Horn with all hands lost. The unit's final success of the war came the same day when U-1008 had to be scuttled after being damaged by ten depth charges.

Both Liberator squadrons spent the last few days of the war shepherding surrendering U-boats and gently reminding those who were not aware that the conflict was finally over. It was not until 6 August 1945 that 311 Squadron left Tain for Manston and a new role in Transport Command. The same fate awaited 86 Squadron, which left for Oakington three days later.

The airfield then became the home of 519 Squadron, which continued its meteorological tasks having arrived from Wick on 17 August; its Fortresses, Halifaxes and Spitfires were moved to Leuchars by 9 November. Another meteorological unit, 518 Squadron, was also detached here on

Tain seems to be reasonably complete from the air, and the main runway is almost at its complete length of 2,000 yards.

two occasions during 1945, but it was 280 Squadron, with Warwicks, that was destined to be the airfield's last unit. The ASR squadron that was detached from Thornaby had left by April 1946, and by November the airfield was relegated to C&M.

While RAF Tain still exists, with the current bombing range to the east, the wartime airfield now presents a very bleak picture. Until recently many buildings still stood in various states of preservation, but a recent purge by a local farmer has seen many of them reduced to rubble. On my last visit a few years ago the operations block was still intact, as was the control tower; the latter I fear is in a fairly tenuous position.

Main features:
Concrete runways: QDM 256 2,000 yards (extended), 316 2,000 yards (extended), 199 1,462 yards. *Hangars:* two T2, three Bellman, eight EO blister. *Hardstandings:* seventeen loop, three frying pan, eleven fighter standing. *Accommodation:* RAF: 1,851; WAAF: 381.

TALLAGHT (COOKSTOWN), Dublin

53°15'45"N/06°22'30"W; O083283; 6 miles SW of O'Connell Street Bridge off Belgard Road

Tallaght was one of many airfield sites surveyed for the use of the RFC in mid-1917. Work began later that year, with several Belfast Truss-type hangars and a large technical and domestic site. Complete in August 1918, Tallaght was ready for occupation the following month. First to arrive was 9 TS from Sedgeford on 1 September, only to be disbanded the same day into 25 TDS. This would be the main resident unit during the RAF's tenure.

This nice view across the flying field at Tallaght shows large aircraft sheds to the left and nine Bessoneau hangars to the right, with technical buildings in the distance.

244 Squadron visited from Bangor with its DH.6s in September. 530 Flight, also from Bangor, arrived on 18 October with its DH.6s, returning on 11 December.

March 1919 saw three operational squadrons arrive, and all would stay for several months. First was 141 Squadron from Biggin Hill on 1 March, followed by 117 Squadron on the 23rd, then three days later a cadre of 149 Squadron from Bickendorf. By April 117 Squadron's DH.9s arrived from Gormanston, while 141 Squadron's F.2bs began detachments to The Curragh and Birr.

24 TS with 504Ks moved in from Collinstown on 1 May, joined by a detachment of 105 Squadron from Oranmore in August. The same month it was the beginning of the end for Tallaght as 24 TS and 149 Squadron were disbanded. 55 Wing followed on 25 September, and the last RAF unit to use the airfield was 141 Squadron, which left Baldonnel on 14 December.

Offered to the IAC in 1922 but not taken up, much of the land was bought by a Mr Gallagher, who set up the Urney Chocolate Factory in the disused aerodrome buildings.

This traditional shot from the top of a hangar gives us an excellent viewpoint of the main technical site at Tallaght in 1918.

TEALING, Tayside

56°31'23"N/02°58'12"W; NO405370. 3 miles N of Dundee off A90, W of Inveraldie

Tealing was a typical example of a hurriedly built airfield with little thought given to the surrounding terrain or its history of poor weather conditions. Neither of these two factors was ideal for flying training, but this did not prevent 56 OTU from moving from Sutton Bridge on 27 March 1942.

The OTU's job was to train fighter pilots on the Hurricane, supported by Masters and Lysanders. Tealing was not a big airfield, and the allocation of Kinnell as a satellite two days after the OTU arrived was appreciated.

An unfamiliar four-engined bomber landed at dawn on 29 April. It was a Tupolev TB.7 with the Soviet Minister of Foreign Affairs, Vyacheslav Molotov, and a military mission on board. Little is known about the minister's meeting with Winston Churchill at Chequers that followed, or what was discussed, but Tealing would have provided a very low profile for such arrivals to take place. A second TB.7 arrived on 20 May before continuing on to the USA via Prestwick on the 24th.

The Tupolev TB.7 at Tealing that brought the Soviet Minister of Foreign Affairs, Vyacheslav Molotov, and a military mission on 29 April 1942.

With an average of forty pilots per course passing through the OTU, Tealing was a very busy place. Accidents were regular, and typical of inexperienced pilots trying to cut their teeth on a powerful single-seat fighter. The task was made all the more difficult by the fact that most of the 56 Hurricanes on strength at this time had already seen a great deal of action, a lot of it during the Battle of Britain.

Most of the pilots who graduated from 56 OTU were posted to the Middle East, where the Hurricane was used for ground-attack duties rather than air superiority. Elaborate exercises were organised as part of the course to give the pupil pilots as much experience as possible of low-level close-quarter attacks. By the end of 1942 operational tactics featured prominently on every course and formations of up to thirty Hurricanes would fly escort to the OTU's Masters, acting as bombers, to attack targets such as Kinnell, Royal Navy ships and the Tay Bridge. 'Roadstead' practice was also carried out from Tealing from early 1943, with Hurricanes detailed to fly as fighter-bombers, accompanied by anti-flak flights and even more aircraft flying in support. 2 TEU from Grangemouth often took part in these well-organised exercises with their pilots gaining experience of their own flying top cover.

56 OTU was renamed as 1 CTW from 5 October 1943, but this was to be short-lived, being redesignated 1 TEU from January 1944. Pilots yet to complete their training were transferred to 55 OTU at Annan. They were replaced by a fresh intake who had just completed their OTU training and would then take part in a new TEU course that would teach them a host of specialist tasks. These specialisms were divided into three squadrons within 1 TEU: 1 Squadron was based at Kinnell and taught air-firing; 2 Squadron carried out low-level navigation and flew mock 'Rhubarbs'; and 3 Squadron trained the pilots to perform 'Circus' and 'Roadstead' operations. Both 2 and 3 Squadrons operated from Tealing. and once again 2 TEU was heavily involved in all of the exercises.

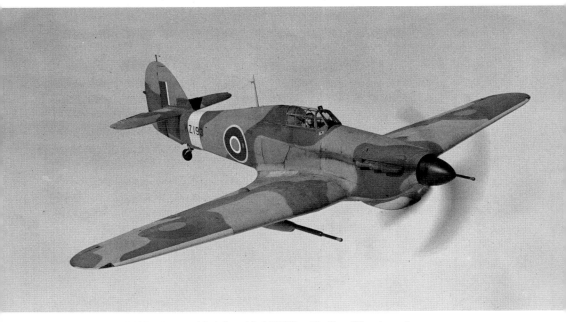

Hurricane Mk V KZ193 served briefly with 1 TEU at Tealing. The Aeroplane

During early 1944 1 TEU had nearly 110 aircraft on strength, the majority of which were still Hurricanes. A couple of Typhoons were also on strength around this time for conversion training. By February the Hurricane strength was reduced dramatically when forty of them were swapped with thirty-eight Spitfires from Grangemouth.

More general exercises were commonplace during the build-up to D-Day, and nine Mustangs from 63 Squadron from Turnhouse joined the TEU in March to take part in one of them. 1 TEU was directly affected by the invasion when, in late May through to mid-June 1944, several sections were put on operational readiness in support of the few remaining front-line squadrons in the area. It was thought that a counter-attack from Germany might occur during the invasion, but in the end all of the enemy's attention was focused on Northern France. Many of the pilots that passed through the TEU went on to serve with squadrons supporting and fighting beyond D-Day, but by 31 July the unit's work was deemed to have been done and it was disbanded.

The airfield was taken over by Flying Training Command in August, and in September Tealing became an RLG for Masters of 9 PAFU as well. The Masters gave way to Harvards during October and their rasping sound continued until the PAFU was disbanded in June 1945.

Maintenance Command took over on 21 August 1945 when the airfield became a sub-site for 260 MU. Four days later 70 Wing also moved in from Inverness, bringing an Oxford and a Tiger Moth. These were the last military aircraft to use Tealing when 70 Wing disbanded on 31 May 1946, leaving just 260 MU, which remained until 1948.

Looking north-east, with Tealing village in the distance, the airfield is now the home to a collection of poultry sheds and a large electricity substation.

Only the eastern section of the main runways is extant thanks to it providing solid bases for several poultry sheds, which also take advantage of the old technical site. Within the latter area several wartime buildings still stand, including the control tower.

Main features:
Concrete and wood chipping runways: QDM 272 1,500 yards, 212 1,100 yards. *Hangars:* three T3, eight over blister. *Hardstandings:* fifty-two. *Accommodation:* RAF: 1,512; WAAF: 380.

THE CURRAGH, Dublin

59°09'29"N/06°50'61"W; N77354 12232; 1½ miles E of Kildare

The Curragh can trace its aviation roots back to November 1915, but it was not until mid-1918 that the RFC arrived. On 27 June it became the home of 19 TS from Fermoy, which flew a wide selection of aircraft, and the amount increased when the Irish FIS was formed on 22 October with 504s and DH.9s. Both units remained here until 13 April 1919, when they were disbanded.

The Curragh on 22 July 1918, with a row of six Bessoneau hangars and a host of temporary and semi-permanent buildings beyond.

THURSO, Highland

NO121689

This airfield existed briefly in response to the potential U-boat threat at the beginning of the First World War. Thurso and Scapa Flow were chosen as sites for seaplane stations in August 1914 to help protect the Fleet. Not long afterwards an S.38 biplane was delivered by rail to Thurso, but by the end of the month had already gone. Before the end of 1914 all plans to establish a station here had been dropped, and all equipment and personnel were merged with Scapa.

TIREE, Strathclyde (Argyllshire)

56°29'56"N/06°52'12"W; NM000445. 3 miles W of Scarinish on B8065

Midland & Scottish Airways was the first to establish an airfield on Tiree in 1934. Laid out on an area known as The Reef, the service operated between Glasgow and Skye. It was more regular from 1937 onwards after a rental dispute was resolved, and continued intermittently throughout the war.

By 1940 the civilian aerodrome had been requisitioned and plans were drawn up to construct a Coastal Command airfield. Tiree's population swelled overnight as contractors and labourers poured onto the island.

By early 1942 the airfield was nearly complete and had already attracted several aircraft, including a 120 Squadron Liberator on 20 February. A Harrow from Limavady on 8 April marked the arrival of the first unit; 224 Squadron with Hudsons. A second, 304 Squadron, arrived on 10 May from Lindholme with Wellingtons. Both squadrons began A/S patrols, but they did not yield any targets. 304 Squadron's tour here was short, but this Polish unit must have made an impression as Tiree's station commander Gp Capt Tuttle arranged for the Coastal Command band to see them off to Dale on 15 June. 304 Squadron's CO Wg Cdr Poziomek received a letter from Tuttle a fortnight later, which included the following: 'I must write and express my appreciation to you and the whole of your squadron for their magnificent work here. I was amazed the whole time at the enthusiasm with which they tackled anything, and at their cheerful acceptance of the living conditions here.'

The new airfield at Tiree is seen not long after completion in 1942, photographed by a 1 OTU Hudson from Silloth.

The Hudsons of 224 Squadron had served it well since 1939, but in July 1942 the squadron received the Liberator, with a range of 2,000 miles. Before the squadron could get into its stride with the new aircraft it was moved to Beaulieu, and the Liberator units based in Northern Ireland now took on the task of convoy protection and A/S operations.

This exposed, windswept airfield was then placed under C&M, which would have been a good opportunity to upgrade many of the buildings that were not standing up to the weather very well. Accommodation was particularly susceptible to the weather, with many Nissen huts being stripped of their steel sheet covering.

It was not until September 1943 that Tiree was brought back to life with the arrival of 518 Squadron from Stornoway. This was a meteorological reconnaissance unit, which operated the Halifax far out into the Atlantic to provide weather reports as up-to-date as possible for other Coastal Command units. The MCU was also formed here on 28 October to train all initial crews for the Halifax meteorological squadrons. The life of the MCU was short as it was absorbed into 517 Squadron at Brawdy on 14 February 1944.

The SE for 281 Squadron was formed here in October 1943 to service the squadron's Warwicks. However, it was not until 27 February 1944 that the squadron moved in from Thornaby. Its area of operations was extensive, and to make sure ASR cover was available detachments were maintained all over the British Isles. 281 Squadron and its SE moved to Mullaghmore on 7 February, although a detachment was left behind until September 1945.

518 Squadron carried out a couple of detachments of its own during its tour here, including one at Wick and another at Tain. The squadron was moved to Aldergrove on 18 September 1945, leaving Tiree devoid of all military units other than a C&M party.

518 Squadron carried out long-range meteorological flights from Tiree with the Halifax until the unit was moved to Aldergrove in late 1945.

By 1 July 1946 Tiree was in the hands of the MoCA, which maintained the runways in a useable condition. The infrastructure of the airfield was already in a sorry state but in recent years the derelict wartime buildings have been cleared to make way for modern structures. Unfortunately one of the buildings that was swept was the pre-war clubhouse and control tower, which has been replaced by a modern version. It is very difficult to argue against such a move on an airfield as remote as this, were a practical modern building is a much better option than trying to maintain a decaying relic.

Main features:
Concrete runways: QDM 181 2,000 yards, 062 1,840 yards, 122 1,400 yards.
Hangars: ten half T2. *Accommodation:* RAF: 1,249; WAAF: 162.

TOOME, Londonderry

54°45'28"N/06°29'39"W; H970905. 1 mile W of Toome off A31

Originally planned in 1941 for a bomber OTU, construction was held up because at least fifty landowners were involved in the requisitioning. It was not until January 1942 that work began and it was not an easy project, progress being aggravated by its location close to the shores of Loch Neagh and bordered by the Bann and Moyola rivers.

By early 1943 the airfield was complete, but only a handful of RAF personnel arrived to open it. The USAAF showed an interest in March, but it was an RAF unit that made the airfield its home on 10 July when 'A' Flight, 104 (Transport) OTU, brought eight Wellingtons from Nutt's Corner. Toome was then handed over to the USAAF and redesignated as Station 236 on 26 July, although 104 OTU did not leave until early September.

Toome would now become the home to a CCRC, preparing combat crews to serve in the medium bombardment groups of the 9th AF in England. On 23 August 1943 the CCRC units were activated, and by 21 November it had been renamed the 3rd CCRC Group.

The first crews arrived in September for the three-week course and a large number of A-20s and B-26s were also here. By the beginning of 1944 the 9th AF added three more A-20 groups and four B-26 groups to its own inventory, and the number of crews needed for these units was instantly felt. By March the maximum number, 100 crews, was passing through Toome, although this figure was eclipsed in August when 112 B-26s and forty-two A-20s were prepared for operations.

Toome, pictured twenty years ago, has since been encroached upon further by industry from all angles. It is doubtful whether the site will be recognisable as an airfield in another twenty years.

While the CCRC was in full swing, further expansion of the airfield was taking place in support of the 3rd BAD at Langford Lodge. The BAD needed as much storage as it could muster, and in early 1944 five MAP dispersals were built capable of storing up to fifty bombers.

The 3rd CCRC is credited with training up to 800 combat crews for the 9th AF. There is no doubt the work carried out here would have helped many 'green' crews to settle in much quicker than if they had been thrown in at the deep end. The 3rd CCRC moved to Cheddington in October, and by 7 November Toome was back in RAF hands. No more flying units would make use of it before the end of the war, and on 24 November it was closed to flying. This did not stop it being inspected on at least two occasions for prospective use, first by Bomber Command in February 1945; it was then considered as a bomber OTU again, but the domestic site was not up to it despite the amount of American servicemen who had passed through it only months before. Toome was also looked at by 109 OTU, flying Dakotas, but once again was found lacking.

Toome languished until June 1945 when 257 MU was formed here; this EDD MU also had a sub-site at Langford Lodge from March 1946. 217 MU, an MTSU, arrived from Holyrood in October 1945, but only until February 1946, when it was disbanded into 257 MU. The latter only remained until March 1947, and the airfield fell silent again. The following day Toome was transferred to the Royal Navy as a reserve station for Eglinton until 1954, but the FAA never used it.

The reformation of 2 FTS at Cluntoe on 1 February 1953 brought new activity to Toome. Designated as a satellite for the FTS, a large proportion of Toome's runways were resurfaced and the prospect of a lengthy continuation of flying looked promising. It was to be short-lived, however, as 2 FTS was moved to Hullavington in May 1954 and what little flying did occur was brought to an abrupt halt.

The airfield finished its days under Admiralty control serving as a Naval Repair Yard specialising in gun turrets until early 1959. Two years later the process of returning Toome to its original owners began. Today a surprising large amount of original buildings still remain, including the control tower, which has been converted into a dwelling. The majority of buildings can be seen from the Creagh Road, many of them from the CCRC period, including a bombing teacher.

Main features:
Concrete and wood chipping runways: QDM 270 1,920 yards, 330 1,400 yards, 220 1,400 yards. *Hangars:* four T2. *Hardstandings:* thirty-one loop.

TURNBERRY, Strathclyde/Ayrshire

55°19'32"N/04°49'27"W. S of Maidens, N of Turnberry, traversed by A719

It is very unusual to record an airfield that has a history covering almost a century, which has been used in four different guises, and which is still used in a limited capacity today.

For those who are subservient to the world of golf, it would seem sacrosanct to plant an airfield in the middle of one of the most historic courses in Scotland. Established formally on 6 July 1901, Turnberry was quickly acknowledged as a great golf course, but the outbreak of the First World War focussed a great deal of attention away from the sport.

The course and level ground was not overlooked by the RFC, and in January 1917 an SoAG was formed. Designated as 2 (Auxiliary) SoAG, the unit flew various types and was joined on 17 September by 1 SoAF, also formed here. The SoAF also operated a lot of aircraft, although, like those of the gunnery school, all were very tired and poorly maintained, resulting in a high casualty rate.

Both units were disbanded and joined to form 1 SoAF&G, which operated between here and Ayr. Aircraft types had now been streamlined to the DH.9, SE.5a and Fe.2b, but despite some improvements in maintenance pilots were still losing their lives before getting anywhere near the front. A final change of name came in May 1918 when the SoAF&G became 1 FS, before disbanding on 1 April 1919. The aerodrome closed down not long after.

During the 1930s the LG was recorded on the AA listing, probably for those golfers who could afford to fly in for a round or two. The golf course was given no such consideration during the Second World War, and work began on a more substantial airfield in mid-1941.

A brightly coloured BE.2C has its prop swung at Turnberry in late 1917.

The new airfield was complete by early 1942, and in February personnel began to arrive. However, it was not until 3 May that the first unit appeared when 5 (Coastal) OTU Beauforts and later Hampdens moved in from Chivenor. The unit's task was operational crew training, but by November torpedo training was also introduced. To help cater for this, the TTU moved here from Abbotsinch on 11 November and would later be dissolved into a 1 TTU, formed here in January 1943. In the meantime 5 OTU departed for Long Kesh, leaving Turnberry as the specialist for torpedo training.

A 5 OTU Beaufort I on a training sortie from Turnberry in June 1942.

1 TTU was one of the principal elements in the expansion of torpedo training within the RAF during 1943, providing advanced training for crews who had already passed through an OTU. Both TTUs (2 TTU was based at Castle Kennedy) were concentrated in one area, utilised the same targets and recovery vessels, and used the ranges on the Clyde. By March the unit also absorbed the TT Flight and its Wellingtons at Limavady. Hampdens, Beaufighters and Lysanders were also used, although by September much of the training was transferred to the Middle East and 1 TTU was

reduced in size. The same month, 2 TTU was absorbed, as the requirement for RAF torpedo units began to decline. The unit continued until on 22 May 1944 it was absorbed into the one from which it had been created.

5 OTU returned from Long Kesh in February 1944, still flying Beauforts together with Hudsons and Venturas. After absorbing the ASRTU from Thornaby on 15 May, the unit also began to receive the Warwick ASR to carry out another area of specialised Coastal Command training. When 1 TTU was absorbed, Beaufighters began to replace the tired Beauforts. The unit continued to juggle its specialist tasking until it was disbanded here on 1 August 1945.

RAF Turnberry is seen after its closure in the late 1940s. Despite the size of the airfield, the golf course survived surprisingly well and today's course works around the large sections of concrete that still remain.

10 GS flew its Cadets from here until January 1948, then not long afterwards Turnberry was closed, but by the mid-1960s was partly reactivated to light aircraft thanks to the golf course establishing itself. Today, helicopters are the only flying visitors.

A few wartime buildings still remain including the control tower, which has been developed into a private dwelling to such an extent that its previous identity has almost been lost. Large sections of all three runways still remain, in particular a 1,000-yard piece of the main runway; this can be followed along the A77, which now traverses the site. One poignant memorial to those who lost their lives at the airfield during the First World War was erected in 1923 on the seaward, western side of the old airfield. The large double Celtic cross was paid for by the people of Kirkoswald parish, and in 1990 the names of those lost during the Second World War were added.

Main features:
Tarmac-covered concrete runways: QDM 222 1,600 yards, 181 1,400 yards, 275 1,250 yards. *Hangars:* two T2, two half T2, twenty-four EO blister. *Hardstandings:* thirty-one 100-foot diameter, three fighter HS. *Accommodation:* RAF: 2,345; WAAF: 437.

TURNHOUSE (EDINBURGH), Mid-Lothian

55°57'09"N/03°21'46"W; NT60735. 5 miles W of Edinburgh off B9080

This once busy fighter station is still bustling as Edinburgh Airport after ninety-six years of almost continuous activity. Steady development over the years has changed the airfield, and today it is an international airport that can cater for all modern airliners.

Requisitioned in 1914, the first unit can be traced back to 1915 when the Aeroplane Barrage Line constructed a Flight Station for the RFC here. 44 Squadron arrived on 18 April 1916, but was disbanded into 26 TS a month later.

This is Turnhouse not long after it opened in 1916, with aircraft of 26 TS. Via Stuart Leslie

By 1916 Zeppelin raids were on the increase, but they still remained rare over Scottish soil. A raid on Edinburgh during the night of 2/3 April saw 77(HD) Squadron being based here. During 1917 two Canadian units were formed out of 26 TS: first 84 (Canadian) TS, which left for Toronto, then 89 (Canadian) TS, which moved to Beverley in April. 73 TS moved here with Camels from Thetford on 17 July 1917, and 26 TS left for Stamford in September. 73 TS left for Beaulieu in February 1918. 77 Squadron's responsibilities began to shrink by 1918 and the squadron moved to Penston; after re-equipping with the 504K, it disbanded in June 1919. The airfield was also home to 103 Squadron, which arrived from Maisoncelle in February; by 3 March it had moved to Crail.

It was here that 'Edinburgh's own' squadron was formed on 14 October 1925. 603 (City of Edinburgh) formed as a bomber unit and its first aircraft was the DH.9A, replaced by the Wapiti in March 1930, then the Hind.

The subject of municipal airports was being discussed by most councils in Great Britain during the late 1920s and 1930s, and Edinburgh was no exception. While many sites were surveyed, Turnhouse stood out as an obvious choice. After a false start with London, Scottish & Provincial

Sopwith Camel N7149 Swillington *poses at Turnhouse in 1919. This presentation aircraft was delivered to 6 AAP at Renfrew in January 1919 before arriving at Turnhouse.*

A formation of 603 Squadron Harts flies past Bass Rock lighthouse during the mid-1930s.

Airways Ltd in 1934, the first service took place in June 1935. The route was from Dyce to Turnhouse, using an Aberdeen Airways DH.84. North Eastern Airways began flying a twice-weekly service from Heston via Leeds and Newcastle, with one flight continuing to Turnhouse, using an Envoy.

A change of role for 603 Squadron occurred during October 1938 when the unit switched to fighters and re-equipped with the Gladiator. Turnhouse became a Sector Section airfield from September 1939 to control the operational activities of 603 Squadron and 602 Squadron based at Abbotsinch.

83 Squadron Hinds line up at Turnhouse on 29 May 1937, with the only Type C hangar providing the backdrop.

Flt Lt G. L. Denholm flew the first wartime patrol from here on 5 September in a Gladiator of 603 Squadron. Ten days later the unit received its first Spitfire. 141 Squadron was re-formed on 4 October 1939 as a night-fighter unit, gathering together whatever aircraft it could find, including Gladiators from 603 Squadron, before moving to Grangemouth on 19 October.

16 October was not only a historic day for 603 Squadron, but also for the AAF. Yellow Section, made up of Flt Lt Denholm, Plt Off Gilroy and Plt Off Morton, was scrambled to patrol over the Firth of Forth. A German aircraft was sighted, and a message intercepted from this machine indicated that a heavy enemy air raid was inbound, the targets being the Forth Bridge and the Rosyth Dockyard. Red Section 603 Squadron and a section of 602 Squadron, now operating from Drem, also joined Yellow Section over the Firth of Forth. The enemy turned out to be twelve He 111s, which reached the entrance of the Firth and attacked naval vessels near the bridge. The enemy raiders adopted dive-bombing tactics and released approximately forty bombs, causing some naval casualties. The bombers were quickly intercepted by the fighters; the first was sighted east of Dalkeith and was shot down into the sea by 603 Squadron's Spitfires. More success was to follow that day for 603 Squadron. Red Section, which included Plt Off Morton and Plt Off Robertson, attacked an He 111 near Rosyth. The rear gunner of the enemy bomber was silenced and one engine had stopped by the time Morton and Robertson broke off their attack. Flg Off Boulter engaged another He 111 east of Aberdour, and Flt Lt Gifford, accompanied by Plt Offs Morton and Robertson, was directed to a convoy that was being attacked off St Abbs Head. Another He 111 was attacked by the trio, which quickly attempted to escape out to sea after being hit several times. The damage caused by the 603 Squadron Spitfires was severe enough for the German bomber to turn back towards the Scottish coast, the crew realising that they had no chance of making it back to their home airfield. The four-man crew of the He 111 were found alive not far from the spot where they had originally been attacked by Red Section.

On 28 October 1939 602 and 603 Squadrons brought down this Heinkel He 111 near Humbie.
This was the first enemy aircraft to be shot down over British soil during the Second World War.

Another significant event for the squadron took place on 28 October 1939. While on patrol over the Firth of Forth, Red Sections of both 602 and 603 Squadrons spotted an He 111, which was attacked by both and crash-landed east of Humbie. This shared victory was the first enemy aircraft to be brought down on British soil.

By mid-November it was becoming obvious that both the runways and the general condition of the airfield were suffering. Up to now the runways had been turfed, and after a visit by the AOC of 13 Group on 22 November it was decided that Turnhouse should be upgraded with solid runways. To make way for the work, 603 Squadron left for Prestwick on 16 December.

On 4 May 1940 the runways were opened and 603 Squadron returned from Drem the following day. Hurricanes of 245 Squadron also moved in from Drem in June. The squadron spent most of its time detached to Hawkinge, from where it patrolled over the Channel and Dunkirk. After returning from there on 1 July, the squadron was moved to Aldergrove on the 20th.

While FAA squadrons were a common sight, it was not until 13 February 1942 that the first arrived here. 882 Squadron was briefly at Turnhouse flying the Sea Hurricane and the Martlet, then left on 17 March to be replaced by 884 Squadron from Yeovilton, flying the Fulmar.

Two more Seafire units arrived in June, first 808 Squadron on the 14th, then 895 Squadron the following day. 808 Squadron arrived from HMS *Battler* where it had been practising flying under battle conditions at sea. The squadron left for Andover on 20 July, although four of its Seafires embarked on HMS *Battler*.

603 Squadron returned on 28 April 1945, now equipped with the Spitfire XVIE, but it was only at its home airfield for a few weeks before moving to Drem on 7 May. The same day, and only hours before the war came to an end, several new units were reorganised and formed here. 88 Group CF was the first, formed from a detachment of 116 Squadron, which slipped into Turnhouse on 12 March. The new flight, equipped with Ansons, was formed to support 88 Group, which had recently formed at Kinella House, Murrayfield Rd, Edinburgh, on 10 April.

Before 7 May had ended, a long-term resident at Turnhouse, 289 Squadron, moved to Acklington. Finally, seventeen Mustangs of 611 Squadron transited through the airfield en route to Peterhead.

164 Squadron, which had been operating the Typhoon across Europe, arrived on 17 June from Milfield. The plan was for the unit to re-equip with Spitfires provided by 451 Squadron, based at Skeabrae. This Australian squadron arrived on 13 June, leaving by road and rail to Lasham and onwards to serve in Germany. 164 Squadron remained here until November 1945, but would return again the following year.

603 Squadron was back on 28 July, this time from Skeabrae, and was one of several fighter squadrons covering the arrival of surrendered German vessels into Scapa Flow. With the defeat and final surrender of the Japanese on 15 August, 603 Squadron was ordered to disband.

Mustangs of 303 Squadron were the only significant arrival at the airfield during late 1945, but by May 1946 603 Squadron was recruiting again. Re-formed on 10 May under the command of Sqn Ldr G. K. 'Sheep' Gilroy, the squadron was equipped with the Spitfire LF.XVIe, but the F.22 replaced these in 1947. In May 1951 the squadron entered the jet age with the arrival of the Vampire. This new type of aircraft required longer runways and Turnhouse's was extended during late May through to late September. The squadron relocated to Leuchars while the work was carried out, returning on 15 October. The final hammer fell for all RAAF squadrons on 10 May 1957; 603 Squadron was destined to become the first and last jet fighter squadron to be based here.

Meanwhile, civilian airliner activity was on the increase, especially since a new terminal building was built in 1956. Four years later the MoD transferred ownership of the airfield to the MoA, while maintaining an RAF presence here. By 1971 control of the airport was moved to the British Airports Authority, under whose management a large-scale extension and reconstruction was begun. A new 8,400-foot runway was completed in 1977, which was more than capable of handling the world's biggest airliners. Another state-of-the-art terminal was constructed, and the old one was converted into a new cargo centre. By 2007 more than nine million passengers were passing through Edinburgh Airport, and it continues to evolve. Passenger numbers are projected at 20 million by the year 2020!

A regular sight at Turnhouse during the 1960s and 1970s was Canberra WJ643, which served with Ferranti on various trials for several years.

This view of Edinburgh Airport in the mid-1990s shows how much it has expanded beyond the original RAF Turnhouse to the right of the photo.

The original wartime location of the airfield and technical area was still known as RAF Turnhouse until 1 April 1996, when the station was closed. Virtually all of the military buildings remain, including the control tower, Type C hangar and a host of technical and domestic buildings, many being put to alternative civilian use. A vital airfield during the Second World War, Turnhouse will continue to serve the Scottish people for many decades to come.

Main features:
Concrete runways: QDM 310 1,156 yards, 260 1,133 yards, 220 716 yards. *Hangars:* one C, six blister. *Hardstandings:* four frying pan, twelve SE double pens. *Accommodation:* RAF: 1,340; WAAF: 643.

The modern £10 million control tower at Edinburgh's International Airport. Author

TWATT, Orkney

59°05'13"N/03°17'12"W; HY265230. 9 miles N of Stromness off A967, 1 mile N of Skeabrae

Described as little more than a 'clearing in primeval heather', this airfield was between the Loch of Isbister to the west and a main road to the east. There was some concern about the name attached to this latest addition to the Royal Navy's inventory, suggesting that it may create some ridicule. Regardless, the airfield would be named Twatt, which was marginally concealed when the site later became HMS *Tern*, 1 April 1941.

The first unit to arrive was 812 Squadron with its Swordfishes on 25 June, leaving for HMS *Furious* on 16 July. The same month the Sea Hurricanes of 880A Squadron arrived, as did the Swordfishes of 818 Squadron. 821 Squadron came next from Hatston with its Swordfishes, briefly departing for Machrihanish then on to Sumburgh by 5 November. The Martlets of 802 Squadron made Twatt their home between 25 August and 10 September before embarking on HMS *Audacity*, followed by brief detachments by 817 and 832 Squadrons, both flying Albacores from HMS *Victorious*.

A Fairey Swordfish at Twatt in 1942.

It was a fighter squadron from HMS *Victorious* that would become the airfield's first permanent unit, although Twatt was little more than a resting place between trips at sea. 809 Squadron's Fulmars arrived from *Victorious* in October. The squadron was destined to come and go from here at least seven times until it left in July 1942, and saw a great deal of action during its voyages in Arctic waters escorting the Russian convoys.

Apart from a another brief visit by 819 Squadron from Crail in late January 1942, it was not until 22 June that a proper role was found for Twatt. On that day 'A' Flight of 700 Squadron, which consisted of its HQ and Training Flight, moved in from Hatston with more than sixty Walruses. Its role was train pilots for catapult flights, which was covered in a ten-week course. Three weeks of this was carried out at Donibristle, with another three weeks spent at Dundee, one week on HMS *Pegasus* and another week at Donibristle. The last two weeks of the course were spent with 'A' Flight at Twatt before the fully trained crews were allocated to a ship. Various sub-units were created from 700 Squadron, which not only operated the Walrus but also the Seafox and Kingfisher. Eventually the increased availability of MAC ships and escort carriers reduced the need for catapult aircraft, and on 24 March 1944 the unit was disbanded.

Another long-term resident at Twatt was 771 Squadron, an FRU that arrived from Hatston on 1 July 1942. This unit brought a large collection of aircraft with it, including the Skua, Defiant, Swordfish, Henley, Roc, Blenheim, Sea Gladiator, Maryland and Chesapeake, all bringing an element of the unusual and exotic to Twatt. By early 1945 the unit also had a handful of Hoverfly helicopters on strength before the unit moved to Zeals on 25 July.

Target-towing Swordfish II DK711 climbs away from Twatt in early 1943.

Until 21 June the Seafire was a rare sight, but 802 Squadron changed that when it arrived from Arbroath. It was not a long stay as the naval fighters left for Ayr on 18 July, to be replaced two days later by 846 Squadron from Hatston. Flying Avengers, it was to become the last FAA squadron to make use of Twatt, leaving for Crail on 1 August.

Twatt remained in the hands of the Admiralty until it was paid off in September 1946. It was retained under C&M and controlled by Lossiemouth until January 1957, when the site was sold off.

Due to its location there is a large collection of semi-derelict buildings around Twatt, and several, if not all of the original fighter pens are extant. The most notable feature on the old site is the unique control tower, which is positioned on top of the operations block. The building is in very good condition and there is talk of it being fully preserved or possibly restored for generations to come.

Main features:
Tarmac runways: QDM 153 1,200 yards, 113 1,030 yards, 058 1,000 yards, 013 1,000 yards. *Hangars:* twelve 60 x 60 feet squadron, nine 60 x 70 feet, seven 60 x 70 feet storage, one 186 x 105 feet workshop. *Accommodation:* RN: 1,119; WRNS: 182.

TYNEHEAD, Midlothian

55°49'N/002°58'W; NT380585. 5 miles SE of Gorebridge

Little more than field with a few tents, this LG was used by 77(HD) Squadron during 1917 and 1918.

URQUHART, Invernesshire

4 miles E of Elgin

This was an RLG for the use of 15 SFTS from October 1939 until April 1940.

VALENCIA HARBOUR, Kerry

51°55'92"N/10°17'41"W; V425780. 2½ miles WSW of Cahersiveen

The Royal Navy operated seaplanes from the harbour from 1918. A stretch of water, in an east-west direction, 2,000 yards in length and 400 yards wide, made this a good area from which to fly.

WAKEFIELD, Kincardineshire

2 miles SW of Laurencekirk

The exact location of this FLP is not clear owing to the nature of its use. From 1940 it was used by 8 FTS, followed by 2 FIS until the end of the war.

WEST CAIRNBEG, Aberdeenshire

3 miles W of Fordoun airfield off B966

One of potentially three FLP areas used by 8 FTS and later 2 FIS, the exact location is vague but it was probably located near a place called Gallows knap, south of West Cairnbeg. It was brought into use from 1940 and continued until 1945.

WEST FREUGH, Dumfries and Galloway

54°51'03"N/04°56'52"W; NX110545. 5 miles SE of Stranraer off A757

Still in the hands of the MoD, although now operated by QinetiQ, West Freugh has been used for weapons training and experimentation since it opened in 1937.

In August 1936 2,700 acres of land was purchased for the construction of an airfield and nearby ranges at a cost of £19,400. The ranges were located very close to the airfield along the north-western edge of Luce Bay, stretching from Clayshant to Torrs Warren, and this still remains a 'Danger Area' today. Work on the airfield began not long after, while bombing targets were constructed on the range.

On 1 January 1937 4 ATC was formed with Wallaces and Tutors. In May 1938 the ATC was redesignated 4 ATS, and gained a few Wellesleys followed by Heyfords later in the year. Such was the increasing demand for target-towing duties that 'E' Flight, 1 AACU, moved in on detachment from Farnborough in May. During this first summer at West Freugh the unit worked closely with the Royal Artillery, TA Battalion, at Burrow Head before returning to Farnborough on 15 September. The following year 'E' Flight returned, on 20 May 1939, but this time it was permanent. Although initially affiliated to Fighter Command, the flight, which operated Henleys, spent a great deal of time towing targets up and down Luce Bay while trainee observer/air gunners let loose at the drogue behind. Once again, though, the flight also worked with 2 HAAPC at Burrow Head before it was disbanded here on 1 October 1942, although it lived on in 289 Squadron.

4 ATS was renamed again on 17 April 1939, this time to 4 AOS, which was to be short-lived as it became 4 B&GS from 1 November. The B&GS began to re-equip with Bothas, while several Battles were still retained for target-towing duties, the Wallace being finally withdrawn. On 14 June 1941 4 B&GS reverted to 4 AOS, again with an establishment of seventy-eight Bothas, although the total at West Freugh never exceeded sixty-six. Much to the relief of many instructors, the Bothas began to be replaced by Ansons from the end of the year, and the Battles were being superseded by Lysanders.

Several aircraft from Bomber Command had been visiting, making full use of the ranges. It was clear that there would be more benefit in establishing a permanent unit that could focus on the development of aerial ordnance, so on 1 August 1942 the BTU was formed with Hampdens under the control of the MAP. The BTU also operated Lancasters, and by 1945 also had Mitchells and Mosquitoes on strength. As well as using the local ranges, a fake factory made of concrete was constructed on the moors near Stranraer, providing a very realistic target for the BTU. The unit moved to Wigtown on 16 June 1947, but it would not be long before it would return.

One of many aircraft that served with the BTU was Lincoln II RA716, seen here at West Freugh in 1953.

4 AOS was redesignated as 4 PAFU on 11 June 1943 and was now equipped with more than fifty Ansons. The last Bothas clung on until July, and target-towing duties were still carried out by Lysanders until November, when they were replaced by Martinets.

The long-serving – albeit in many forms – 4 OAFU was disbanded on 21 June, and after a short period of quiet the airfield was taken over by Maintenance Command on 31 July 1945. The same day West Freugh became the home of 103 SSS under the control of 57 MU at Wig Bay, and remained so until early 1946. The BTU and 1353 Flight continued to use the airfield, although by now the majority of the hangars were filled with up to seventy-five Mosquitoes, all of which were destined never to fly again. 275 MU moved in from Cairn Ryan on 10 November 1947 but only remained until early 1948. The airfield was also briefly used by 249 MU at Great Orton as a sub-site until mid-1952, by which time Maintenance Command had no further use for West Freugh.

In the meantime the BTU had left, but was back from Wigtown by May 1948. It continued to operate a diverse range of aircraft, which by this time included the Mosquito B.35 and the Lincoln B.2. On 1 January 1957 the BTU was redesignated as the AATE, and was now under the control of the Ministry of Supply. Under its new title its role was brought to an end on 10 June 1959 when it was disbanded following absorption into the RAE.

West Freugh today is a neat arrangement of runways and technical buildings. Luce Bay airship station was located in the area of the bomb dump towards the top of the photograph.

The work that the BTU and subsequent AATE carried out was encompassed under a new title from 1 May 1956. The airfield was now referred to as RAE West Freugh, and continued to carry out weapon development trials with new aircraft for decades to come. On 1 April 1992 the airfield became the Test & Evaluation Establishment, West Freugh, under the Air Flight Ranges Division of the Directorate General of Test and Evaluation. The unit operated a Devon, carried over from the RAE days, and a Jetstream. Today the Jetstream serves with the DT&EO WF, and the RAE continues to support weapons development projects and testing, thanks to the nearby range, which is still used.

Main features:
Tarmac runways: QDM 070 1,500 yards, 120 965 yards. *Hangars:* one F, seven Bellman, one Bessoneau, nine EO blister. *Hardstandings:* three twin fighter pens, 200 x 120 feet tarmac area. *Accommodation:* RAF: 1,376; WAAF: 428.

WEXFORD (FERRYBANK), County Wexford

52°20'79"N/02°21'6"W; T05248 22772. 1 mile N of Wexford

Originally an RNAS seaplane station, Wexford was taken over by the USN; work began on upgrading the site for the H.16 Large America from 2 May 1918, and the station was operational on 18 September. All of the construction was carried out by American labour, which must have upset the locals at a time when that type of work would have been sought after.

The station's main task was to protect the southern entrance to the Irish Sea, but with the Armistice just around the corner very few operations would have been flown from here. USNAS Wexford was closed down in February 1919, and only a single concrete slipway remains today.

WHELANS FIELD (BALLYMULLEN BARRACKS), Kerry

52°16'21"N/09°41'35"W; Q847145. 1 mile SE of Tralee town centre

Described as a grass airstrip with a single NW/SE runway, 400 yards long, this airfield was active from late 1922 through to 1923, and both the RAF and IAAC used it.

WHIDDY ISLAND, Cork

51°41'48"N/09°29'21"W; V972498. 1½ miles W of Bantry in Bantry Bay

With the First World War drawing to a close, the USN decided to establish a seaplane base in south-western Ireland. Work began from July 1918 and it was an operational USNAS by September. Aircraft stationed here were at least five H.16s allocated to patrol around Fastnet.

After the war some flying continued, but it was clear that Whiddy's days were numbered and the station was closed down in January 1919.

WHITEBURN (GRANTSHOUSE), Borders

55°52'07"N/02°22'37"W; NT765639. 1 mile N of Abbey St Bathans, 15 miles NW of Berwick

Positioned on 120 acres of open moorland on the fringe of the Lammermuir Hills, Whiteburn was opened in 1916. One of the highest aerodromes of the war at 750 feet above sea level, Whiteburn became the home of 'C' Flight, 77 (HD) Squadron, which arrived from New Haggerston in November. Aircraft flown by the flight were mainly BEs.

In August 1917 'B' Flight arrived, followed in early 1918 by 'A' Flight, making the unit complete for the first time in its short history. Despite the aerodrome being so well equipped, the sortie rate was not high and meteorological observations carried out during 1917/18 revealed that flying was only possible during 25% of daylight hours.

In May 1918 the entire squadron left for Penston, returning a few weeks later for a detachment. Not long after the end of the war the site was abandoned.

WHITEFIELD, Perth and Kinross

56°29'42"N/03°20'23"W; NO170345. S of Meikle Whitefield, 3 miles SW of Burrelton

The RLG at Whitefield must have been a very pleasant environment from which to fly for fledgling pilots. To help dilute the already overcrowded circuit at Perth, Whitefield was quickly brought into use for the Tiger Moths of 11 EFTS. 5 FIS was also here from December 1939 to train flying instructors on Tiger Moths and Magisters, but was disbanded in November 1942.

Whitefield served as an RLG for 11 EFTS, and is pictured in August 1943.

Whitefield was closed on 9 July 1945, having served longer than many of its larger and more complex compatriots. The site reverted to farmland and the vast majority of the buildings were either sold off or destroyed. Only the flight office stood the test of time, surviving until at least the mid-1980s. Any evidence of its existence today has vanished, otherwise the flying field has not changed since it was requisitioned back in 1939.

Main features:
Grass runway: 900 yards. *Hangars:* eight EO blisters. *Accommodation:* RAF: 36.

WICK, Highland

58°27'32"N/03°05'35"W; ND360525. 1 mile NW of Wick

The Second World War was an incredibly busy time for Wick, which saw constant military activity from September 1939 right through to early 1946. It was a far cry from the peaceful comings and goings of Highland Airways before the war.

It was 1933 when Highland Airways began to use a small aerodrome on land belonging to Hillhead Farm. On the outbreak of war the aerodrome was taken over by the Air Ministry and plans were made to expand the site into a fighter station complete with its own satellite at Skitten and decoy at Scarlet, 5 miles to the south.

In preparation for the first resident unit, SHQ was opened here on 15 September 1939 while the rest of the airfield was far from finished. In October 269 Squadron moved in from Montrose, with Ansons, tasked with flying patrols along the coast and as far north as the Faeroe Islands. The unit briefly re-equipped with Hudsons during April and May 1940 for attacks against shipping off Norway, but this was only temporary and the Anson would serve the squadron until well into 1941.

Rocs and Skuas of 803 Squadron joined the RAF contingent on 31 October but saw no action and, after one detachment to Hatston, moved there permanently on 10 February 1940. Bomber Command also made its presence felt when 50 Squadron from Waddington and 61 Squadron from Hemswell brought their Hampdens to Wick on 24 November. Under Coastal Command control, neither saw any action before they returned at the end of the year.

By December 1939 Wick became a Sector Station for 13 Group, opening the door for a host of fighter squadrons to serve here in defence of Scapa Flow. This began on 26 February when three units, 43, 111 and 605 Squadrons, all flying Hurricanes, arrived from Acklington, Drem and Leuchars. During these early months of the war the RAF was treating all threats of an attack against the Fleet seriously, and this was justified when the Luftwaffe launched its first attack on 28 March. Fg Off P. G. Leeson of 605 Squadron, accompanied by Plt Off K. S. Law and Sgt Stephen, spotted an He 111 entering cloud at 6,000 feet and flying at about 250mph. Leeson managed two short bursts of fire and witnessed the bomber catch fire before heading down towards the sea. Once the Hurricanes had returned back to Wick satisfied that they had achieved their squadron's first kill of the war, they learned that 43 Squadron had also claimed the same bomber once it was down to 1,000 feet! So it was a half-destroyed each for the two squadrons.

These 111 Squadron Hurricanes at Wick in early March 1940 are being refuelled by a triple-boom bowser immediately after coming to a halt. A third Hurricane, out of shot to the right, is also being refuelled. Via author

43 Squadron was in action on 8 April 1940 when it claimed three He 111s and two damaged, one of which landed at Wick with two dead crew on board. The following day the Germans invaded Denmark and Norway and declared war. On 10 April the Luftwaffe arrived over Scapa in force. 605 Squadron was in the thick of it, the day starting when Plt Off I. J. Muirhead attacked a reconnaissance aircraft before it escaped into cloud. Fg Off Leeson added to his tally when a raider was shot down into the sea; only two of the crew bailed out before the bomber hit the water. The evening brought

more raids, and all of Wick's squadrons were over Scapa fighting it out while the FAA's Skuas were lower down putting the damaged aircraft out of their misery. Seven enemy bombers were destroyed, with claims by all three Hurricane squadrons, the FAA and local anti-aircraft units. Regardless, high praise was showered by senior staff on all who took part in the action.

605 Squadron was successful again on 9 May when Fg Off G. R. Edge, G. W. B. Austin and R. Hope shot down a bomber off Dunnet Head. 111 Squadron moved to Northolt on 13 May, 605 Squadron departed for Hawkinge on 21 May, and 43 Squadron left for Tangmere on 31 May.

Wick's vulnerability to air attack was highlighted on 1 July 1940 when the town was bombed. The airfield's hangars could be seen from miles away, and without difficulty Wick was singled out for the first time on 26 October. Initially the decoy site at Scarlet did its job well, receiving the first wave of the attack, but when the Luftwaffe realised its mistake several He 111s dropped their bombs across Wick. Three civilians were killed in the raid while one aircraft was destroyed and one hangar damaged. On 17 March 1941 the airfield was hit again, killing one airman and narrowly missing the torpedo store. A Hudson was closely followed by a lone raider at night on 26 April, which then dropped its bomb load on the flarepath, killing another airman before making its escape.

This is Wick in June 1941 during a period when several different attempts were experimented with to try and camouflage the airfield from the air. Regardless, there was no hiding the giant Type C hangars, which could be seen from miles around, and Wick suffered its fair share of bombing raids.

The worst and final raid came on 4 June 1941 when a Ju 88 dropped its bombs onto one of the hangars. One 612 Squadron Whitley was destroyed and four others were damaged. Without a thought for their own safety, personnel pushed three aircraft from the blazing hangar. Unbeknown to all involved, one of the enemy's bombs had failed to explode and was not discovered until the next day!

612 Squadron had arrived from Dyce on 1 April 1941, joined by the Hudsons of 220 Squadron from Thornaby on the 28th. The airfield was busy over the coming weeks before Wick's long-term resident, 269 Squadron, left for Kaldadarnes on 31 May. 220 and 612 Squadrons flew several joint operations from Wick, the first taking place on 7 June. The target was the U-boat berths and workshops that had been established at Bergen. Luckily, any defending fighters were caught off guard as the Whitleys and Hudsons reduced the target to rubble before returning to Wick with loss or damage to all involved. 612 Squadron even managed to damage a Do 17 when Plt Off Carter's aircraft emptied its guns into the enemy aircraft.

By July 612 Squadron was also operating a detachment from Limavady, followed by more from St Eval and later Reykjavik. It was for Iceland that the squadron left Wick on 15 December, 220 Squadron having moved on earlier in the month.

Wick remains a reasonably busy regional airport thanks to HIAL operations and, as can be seen from this modern aerial view, retains many of its wartime features.

608 Squadron moved its Hudsons here from Thornaby on 2 January 1942, followed four days later by 48 Squadron from Skitten, also flying Hudsons. Both were operating in the anti-shipping and A/S roles and neither wasted any time in getting on with the job. 608 Squadron scored three direct hits on an icebound vessel on 26 February, and an MV was damaged at Egersund a few days later. On 17 May eight Hudsons took part in a shipping strike off Norway, one being damaged by a Bf 109, although the pilot skilfully outmanoeuvred the enemy fighter while his colleagues fired more than 250 rounds in support of him. On 3 June a tanker was hit in the Skaggerak, and a week later a U-boat was attacked with three depth charges that fell short of their quarry. Finally both 48 and 608 Squadrons took part in the attack on the *Prinz Eugen* on 17 May, but despite the fact that nearly fifty aircraft were involved no hits were scored on the battleship.

48 Squadron left on 23 September 1942, its place taken by 612 Squadron, which returned from Thorney Island still equipped with the Whitley. It was partnered by torpedo-carrying Hampdens of 489 Squadron, which moved in from Skitten on 24 September. The New Zealanders only remained for a few days before leaving for Leuchars on 6 October.

The first element of the 'Wick Strike Wing' arrived on 20 April 1943 with the Beaufighters of 404 Squadron from Tain. They were joined by the 'Torbeaus' of 144 Squadron on detachment from Tain a few days later, and between them they began to wreak havoc among enemy shipping along the Norwegian coast. The 'wing' was joined in September by the Mosquitoes and Beaufighters of 618 Squadron, detached here from Skitten, and 144 Squadron moved in permanently on 23 October. All three squadrons scored successes against the enemy, but also suffered high casualties thanks to the close-quarter nature of the attacks. Both 144 and 404 Squadrons were moved to Davidstow Moor in early May 1944 to play their part in the Normandy invasion.

An unusual arrival from Reykjavik on 1 June 1943 was a squadron of 162 Squadron's RCAF Canso amphibians. Until now they had been having a very quiet war traversing the open seas of the North Atlantic, but this was all about to suddenly change, and on 3 June Flt Lt R. E. MacBride and crew, in 9816, claimed the squadron's first enemy submarine when U-477 was sunk west of Trondheim. A second was sunk on 11 June when Fg Off L. Sherman and crew, in 9842, dispatched U-980 north-west of Bergen, only eleven days into its first patrol.

Incredibly, the squadron's lucky streak continued, although it was not so straightforward for the unit's CO, Wg Cdr C. G. W. Chapman and crew in 9816 on 13 June. Chapman caught U-715 on the surface north-east of the Faroes, and rather than dive it chose to fight it out with its anti-aircraft guns. The U-boat's gun crews succeeded in forcing the Canso to ditch. but not before the submarine was sunk by its depth charges. After spending 9 hours in a dingy, the Canso crew were rescued.

On 24 June 1944 it was the turn of Flt Lt D. E. Hornell and crew in Canso 9754 to take on a U-boat. U-1225 was caught on the surface north-west of Bergen, but accurate fire from the submarine set the Canso on fire. Once again, with Canadian perseverance, Hornell pressed home his attack and the U-boat was sunk. Hornell ditched the flaming Canso in the sea, but before the amphibian quickly sank only one dingy could be recovered for the eight crew to huddle in. The crew took turns in the water to make room, but sadly two of them died of exposure before rescue finally arrived 21 hours later. Hornell died from the effects of exposure not long after being rescued, and for his inspired leadership and devotion he was awarded a posthumous VC.

Early 1945 saw detachments from 279 Squadron with Warwicks, and 518 Squadron passed through in April, leaving Wick a fairly quiet airfield as peace descended upon it for the first time. After the war 122 Squadron served here on two occasions, first from Dyce in August, then from Hawkinge in October, before taking its Spitfires to Dalcross in January 1946.

Mustangs served here for the first time from 28 November 1945 when 316 Squadron arrived from Andrews Field to take part in 'Dodgem' exercises. It was joined by 303 Squadron from Turnhouse in January; this unit also took part in the exercises, which involved simulated raids on several high-profile Scottish targets. 303 Squadron left for Charterhall on 6 March 1946, and nine days later 316 Squadron brought military flying to a close at Wick when it left for Hethel on the 15th.

518 Squadron Halifax Met.III PN396 on detachment at Wick in early 1945.

After the war civilian aviation returned with BEA taking over routes throughout Scotland; found to be unprofitable, they were taken over by Loganair in the late 1970s. The airfield's infrastructure had been steadily declining right up to the 1990s; two of the Type C hangars had been demolished and the two remaining were in a sorry state. However, in recent years Wick has received a great deal of investment thanks to HIAL and, with a new terminal and tower, is a much more inviting place to visit for the modern traveller.

Main features:
Tarmac runways: QDM 326 1,570 yards, 268 1,150 yards, 193 1,110 yards.
Hangars: four C, two Bellman. *Hardstandings:* forty-three 100-foot diameter.
Accommodation: RAF: 3,062; WAAF: 544.

WIG BAY AND STRANRAER (including CAIRN RYAN), Dumfries and Galloway

Wig Bay: 54°58'07"N/05°04'16"W; NX035680. 5 miles N of Stranraer off A718

Stranraer: 54°54'40"N/05°02'16". Half a mile NW of town, between W Pier and McCulloch's Point

Now little more than a collection of hardstandings, Wig Bay was one of the busiest RAF flying boat stations. However, this was not for operational reasons – it was because its maintenance facilities would become the last resting place for hundreds of Catalinas and Sunderlands. However, before this task befell the station Loch Ryan had supported several units that had been posted here at Stranraer, which was a separate station in its own right.

The first unit to arrive at Stranraer was 209 Squadron on 22 May 1939, with Stranraers. Its stay was brief, leaving for Felixstowe in June, and leaving the loch free of aircraft until January 1940. During that month the STS moved to Wig Bay from Invergordon with various aircraft. It is possible that the station at Stranraer was not yet completed, and the STS had returned to Invergordon by March.

Another training unit, the FBTS, arrived on 24 June from Calshot, as that station was now exposed to enemy bombers based in France. The training squadron operated a large array of flying boats and, from July 1940, introduced WO/AG training in addition to pilot training. The FBTS continued to grow and diversify its training, and on 16 March 1941 was used to create 4 (Coastal) OTU. It was clear by now that Loch Ryan was being used by more operational squadrons, and on 15 June 4 COTU began to make way for them by moving to Invergordon. Five Sunderlands and seven Catalinas were later dispersed here by 4 COTU during early 1942 and throughout the remainder of the war.

A Sunderland and a Stranraer are moored out in Loch Ryan, RAF Stranraer. The flying boat station's slipways are in the extreme bottom right of the photograph.

240 Squadron's Catalinas made Stranraer their home on 3 July 1940 from Pembroke Dock. The squadron was joined by 'G' Flight from Helensburgh in November, which operated S.26 flying boats, and flying operations commenced over the Atlantic from December. Only nine days later the flight was moved to Bowmore, although a detachment of 210 Squadron's Sunderlands remained during late 1940 and early 1941.

The elements probably claimed more flying boats than the enemy could have hoped for. This Stranraer sank at its moorings during a severe gale.

209 Squadron with its Lerwicks was the next unit to arrive, on 3 January 1941 from Pembroke Dock. The squadron was having an uncomfortable relationship with the twin-engined flying boat since receiving it in December 1939. Once at Stranraer several patrols were flown over the Atlantic and the north-west approaches, but this came to a halt on 22 February following the loss of L7263 with fourteen on board including the pilot and CO of 209 Squadron, Wg Cdr J. E. M. Bainbridge. 209 Squadron left for Lough Erne on 23 March to re-equip with the Catalina, and five days later 240 Squadron was moved to Killadeas.

It was not until 23 June 1941, when 413 Squadron was formed here with Catalinas, that any significant activity returned. The Canadian squadron began the task of working up but was moved to Sullom Voe on 1 October before becoming operational. Eight days later 228 Squadron was re-established here with the Sunderland and was quickly operational again. Several patrols were flown from Stranraer before the squadron was moved to Oban on 10 March 1942.

It was during early 1942 that the site known as Wig Bay began to be developed to house an unit independent of those serving at Stranraer. Large hangars were built on the shore as well as the dispersals that are visible today. Aircraft moorings stretched out from Scar Point following the formation of the FBSU here on 12 March.

302 FTU was the next flying unit to arrive from Castle Archdale on 1 December with Catalinas and Sunderlands. It was joined by 490 Squadron from Jui in the spring of 1943 before it was moved to Oban in late July to make way for the expansion of the FBSU.

By 25 September 1942 the FBSU had become 1 FBSU, and was joined by 11 FBFU on 15 May 1943. The workload of both units was increasing as flying boats arrived on a daily basis for servicing and modifications. Indeed, the task was getting so large that it was decided to absorb the FBSU into a new unit. Thus on 8 October 57 MU was formed at Wig Bay and, as the war progressed, it would be responsible for anything up to fifty flying boats moored in Loch Ryan as well as many on shore.

The MU was also responsible for receiving new aircraft and preparing them to an operational standard. Repairs were also carried out, and later storage, which would feature during the post-war years. The storage element of 57 MU increased from 1 February 1944 when 1 FBSU was also absorbed, making the unit the biggest of its kind. It was also at this point that Stranraer ceased to exist and was disbanded as a station and taken over by Wig Bay.

57 MU became specialists in Catalina conversions and modifications, and by late 1944 was also carrying out Sunderland III to Mk V work; the first Mk V was test-flown from here on 18 May 1945. Smaller types such as the Walrus and Sea Otter were being handled in large numbers during 1944, and the entire Mariner fleet was also stored here.

In a typical scene at Wig Bay after the end of war, this part-dismantled Sunderland is destined for the scrapman.

As the war drew to a close 57 MU began to receive aircraft by the dozen as squadrons were disbanded. The MU had to expand into other airfields as land-based aircraft, such as the Mosquito, were also being received from late June 1945. 104 SSS was created at Castle Kennedy and 103 SSS at West Freugh to cope with the number of Mosquitoes that had been transferred to 57 MU.

Scores of Sunderlands, Catalinas, Walruses and Sea Otters all await their fate at Wig Bay in 1947.

Worthy of note is the formation of 275 MU across the loch at Cairn Ryan on 17 November, which came under the parentage of Wig Bay. Back at the parent station, the MU settled into the post-war period storing up to 160 Walrus, Sunderland, Mariner, Coronado and Catalina aircraft. Several Norwegian Catalinas were overhauled here, and sixteen Sunderlands were reconditioned for service with the RNZAF. Such was the quality of the work carried out at Wig Bay that it was taken over by Short & Harland on 1 October 1951 when 57 MU was disbanded.

Meanwhile, at Cairn Ryan, 275 MU was moved to West Freugh in November 1947, but the site was reactivated again in March 1955 when it became a sub-site for 31 MU. It was closed in September 1956 and the small contingent that remained at Wig Bay was gone by September 1957.

Traces of Wig Bay are more in evidence than at Stranraer, whose wartime jetty has been obliterated by the modern ferry terminal. At Wig almost all of the shore dispersals are still in place, as well as the bases of many buildings, including the hangars.

Only the dispersals and a trace of at least two slipways remain at Wig Bay today.

WIGTOWN (BALDOON), Dumfries and Galloway

54°50'57"N/04°27'02"W; NX435535. 1 mile S of Wigtown

In 1938 it was decided to turn an area of land south of the River Bladnoch, hemmed in by Lane Burn on the edge of Wigtown Bay, into an LG. No aircraft made use of it before the outbreak of the war, or after, as it was blocked with obstacles to prevent the enemy using it.

The site was inspected in 1940 and work began not long after to turn Wigtown into a training airfield. By late July 1941 it was close to completion, and on 13 September the airfield's first unit, 1 AOS, was re-formed here with Ansons, Blenheims and Lysanders. In the meantime 1 AOS was redesignated 1 OAFU from 1 February 1942.

The autumn of 1941 saw unseasonable weather during October and November and the airfield became flooded, so work began on building concrete runways during early 1942. The work did not deter 114 Squadron's Blenheims from detaching here from West Raynham around the same time.

Bothas were introduced to the OAFU from July 1942 onwards. Luckily, the unit only received thirteen of them, and the Anson remained the main type. This was confirmed in 1943 when 1 OAFU was standardised on the Anson and the last Bothas that could be withdrawn had gone by July 1943.

Three squadrons of Typhoons arrived between 18 and 22 September 1943. As part of the lengthy build-up to D-Day numerous exercises were held across Scotland, and this one simulated a large sea-borne invasion on the west coast. 174, 175 and 182 Squadrons all took part in the exercise, and all three would go onto distinguish themselves over Normandy nine months later.

The Lysanders had gone by November, to be replaced by Martinets, while the Ansons would remain until 1 OAFU was disbanded in November 1945, having trained thousands of aircrew.

The airfield was then handed over to Maintenance Command, and in December 1945 Wigtown became a sub-site for 220 MU. It remained so until 30 June 1946, and was replaced the following day by 14 MU, which also used Wigtown as a sub-site until it was closed down in May 1948.

It was not quite over for flying at Wigtown, though, and the arrival of the BTU from West Freugh on 16 June 1947 brought several interesting aircraft; the Mosquito would have been the predominant type, as well as a handful of Lancasters. As the unit's name suggests, various trials were flown from here, making full use of the local bombing ranges. The BTU returned to West Freugh on 6 May 1948, becoming the last RAF unit to serve here.

This is Wigtown in 1992, with many of the original buildings still in place, and runways and perimeter track extant.

By the 1980s the airfield's future was a rather gloomy one, with the threat of the infrastructure being removed for hardcore for a new harbour project. It appears that this never came to fruition, as many of the original buildings still survive and runways and perimeter track are still in place. The site was returned to agriculture many years ago, and the Type 12779 control tower now looks across empty fields.

Main features:
Concrete runways: QDM 070 1,750 yards, 160 1,380 yards. *Hangars:* seven Bellman, fourteen EO blister. *Hardstandings:* thirty circular. *Accommodation:* RAF: 1,975; WAAF: 492.

WINFIELD (HORNDEAN), Borders/Berwickshire

55°44'57"N/02°09'48"W. 6 miles W of Berwick upon Tweed, N of B6461

Surveyed in 1941, there is no doubt that the Air Ministry officials, drawn to the sloping plain of the Merse, were aware that the area had supported LGs during the First World War. 77(HD) Squadron had operated from Horndean during 1916 and 1917, and this site was to be swallowed up by a more complex Second World War airfield.

Charterhall was surveyed at the same time, and the site selected at Horndean was destined to become known as Winfield, planned as a satellite. Without ceremony, a small party from 54 OTU pronounced Winfield open on 30 April 1942. The unit was established to train night-fighter crews on the Beaufighter, but during the early days the Blenheim was also still being used and it was this type that first operated from here in May.

There is no doubting Winfield's past when viewed from this angle, and thanks to a minor road crossing the site a good view can be had by all.

After a reorganisation at Charterhall, it was decided to establish the 'Advanced Squadron' here from 1 July. Later redesignated 'C' Flight, its specialist task was AI training.

Two operational squadrons arrived in August 1942 to take part in local exercises. On the 4th 222 Squadron arrived from North Weald, and the same day 88 Squadron arrived from Attlebridge with Bostons, although it had departed eight days later, and 222 Squadron left for Drem on the same day.

Mosquitoes arrived from May 1944, a batch of six serving with 54 OTU's 'C' Flight. However, it would be the Beaufighter, and the number of accidents in which it was involved, that would be associated with Winfield.

Winfield continued as a satellite for Charterhall and 54 OTU until 31 May 1945, when the airfield was closed. As with so many airfields during the immediate post-war period, Winfield was considered for use by the FAA but nothing ever came of it.

It is not clear when the military relinquished Winfield, but on 21 July 1951 it was the venue for the Scottish Grand Prix. The 50-lap 100-mile race was won by Philip Fotheringham-Parker in a Maserati. Sadly, the event was never repeated, but the airfield is still used for autotest events organised by the Berwick & District Motor Club.

Flying did return in 1963 when the airfield was reopened by the Border Reivers Flying Club, but the runways are in such a poor state that this no longer continues. Very few buildings remain standing, but the usual bases are plentiful, together with large sections of runway and perimeter track.

Main features:
Tarmac runways: QDM 064 1,600 yards, 127 1,160 yards. *Hangars:* four EO blister. *Hardstandings:* thirty-seven. *Accommodation:* RAF: 686; WAAF: 56.

WINTERSEUGH, Dumfries and Galloway

55°01'19"N/03°18'38"W; NY165705. 3 miles NW of Annan

Winterseugh was brought into service as a result of events occurring at Dumfries in July 1940. 10 B&GS found that the grass runways at Dumfries were not up to the job, and 18 MU also realised that it would need additional SLGs for its own operations. Between the two units, Winterseugh was selected as an RLG for 10 B&GS and later an SLG for 18 MU.

The site was fairly level and, without the lengthy and costly task of grading involved, only took a few weeks to prepare. Facilities were sparse, and while construction continued at Dumfries the bombing school was ordered to use the RLG as much as possible. Only a single tent was provided for the instructors and pupils, purely to provide cover when the weather was inclement. By the end of 1940 the runways at Dumfries were completed and Winterseugh barely saw another aircraft until 18 MU showed an interested the following year.

A test landing was made by an Oxford in April 1941 and Winterseugh was renamed 36 SLG. Minor expansion of site included the use of a wood to the north, and two Super Robins were also built. The first aircraft to arrive were Battles, Blenheims and Beauforts; with an extension of the runway, Wellingtons were also accommodated. However, by November 1941 the condition of the SLG was poor and at least one Wellington became stuck in 2 feet of mud after landing. By the following month the site was abandoned to the winter.

In the spring of 1942 it was hoped that the SLG would have recovered and plans to improve the airfield were considered. It is not clear if any more of 18 MU's aircraft were accommodated at the SLG during 1942, but no further work was carried out and the Dumfries-based unit had relinquished any control of Winterseugh by October.

36 SLG remained under Air Ministry control until 20 April 1944, when the site was handed back to the land-owners. No time was wasted in reverting the SLG to agriculture, and it is quite possible that the Super Robins were dismantled and reconstructed elsewhere before the end of the war.

WOODHAVEN, Fife

56°26'00"N/02°57'29"W; NO408271. 1 mile SW of Newport on Tay

During February 1942 a brief detachment of 210 Squadron passed through Woodhaven, and a single Catalina was left behind to form a Norwegian detachment. The aircraft was quickly put to work, flying along the Norwegian coast, delivering and picking up agents and supporting the resistance. It was also engaged in submarine hunting, convoy escort duties and transport flights to Murmansk in the northern Soviet Union. The small flight's important role was recognised on 7 May when His Majesty King Haakon VII of Norway visited Woodhaven to inspect the unit.

Other Norwegian units passed through Woodhaven on a regular basis from mid-1942. 330 (Norwegian) Squadron, which had just converted to the Catalina, was a regular visitor, and on several occasions the unit's Catalinas and, later on, Sunderlands began their reconnaissance sorties of the Norwegian coast from here.

The title of 1477 Flight was to be short-lived, as in May 1943 it gained squadron status. Redesignated 333 (Norwegian) Squadron, it was the fourth Norwegian unit to be formed within the framework of the RAF. With the squadron in two locations, the Catalinas at Woodhaven became 'A' Flight and the Mosquitoes at Leuchars became 'B' Flight.

No more U-boat attacks were recorded until 17 May 1944, when a Catalina caught an enemy vessel on the surface. The U-boat put up a strong defence with its deck gun and the Catalina was seriously damaged in the process. One crew member was killed and, on return to base, the aircraft was considered sufficiently damaged to warrant repairing.

Lt C. F. Krafft and crew were on patrol 100 miles WNW of Stadtlandet when they spotted U-423 under the surface. The submarine was straddled by four depth charges, which lifted the vessel out of the water; it stood no chance, and before a rescue could be carried out the icy northern waters claimed the lives of all the crew.

With the Germans on the back foot in Norway, much of 333 Squadron's time was taken up flying transport missions. When hostilities ceased, 333 Squadron moved its four Catalinas to Fornebu near Oslo on 11 June 1945, only four days after King Haakon returned to his country. The squadron was disbanded on 21 November 1945 and transferred to the Norwegian Air Force. The unit's trusty Catalinas, which still belonged to the RAF, were handed back and the squadron continued to operate with a variety of captured German Arado and Dornier flying boats.

The exact date of Woodhaven's closure is unknown but, with 333 Squadron's departure, no other units were recorded as having used the flying boat station. It can only be presumed that, by the end of June 1945, Woodhaven was closed and consigned to history. Today the slipway is still in place as well as a protective pier. Looking across the Tay, it is not too hard to imagine Sunderlands and Catalinas on the step about to take to the air.

Bibliography

Bowyer *The Stirling Story* (Crécy)

Chorley *RAF Bomber Command Losses, HCUs* (Midland)
   RAF Bomber Command Losses, OTUs (Midland)

Chorlton *Scottish Airfields in WW2: Vol 1 Lothians* (Countryside)
   Scottish Airfields in WW2: Vol 2 Fife (Countryside)
   Scottish Airfields in WW2: Vol 3 Grampian (Countryside)

Fife *Scottish Aerodromes* (Tempus)

Franks *Fighter Command Losses 1939-41* (Midland)

Franks and Zimmerman *U-Boat v Aircraft* (Grub Street)

Halley *The K File* (Air Britain)
   The Squadrons of the RAF (Air Britain)

Hunt *Twenty-One Squadrons* (Garnstone Press)

Jefford *RAF Squadrons* (Airlife)

McNeill *RAF Coastal Command Losses 39-41*(Midland)

Rawlings *Fighter Squadrons of the RAF* (MacDonald)

Sharpe *U-Boat Fact File 1935-1945* (Midland)

Smith *British Built Aircraft* (Tempus)

Sturtivant *RAF Flying Training & Support Units* (Air Britain)
   The Squadrons of the FAA (Air Britain)

Sturtivant, Burrow and Howard *FAA Fixed Wing since 1946* (Air Britain)

Willis and Hollis *Military Airfields* (Willis/Hollis)

The National Archives

Index

Aircraft

1½ Strutter..........................132, 264

184 (Short) 123, 168, 171, 268

IIIA (Fairey) 211

IIIF (Fairey)......................146, 193

XI (Bleriot)................................223

504 (Avro) 40, 51, 53, 55, 96,
98, 192, 265-266,
282, 285, 292

737 (Boeing) 104, 142

747 (Boeing) 39

XI (Bleriot)................................223

A.7 (Saro) 41

A-20 ....163, 189, 288

A-28 163

A-35 163

Aerovan.......................................233

Albacore...............11, 45, 84, 98-99,
111-112, 137, 145,
149, 166, 266, 297

Albemarle 145

Airbus.......................142, 190, 250

Anson 32, 35, 37, 63, 74, 76,
89, 103-104, 116, 119-121,
128, 141, 143, 147, 149, 159,
176, 178, 186, 193, 220, 238,
245-246, 257-258, 263, 266,
275, 295, 299-300,
303, 311-312

Arado 315

AS.4 Ferry....................................83

Audax................147, 159, 176, 224,

Auster............33, 49, 121, 124, 173,
220, 238, 254

Avenger...........33, 46, 60, 100, 168,
186, 200, 211, 228, 254, 298

Aztec 155

B-17.............94, 114, 140, 157, 164,
188-189, 204, 248

B-24 ....94, 114, 163-164, 182,
189, 204, 245, 248

B-25 Mitchell 248, 299

B-26 ....228, 288

Baby (Hamble)...........................123

Baby (Sopwith)...........123, 168, 244

BAe 146 ....104, 245

Barracuda 11, 33, 46, 57, 59,
99-100, 127, 137, 142, 149-150,
186, 211, 218-219, 228,
251-253, 260, 277, 280

Battle..............76, 89, 120-121, 124,
147, 173, 191, 210, 231, 238,
275, 299, 314

Beaufighter 37, 49-50, 55-56,
63-65, 76, 89, 92, 105-109,
114, 118, 130, 133-134,
190, 195, 205, 215,
240-241, 245-246,
256, 274, 290-291,
306, 313-314

Beaufort 32, 37, 58, 89, 92,
125, 134, 195, 199, 202, 215,
220, 245, 256-257, 273-274,
290-291, 314

BE.2A.................................201, 227

BE.2C 11, 40, 82, 85, 88, 109,
213, 223-224, 253,
265-266, 290

BE.2E....................11, 40, 253, 266

BE.12 ....11, 266

BE.12B...11

Beaver 39, 81

Belfast....................................39, 277

Beverley 81

Bf 109 ....65, 156-157, 206,
241-242, 260,
270, 306

Blackburn (Blackburn) 146

Blenheim........35, 37, 52, 90, 92-93,
121, 124, 127-130, 133-134,
143, 147, 183, 191, 194-195,
199, 202, 204, 206-207,
210-211, 213-215, 225,
246, 254, 261, 273-275,
297, 311-314

Boat Pusher (Sopwith)................258

Borel Seaplane 102, 245

Boston 52, 202, 245, 275, 314

Botha 32, 89, 120-121, 147,
246, 299-300, 312

Britannia 277

Buccaneer 109, 209, 277

Buckmaster 257

Bulldog (SA)..............................249

Bv 138................................169, 275

C.30A (Cierva) 204

C-47 ....104, 182, 228, 249

C-53 228

C-87 234

Cadet.........102, 114, 145, 153, 184,
238, 268, 291

Camel..........40, 109, 116, 132, 138,
263-264, 292

Canberra............177, 235, 277, 296

Catalina 41-42, 71, 76-77, 86,
88, 164-165, 169, 174, 190,
236-237, 248, 256, 270-272,
307-310, 315

Caudron......................................40

CF-100..............................250, 254

CF-104......................................250

Chesapeake 118, 127, 211, 297

Chinook 10

Cloud...236

Comet 136

Concorde.............................136, 212

Constellation.............................249

Coronado...........169, 190, 258, 310

Corsair .57, 137, 139, 141, 186, 234

Cuckoo 69-70, 132, 172

Dakota 89, 168, 196, 204, 248,
259, 275, 289

DC-3 187

DC-4 249

Defiant 49, 55, 79, 89, 103,
133, 160, 183, 190, 211,
220, 232, 252, 256, 297

DH.4...266

DH.6 ....82, 211, 264, 282

DH.9............31, 53-54, 85, 96, 110,
159, 172, 254, 282,
285, 289, 292

DH.84 ....230, 293

DH.86 ....46, 230

Do 18 194

Dominie 32, 43, 112, 121, 204

Dragon................................83, 266

Envoy...293

F-86...254

F.2a (Felixstowe) 123, 170-171

F.2b.........34, 53-54, 74, 85, 96, 98,
151, 237-238, 282

F.3 (Felixstowe) 92, 123,
170-171, 244, 265

F.5 (Felixstowe) 41

FB.2 (Porte)................................92

Firefly 33, 46, 118, 141, 186, 211

Firebrand 150, 253

FK.3....................................265-266

Flamingo....................................112

Flying Fortress 37, 58, 70-71,
234, 263, 271, 280

Fokker 246

Aircraft continued...

Fox Moth 83, 213
Freighter (Type 170) 89, 233
Fulmar 45, 52, 56-57, 90, 113,
        118, 167, 182, 207, 211,
        240, 276, 295, 297
Fury...225
Fw 190 ....65, 107, 241
Fw 200 233
Gannet 60, 145, 207
Gauntlet 31
Gladiator...........111, 116, 259, 273,
        293-294
Gordon 147
H.16 Large America ..123, 170, 301
Halifax 38, 44, 76, 79, 178,
        185, 191, 215, 228, 262,
        266-267, 280, 287, 307
Hampden 35, 147, 177, 195,
        202, 206, 215, 261, 290,
        299, 303, 306
Harrier (HS)...............................223
Harrow.....................120, 147, 286
Hart......31, 116, 147, 176, 224, 293
Harvard 52, 94, 113, 118-119,
        141, 144-145, 176,
        185, 205, 253, 285
Hastings 38
Havoc..185
He 111 ....27, 90, 116-117,
        128-129, 195, 225, 274,
        294-295, 303-304
He 115 ....118, 169, 270
He 177 274
Hector 31
Hellcat 57, 118-119, 139, 141, 186
Henley 49, 120-121, 147, 173,
        231, 297, 299
Henry Farman 258
Hercules...........................223, 259
Hereford 275
Heyford...........................147, 299
Hind.....................35, 159, 292-293
Hornet Moth 204
Horsa 262
Hoverfly....................................297
HU-16.......................................250
Hudson 35, 37, 52, 58, 70,
        139-140, 193-194, 196, 199,
        202, 213, 215, 246, 261-263,
        266, 274, 286-287,
        291, 303-306
Hunter 177, 197

Hurricane 11, 32-33, 35-36,
        43-45, 49, 51, 55, 90, 117, 119,
        124, 127-130, 139-140, 143,
        145, 157, 181, 183, 190-191,
        199, 202, 205, 210-211, 213,
        220, 232, 240-241, 246, 252,
        259-261, 268, 274, 279,
        283-284, 295, 303-304
Hyderabad...................................35
Islander 39, 114, 187
Jaguar.....................7, 205, 207
Javelin 197
Jetstream 249, 301
Jet Provost.................................277
Ju 52...................104, 119, 204, 238
Ju 188..................................91, 157
Ju 88 ....90, 116-118, 130, 140,
        207, 225, 259-260,
        274, 303
Kangaroo 253
King Air 155
Kingfisher 123, 297
L-4 94
Lancaster 11, 59, 143, 178-179,
        205, 207, 222, 234, 248-249,
        258, 280, 299, 312
Lerwick 41, 86, 164, 169,
        236-237, 309
Liberator..............37, 58-59, 74, 88,
        196, 221-222, 228, 233-234,
        241, 246-249, 280, 286-287
Lightning 197
Lincoln..............................177, 300
Lodestar 196
London 41-42, 269-270
Longhorn Seaplane 245
Lynx.............................9, 60, 218
Lysander 32, 41, 43, 49, 56, 62,
        68, 79, 84, 89, 91, 103, 121,
        124, 126, 143, 147, 151, 159,
        163, 178, 181, 183, 202, 204,
        213, 215, 226, 231-232, 234,
        254, 256, 269, 274, 276, 283,
        290, 299-300, 311-312
Magister.............184-185, 204, 225,
        238, 275, 302
Mariner.........169, 190, 237, 273,
        309-310
Martinet........42, 49-51, 74, 89, 93,
        141, 202, 211, 232, 253,
        256, 258, 300, 312
Martlet 33, 45, 182, 215, 245,
        259, 261, 295, 297
Maryland...................166-167, 297

Master............43-44, 49, 51, 74, 91,
        93, 116, 145, 151, 159, 161,
        183, 205, 224-225,
        268, 283, 285
Me 110................................65, 270
Me 210.....................................274
Messenger 203, 233
Meteor 93, 190, 197
MF7...88
MF Seaplane..............................102
Mosquito........38, 46, 50, 59, 63-67,
        89, 92, 106-107, 130, 134, 136,
        156-157, 196, 215, 241-242,
        245, 248, 256, 259, 274,
        299-300, 306, 310,
        312, 314-315
Mustang 32, 52, 56, 65, 93,
        106-107, 124, 126, 140, 151,
        183, 213-214, 240-243,
        284, 295, 306
N3P-B (Northrop).....................237
Neptune 59, 179
Nightjar....................................194
Nimrod (Hawker)...............147, 193
Nimrod (HS) 7, 67, 109,
        179-180, 267
One-Eleven........................104, 136
Osprey.................................147, 193
Oxford 42, 63, 79, 92, 100,
        103-105, 116, 139, 143, 148,
        152, 156, 176-177, 181, 183,
        190, 202, 204-205, 224-225,
        232, 285, 314
P-38 Lightning 140, 188, 217,
        245, 254
P-39...188
P-47...163
P-51...254
Perth 236
Phantom 197
Pioneer....................................249
Prentice....................................94
Proctor 45, 139
Puma...9
Pup.........................132, 138, 264
Q.6...33
Queen Bee 173
Rapide 104, 238, 273
RE.8.........51, 82, 85, 151, 237-238
RE.9...51
Reliant................................33, 141
Ripon 193
Roc...........45, 98-99, 111, 141, 147,
        166, 204, 245, 297, 303
S.23.....................................77-78
S.26 ....77, 170, 208

S.38 286
S-76 (Sikorsky) 243
Sabre 177
SC.1 277
Scout 10
SD330 277
SD360 277
SE.5A 53, 138, 289
Sea Fury 47, 141-142
Sea Gladiator 111, 259, 297
Sea Hawk 33-34, 277
Sea Hornet 46, 142
Sea Hurricane 156, 186, 211,
            276, 279, 295, 297
Sea King 7, 207, 250, 267
Sea Otter 33, 65, 200, 277,
                                  309-310
Sea Venom 33-34
Sea Vixen 33, 277
Seafire 33, 46, 56-57, 124, 137,
            141, 150, 182, 186, 202, 211,
            219, 223, 234, 277, 295, 298
Seaford 277
Seafox 123, 167, 297
Seal 45, 120, 146
Seamew 277
Seaplane (Sopwith) 102
Shackleton 38, 59-60, 62,
                      179-180, 207-208
Shark 32, 45, 98, 111, 147
Shrimp 169
Singapore 41-42, 164
Skua 45, 111, 147, 165-166,
                      211, 297, 303-304
Skymaster 249
Skyraider 33, 113
Skyvan 277-278
Solent 277
Sperrin 38
Spitfire 11-13, 31, 33, 38, 49-51,
            55-57, 68, 90-91, 93, 104,
            116-119, 124, 128-131, 140-
            141, 149, 159-161, 169, 181-
            182, 185-186, 190, 213, 217,
            225, 240, 246, 256, 258, 260,
            263, 274, 279-280, 284,
                      294-296, 306
Stirling 215-216, 220, 224, 234,
                                  276-277
Stranraer 41-42, 85, 164, 170,
                  236, 269, 307-308
Sturgeon ....277 -278
Sunderland 41-43, 76-79,
            86-88, 164-165, 170, 174-176,
            201, 230, 236-237, 256,
            269-271, 273, 307-310, 315

Swordfish 32-33, 45-46, 49, 84,
            87, 98-99, 105, 111-112, 123,
            126-127, 137, 141, 145, 147,
            149, 156, 165-167, 182, 186,
            200, 211, 217-218, 228, 245,
                      270, 297-298
Sycamore 38
T-33 250
Taylorcraft 121, 173, 202
TB.7 283
Tempest 254
Tiger Moth 159-160, 162, 181,
            184, 231, 238, 246, 259,
                      276, 285, 302
Tomahawk 52, 202, 215, 234
Tornado 7-8, 197, 205, 209, 267
Traveller 141
Trident 104
Tucano 277
Tutor 147, 183, 225, 299
Twin Pioneer 249
Typhoon (Eurofighter) 7, 197
Typhoon (Hawker) 44-45, 49,
            119, 280, 284, 295, 312
V/1500 ....34, 109
Valetta 74-75
Vampire 33, 38, 131, 139, 197,
                      255, 267, 295
Varsity 74
Vengeance 277
Ventura 139, 202, 215, 263, 291
Venture 74
Vigilant 233
Viking (Vickers) 239
Viking 184
Vimy 35
Virginia 35
Viscount 34, 104, 136, 187,
                                  255, 275
Vulcan 136
Wallace 35, 299
Walrus 32-33, 45, 123, 167,
            211, 218, 258, 266, 270,
                  297-298, 309-310
Wapiti 31, 292
Warwick 59, 65, 76, 79,
            105-106, 156-157, 179, 185,
            200, 207, 228, 281,
                  287, 291, 306
Wasp 81
W.B.1 110
W.B.2 109-110
Welkin 191
Wellesley 246, 299

Wellington 32, 35, 37, 44, 71,
            74, 89, 92, 104, 121, 124-125,
            139, 143-144, 154, 178, 185,
            190-191, 199-200, 206-208,
            215, 220-222, 228, 234, 256,
            262, 266, 268, 280, 286,
                      288, 290, 314
Wessex 39, 60, 74, 81, 207
Whirlwind (Fighter) 117, 142
Whirlwind (Helicopter) 142, 220
Whitley 13, 37, 58, 79, 103,
            129, 154, 177-178, 185, 199,
            246, 266, 305-306
Wildcat 33, 112, 141, 186, 200,
            211, 228, 245, 260
Wright 155
York 234

**Airfields/Airship Stations/
    Flying-boat Stations**
Abbeyfarm 94
Abbotsinch 31-34, 84, 113,
            124, 238, 254-255, 291, 293
Abingdon 178
Acklington 45, 49, 90, 93,
            116-117, 243, 273, 295, 303
Albar 48
Aldergrove 8-10, 34-39, 44, 55,
            57-58, 63, 70-71, 74, 114, 194,
            199-200, 202-203, 222,
            230-231, 234-235, 245,
                  275-276, 287, 295
Alloa 40
Alness 7, 40-42, 174, 237
Andreas 228
Andrews Field 241-242, 306
Angle 140
Anglesey 217
Annan 43-45, 121, 284
Anthorn 46
Arbroath 8, 45-47, 112, 123,
            137, 139, 234, 298
Ards 230
Armagh 48
Askernish 48
Aston Down 45
Atcham 202
Athlone 48
Attlebridge 202, 314
Aught Point 48
Auldbar 48
Ayr 13, 33, 48-51, 57, 68, 93,
            102, 118, 124, 150-151, 186,
            211, 214, 218, 220, 228, 237,
            246-248, 280, 289, 298
Balado Bridge 8, 51-52, 160

**Airfields/Airship Stations/
Flying-boat Stations
continued...**

Baldonnel.............10, 53-54, 85, 96,
                159, 238, 282
Baldoon.....................................311
Balhall......................................54
Balivanich 70
Ballincollig............................54-55
Ballycastle 10, 55
Ballydonagh..............................48
Ballyhalbert 37-38, 55-58, 137,
                140-141, 182, 231-232,
                234, 256
Ballykelly 8, 33, 37, 58-62, 74,
                141, 200, 232, 234
Ballyliffin...................................62
Ballymena 62
Ballyquirk...................................63
Ballywalter Park..........................63
Balmain......................................63
Balta Sound................................63
Banff...........13, 63-68, 79, 105-106,
                108, 156-157, 241
Bangor 10, 68, 211, 282
Bantry 68
Barassie......................................68
Barrhead....................................69
Barrow 74, 89
Barry 69
Barry Buddon 81
Barton.......................................218
Bassingbourn 88
Bearhaven...................................73
Beaulieu....................................287
Belhaven Sands...........................69
Benbecula 7, 37, 70-73, 105,
                200, 228, 268
Benone Strand 114
Benson 39, 130
Bentra 10, 73
Bentwaters 131, 242
Berehaven...................................73
Berneray 74
Beverley 224, 292
Bickendorf................................282
Biggin Hill................................282
Bircham Newton 35, 129, 199, 266
Birr....................................74, 282
Bishops Court 9, 74-75
Black Isle....................................76
Blackstand Farm..........................76
Blaris...76
Boa Island..................................76
Bognor.......................................91
Bogton.......................................77

Bowmore 77-79, 169, 236, 308
Boyndie.....................................63
Brackla..............63, 79-80, 103-104,
                143, 177, 185,
Brawdy.....................................287
Brims Mains...............................80
Broomfield 223
Broughty Ferry 80
Bryansford 10, 80
Buddon......................................81
Burscough 46, 50, 57, 150, 234
Buttergask..................................81
Buttevant....................................81
Caird's Yard...............................164
Cairncross..................................82
Cairn Ryan 300, 307, 310
Caldale..................................82-83
Calshot..................41, 88, 165, 307
Campbeltown 32, 83-85, 112,
                211-212
Cardross.....................................85
Carew Cheriton 58
Carmunnock...............................85
Casement....................................53
Castle Archdale 85-88, 174, 309
Castlebar...............................53, 85
Castle Kennedy 88-89, 290, 310
Castletown 80, 90-91, 118,
                143, 259-261, 274, 279,
Castletownbere 73
Castletownroach 85
Catfirth 63, 92
Catfoss..................................35, 146
Cathcart.....................................85
Catterick 49, 90, 224, 246,
                266, 279
Chalgrove 190
Charterhall 13, 92-93, 306,
                313-314
Cheddington 163, 228
Chelveston 89
Chilbolton..................................55
Chipping Warden 121
Chivenor 37, 59, 65, 71, 195,
                200, 262, 280, 290
Church Fenton 55, 92, 147
Church Lawford 79, 103
Clifton...............................140, 234
Clongowes Wood College............93
Clonmel 94
Cluntoe 94-95, 248, 289
Coleraine 114
Colerne 279
Colinton.....................................95
Collinstown..............10, 54, 96, 282
Coltishall................140, 241, 274

Connel 97
Corsewell 181
Couplaw Farm...........................268
Crail..........45-46, 97-101, 112, 116,
                119, 126-127, 150, 266,
                292, 297-298
Cramlington 266
Cranfield (Beds)..................133, 177
Cranfield (Greencastle) 162
Creetown 102
Crinkill......................................74
Croft..280
Cromarty 102, 155
Crosby-on-Eden...........................37
Culdrose.....................46, 113, 250
Culham......................................33
Dalcross 79, 103-104, 183, 190,
                204, 306
Dale 118-119, 286
Dallachy...........13, 63, 65, 105-109,
                156, 251
Dalmellington 77
Dalmore..................................41-43
Dalmuir...........................109-110, 172
Davidstow Moor.......................306
Debden 35, 117
Delny House 110
Detling.....................................260
Digby 34, 91, 151
Dishforth..................................177
Docking....................................275
Donibristle 13, 33, 84, 90,
                98-100, 110-113, 147, 149,
                172, 182, 204, 219-220,
                256, 297
Dornoch....................................114, 149
Dounreay 114
Downhill...................................114
Drem..........11, 49, 56, 92, 116-120,
                127-128, 132, 213, 241, 261,
                274-275, 294-295, 303, 314
Driffield....................................275
Dumfries.............13, 120-122, 125,
                173, 191, 210, 314
Dunbar.....................................265
Dundee 123, 152, 155, 256,
                268, 297
Dundonald......13, 32, 123-124, 246
Dundrum.............................124, 163
Dungavel....................121, 125, 268
Dunino.........99, 126-128, 151, 204,
                254, 269
Dyce..............37, 51, 117, 128-131,
                139, 156, 225, 243, 261, 274,
                293, 305-306
Earls Colne 228

East Fingask.............................132
East Fortune...................13, 15, 69,
132-137, 192, 215
East Haven 45, 57, 137-138,
223, 252
East Moor 92
East Wretham 37
Eccles Tofts..............................138
Edinburgh...................................11
Edzell 8, 47, 104, 131,
138-139, 224-225, 228
Eglinton 9, 57, 59, 140-143,
150, 182, 217, 219, 232,
234, 245, 256, 277, 289
Elgin...................13, 104, 143-145,
205-206, 220, 261,
279, 298
Errol..........................145, 151, 181
Evanton 41, 103-104, 110-111,
146-148, 165-166
Exeter...........................91, 117, 150
Fair Isle 148
Fairlop......................................130
Fairwood Common 49, 131
Falleninch Farm.......................265
Farmacaffly.................................48
Farnborough 34, 54, 227, 299
Faughanvale................................55
Fearn.....57, 104, 148-150, 252, 280
Felixstowe 41, 169-170, 307
Fermoy...51, 74, 150-151, 238, 285
Fersfield....................................228
Fifteen Acres 151
Findo Gask 126, 145, 151-152,
183, 214
Finningley 147
Fliergerhorst Hedia.....................65
Ford 45, 47, 84, 168
Fordoun 152-153, 184, 240, 299
Forres............13, 104, 154-155, 177
Fort George.......................102, 155
Fortrose......................................76
Fowlmere 140
Fraserburgh.................63, 99, 105,
155-157, 240
Ganavan 13, 157, 236
Gander.....................................248
Gargunnock..............................265
Gatwick...............................38, 126
Gifford 158
Gilmerton 158
Goose Bay.................................267
Gormanston.......................158, 282
Gourock Bay.............................164
Gosport 32, 46, 128, 148, 194, 274
Goxhill 140, 217

Grangemouth..........13, 31, 51, 121,
143, 147, 159-162, 184,
213, 246, 284, 294
Granton Harbour 162
Grantshouse..............................301
Grasnaya...................................271
Gravesend..........................49, 119
Great Orton 44, 300
Greencastle...............................162
Greenock 164-165
Grimsetter.................186, 202, 260
Groomsport 68
Grove 215
Gullane 116
Gütersloh 254
Haddington...............................191
Harlaxton..................................97
Harrowbeer...............................260
Hatston 84, 111-112, 114,
126-127, 147, 149, 165-168,
186-187, 228, 259-260, 273,
297-298, 303
Haverfordwest...........108, 130, 134,
200, 228
Hawarden 182
Hawkcraig.................................168
Hawkinge 93, 260, 295, 304, 306
Heathfield 48, 50
Heathhall 120
Helensburgh 77, 169-170, 308
Hemswell 303
Hendon 40
Henstridge 57, 124
Herdla.......................................207
Heston..........................56, 188, 293
Hethel 93, 306
Hibaldstow...............................259
High Ercall.................................84,
Holmsley South 266
Honiley 45, 56
Honington..................................209
Hooton Park 199, 245-246, 266
Hoprig Mains............................170
Hornchurch 91
Horne...56
Houton Bay 123, 170-171, 244,
264-265
Hoy...264
Hullavington 94, 145, 289
Hunsdon 242
Hutton Cranswick......................56
Ibsley...91
Inchinnan...................109, 172, 253
Inskip 84, 127, 149
Invergordon............41-42, 146-147,
169, 236, 269, 307

Inverkeithing Bay......................172
Inverness 13, 104, 114, 126,
143, 159, 204, 266, 285
Ipswich.......................................49
Johnston Castle.........................172
Jui 236, 309
Jurby 121
Kaldadarnes..............................305
Kayshill 121, 173
Kearney 55
Keflavik...............................157, 267
Kenley...49
Kidsdale 121, 173-174
Kilconquhar.............................174
Kilkenny....................................174
Killadeas 42, 174-176, 237,
256, 309
Killeagh......................................63
Killingholme 123
Kincairn....................................265
King's Cliffe 140
Kinloss............7, 11, 13, 24, 38, 67,
79, 117, 154, 176-180,
207, 259, 280
Kinnell 181, 283-284
Kinross 265
Kinrush 94
Kirkandrews...............................181
Kirkcolm 181
Kirkistown 55-56, 140, 182-183
Kirknewton 8, 152, 183-184, 204
Kirkpatrick................................184
Kirkton......................................185
Kirkwall 168, 186-187, 204, 259,
Kirkwall Bay 187
Kirriemuir..................................228
Lagons..71
Langford Lodge...........13, 163-164,
187-190, 215, 289
Langham...................105, 195, 200
Largs Channel 190
Larne...73
Lasham 260, 295
Leanach 104, 114, 143, 190-191
Leconfield 132, 259
Lee-on-Solent 33, 45-46, 99,
124, 147, 150, 182, 276
Leeds..293
Leeming 246
Lenabo 48, 204
Lennoxlove 191
Lerwick 191
Leuchars 7, 13, 33, 35, 100,
139, 146, 192-199, 258, 274,
280, 295, 303, 306, 315
Leven 199

**Airfields/Airship Stations/
Flying-boat Stations
continued...**

Lews Castle 266
Limavady 37, 58, 62, 71, 194,
199-201, 228, 266,
286, 290, 305
Limerick....................................201
Lindholme 286
Linton-on-Ouse 178, 246
Lisburn..76
Little Snoring 50
Llanbedr 140, 202
Loch Baghasdail 201
Loch Doon................................202
Long Hope................................264
Long Kesh 10, 13, 86, 202-203,
215, 231-234, 236,
290-291
Longman 13, 103-104, 190, 204
Longside 13, 204-205, 240,
243-244
Longtown................37, 44, 234
Lossiemouth............7, 8, 11, 65, 76,
109, 114, 143-145, 178, 197,
205-209, 214, 220-222, 253,
279-280, 298
Lough Erne 85-86, 174-176,
236-237, 256, 270, 309
Low Edrig 210
Luce Bay............8, 62, 73, 210-211,
299-300
Ludham 90
Luqa..................................60, 250
Luton 231
Lympne....................................280
Lyneham....................................234
Machrihanish..............8, 45, 50, 57,
83-85, 99, 112, 126-127,
149-150, 156, 182, 186,
200, 210-212, 217-218,
245, 280, 297
Macmerry 51, 84, 117, 119,
126, 132, 143, 160,
170, 213-215
Maghaberry 125, 188, 202,
215-216, 234
Malahide...................................217
Manston....................93, 146, 280,
Martlesham Heath.......49, 186, 238
Matlaske....................................241
Maydown..............49, 140-141, 186,
217-220
Melton Mowbray..............215, 245
Methven...............49, 139, 220
Middleton St George 74, 280
Middle Wallop......................50, 56

Mildenhall................................147
Milfield.....................................295
Millisle 63
Milltown 8, 11, 37, 207, 220-223
Molesworth 243
Montrose.........13, 32, 54, 117, 128,
139, 143, 201, 203, 223-227,
265-266, 268, 303
Moorpark.................................253
Moreton Valence 183
Mount Batten............................269
Muirhouses 228
Mullaghmore 200, 228-229,
234, 255, 287
Murlough..................................124
Musgrave Channel 230
Myreside 230
Netheravon 193, 223, 265
Newcastle....................................80
Newtownards 10, 56, 62, 68,
114, 182, 202-203,
230-233, 275
Nigg 233
North Coates 65, 199
North Luffenham.......................195
Northolt 56, 196, 304
North Queensferry.....................233
North Weald 118, 129, 131, 314
Novar 110, 146
Nutt's Corner 38, 46, 56, 58,
202, 215, 233-235, 277, 288
Oakington 197, 280
Oban..............13, 41-42, 77, 86, 97,
157, 165, 174, 201,
236-237, 271, 309
Odiham 124, 159, 213-214, 240
Old Sarum 121, 202
Omagh...................51, 85, 237-238
Orangefield..............................237
Oranmore 53, 85, 151,
237-238, 282
Ørlandet 65
Orphir......................................170
Ossington 63, 105
Ouston 32, 49, 118
Paisley......................................238
Pembroke.................................172
Pembroke Dock 41-42, 77,
86-88, 236, 269, 271, 308-309
Penston 170, 292, 301
Perranporth 50, 186, 200
Perth (Scone).........33, 81, 160, 162,
190, 204, 238-240,
254, 259, 302
Peterhead.............13, 91, 128, 130,
156, 204, 225, 240-244, 295
Peterhead Bay...........................244

Phoenix Park.............................151
Pierowall 244
Polebrook.................................248
Port Ellen 245
Port Laing 245
Portland 84
Portobello Barracks.......10, 25, 246
Portreath 55, 64, 195, 256
Predannack................................280
Prestwick.........8, 32, 34, 48, 50-51,
75, 98, 114, 117, 128, 145,
159, 246-250, 283, 295
Queenstown 250
Raeburnfoot..............................250
Raploch....................................265
Rathbande House 250
Rathmullan 251
Rattray......8, 46, 150, 194, 251-253
Redhill...............................91, 124
Renfrew 13, 31, 33-34, 85, 126,
172, 204, 253-255, 292
Rerrin.......................................255
Reykjavik 59, 86, 199, 236-237,
249, 270, 280, 305-306
Rhu...169
Riccall......................................234
Rinenore Point............................48
River Bann 255
River Foyle 256
Robertson Field 109
Roborough................................273
Rochester..................................275
Ronaldsway......................141, 150
Rosyth......................................256
Royal Barracks...........................256
St Angelo 9-10, 79, 174, 176,
256-258
St David's..................................266
St Eval 37-38, 59, 71, 98, 140,
196, 199, 217, 221-222,
266, 305
St Inglevert 53
St Merryn..................141, 150, 251
Sandy Bay.................................258
Sawbridgeworth.........121, 124, 220
Scampton.........................147, 177
Scapa Flow 90-91, 114, 147,
166-167, 244, 258-260, 263-
264, 286, 295, 303-304
Scatsta..............................258-259
Schiphol 71
Scone 145, 238-239, 259
Seahouse 82
Sealand......................................84
Sedgeford 281
Shallufa 58
Shawbury..................................103

Shotwick 253
Silloth.....................37, 44, 202, 286
Skateraw 259
Skeabrae 90-91, 104, 186,
        259-260, 274-275, 279, 295
Skitten 13, 90, 143, 259,
        261-263, 303, 306
Slidderyford Bridge..............10, 263
Smoogroo 155, 263-264
Snelsetter..................................264
Sollas 264
Southend....................................49
South Belton 265
South Carlton 224
South Kilduff 265
South Uist 7, 48, 72
Spittlegate 54, 97
Squires Gate.........................55, 156
Stamford 292
Stannergate................................123
Stansted....................................228
Stanton Harcourt.......................143
Stenness Loch 265
Stirling 265
Stornoway.........7, 13, 72, 199, 261,
        266-267, 287
Stracathro 268
Stranraer..............42, 73, 77, 85-86,
        170, 236-237, 270,
        299, 307-310,
Strathaven..................................268
Strathbeg...................123, 251, 268
Straughroy 237
Stravithie 268-269
Stretton 113
Strubby 64, 105
Sullom Voe 41, 86, 236-237,
        258-259, 269-273, 275, 309
Sumburgh..............37, 90, 128-130,
        166, 186, 204, 266,
        273-275, 297
Sutton Bridge............................283
Swanton Morely 275
Sydenham 39, 56, 124, 188,
        202, 230, 232, 235, 275-279
Tain.............8, 42, 49, 58, 104, 143,
        147, 150, 178, 279-281,
        287, 306
Talbenny.............................37, 266
Tallaght 74, 96, 159, 281-282
Tangmere 117, 119, 160, 304
Tarrant Rushton.......................215
Tealing...............181, 204, 283-285
Ternhill 84, 145
The Curragh..............151, 282, 285
Thetford............................224, 292

Thirsk.......................................275
Thornaby........37, 65, 92, 105, 130,
        147, 179, 193-194, 281, 287,
        291, 305-306
Thorney Island 37, 59, 90, 149,
        186, 261, 266, 273, 306
Thruxton............................121, 213
Thurso 114, 286
Tinwall Downs...........................120
Tiree..............38, 97, 200, 228, 266,
        286-287
Toome 94, 233, 288-289
Topcliffe..............................59, 84
Townhead................................158
Tranent 170
Turnberry 32, 42, 51, 89, 200,
        202, 215, 257, 289-291
Turnhouse.........7, 35, 90, 103, 116,
        118-119, 122, 124, 128, 136,
        159, 162, 183, 186, 202, 204,
        214, 240, 260, 280, 284,
        291-296, 306
Twatt 46, 99, 114, 167-168,
        260, 297-298
Tynehead..................................298
Unst 63
Upper Dysart........88, 223, 227-228
Urquhart...................................298
Usworth 43, 213, 220, 246
Vaernes 93, 131
Valencia Harbour......................299
Valley....................56, 177, 200
Waddington 177, 234, 303
Wakefield..................................299
Warmwell....................88, 120
Warton 163, 188
Wattisham.......................194, 275
Watton 143, 206
WB.X...254
Wellingore...................................90
West Cairnbeg 299
West Fenton..............................116
West Freugh............8, 89, 210, 233,
        299-301, 310, 312
Westhampnett......................56, 246
Westley.......................................121
West Raynham 207, 213, 312
Wexford 172, 301
Whelans Field 301
Whiddy Island 301
Whiteburn.................................301
Whitefield...........................238, 302
Whitehead...................................73

Wick 90, 93, 104, 114, 117,
        129, 149, 166, 195, 199, 204,
        234, 261, 263, 273-275, 280,
        287, 302-307
Wig Bay 41, 300, 307-311
Wigtown 299-300, 311-312
Winfield 92, 313-314
Winterseugh......................120, 314
Wittering...........................55, 104
Woodhaven.................................315
Woodvale 57, 206
Woolsington...............................225
Worthy Down 90, 126
Wyton 143
Yeovilton........39, 98, 211, 276, 295
York 213
Zeals..297

Airships
R 24 172
R 27 172
R 29 132
R 34 ....13, 132, 136, 172
SS-20..73
SS-41....................................82-83
SS-43..82
SSP...82
Zeppelin.....10-11, 95, 265-266, 292

Flights, RAF
300 Flt..92
301 Flt..92
302 Flt..92
303 Flt..92
304 Flt..92
305 Flt..92
306 Flt.....................123, 171, 244
309 Flt......................................265
310 Flt......................................265
311 Flt......................................265
318 FB Flt 123
319 FB Flt 123
400 FB Flt 123
401 Flt...............................194, 268
401 (Seaplane) Flt 123
416 Flt......................................231
430 Flt......................................171
450 (Baby) Flt............................123
523 (SD) Flt...............................211
524 (SD) Flt...............................211
529 Flt......................................211
530 Flt......................................282
531 Flt......................................211
532 Flt......................................211
533 Flt......................................211
1353 Flt....................................300

Flights, RAF continued...
1402 Flt 38, 57
1441 Flt 32, 124
1445 Flt 234
1476 Flt 186
1477 Flt 165, 315
1480 Flt 231-232
1490 Flt 49-50, 91
1493 Flt 56, 231-232
1494 Flt 56-57, 202
1497 Flt 214
1617 Flt 232
1680 Flt 32, 145
1693 Flt 263, 266, 275
1966 Flt 238
1967 Flt 33, 238, 254
1968 Flt 33
'G' Flt 77, 164, 170, 308
SD Flt 77, 169, 211, 238

Land-bases, Royal Navy
Condor 8, 45, 47, 123
Corncrake 57, 182
Wagtail 50

Maintenance Units, RAF
14 MU 45, 312
18 MU 120-121, 173, 191, 210, 314
23 MU 35, 38-39, 63, 124-125,
              187, 216-217, 256
31 MU 310
40 MU 120
44 MU 139, 143, 151-152, 181,
              220, 268-269
45 MU 76, 79, 114, 144,
              177-178, 185
46 MU 76, 114, 143, 190,
              205-206, 208
55 MU 62
56 MU 204
57 MU 89, 300, 309-310
62 MU 170
63 MU 191, 203, 225
97 MU 165
98 MU 153
213 MU 165
215 MU 121
217 MU 62, 289
220 MU 312
226 MU 125
243 MU 153, 162, 184
244 MU 97
249 MU 45, 300
257 MU 189, 289
260 MU 145, 152, 181,
              225, 268, 285

272 MU 176, 257
275 MU 300, 310

Miscellaneous units, RAF
1 AACU 173, 231-232, 299
1 AONS 246
1 AOS 246, 311
1 ATS 35
1 CANS 246
1 CTW 181, 284
1 FBSU 309
1 FIS 103
1 FS 51, 289
1 FTS 193
1 GS 121, 125, 268
1 MRS 179
1 OAFU 311-312
1 RFTS 183
1 RSS 204
1 TEU 181, 284
1 TTS 132
1 TTU 32, 89, 200, 290-291
2 AGS 79, 103-104, 204
2 ANS 74-75
2 ATC 35
2 ATS 35, 258
2 CFS 79, 103
2 CTW 51, 160
2 FBSU 165
2 FIS 54, 63, 103, 139, 152,
              181, 224-225, 268, 299
2 FTS 94, 289
2 Group 145, 207
2 GS 97, 162
2 HAAPC 173, 299
2 TEU 51, 160, 284
2 TTU 290
3rd Wing 96
3 AOS 35
3 AGS 89
3 APC 258
3 APS 93
3 B&GS 35
3 GS 119
3 RDFS 246
3 RS 246
3 SGR 156
3 TEU 44-45
4 AOS 299-300
4 ATC 299
4 ATS 299
4 B&GS 299
4 FBSU 157
4 GS 162, 238
4 OAFU 300
4 PAFU 300

4 RFU 228
4 TEU 44
5 ANS 189
5 FBSU 41
5 FIS 238, 302
5 GS 139, 153
6 AACU 276
6 AAP 172, 292
6 FTS 147
6 GS 162
7 AOS 73-74
7 ANS 74
7 AONS 238
7 CANS 238
7 OAFU 74
8 AFTS 104
8 AGS 147
8 AOS 147
8 APC 177
8 ATC 147
8 ATS 147
8 B&GS 147
8 COTU 130, 134
8 FPP 276
8 FTS 63, 104, 139, 147-148,
              150, 224-225, 268, 299
8 SFTS 224-225
8 GS 102
9 Group 44
9 GS 145
9 PAFU 52, 145, 151-152,
              181, 285
10 AGS 89
10 ANS 121
10 AONS 159, 246
10 AOS 120-121
10 B&GS 120, 314
10 CANS 159
10 GS 291
10 OAFU 121
11 E&RFTS 238
11 EFTS 81, 238-239, 259, 302
11 FBFU 309
11 (Irish) Group 54
11th (Irish) Wing 54
11 RFS 162, 238
11 SFTS 103
12 AGS 74-75
12 E&RFTS 246
12 EFTS 123, 246
12 FIS 174
12 (O)FIS 256
13 FTS 116
13 Group 50, 103-104, 128,
              159, 183, 186, 214, 295, 303
13 Group AACF 103, 183, 204

13 Group CF 204
13 Group HQ 104, 159
13 RFS 162
13 SFTS 116
14 APC 50
14 FTS 176-177
14 Group CF 204
14 PAFU 13, 63, 79, 156
14 SFTS 177
15 EFTS 181, 184-185
15 FTS 205
15 Group....................................58
15 SFTS 298
16 AAP 34
17 BB 73
17 LAAPC 231
18 Group..........................157, 259
18 Group CF 259
18 HAAPC................................232
19 PAFU.......79, 103, 143, 190-191
20 BB 83
21 ACHU 108
21 PAFU 104
22 ACHU 200
22 RC..202
23 E&RFTS 275
24 E&RFTS 275
24 EFTS..........................231, 275
25 Group...................................211
28 Group.............................92, 265
29 Group...................................265
32 Wing 183
35 E&RFTS 159-160
35 Recce Wing...........................126
41 Group...................................114
42 Group...................................184
42 SFTS 224
44 Group...................................234
55 Wing 282
70 (Signals) Wing 204, 285
78 Wing 123
81 SU..223
82 Group CF 231
88 Group...................................295
88 Group CF 295
102 SSS 79
103 PDC....................................202
103 SSS 300, 310
104 SSS 89, 310
105 SSS 143
106 SSS 257
201 GS 76, 203, 233
203 GS 114, 203, 233
302 FTU 42, 86, 165, 174, 176, 230, 237, 309
303 FTU 266

304 FTU 245
305 FTU 145
306 FTU 215
308 FTU 237
661 VGS 8, 184
662 VGS 47, 139
663 VGS 33, 223
664 VGS 10, 74, 233
666 VGS 33, 121
671 VGS 74, 203
1100 MC.....................................42
1332 CU 234
1480 AACF 231-232
1493 TTF 56, 231-232
1512 BATF 63-64
1541 BATF 268
1542 BATF 105
1674 HCU 37, 44, 207, 222, 234
3201SC 124
8330 SE....................................165
A&AEE 238
AATE 300-301
AMMT 38
ASWDU......................................59
Belfast UAS...............................276
BTU 299-301, 312
CCDU 58, 280
CCFIS.................42, 174, 257
CGS 88-89
CPF 223
DPHU..44
'F' Boat STF 171
FBSU 157, 164, 309
'G' Flight 77, 123, 164, 170, 308
Glasgow UAS 33
Irish FIS 285
Irish Flight 54, 96
JASS 59
Liberator CF...............................37
LORAN TU 228
LTU 200
MAEE..........77, 169-170, 230, 245
MCRU.......................................165
MCU 287
MOTU 179
RDF 238
Roc Flight 204
St Andrews UAS 100
STS 307
TTF 200, 256

Miscellaneous units, USAAF/
  USAF and USAF Wings
2 CCRC 94, 163
3rd BAD 188-189, 289
3 CCRC 288

4 CCRC 94
4th G&TTF 163
4th R&TS (Bomb) 163
5 CCRC 163
6 CCRC 228
6th R&TS (B) HQ 228
7th ADG 188
8th AFCC 163
8th AFSC 163
8th Composite Command 94
17th SSS 139
27th ATG 215
37th RSM 184
42nd DRS 163
42nd DSS 163
67th ARS 250
311th Ferry Sqn.................94, 188, 215-216, 248
312th Ferry Sqn................188, 215
321st Ferry Sqn.........................215
325th Ferry Sqn................188, 215
1631st ABS 50, 250
6852nd RSM 184
7535th Air Base Sqn 184
AAU 188

Operational Conversion Units,
  RAF
226 OCU 207
228 OCU 197
236 OCU 179
237 OCU 209

Operational Training Units, RAF
1 (Coastal) OTU 37, 202, 286
3 (Coastal) OTU 245
4 (Coastal) OTU 41-42, 87, 174, 307
5 (Coastal) OTU 202, 215, 290-291
6 (Coastal) OTU 44, 92, 179
7 (Coastal) OTU 199-200, 228
8 OTU 149, 156
9 OTU 37
19 OTU 79, 103, 129, 154, 177-179
20 OTU..............143-145, 206-208, 221-222
42 OTU 177
51 OTU 133
54 OTU...................92-93, 313-314
55 OTU 43-44, 284
56 OTU 181, 283-284
58 OTU.........13, 51, 159-161, 213
60 OTU 132-135
62 OTU 246

Operational Training Units, RAF
continued…
104 OTU 215, 228, 234, 288
109 OTU 289
111 (Coastal) OTU 207, 222
131 (Coastal) OTU 42, 76, 165,
174, 176, 256
132 (Coastal) OTU 133-135, 215

Organisations, civil
Aer Lingus....................................38
Allied Airways....................128, 273
ATA 157, 191, 215, 220
BAe Systems 7-8, 250
BEA...............34, 71, 104, 168, 204,
212, 235, 245, 254-255,
275, 307
BOAC 38, 77, 196, 246, 249
Blackpool & West Coast 230
Bombardier.190, 220, 275, 277-278
Bond Helicopters 243
Bristow Helicopters....................243
British Airways...104, 142, 226, 238
CRO 32, 52, 68, 139, 165,
246, 254
Dan-Air......................................104
Defence Estates.............................8
Edinburgh Flying Club.............170,
213, 215
Ferranti 47, 296
Flybe 187
Goodrich.....................................190
Hebridean Air Services...............97
HIAL...........72, 104, 187, 212, 245,
267, 305, 307
Highlands Airways..............190, 303
Icelandic Airways.......................190
KLM 71, 246, 249
LMS..68
LOC 188-189
Loganair..............97, 114, 142, 149,
187, 212, 245, 307
Martin-Baker.......................189-190
Midland & Scottish
Air Ferries Ltd.........................83
Midland & Scottish Airways 286
North Eastern Airways 293
NEAM 220
Northern & Scottish Railway Air
Services...................................230
Northern Island Flying Club 230
North Scottish Helicopters 243
Oley Air Services 230
QinetiQ.............................8, 299
Randox 190
Raytheon......................................250

Ryanair 75, 142, 278
SAS 249
Scottish Aero Club......................240
Scottish Airways Ltd 70, 83,
103-104, 204
Scottish Aviation Ltd 139, 159,
165, 190, 213, 246,
249-250, 254
Scottish Flying Club 254
Silver City Airways 89, 233
SMT...................................139, 213
Spirit AeroSystems.....................250
Trans-Canada Airlines 248
UKMATS.......................................74
Ulster Aviation Society 13, 203
Vector Aerospace.......................220

Organisations, military
Irish Air Corps............................10
MATS...................................50, 250
MoD 8, 52, 97, 139, 150, 184,
203, 212, 216, 223,
253, 295, 299
NATO.............................8, 52, 205
Polish Army 32, 126, 152, 154

People
Chamberlain, Neville MP 275
Churchill, Winston MP 11, 283
Clark, Jim 253
Cobham, Alan 40, 54
Dunlop, Joey 216
Fotheringham-Parker, P 314
Fox, Liam MP 7
Fresson, Ted.13, 103, 165, 266, 273
Gandar-Dower, E L.......... 128, 273
Haakon, King 315
Kent, Duke of 42
Londonderry, Lord....................230
Pilcher, Percy 85
Reid, Margaret 77
Starling, Eric................................34
Swinton, Lord 238

Personnel, military
Aitken, Max 64
Atcherley, Richard.................11, 90
Austin, G. W. B.........................304
Bainbridge, J. E. M....................309
Bend, Capt.................................244
Bishop, A. A.................................87
Boulter, Fg Off...........................294
Bourne, Plt Off 117
Brancker, Sefton 202
Briggs, D. A..................................86
Bruneau, A. A. 196

Bulloch, T. M. 58, 233
Burcher, C. 37
Burdett, A. P. 280
Burke, J......................................223
Campbell, J. C. 271
Carter, Plt Off.............................305
Carver, Lt 259
Chapman, C. G. W. 306
Crosland, B.................................271
Cruickshank, J. A........................271
Davenport, J. N. 196
Davison, H..................................165
Denholm, G. L............................294
Douglas, Sholto.................10, 53, 96
Dunning, E. H. 263-264
Edge, G. R. 304
Ensor, M. A. 266
Farquhar, A. D. 116
Foxley-Norris, Wg Cdr 65
Garret, J.....................................271
Gibbs, Flt Lt...............................270
Gilroy, G. K. 294-295
Goddard, N. E. 166
Gouldie, T. H. 222
Hall, Flt Lt 87
Hatherley, G. 37
Hearne, Sqn Ldr.......................242
Heath, W. E. C. 77
Hess, Rudolph 125
Hillary, Richard............................93
Hitler, Adolf.................................11
Holmes, J. A................................271
Hood, M. 149
Hope, R......................................304
Hornell, D. E. 306
Hyland, J. M. 114
Isted, Sqn Ldr 37
Johnsen, C. T..............................271
Krafft, C. F. 315
Lane, E. H. 87
Law, K. S. 303
Leeson, P. G. 303
Lever, E. J....................................77
Longcroft, Capt 227
Longmore, A......................102, 155
Lucy, W. P. 166
Macbride, R. E. 306
McKellar, A. A. 116
Mannock, Edward.................54-55
Marryshow, J. A...........................241
Milson, C. G. 196
Moffat, G. 37
Molotov, Vyacheslav 283
Moreton, J..................................156
Morgan, T. F. D. 117
Mortimer, Lt Cdr 165

Morton, Plt Off.........................294
Muirhead, I. J. 303
Musgrave, J..............................87
Owen, Fg Off.............................70
Palmer, E. G. 77
Parke, Sub Lt 259
Partidge, R. T. 166
Paynter, M. H..........................200
Philips, F. 269
Phillips, G. C. 77
Pinkerton, G. 116, 268
Poziomek, Wg Cdr 286
Pretlove, Flt Lt 222
Pryor, G. 206-207
Ramsden, Plt Off.......................58
Rayner, H. J............................222
Robertson, Plt Off...............58, 294
Russell, A. H. 87
Sargent, P. T............................. 79
Sherman, L. 306
Sikorski, W..............................32
Smith, L. B..............................86
Stephen, Sgt............................303
Thomson, R. B. 71
Thorne, Sgt..............................91
Turner, R..................................37
Tuttle, Gp Capt 286
Waslyk, Fg Off..........................91
Wiggins, A. L. 196
Womersley, A. L. 194

Satellite Landing Grounds
9 121
11 ....121, 210
16 ....63, 216
17 217
18 256
19 ....124-125, 216
24 ....139, 220
25 ....139, 151
26 ....139, 268-269
27 ....121, 191
32 245
36 ....121, 314
40 ....114, 177, 191, 205
41 ....177, 185
42 ....76, 205
43 ....190, 205
101 ....125, 216
102 Super..........................79, 185

Ships, Royal Navy
Activity 45, 50, 217
Albion 81
Archer 33
Argus.............45, 98, 126, 132, 217

Ark Royal........45, 98, 147, 165-166
Attacker...................................202
Audacity..................................297
Barham 110
Battler 49, 295
Begum..............................277, 280
Biter 87, 200,
Bulwark...................................250
Caroline 276
Centaur 60, 142
Colossus 57
Cossack 194
Courageous.......................146-147
Dale...202
Devonshire..............................108
Drury 79
Fearless 81
Furious............32, 45, 84, 111, 147,
                         263-264, 297
Glorious 147, 166
Hermes.............................102, 250
Hunter 57
Illustrious 84, 99, 245
Implacable 46, 141
Indefatigable 99
Nairana....................................57, 127
Norfolk....................................270
Ocean 254, 277
Pegasus............................123, 297
Premier 57, 137, 168
Ravager..............................137, 168
Ruler.......................................277
Searcher.............................168, 186
Smiter 168
Stalker......................................57
Theseus 47, 141, 219
Triumph...................................277
Trumpeter.................................33
Victorious..........................167, 297
Vindex................................200, 228
Warspite...................................110

Ships, civilian
Princess Maud 73

Ships, other military
Altmark....................................194
Bismarck 11, 86, 167, 270
Drumheller, HMCS 87
Fort Austin, RFA 278
Gneisenau................................166
Königsberg...............................166
Magnificent, HMCS..................142
Prinz Eugen 306
Rapana, MV 218
Scharnhorst.................166, 270, 273

Sydney, HMAS..........................142
Tidespring, RFA 278
Tirpitz 11-12, 99, 130, 178,
              207, 222, 258-259, 280

Squadrons, AAC
655 60

Squadrons, FAA
700 ....167, 218, 270, 297
702 276
703 ....47, 123
708 ....150, 253
711 99-100
712 168
714 ....150, 252
717 ....150, 252
718 57
719 ....141-142, 150
725 141
730 33
732 119
744 ....59, 141, 219
746 168
747 149-150
751 ....45, 123
753 ....45-46, 253
754 45-46
758 45
759 141
763 45
764 223
766 ....84, 223, 253
767 ....45, 111, 137, 223
768 ....45, 57, 137, 141
769 ....45, 111, 137, 252
770 ....92, 99, 127
771.......147-148, 165-168, 250, 297
772 ....46, 50, 84, 93, 211, 234
774 251-252
778 45-46
782............................112-113, 204
783 46
784 ....57, 118-119
785 98-100
786 98-100
787 ....46, 57
791 45
794 141
799 211
800 ....98, 147, 165-166, 186, 202
801 ....46, 111, 147, 202, 234,
                      260, 279-280
802.....33, 46-47, 193, 234, 297-298
803 ....46, 142, 147, 166, 234, 303
804 ....111, 219, 259, 261, 276

Squadrons, FAA continued...
805 141-142
806 142
807 ....202, 234, 277
808 ....90, 124, 182, 276, 295
810 ....84, 99, 147, 193, 250
811 ....111, 147, 182, 193, 200
812 ....57, 84, 277, 297
813 33
814 ....46, 250
815 ......84, 142, 150, 228, 253, 280
816 ....32, 84, 112, 141-142, 150
817 ....112, 150, 280, 297
818 ....32, 84, 147, 150, 182, 297
819 ....33, 49, 60, 75, 99, 112,
142, 149, 250, 267, 277, 297
820 ....46, 84, 99, 146-147, 250
821 ....33, 146-147, 150, 166,
253, 274, 297
822 .....112, 147, 150, 192, 218, 280
823 ....99, 146-147, 150, 156, 166
824 ....33, 50, 149
825 ....47, 112, 126, 142, 147,
149, 200, 228, 252
826 ....84, 99, 150, 250
827 ....57, 98, 112, 127, 266, 277
828 ....84, 99, 112,
829 ....84, 98, 280
831 ....60, 99
832 ....33, 297
834 ....141, 218
835 ....33, 49, 141, 182
836 217-218
837 ....126, 141
838 ....105, 127, 217-218
840 218
841 ....46, 260, 267
842 228
845 ....39, 81, 250, 278
846 ....186, 200, 298
847 150
848 186
849 ....113, 186, 207
850 ....200, 228
852 33
860 ....112, 127, 150, 218
878 245
879 ....202, 234
880 ....57, 297
881 182
882 ....186, 202, 260, 295
883 ....142, 156, 234
884 ....186, 260, 295
885 ....124, 182
886 276
887 ....56-57, 182, 276

890 ....223, 245
891 234
892 ....33, 119
894 57
897 124
898 57
899 202
1702 33
1771 228
1772 277
1791 119
1792 119
1830 ....33, 100, 113
1835 234
1837 234
1840 57
1843 33
1846 57
1852 234

Squadrons, RAF
2 ....34, 54, 85, 88, 124, 151, 201,
223, 227-228, 238, 284
3 ....90, 128, 259, 274, 284,
4 ....34, 54, 140
6 ....7, 197, 207
7 147
9 ....11, 130, 207
10 ....177-178, 280
10 (RAAF) 201
12 ....7, 209
14 ....7, 65, 209
15 ....7, 209
17 ....143, 279
18 124
19 ....65, 107, 242-243
21 ....143, 206-207
25 ....55, 224
26 56
33 254
35 178
36 ....71, 111
41 ....104, 140
42 .... 195, 273
43 ....117, 197, 224, 265-266,
303-304
44 ....234, 291
47 81
48 ......199, 245, 261, 266, 274, 306
49 177
50 ....177, 206, 303
51 177
53 ....140, 199
54 ....90, 207, 267
55 253
56 197

57 ....143, 206
59 58-59
61 ....266, 303
63 ....57, 124, 214, 240, 266, 284
64 ....118, 147
65......................106-107, 241-242
66 91
68 240
72 39
74 ....197, 202
76 ....178, 280
77 ....10-11, 82, 95, 110, 116, 138,
158, 162, 170, 174, 191, 230,
259, 265-266, 292,
298, 301, 313
78 177
80 ....224, 254
83 ....147, 224, 293
85 35
86 ......37, 58-59, 194, 222, 274, 280
88 ....124, 202, 275, 314
91 131
96 118
99 149
100 ....53-54, 85, 238
102 ....177, 246
103 292
104 97
105 ....51, 85, 151, 237-238, 282
106 ....51, 74, 147, 151, 238
107 ....195, 206
110 206-207
111 ......117, 128-130, 197, 303-304
114 ....207, 312
116 295
117 ....159, 282
118 ....38, 91, 275
119 ....77-78, 86
120 ....13, 37-38, 58-59, 179-180,
233-234, 247, 286
122 ....104, 242-243, 306
123 ....90-91, 118, 279
125 56
129 ....131, 186, 260, 274
130 ....56, 93, 131
131 91
132 ....91, 186, 240, 260, 274
133 ....140, 256
134 ....140, 256
141 ....49, 53, 74, 118, 120,
159-160, 282, 294
143 ....37, 64-65, 130, 156, 274
144 ....64-65, 105-106, 108,
195, 306
149 282
152 ....140, 273

153 ....55, 140, 256
159 234
160 234
164 ....260, 295
165 ....93, 131
167 90
169 49-50
172 ....200, 262
174 312
175 312
179 ....71, 262
182 312
185 132
186 ....49, 280
190 ....71, 165, 271
197 119
201 ....13, 41, 86-88, 180,
                                269-270, 273
202 ....7, 38, 88, 165, 207
203 ....60, 270
204 ....60, 269-270
206 ....13, 37, 70-71, 196-197, 271
208 209
209 ....41, 86, 230, 236, 307
210 ....41, 59-60, 165, 179, 236,
                        271-272, 308, 315
217 274
220 ....37, 58, 71, 194, 234, 305
221 199
222 314
224 ....35, 38, 60, 193-194, 199,
                   221-222, 266, 286-287
225 ....121, 213
226 275
228 ....41-42, 77, 86-87, 164, 236, 309
231 ......56, 190, 202, 215, 231, 234
232 ....32, 90, 143, 261, 274
233 ....35, 193-194
234 ....65, 186, 242-243, 274
235 ....35, 64-65, 106, 129-130,
                   157, 195, 256, 274
236 274
240 ....38, 41, 59-60, 85-86, 94,
                   174, 269-270, 308-309
241 204
242 ....118, 143
244 ....211, 282
245 .....35-37, 55, 119, 199-200, 295
246 ....77-78, 175
247 273
248 ....59, 64-65, 128-129,
                        157, 225, 274
249 ....123, 268
252 ....37, 130
253 ....35, 259-260
254 ....37, 128, 273-274

255 211
256 ....55, 82
257 123
258 211
260 ....90, 261
263 ....93, 117, 213, 246
269 ....32, 59-60, 271, 303, 305
272 ....199, 211
278 ....211, 274
279 ....65, 156-157, 306
280 ....207, 281
281 .....65, 105, 156, 200, 228, 287
289 ....183, 204, 295, 299
290 ....202, 232
303 ....56, 93, 295, 306
304 ....71, 200, 286
307 274
309 ....32, 126-127, 151, 183, 204,
                        214, 241-242, 26
310 ....91, 130
311 ....37, 280
312 49
313 275
315 ....56, 241
316 306
329 ....50, 260
330 ....77, 165, 237, 271, 315
331 ....90, 131, 260, 274
333 ....64-66, 315
334 65
345 50
402 49
404 ....64-65, 90, 105-107, 130,
                        261, 274, 306
407 ....200, 262
410 49
413 ....270-271, 309
414 ....124, 240
416 ....130, 225, 231
417 279-280
422 ......77, 79, 86-87, 175, 236, 256
423 ....86-88, 236, 315
430 240
441 260
451 ....260, 295
455 ....105-106, 108, 195-196
461 271
485 ....140, 182
489 ....65, 105-106, 108,
                        195, 261, 306
490 309
500 ....199, 266
501 ....56, 140, 232
502 ....35, 37-38, 199, 266-267
504 ....55, 90-91, 140, 182
516 124

518 ....38, 268, 280, 287, 306-307
519 ....263, 280
524 237
526 204
527 204
540 ....12, 130
547 ....196-197, 280
555 45
600 246
602 ......31, 33, 48-49, 116-117, 225,
                   241, 246, 254, 260,
                        274, 293-295
603 ....13, 116, 119, 128, 130,
                   159, 225, 260, 292-295
605 ....117, 303-304
607 ....90, 116, 213, 261
608 ....274, 306
610 90-91
611 ....242-243, 260, 275, 295
612 ....128-129, 131-132, 139,
                   199-200, 305-306
614 ....84, 121, 126, 143, 147,
                   159-160, 213-214
615 124
617 ....7, 11, 130, 207, 209, 258
618 306
644 215
651 ....121, 173, 202
652 ....49, 121, 220
666 ....33, 238, 254

Squadrons/Units, USAAF/USAF

2nd FS...217
95th FS...140
96th FS...140
97th FS...................................140, 217

**Training Schools/units,
    RFC/RNAS**

1 SoAF 51, 289
1 SoAFG 51
1 SoAF&G 289
2 SoAG 289
SoAG 77, 289

**Training Stations/Squadron
    Depots**

2 TDS 116
6 (Glasgow) AAP.......................172
6 TS 224
8 (Irish) ARD 53
9 TS 281
18 TS 224
19 TS 151, 285
22 TDS 158
22 TS 158-159

Training Stations/Squadron Depots continued...

23 TDS 53
24 TDS 96
24 TS 96, 282
25 TDS 281
26 TS 158, 291-292
26 TDS 138, 224
27 TDS 97-98
31 TS 53
32 TDS 224
36 TS 138, 224
39 TS 224
51 TS 53
52 TS 224, 266
58 TS 97
59 TS 96
64 TS 97
69 TS 158
73 TS 292
74 TS 138
82 (Canadian) TS.....................224
84 (Canadian) TS.....................292
89 (Canadian) TS.....................292
208 TDS 132
210 TDS 171

U-boats

U-109......................................37
U-214......................................58
U-231....................................271
U-265......................................58
U-281......................................79
U-292......................................59
U-297......................................88
U-361....................................271
U-387....................................271
U-417......................................71
U-423....................................315
U-440......................................87
U-448......................................79
U-476....................................271
U-477....................................306
U-489...........................87, 271
U-518......................................87
U-529......................................37
U-531....................................271
U-534....................................280
U-545....................................200
U-579....................................196
U-594......................................37
U-610......................................87
U-623......................................37
U-624......................................58
U-632......................................37
U-635......................................37

U-653......................................58
U-667....................................271
U-668....................................271
U-714....................................200
U-715....................................306
U-733....................................196
U-753......................................87
U-865....................................280
U-867....................................222
U-980....................................306
U-990......................................59
U-1008..................................280
U-1060..................................266
U-1225..................................306
U-3523.........................222, 280

Units, British military

45 Commando.....................8, 47

Units, FAA miscellaneous

1 NAFS 141
1 NOTU 100
1 OTU (Naval).......................149
1 TRS....................................280
2 OS....................45-46, 123, 251
3 NFW 141
4 NAFS 57
19th CAG 46
20th CAG 141
24th FW 57
Firebrand TTU.......................150
Fleet ARD..............................111
FRU 46, 141, 297
RFTU 211
RNHF 218
Shetlands Flt 270
X Flight..................................165

Units, Luftwaffe

12/ZG.......................................65

Units, miscellaneous

1 Sqn RCAF 247
41st Aero Squadron 116, 224
162 Sqn RCAF 306
168 Heavy Transport Sqn,
   RCAF 248

Units/Groups, USAAF

20th FG...................................245
52nd FG...........................140, 217
82nd FG...........................140, 217
97th BG 248

Units, USN

VP-84......................................71

Action Stations Revisited vol 1
East Anglia
Michael J F Bowyer

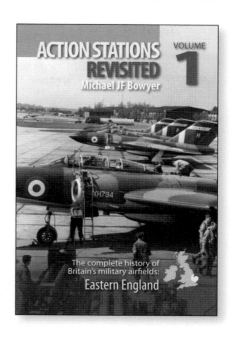

Nothing is forever, not even diamonds. Fundamental changes in international relations, changing threats and limited resources have led to a slim, overworked Royal Air Force, a modern, sleek equivalent of its earliest days and eastern England's elaborate airfields have a new role as home bases for expeditionary activities.

It has not always been like that. Cranwell was a naval base for much of WWI and Duxford, a 225-acre site, developed into a typical RAF fighter station of the 1920s and early 1930s. Fowlmere was too far from the Continent to allow its use as a starting point for offensive operations but its Spitfires tangled with Bf 109s in WWII. Lakenheath became a USAF Air Base with F-84Gs of the 508th Strategic Fighter Wing and Bentwaters accommodated F-16s and grisly green A-10s.

Michael JF Bowyer has drawn on over sixty years of personal recording, recollection and official sources to produce a definitive record of eastern England's airfields from today's major international airports and huge air bases down to tiny airstrips or disused remains. This fully revised second edition incorporates over 200 new photographs and much fresh information. *Action Stations Revisited – Eastern England* provides a vital record of the many advances witnessed in the region with Britain's busiest skies.

480 pages, hardback
234mm x 156mm
Over 400 photographs, maps and plans
9 780859 791458
£24.95

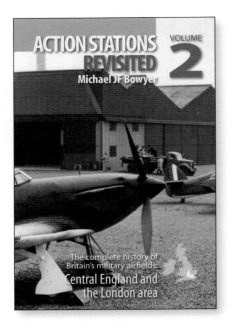

Action Stations Revisited vol 2
Central England and the London area

Michael J F Bowyer

The second volume in the highly successful Action Stations Revisited series updates the histories of over 140 airfields with military associations around the central England and London area. RAF Fighter Stations, training bases, contractor airfields such as those of De Havilland, Hawker and Vickers, plus the bases of the paratrooper units who played a large part in the D-Day landings all contributed to the aviation history of the area.

Included among the numerous well-known sites are Wittering, home of the Harrier; Benson, of photo reconnaissance fame; Brize Norton, now the RAF's in-flight refueller base; Cardington, still the departure point for airship voyages; Eastchurch, where naval aviation was pioneered and London Heathrow where the jet-set age was born. Legendary names from the Battle of Britain such as Biggin Hill, Kenley, Hornchurch and many others also lie among the plentiful stories recounted.

Action Stations Revisited No 2 Central England and the London Area contains over 280 photographs, most previously unpublished. The depth of research and the wealth of personal insight make the Action Station Revisited series a major contribution to aviation literature.

416 pages, hardback
234mm x 156mm
Over 280 photographs, maps and plans
9 780947 554941
£24.95

Action Stations Revisited vol 3
South East England
David Lee

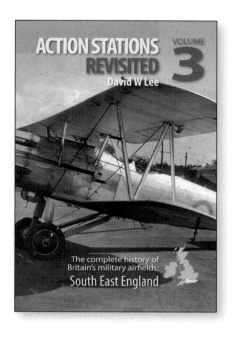

The military airfields of the south east of England including those in Kent, Sussex, Hampshire and Wiltshire are all in the third volume of the new 'Action Stations Revisited' series.

These are the airfields from which the flimsy biplanes and blimps of World War One rose to defend Britain from Zeppelins and U-boats, the airfields from which Hurricanes and Spitfires took on the Luftwaffe in the Battle of Britain and which later took the fight to the enemy's home territory. Airfields from which the RAF stood ready at the most dangerous moments of the Cold War and which have become household names in more recent conflicts.

Within these pages well-known airfields such as Manston, Hawkinge, Odiham, Tangmere, Lee-on-Solent, Greenham Common, Thorney Island, Farnborough and Wroughton mingle with the almost-forgotten Bekesbourne, Welford, Grain, Hartford Bridge, Throwley, Ramsbury and Woodchurch.

The relics of the Sound Mirrors, Britain's early warning system before radar, is also covered amongst the many previously unpublished accounts and photographs which illustrate this comprehensive coverage of Britain's front line airfields.

Arranged in alphabetical order with maps and map references, directions, plus a comprehensive index, Action Stations Revisited No 3 South East England provides a fascinating wealth of information on south-east England's aviation heritage.

344 pages, hardback
234mm x 156mm
Over 150 photographs, maps and plans
9 780859 791106
£24.95

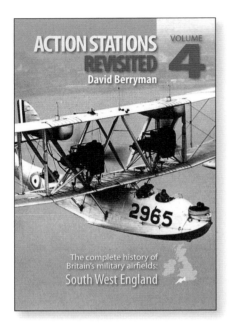

Action Stations Revisited vol 4
South West England
David Berryman

Over 120 military airfields of the south west are the subject of the latest volume of the new Action Stations Revisited series. The area covered includes most of the counties of Gloucestershire, Hampshire and Wiltshire, along with those of Dorset, Somerset, Devon, Cornwall, the Isles of Scilly and the Channel Islands.

The whole of British aviation history is reflected from the birth of military aviation at Larkhill, flying training at Old Sarum during the First World War and at Upavon during the 1930s, to fighter operations from Charmy Down during the Second World War. Postwar developments at Filton and Boscombe Down are supplemented by recent activities at Culdrose, St.Mawgan, Yeovilton and Lyneham.

Detailed accounts of the construction and operational use of the stations, with the aircraft types flown and units involved are copiously illustrated by over 340 photographs, many of them previously unpublished.

Fully indexed, this volume contains a wealth of information for any airfield visitor, modeller or aviation historian.

368 pages, hardback
234mm x 156mm
Over 150 photographs, maps and plans
9 780859 791212
£24.95

Action Stations Revisited vol 5
Wales and the Midlands
Tim McLelland

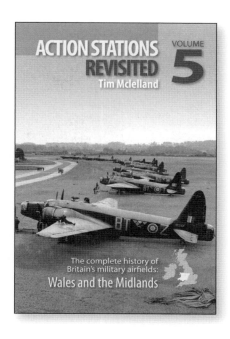

The detailed histories of over 120 military airfields of Wales and the Midlands are the subject of this latest volume in the best-selling *Action Stations Revisited* series. The airfields covered in *Action Stations Revisited 5* include those in Cheshire, Derbyshire, Gloucestershire, Leicestershire, Nottinghamshire, Shropshire, Warwickshire, West Midlands, Wiltshire, Worcestershire, all of Wales and Anglesey.

The whole of British aviation history is reflected in the stories of these airfields, from the use of airships at Llangefni and the Isle of Man and flying training at Hooton Park during the First World War; through the interwar years and into the Second World War, supporting the battle of the Atlantic from Talbenny, Fairwood Common (Swansea) and Pembroke Dock. Thousands of WWII aircraft were built at Coventry, Hawarden and Castle Bromwich and St Athan and Shawbury saw use during the Cold War. In the millennium age the region still embraces the so-called super bases such as Fairford, Valley and Lyneham.

Detailed accounts of the development and operational use of the stations, including the aircraft types flown and units based at each, are copiously illustrated with over 350 photographs, many of them previously unpublished.

Personal accounts and a full index ensure *Action Stations Revisited 5* is the definitive reference to the military airfields of Wales and the Midlands and contains a wealth of information for any airfield visitor, historian, modeller or aviation enthusiast.

280 pages, hardback
234mm x 156mm
Over 150 photographs, maps and plans
9 780859 791113
£24.95

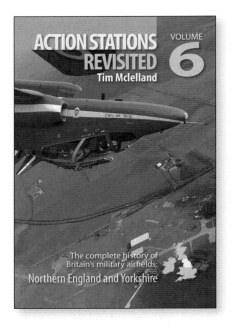

Action Stations Revisited vol 6 Northern England

Tim McLelland

The dark days of World War II brought military activity to every corner of the United Kingdom with Lincolnshire and the surrounding areas providing a home for the Royal Air Force's bomber force. The lush, rolling fields that stretch across the country to the coast offered a home for the RAF's ever-growing fleets of Wellingtons, Halifaxes, Stirlings, Manchesters, Hampdens and, of course, the immortal Lancaster.

Many of the almost countless wartime bomber airfields are now long gone, but some still survive. Scampton, from where Guy Gibson led the famous attack on the Ruhr dams and where the RAF later established a major part of its post-war nuclear deterrent force in the shape of the mighty Vulcan. Manby was the home to a wide variety of aircraft employed on evaluation duties including the Wyvern , Canberra, Dominie, Jet Provost and the Wellington's post-war derivate, the ubiquitous Varsity. A few miles to the north at Binbrook the Canberra, the RAF's first jet bomber was introduced into service and the supersonic interceptor Lightning found a home.

Further to the west, the huge expanses of Sheffield-Doncaster's Airport reveal the traces of its former incarnation as RAF Finningley, home to wartime bombers and the post-war Vulcan nuclear bombers.

But perhaps the most unusual and disturbing traces of the region's military history can be found amongst the former airfield sites at Ludford, Caistor and Breighton, where a careful examination of the landscape will reveal the stark, concrete assemblies which once supported the Thors - huge intercontinental ballistic missiles armed with thermonuclear warheads aimed at the heart of the Soviet Union.

Arranged in alphabetical order with maps and map references, directions, plus a comprehensive index, Action Stations Revisited No 6 Northern England provides a fascinating wealth of information on our 'Bomber Country' heritage.

336 pages, hardback
234mm x 156mm
Over 300 photographs, maps and plans
9 780859 791120
£24.95